'Adrian Perkel takes us on an adventurous journey through psychoanalysis and contemporary neuroscience in this bold book. He narrates a story in which the protagonists are aggression and the paradoxes of destruction and conservation of the death drive. Their integration and interpretation lead to innovative emphases about how to understand various psychopathologies and why this necessitates changes towards a more active psychotherapeutic technique to reckon with Freudian dual-drive theory. The argument is often surprising and inspiring when exploring clinical depths and widths. Put playfully, Perkel presents a psychoanalytic Bob Dylan affronting Velcro phenomena implied in every 'paradogma'.'

Dr Mark Kinet, MD, *psychiatrist, psychoanalyst and author of various books on Psychoanalysis and Neuropsychoanalysis, including* The Spirit of the Drive in Neuropsychoanalysis (Routledge).

'Adrian Perkel's new book, "Neuroscience and the Death Drive: The Nature of Symptoms, From Formulation to Treatment," reconfigures our understanding of the death drive in terms that will probably render it both more accessible and plausible to psychoanalytic theoreticians. It is, simply, conceived to be a manifestation of the self's drive to protect itself from the annihilatory experiences that threats originating from both within the organism and outside it can occasion. In response, the self mounts a counterattack, much like an immune system would, against perceived invaders, employing automatized defenses often established in the preverbal era, before memory can be encoded with language. Interestingly, consciousness is also conceived as originating in the brainstem, rather the cortex, the cortex representing that part of the brain which is responsible for creating representational thought that allows the organism to differentiate the various compromises that it faces. Perkel also provides a thoughtful and carefully documented review of libido as a source of psychopathology, noting that Freud unfortunately neglected the dual drive theory that he established in "Beyond the Pleasure Principle." Perkel's work paves the way for us to reconsider defense as a consequence of trauma rather than a response to unacceptable libidinal urges. This is a remarkably important paradigm shift for us to undertake and one that has profound implications for our work, as Perkel demonstrates. He ably ties in contemporary conceptions of neuroscience with his thesis.'

Dr Richard Wood, PhD, *psychoanalytically oriented clinical psychologist and author of* A Study of Malignant Narcissism: Personal and Professional Insights' (Routledge)

'Dr Perkel's new book, Neuroscience and the Death Drive, is a bold offering whose chief aim is to complete Freud's death drive. As an extension of his brilliant work on aggression, this exciting new work incorporates classical psychoanalytic writing and theorising situating it within contemporary neuroscientific thinking, and expertly rises to the work's two-fold challenge, namely: outlining new and detailed formulations around aggression's central role in psychic life, and providing novel approaches to treatment. This is essential reading for all mental health professionals curious about the enduring presence (and importance) of an essential drive.

Dr Michael Owen, PhD, Editor of *Psychoanalytic Practice, Lecturer/ Clinical Psychologist*

Neuroscience and the Death Drive

In this book, Adrian Perkel seeks to expand upon Freud's theory of the death drive by locating it within modern neuroscience, arguing for the centrality of the aggressive drive in the formation of mind, and the genesis of symptoms and psychopathology.

Neuroscience and the Death Drive reformulates the function of defence mechanisms as they link to the aggressive drive and their role in the binding of free energy. Filling an important gap in both formulation and treatment, this book completes Freud's self-confessed incomplete theory of aggression through the lens of modern psychoanalysis and neuroscience, updating these concepts with current scientific insights, and introduces a refreshed view on psychotherapeutic treatment implications based on these developments. Perkel explores the treatment of patients experiencing eating disorders, anxiety, depression, addiction, personality disorders and sexual dysfunction.

This invigorating and approachable book will be of interest to all psychoanalysts, psychiatrists, psychotherapists and counsellors, and will help readers reach new understandings of this key theory of the mind.

Dr **Adrian Perkel** is a registered practicing Clinical Psychologist based in Cape Town. Since 1989, he has been lecturing, writing, supervising other professionals, and has deep and wide experience as a clinician practicing psychotherapy. His work is deeply informed by psychoanalysis and neuroscience.

The Routledge Neuropsychoanalysis Series

Series editor: Mark Solms

The attempt to integrate the findings and methods of psychoanalysis with those of the neurological sciences can be said to have begun in 1895, with Freud's Project for a Scientific Psychology. Ongoing, sporadic efforts continued throughout the 20th century. However, the field really took off when the journal Neuropsychoanalysis was founded in 1999 and the International Neuropsychoanalysis Society was established in 2000. Ever since, a themed annual congress has been held in different cities around the world. Today, it is fair to say that these efforts have generated the most rapidly growing and influential body of knowledge and clinical practice in the broader field of psychoanalysis.

The establishment of this book series in 2023 marked another important milestone in the development of the field. Under the editorship of Mark Solms, the co-chair of the International Neuropsychoanalysis Society, it publishes books by leading proponents - and critics - of neuropsychoanalysis. The books in this series focus not only on the scientific findings of neuropsychoanalysis and on its theoretical yield, but also on its history, its philosophical implications and its clinical practice, as well as its ramifications for neighbouring disciplines and for the mental and neurological sciences as a whole.

The Spirit of the Drive in Neuropsychoanalysis
Mark Kinet

The Unconscious in Neuroscience and Psychoanalysis: On Lacan and Freud
Marco Máximo Balzarini

Explorations Between Psychoanalysis and Neuroscience: At the Edge of Mind and Brain
David D. Olds

Neuroscience and the Death Drive: The Nature of Symptoms, from Formulation to Treatment
Adrian Perkel

Neuroscience and the Death Drive

The Nature of Symptoms, from Formulation to Treatment

Adrian Perkel

Routledge
Taylor & Francis Group

LONDON AND NEW YORK

Designed cover image: Getty Images © Benjavisa

First published 2026
by Routledge
4 Park Square, Milton Park, Abingdon, Oxon OX14 4RN

and by Routledge
605 Third Avenue, New York, NY 10158

Routledge is an imprint of the Taylor & Francis Group, an informa business

© 2026 Adrian Perkel

The right of Adrian Perkel to be identified as author of this work has been asserted in accordance with sections 77 and 78 of the Copyright, Designs and Patents Act 1988.

British Library Cataloguing in Publication Data
A catalogue record for this book is available from the British Library

Library of Congress Cataloging-in-Publication Data
A catalog record has been requested for this book

ISBN: 978-1-041-04586-1 (hbk)
ISBN: 978-1-041-04588-5 (pbk)
ISBN: 978-1-003-62897-2 (ebk)

DOI: 10.4324/9781003628972

Typeset in Times New Roman
by Taylor & Francis Books

To the pioneers
Who notice simple things
Ask simple questions
And formulate simple answers
To all the glorious complexity

Contents

Contributors

Adrian Perkel (M.A. Clin. Psych.; D.Phil.) is a clinical psychologist and former senior lecturer in Psychology at the University of the Western Cape. He has been immersed in psychoanalytic theory, writing, and clinical practice, specialising in individual adult and couple psychotherapy for 35 years. He has been involved in numerous psychoanalytical, neuroscience, and editorial organisations both in South Africa and abroad, including the South African Psychoanalytic Confederation and the South African Psychoanalytic Initiative (SAPI) Psychotherapy College, and is a founding member of the Association of Couple Psychoanalytic Psychotherapists (ACPP). He is also on the editorial board of the professional journal *Psychoanalytic Practice* (formerly *Psychoanalytic Psychotherapy in South Africa*) and is a member of the International Advisory Board of the *Couple and Family Psychoanalysis* journals. He has focused his research over the past years on the aggressive drive in symptom formation and couple conflict. His most recent publication is the book *Unlocking the Nature of Human Aggression: A Psychoanalytic and Neuroscientific Approach*, published by Routledge in 2023.

Preface

"*Why* did you do it?", the psychiatrist asked the 17-year-old schoolboy again, this time leaning forward onto his hospital-issue desk, his tone cooling.

The patient paused for some time, eyes averted, shoulders drooping, sighed deeply. "To stop the pain", he said finally, swallowing against his throat inflamed from the emetic and subsequent emesis.

Thus ended the 15-minute psychiatric intake.

In the government-issue brown file was noted:

Axis 1: Major Depressive Episode, Episode Current;

Axis 2: Borderline traits;

Axis 3: Overdose-induced disorientation/ hallucinations (sleeping pills). Probable cause: breakup with girlfriend.

Current treatment: Amitriptyline (Tryptanol), Lorazepam (Ativan), Rohypnol (flunitrazepam), Methylphenidate hydrochloride (Ritalin), Prolintane (Catovit).

It was the second overdose he had taken, said it made him feel at peace for the first time ever. He was understood to be tormented, bereft, suffering anguish. He felt some of these feelings, it was true. But he suffered, as it turned out years later in psychotherapy, from something that predated an adolescent breakup and a betrayal by his best friend, predated difficult sibling dynamics and a sadistic older brother, predated parental bickering and the loneliness it engendered, predated an oppressive school environment and its corporal punishments, predated the complexities of navigating oedipal enmeshments with his depressive and thin-skinned soft-narcissistic mother, finding its earliest roots in a briefly anoxic birth caused by umbilical cord constriction around the neck, followed by struggles with milk supply which ran dry at six weeks.

These early experiences threatened his existence, or at least, *he* felt it did – creating a subjective threat of entropy – he could die before his life began. This early set of experiences came at a time when 'feel-good' and 'feel-bad' was yet *meaningless* – could not be represented as 'mental solids' and so could not be cognitively understood; a time when feeling bad felt *all-bad*.

These primitive experiences triggered surges in mental stress (free-energy), that required to be reduced, psychically bound in some way, to prevent mental fragmentation. These experiences were distressing enough for the infant that they became encoded in a form of early memory that cannot be remembered, and yet were stored for future reference and use.

The only mechanisms at this early stage of development the patient had available for the purpose of binding the excess mental energy was to encapsulate and expel the bad, and, as time evolved, turn some of these affects inwards, attempting to restore balance. This infant had to solve his first problems in life. He had to find a way, according to his primitive and available means, to reduce the excess distress and bind the free energy, to try persist *come what may* according to the pre-programmed pressures of his life drive. But at the same time, he had to preserve the one-and-only mother upon whom dependency meant survival. Mother was the source of life but also the 'source' of the dreadful threats to it – it was, from his perspective, her body that threatened his body, her mind his. It was *she* that provided life and yet *she* that tried to throttle him at birth, *she* that was starving him, from her emanated the feel-bad as well as the feel-good.

How does an infant solve such a complex muddle just out the starting blocks of life? Find a way through these early problems of life? In blunt terms, its mind may still be primitive, but it must nonetheless already do mental *work* on behalf of its body, to solve the problems that push it away from feeling good and toward feeling bad. To survive, the infant must, from the outset, start solving problems, reverse feeling-bad towards feeling-good. But how can it accomplish such a challenge when its available means are so limited? It can only rely on what tools it has to do this difficult task. And at this stage, they are few. It cannot go to the fridge, or find another mother, or solve its problems in the external world, where its needs must be met. In this helpless state, it can cry in an attempt to *induce* his mother to provide a remedy. Or, it can posit or eject the contents from her breast, put them outside of the self. It can ingest or incorporate them, and take in what this nourishment represents, even when the milk is 'sour' because it causes colic or reflux. It can also refuse these contents, close its mouth and deny any link between the inner and outer worlds, experienced as persecutory. These manoeuvres it must use to reduce the level of arousal and distress being caused by its imperfect body and the imperfect mother in an imperfect environment.

So, as time went on, over the next few months, our patient swallowed in his aggression to protect his one-mother, which felt bad, so he put some of this bad outside of himself, ejected and projected it, which felt better, but also, then, made the outside world seem more dangerous. The early over-arousal sensitised him, appeared to engender an infant sensitive in senses but also in his later personality. These processes also raise many questions – what exactly has happened to the mind of this patient, what mechanisms did he use to manage his particular challenges, how did these mechanisms get fixed there through memory, so that one day, 17-years later, he would again turn his aggression against himself and try to commit homicide against his own ego, his own Self?

These mechanisms, which we will be exploring in this book, were not only about being sad, bereft, or suffering anguish from an adolescent breakup. They were also driven by his neurobiological drive aiming at conservation and restoration – namely, the aggressive drive, what Freud termed the death drive, trying-through-crying and mental manoeuvring to unsuccessfully bring about change. His suicide attempts were not only about the pain he felt in his chest. It was about deep rage, a level of heightened aggression and destructiveness that in response to states of early narcissistic threat became endlessly mobilised, but also, endlessly turned inwards to protect the love-objects upon whom he depended. This was what his suicide attempts had to do with. Not the internal victim but the internal 'villain'.

Like many pathologies of the mind, most paradigms of intervention and treatment rely on techniques that reach only half the problem. The most important half, I will aim to argue across the various examples of psychopathology I deal with in this book, is the role of the conservative drive in the genesis of symptoms and psychopathology – what Freud termed the death drive – and which I believe is now corroborated by modern neuroscience. In the example just mentioned, the patient's severe depression did not require empathy for effective treatment, it required mobilisation of an otherwise 'silent' drive, as do most maladies of the mind. And the place this mechanism was first fully understood, in my view, was not in the preceding decades of theoretical breakthroughs Freud made up till the first part of the 20th century. It was in a new work that in some respects upended what had come before – even for the scientific conquistador that discovered and built these techniques. But even he, Sigmund Freud, did not, it seems, fully integrate his later discoveries into his insights regarding the genesis of symptoms and psychopathology, or of their treatment. This book aims to remedy this leaning by revisiting the implications of a now famous previous "little work", and my own treatment of this key drive in my book *Unlocking the Nature of Human Aggression* [1], in which I undertook to deal with these issues in greater depth.

"The latest little work of mine..." [2]

This was how Freud described one of his most brilliant and prescient of works in a 1920 letter to a colleague, Georg Groddeck. This 'latest little work' comes to represent a groundbreaking and integrating treatise on the workings of the mind, and especially so with the hindsight of modern neuroscience. In this work, Freud linked cosmic forces in evolution with the emergence of the forces within the mental apparatus, a grand and courageous endeavour, but elegantly executed. Nonetheless, he wrote humbly at the end of it all, that, "This in turn raises a host of other questions to which we can at present find no answer. We must be patient and await fresh methods and occasions of research." [3]

Fair enough. There can be no quibble with scientific humility and the deferment to what future research, insights, and, of course, evidence brings. Freud wrapped up his work *Beyond the Pleasure Principle* by conceding, "We must be ready, too, to abandon a path that we have followed for a time, if it seems to be leading to no good end. Only believers, who demand that science shall be a substitute for the catechism they have given up, will blame an investigator for developing or even transforming his views".[4]

And yet, did Freud do just that? Did he fully recognise the quantum jump he had created in his own discoveries? A sweeping overview of his lifetime of work suggests he may not have. He did not abandon his earlier path, one painstakingly constructed, and with hindsight, completely right, but also only half-the-right required by his later discoveries. This is a topic to which we shall return in this book since it has significant implications for how we understand psychopathology, symptoms, and treatment. Freud's resistance to fully embrace his later discoveries has had significant knock-on effects through both the theory and practice of mental health and its symptoms and syndromes. He had declared to Groddeck, "I am myself a heretic who has not yet become a fanatic. I cannot stand fanatics, people who are capable of taking their narrowmindedness seriously."[5] But yet, Freud could be said to have remained the 'fanatic' to his cause, his earlier theories of the ascendant role that libidinal forces and sexuality play in the development of both the mind and its derivations and deviations. This observation is not unique to Freud. Many great thinkers have fallen foul of paradigmatic changes, even when their own discoveries have pointed in new directions.

The famous Albert Einstein made a similar sentiment-driven blunder about his own work, when dismissing the brilliant physicist Lemaître's ground-breaking insights into the implications of Einstein's own theories, telling him that despite his calculations being correct his "physics is atrocious"![6] Lemaître's insights later proved correct, and several years later Einstein had to concede his error in resisting the implications of his own discoveries. He had inserted a 'cosmological constant' into his theory of general relativity to force the equations to predict a stationary universe in keeping with general sentiment and physicists' thinking at the time. When it became clear that the universe was not actually static, but was expanding instead, Einstein abandoned the constant, conceding he had made a significant "blunder".[7]

Or, another example of how shifts in thinking invariably meet opposition. "The law of higgledy-piggledy",[8] was how Sir John Frederick William Herschel described the newly released book on *The Origin of Species* in a letter penned to the author a few weeks after it was published in 1859. A reminder that whether from outside sources or inner ones, the evolution of thinking can be met with resistances that aim to conserve what is *felt* to be true. The downside, perhaps, of the vaunted intuition and feelings that great thinkers such Einstein, Hawking, or even Freud punted in their work.

Paradigms are tenacious masters, it seems, that struggle with the tensions of change against conserving what 'is'. Driven by the need to make meaning of experience, deeper emotional needs lead to ideas, and can turn intuition into the 'mental solids' of rationality and theory. Even the brilliant theoretical physicist, Einstein, felt a deep affinity with intuition in his scientific reasoning, leaning into the grand benefits of imagination in science and the power of the intuitive. He noted the "important part played by intuition" in the development of an exact science,[9] and, by intuition, we could also suggest unconscious drivers. "It is a magnificent feeling to recognise the unity of complex phenomena which appear to be things quite apart from the direct visible truth", Einstein commented, a task much more laborious and painstaking for Freud, who for many years grappled with the links of the mental apparatus and its intangibles with the more tangible elements of the natural and neurological-biological sciences.

But the same intuition that drives progress in knowledge and discovery, can also make forward shifts in absorbing new paradigms and ways of thinking most difficult, even for the great masters that move the needle of knowledge, and yet are themselves never quite free from their own prevailing cultural, personal, or scientific worldviews. *Weltanschauung* can exhibit a 'velcro-effect', as can creating knowledge through scientific endeavour to which the creator becomes 'married' and for which divorce can be too costly to concede. What if a lifetime of work and intellectual toil meets with new discoveries of formulations that undo them, even when the disruptor is from their own pen? This can be a painful experience as it can be enlightening, euphoric even. In Freud's case, his dual drive theory was monumental but Freud also carried doubts about himself, and perhaps never thought of himself as comparable to the people he considered great, such as Goethe, Kant, and Darwin. In response to a compliment from Marie Bonaparte comparing him to a mixture of Pasteur and Kant, replied, "That is very complimentary but I cannot share your opinion. Not because I am modest, not at all. I have a high opinion of what I have discovered, but not of myself... So, you see that one may find great things without its meaning that one is really great".[10] Ernest Jones, Freud's official biographer, noted that, "of one thing about himself he was always sure: that he had a poor intellectual capacity. There were so many things, e.g., in mathematics or physics, he knew he should never be able to understand where so many others easily could".[11]

Freud was not arrogant, writes Jones: "If one wished one might use the word opinionated to describe the tenacity with which he held his hard-won convictions...", knowing he had made a "few beginnings" and opened out "a few paths", but where they might lead, he could not judge and did not try to do so. "He was not philosopher enough to imagine he had the capacity for constructing any finished system of thought; beginnings are far removed from anything of the kind".[12]

Interesting to note, in this description, is a duality: Freud's "hard-won convictions" becoming firmly entrenched in his scientific way of being in the world, and becoming part of his personal *Weltanschauung*; but Freud also recognised that time and scientific development would contribute to verifying or refuting his thinking, and taking the next steps in how tenacious his discoveries would be. Theoretically, his hard-won convictions refer, of course, to the ascendancy of the libidinal drive and the centrality of sexuality in its role in human development and psychopathology, and Freud seemed to remain wedded to these convictions to the end of his days. But his scientific brain also gathered tremendous insights into the dual nature of organic life, one drive pushing forward through evolution versus a drive to conserve and maintain what is known to an organism's identity. In more modern terms we would call the need to maintain the Markov blanket of a self-organising entity versus the need to adapt to environmental challenge.

Shifting emphasis from the former to the latter did not rest easily for Freud, despite his insight that the libidinal can, in the service of meeting needs also disrupt balance, rushing forward so as to reach the final aim of life as swiftly as possible; but when a particular stage in the advance has been reached, the other group jerks back to a certain point to make a fresh start and so prolong the journey – the perpetual tussle between adaptation and conservation, or what Freud termed the life and death drives. In his own thinking, this tussle played a role. Whereas his official biographer Ernest Jones suggested that despite Freud's reservations of his work *Beyond the Pleasure Principle* being highly "speculative" and Freud himself putting the idea forward in "a quite tentative fashion",[13] he later "came to accept them entirely". Freud had never written anything of this sort before, suggested Jones, linking it to a "speculative" and "even phantastic side to his nature, one which he had for many years strenuously checked" – but was now surrendering old control and "allowing his thoughts to soar to far distant regions".[14] Of interest, Jones adds, is that this book is noteworthy for a less palatable reason: "This book is further noteworthy in being the only one of Freud's which has received little acceptable on the part of his followers".[15] Despite Freud's initial tentative beginnings in formulating his idea on the death drive and role of aggression, according to Jones he came to accept them with "complete conviction", once telling Jones that "he could no longer see his way without them, they had become indispensable to him".[16]

Did Freud and his followers really accept this work and the role of the aggressive/ death drive in the genesis of mind and its sequelae? I think with hindsight this work represented a paradigm shift, which neither its author nor followers ever fully embraced, despite its central role in the genesis of mind and its symptoms, from the outset of life. Modern neuroscience has come to validate many of these concepts in my view, and the bold vision they brought into science (though not without ongoing contention) – and yet, it remains limited in its role in the field and in treatment approaches. In my experience, this has been a grave omission in both formulation and treatment, an omission I hope to remedy here.

In this book, I aim to show that it is the latter drive, the conservative death drive, that when mobilised in the interests of conservation, triggers an aggressive energy that requires mental mechanisms to manage it. Symptoms emerge due to this mechanism, based on defences that aim to bind excess free energy, which modern neuroscience points out is a requirement of any homeostatic biological system that "they are obliged to minimise their own free energy"[17] and resist entropy, and which Freud had presciently pointed out in his 1920 work, "we infer that a system which is itself highly cathected is capable of taking up an additional stream of fresh inflowing energy and of converting it into quiescent cathexis, that is of binding it psychically".[18]

And yet this central concept is one so easily neglected and oft rejected in psychological thinking and treatment. The aggressive drive seems so odious, unwelcome, unpalatable, destructive – and often rejected by psychoanalysts through its history, or engaged with merely as a theoretical construct, as Jones pointed out. Even later in history than Jone's biography on Freud, authors have lamented this problem. Jon Mills, for example, also noted decades later, that even

> Contemporary psychoanalytic theorists tend to view the death drive as fanciful nonsense, an artefact of imagination... In this relational age, the death drive appears to be a drowning man. Even many classical analysts have difficulty accepting this central postulate in Freud's theoretical corpus. From my account, these attitudes appear to be either based on unfamiliarity with what Freud actually said in his texts, are opposed due to theoretical incompatibilities, or are the result of reactionary defences.[19]

Yet, the death drive finds increasing support from the neuroscientific quarter, despite that field not linking its constructs directly to this drive. Concepts such as homeostasis, free energy, binding, entropy, and so on, all have direct links to the concept. The aims of this aggressive drive are benign – merely serving the mental and biological requirement for restoration and conservation – despite its effects sometimes proving malignant, damaging to self and others. It is this drive, I aim to show, that is the central pillar in the aetiology of symptoms and psychopathology, and where the treatment needs to turn its attention. Modern concepts of free energy, homeostasis, and the function of memory will be explored to narrow the gap between what Freud thought of as speculative metatheory and the hard solutions of current biological and neuroscience, despite the fact that so many of modern neuroscientific notions were already contained in Freud's writings, albeit sometimes using different language. The alignment between modern neuroscience and Freud's work on the death drive is narrow indeed, and by examining how symptoms and syndromes form, hope to bring the reader into this alignment. The benefit is not merely theoretical, or in clinical formulation, but informs treatment and its outcomes as well. I hope the reader will join me on this quest to centralise the aim of the aggressive drive in humans, and where it goes wrong.

Freud, even at the end of his career, had still tended to centralise sexuality in the genesis of morbidity, writing for example, that although recognising the intersection of the sexual and aggressive drive, still argued in a paper published in 1940 (Freud died in late 1939), that:

> Observation shows us invariably, so far as we can judge, that the excitations that play this pathogenic part arise from the component instincts of sexual life. *The symptoms of neuroses are exclusively, it might be said, either a substitutive satisfaction of some sexual impulse or measures to prevent such a satisfaction*, and are as a rule compromises between the two of the kind that arise according to the laws operating between contraries in the unconscious.[20]

He went on the suggest that the gap in our theory cannot at present be filled that theorizing is made more difficult by the fact that most of the impulses of sexual life are not of a purely erotic nature but arise from alloys of the erotic instinct with components of the destructive instinct. "But", Freud strongly asserted,

> it cannot be doubted that *the instincts which manifest themselves physiologically as sexuality play a prominent and unexpectedly large part in the causation of neuroses*—whether an exclusive one, remains to be decided. It must also be borne in mind that in the course of cultural development *no other function has been so energetically and extensively repudiated as precisely the sexual one.* [21]

Freud could acknowledge the limitations of his day, arguing, as always, that he was struck by the fact that he had so often been obliged to venture beyond the frontiers of the science of psychology. "The phenomena with which we have had to deal do not belong only to psychology", he said, "they have also an organic and biological aspect, and accordingly in the course of our efforts at building up psychoanalysis we have also made important biological discoveries and have not been able to avoid making new biological assumptions."[22]

Let us keep in mind the earlier statement 'to prevent such a satisfaction', since the prevention refers ultimately to a mechanism of mind whose job it is to bind excess energy that the libidinal drive fails to remedy through *its* promptings. In other words, when needs are not met in the external world in the interests of homeostasis, frustration builds and activates the aggressive drive whose task is to manage these excess excitations. In fact, we can observe that the task of the death drive is always to manage excess arousal that the libidinal drive cannot remedy through prompting need-fulfilment by the activation of conscious feelings. Nonetheless, in fully engaging with his brilliant dual drive theory of the mental apparatus, so firmly rooted in broader biological and evolutionary dynamics, Freud held fast to the primacy of the sexual drive in the genesis of symptoms and psychopathology. Modern neuroscience and biology, and, of course, evolutionary theory, has, in my view, caught up with Freud's speculations and in so many respects have come to validate many of his concepts, highlighting the role of the death drive, and in fact should have centralised it in the genesis of psychopathology.

In this book, I intend to make a case for why this should be so in both the formulation of psychopathology and its symptoms, and the treatment interventions that flow from this shift in the locus of its causation. The truth oft remains unpalatable and even those in the profession can baulk at elements of the human psyche that strike as unwelcome. Bob Dylan wrote, "Oedipus went looking for the truth and when he found it, it ruined him. It was a cruel horror of a joke. So much for the truth."[23] He added, grumbling poetically, "If I ever did stumble on any truth, I was gonna sit on it and keep it down".

Perhaps Freud did that too – like Einstein, he stumbled on the truth and embraced it, but also, did not, and neither did many of the generations that followed this pioneer of the mind, represented in Abram's comments, that Eigen notes about Winnicott, "When he writes that we can do without a death instinct in psychoanalytic theory because the life instinct 'wreaks enough havoc!'"[24] Eigen went on to add, "One reason Winnicott does not emphasise a death drive is because the life drive wreaks enough havoc. An important theme is, can life survive itself? Life itself has destructive tendencies - territoriality, possessiveness, the assertion of me over you, not just survival but domination, triumph, lust for power. We kill to live." He concluded accordingly, that, "We don't have to go to a death drive to see how life-affirming tendencies destroy life. We don't know what to do with the destructive force of our life drive, let alone a death drive."[25]

But this sort of sentiment, so common in the field, misses the essence of Freud's brilliant conceptualisation, its validation in subsequent neuroscience and biology, and its impact on thinking about formulation and treatment of symptoms. The death drive does not *aim* for destruction – it aims for preservation, conservation, restoration – and only turns to destruction when it cannot fulfil its aims of restoration. It aims to bind excess energy and arousal when needs are frustrated in fulfilling the demands for homeostasis, to feel-good/ pleasure, and return the mind-body to equilibrium. Therein lies much of the confusion about this drive – the two facets, apparently contradictory, of conservation and destruction. Rossella Valdrè, who has written extensively on the death drive, comments in her work, that "Few other concepts in psychoanalysis have caused such a stir, and perhaps none has constituted a breakthrough, such as the so-called watershed of 1920, which changed psychoanalytic theory and the way we conceive humankind".[26]

I invite the reader along an exploration of these discoveries to better intervene in the work we do with those who suffer the challenges and miseries of living life. And, like Mills suggested, "If psychoanalysis is destined to prosper and advance, it must be open to revisiting controversial ideas that gave it radical prominence to begin with",[27] we need to not only revisit but recentralise this vital concept, rather than leave it on the sidelines because it carries an association of being malodorous. I share Mill's sentiment that aggressive elements are so ubiquitous to humanity, and, as he puts it, the "force of the negative is so prevalent in psychoanalytic practice that it becomes perplexing why the death drive would remain a questionable tenet among psychoanalysts today."[28] Like Mills, I concur that "the proponents against the death drive simply do not grasp the inherent complexity, non-concretisation, antireductionism, and nonlinearity of what Freud has to offer us",[29] sentiment borne out by modern neuroscience, and that Freud's attribution to the centrality of death (drive) is the "result of laborious theoretical evolution, a notion that gained increasing conceptual and clinical utility as his ideas advanced based on appropriating new burgeoning clinical data...".[30] Like Mills, I also wish to show the positions that "the death drive is Freud's greatest theoretical contribution to understanding the dynamics of the unconscious mind",[31] and of organic life in general. In particular, I hope to show that it is this mental force of the conservative death drive that plays the central role in the genesis of symptoms and psychopathology.

This "drowning man" death drive[32] is, paradoxically, the central actor in the grand neurobiological play that is the mind, and one which has suffered the misfortunes of ideological and sentimental discontents since its formulation. To my mind, this is like cherry-picking only those data and concepts we find palatable, that feel-good and move us in the direction of the pleasure in the pleasure principle, and try as best we can to move away from those concepts that feel-bad. This is the death drive's own version of resistances that, by dint of its nature, prompts these very resistances in an attempt to hold steady our intellectual and cultural homeostasis, or what Fechner called the principle of constancy,[33] a tendency towards stability, which avoids disruption to our familiar sensibilities. Freud himself, and generations of analysts and psychologists have perhaps fallen foul of Dylan's point, that the truth can be a "cruel horror of a joke", but nonetheless, one we should never shy away from, and certainly so if we are to follow the path to greater insights. How can I possibly argue that the death drive, and its variations of aggression, that threatens and destroys so much we hold dear in life, is the most important element in the maladies of the mind?

This is precisely what I aim to demonstrate in this work.

Notes

1 Perkel, A. (2023) *Unlocking the Nature of Human Aggression: A Psychoanalytic and Neuroscientific Approach*. New York/ London: Routledge.

2 Freud, S. (1920) Letter from Sigmund Freud to Georg Groddeck, November 28, 1920. *The Meaning of Illness: Selected Psychoanalytic Writings Including his Correspondence with Sigmund Freud* 105:56.

3 Freud, S. (1920) Beyond the Pleasure Principle. *The Standard Edition of the Complete Psychological Works of Sigmund Freud* 18:1–64, pp.63–64.

4 Freud, S. (1920) Beyond the Pleasure Principle. *The Standard Edition of the Complete Psychological Works of Sigmund Freud* 18:1–64, pp.63–64.

5 Freud, S. (1920) Letter from Sigmund Freud to Georg Groddeck, November 28, 1920. *The Meaning of Illness: Selected Psychoanalytic Writings Including his Correspondence with Sigmund Freud* 105:56.

6 In the original: "Vos calculs sont corrects, mais votre physique est abominable".

7 Brian, D. (1996) *Einstein: A Life*. New York: John Wiley & Sons, p.195.

8 Hertog, T. (2023) *On the Origin of Time: Stephen Hawking's Final Theory*. London: Torva: Penguin, p.22.

9 Einstein, A. (1995) *Relativity*. New York: Prometheus Books, p. 123.

10 Jones, E. (1963) *The Life and Work of Sigmund Freud*. New York: Anchor Books, p.365.

11 Jones, E. (1963) *The Life and Work of Sigmund Freud*. New York: Anchor Books, p.365.

12 Jones, E. (1963) *The Life and Work of Sigmund Freud*. New York: Anchor Books, p.365.

13 Jones, E. (1963) *The Life and Work of Sigmund Freud*. New York: Anchor Books, p.392.

14 Jones, E. (1963) *The Life and Work of Sigmund Freud*. New York: Anchor Books, p.392.

15 Jones, E. (1963) *The Life and Work of Sigmund Freud*. New York: Anchor Books, p.393.

16 Jones, E. (1963) *The Life and Work of Sigmund Freud*. New York: Anchor Books, p.396.

17 See Friston in Solms, M. (2021) *The Hidden Spring*. London: Profile Books, p.177.

18 Freud, S. (1920) Beyond the Pleasure Principle. *The Standard Edition of the Complete Psychological Works of Sigmund Freud* 18:1–64, p.30.

19 Mills, J. (2006) Reflections on the Death Drive. *Psychoanalytic Psychology*, 23(2), 373–382, pp.373–374.

20 Freud, S. (1940) An Outline of Psycho-Analysis. *International Journal of Psychoanalysis* 21:27–84, p.62 (italics mine).

21 Freud, S. (1940) An Outline of Psycho-Analysis. *International Journal of Psychoanalysis* 21:27–84, pp.62–63 (italics mine).

22 Freud, S. (1940) An Outline of Psycho-Analysis. *International Journal of Psychoanalysis* 21:27–84, p.70.

23 Dylan, B. (2005) *Chronicles. Volume one*. UK: Pocket Books Simon & Schuster, p.125.

24 Abram, J. (2013) Response by Jan Abram. *International Journal of Psychoanalysis* 94:121–124, pp.121–122.

25 Eigen, M. (2012) On Winnicott's Clinical Innovations in the Analysis of Adults. *International Journal of Psychoanalysis* 93:1449–1459, p.1451.

26 Valdrè, R. (2025) *The Death Drive: A Contemporary Introduction*. New York/ London: Routledge, p.87. Valdrè, R. (2019) Psychoanalytic Reflections on the

Freudian Death Drive in Theory, the Clinic and Art. New York/ London: Routledge.

27 Mills, J. (2006) Reflections on the Death Drive. *Psychoanalytic Psychology*, 23(2), 373–382, pp.373–374, p.351.

28 Mills, J. (2006) Reflections on the Death Drive. *Psychoanalytic Psychology*, 23(2), 373–382, pp.373–374, p.374.

29 Mills, J. (2006) Reflections on the Death Drive. *Psychoanalytic Psychology*, 23(2), 373–382, pp.373–374, p.375.

30 Mills, J. (2006) Reflections on the Death Drive. *Psychoanalytic Psychology*, 23(2), 373–382, pp.373–374, p.375 (added word 'drive' in brackets mine).

31 Mills, J. (2006) Reflections on the Death Drive. *Psychoanalytic Psychology*, 23(2), 373–382, pp.373–374, p.377.

32 I want to point out here a technical issue of (mis)translation – the Standard Edition of Freud's works edited by Strachey mistranslates the German word trieb (and todestrieb – death drive) as 'instinct' rather than a more accurate translation of 'drive'. Solms' newly translated Revised Standard Edition corrects this issue. Throughout this book there will be some cross-over of these terms but I lean on the new translation of 'trieb' as 'drive' and use this term conceptually throughout. See Solms M. (Ed), (2024) *The Revised Standard Edition of the Complete Psychological Works of Sigmund Freud*: 24 Volume Set. New York: Rowman & Littlefield.

33 Freud, S. (1920) Beyond the Pleasure Principle. *The Standard Edition of the Complete Psychological Works of Sigmund Freud* 18:1–64, p.9.

Introduction

Introduction

As mentioned in the preface, paradigms can be sticky masters. It is 1920, and Sigmund Freud has just published another significant masterwork. But Freud is not so sure it is significant and writes to his colleague Georg Groddeck, "I cannot stand fanatics, people who are capable of taking their narrow mindedness seriously... Perhaps the latest little work of mine that has just appeared, *Beyond the Pleasure Principle*, will change my image in your eyes a little".[1] This "little work" represents one of the most significant and monumental shifts in the history of science. In fact, one could describe it as a paradigmatic shift, not only in science more broadly, but in Freud's own theoretical development. And yet, like so many great thinkers, he resisted the implications of his own discoveries in this letter, one that shifted the focus from libido to aggression, perhaps showing an unconscious Freudian slip, that his own paradigmatic 'fanaticism' wedding him to his old world-views could be unshakable.

How does this happen? How do paradigmatic shifts get resisted by the discoverers themselves? This question, and resolving it, will allow us to consider moving the needle in our understanding of the genesis of symptoms and psychopathology and the implications these insights have for treatment and interventions. But before building this case, I hope the reader will allow me to take a brief detour from matters of the mind and its symptoms and treatment, to engage with a sub-theme of this book – how paradigmatic shifts are resisted, and in this case, how psychoanalysis and psychotherapies might benefit from taking a step in the direction of new discoveries in neuroscience that validate Freud's own self-understated discoveries. In other fields too, this syndrome can be seen, and since Freud was a neurologist, a neuroscientist ahead of his time, a detour through some related paradigmatic scientific missteps might be enlightening. So too, this brief detour into other branches of the sciences, because ultimately, the mental apparatus and its deviations and derivations can no longer be seen to exist outside of the laws of nature and cosmic forces in physics, evolution, and biology too. These

DOI: 10.4324/9781003628972-1

links will become clearer as the book proceeds and we explore the various syndromes and maladies of the psyche, from the common colds of anxiety and depression, to the more esoteric ones of addiction, sexual dysfunction, and pathologies of personality.

But first, a little detour: In the preface, I mentioned a Belgium priest. Georges Henri Joseph Édouard Lemaître is a name not well known to many people. Yet for a period of five years, beginning 1927, he was, it seems, the only man in the known universe to fully comprehend the implications of the new theoretical physics in the early 20th Century. He did not create this new theory of the cosmos, nor take credit for one of the greatest paradigmatic shifts in the history of science. That accolade, of course, went to Albert Einstein, whose theories of Relativity, he himself explained in an interview in 1929, "reduced to one formula all laws which govern space, time, and gravitation".[2] A gigantic intellectual undertaking, originating from one of the greatest and most imaginative minds in science.

And yet, this same great mind resisted the implications of his own profound insights. Einstein held firm on his view that the universe was a static and unchanging universe, contradicting the implications of his own theories. In fact, "to make his 1919 equations jibe with the *views of most astronomers* - as well as *his own feelings* that the universe is static and unchanging - Einstein had divided both sides of a key equation by a figure close to zero".[3] This so-called 'cosmological constant', was Einstein's attempt to neutralise the implications of his own discoveries, going so far as to first ignore, and later challenge in writing, the Russian mathematician Alexander Friedmann, who regarded the cosmological constant as arbitrary and empirically unsound. Friedmann had suggested that the universe was expanding rather than constant and static, this latter view to which Einstein held fast despite emerging astronomical evidence to the contrary, and which Friedmann tried to demonstrate empirically. Edwin Hubble, the famous astronomer at the time, had begun to observe the expanding universe, based on Einstein's equations, and yet this discovery "seriously threatened Einstein's theory of a static universe".[4] Friedmann died young in 1925 aged only 36 years, and there the matter may have rested were it not for the revival and persistence of the concept in the hands of an unlikely (and, paradoxically, religious) proponent.

Georges Lemaître was born in 1894, a brilliant man who was a Belgian Catholic priest, theoretical physicist, mathematician, astronomer and professor of physics at the Catholic University of Louvain. In the 1920s and 30s, Lemaître proposed what became known as the "Big Bang theory"[5] of the origin of the universe, calling it the "hypothesis of the primeval atom", and later calling it "the beginning of the world". He had published a report in 1927, in the Annals of the Scientific Society of Brussels,[6] under the title "A homogeneous Universe of constant mass and growing radius accounting for the radial velocity of extragalactic nebulae".[7] To put it simply, in his report he presented the idea that the universe was expanding from an original singular point, which he derived from Einstein's theory of General Relativity and other astronomical evidence. The initial state he proposed was taken to be Einstein's own model of a finitely sized static universe. For several years, theoretically shunned by Einstein, Lemaître was the only person in this universe to comprehend this concept of an expanding universe, based on the implications of Einstein's own theory. Lemaître saw that the static universe Einstein had engineered, in defiance of his own theory, was badly unstable. According to Hertog, "It looked much like the cosmological equivalent of a needle balanced on its head; give it the slightest nudge and it begins to move".[8] Most importantly, Lemaître concluded, by designing a static world, "Einstein had defied the most dramatic prediction of his own equation in favour of his philosophical prejudices of how the cosmos *should* be".[9] Further, conceptually reversing time and playing the expansion backwards suggested that the universe started somewhere in a small point of infinite density. How was this even possible, that the great mind that developed the Theory of Relativity *would* not see the implications of it because it defied the prevailing cultural, and his own philosophical narrative?

It is peculiar to imagine that such a scientific and imaginative mind as Einstein would feel repelled at the contradicting of a world-view so firmly held by humanity throughout the millennia. Einstein refused to accept the implications of his own discoveries, not because of any deficit in insight or intellect, but because his *sentiment* obscured his view. The prevailing conviction in science, culture, and even Christian theology at the time, as had been for millennia before this, was that the universe was eternal, static, and unchanging. Ironically for science, only the biblical Genesis had suggested that there was a Beginning, and that the universe had once begun in something the size of a very small point,[10] which science would later describe as the initial singularity, or a speck of infinite density, as counter-intuitive as this is, how could all the matter of the universe be contained, and all the energy of the universe constrained, in one tiny speck of infinite density?

Interestingly, whilst not taking exception to the mathematics of Lemaître's theory, Einstein, in refusing to accept that the universe was expanding, was later recalled by Lemaître as commenting to him, "Your calculations are correct, but your physics is atrocious".[11] Lemaître's proposal also met with scepticism from other fellow scientists. Even Sir Arthur Eddington, a leading English astronomer, physicist, and mathematician in the era, found Lemaître's notion "unpleasant"[12], having 'lost' the copy of his paper that Lemaître had sent him on his findings. Einstein himself thought it unjustifiable from a physical point of view though appreciated Lemaître's argument that Einstein's model of a static universe could not be sustained into the infinite past, and having fiddled with his theory to get the universe to stand still, refused to consider the matter, since a static universe "seemed so much more perfect and emotionally pleasing".[13]

So, as we can see, Einstein had at first dismissed Lemaître out of hand, saying that not all mathematics lead to correct theories. But after Hubble's discovery was published, and the astronomical evidence became incontrovertible, Einstein quickly and publicly endorsed Lemaître's theory, but only in the 1930s, some years later. This helped both the theory and its proposer to get recognition – years after his Relativity theory was originally published – with Einstein later lamenting this theoretical tussle of monumental significance and came to regard his cosmological constant as "the biggest blunder of his life".[14]

However, the lesson of this intellectual sparring is interesting since it provides an important example of how sentiment, the way people feel about things, will determine not just how they think about things (that is, the emotional valence or intensity) but also *what* they think about. The ideologies they choose, when they choose them, and how intensely they will engage with pet causes and theories about the world are often driven by inner emotional experiences of the world and, in neuroscientific terms, the (affective) predictions they make about it.

As a result of this human tendency, paradigms are often tenacious and sticky masters, resistant to revolutions in the *Weltanschauung* of their day, tolerant only of gradual evolutionary steps. Great minds are not immune to this problem, nor exempt from such inner conflicts, even when their own 'sentiment' comes into conflict with their own intellectual insights. In 1859, a mere eighteen days after the publication of his masterpiece, *On the Origin of Species*, Charles Darwin received a letter from the astronomer Sir John Frederick William Herschel, the son of the discoverer of Uranus, "expressed scepticism about the arbitrariness in Darwin's picture of evolution"[15], saying his book was "the law of higgledy-piggledy",[16] struggling with a paradigm shift so great his sentiment could not adapt to it, not necessarily for purely scientific reasons either.

Of course, those familiar with Freud's writings, psychoanalysis, and perhaps even psychology in general, would be comfortable with the notion of the mind in conflict with itself, both knowing and not knowing at the same time, conscious ideas being contradicted and conflicted by inner promptings and instinctual yearnings. More contemporary neuroscience would add to these insights, by suggesting that feeling states confer a significant evolutionary advantage for humans by creating the experience of consciousness, consciousness being the 'system' or mechanism through which the inner world can be registered in the pursuit of biological and psychological balance, homeostatic parameters that are specific. Homeostasis is *the* basic requirement for any organism to continue to exist, rather than suffer the slings and arrows of life's pressures that create threats of entropy, and which move us outside of our viable mental or physical bounds. Therefore, *affects*, although inherently subjective, are, according to Solms, "typically directed toward objects: 'I feel like this *about that*".[17] In other words, human needs can only be fully and healthily met by being internally registered and fulfilled in the environment. But to do so, means that needs must be differentiated, and qualified according to what can fulfil them. One need must be registered as different from another and fulfilled in the different ways that different needs require.

If consciousness emerges in evolution to register the inner world of the *subject*, and enable said subject to differentiate one need from another, then the *valance* and *qualia* of those feelings must be felt in a differentiated way. Gastric hunger must *feel* different from air hunger, and thirst must feel different from sexual arousal, since most needs can only be met in the world 'out there' but from different sources. As Solms puts it, biological systems "*must* test their models of the world, and if the world does not return the answers they expect they must urgently do something differently or they will die".[18] This dialectical relationship between the inner world of the organism and the environment is a crucial component of navigating psychobiological life on earth.

Based on memory and the understanding of how we navigate the world, actioning in the pursuit of meeting needs remains a most crucial aspect of organic continuance. Viable somatic and psychological bounds tend to be narrow, and action required to fulfil the demands to move towards homeostasis and feel-good rather than feel-bad, are usually highly specific. In order for this specificity to become efficient, action plans need to become as automated as possible, so that meeting needs do not require reinvention every time they present themselves. Memory has to work rapidly, efficiently, and be able to predict forward in order to be useful. Based on what has been encoded from past experiences, new experiences can be referenced against them to make forward predictions about what the likely outcome of something would or should be. But as Solms points out, the 'predictive brain' is revealed neuroscientifically to be 'lazy', at least over the long term, "vigilant for every opportunity to achieve more by doing less".[19]

We could suggest that memory serves two critical functions: firstly, memory enables an efficient homeostatic function to effectively navigate a path to the fulfilment of needs in order to reduce or minimise free energy; and, secondly, to register states of disequilibrium in which free energy is increasing and find a way to bind or cathect it. The main mechanism through which this latter function can be accomplished is the subject's internal defence mechanisms, to which they must return through regression, to the developmental point in which these mechanisms fixated in this individual, and through these mechanisms bind excess free energy in the service of homeostasis. Hence, memory serves both the libidinal and aggressive drives in the service of subjective homeostasis.

In addition, memory is entirely subjective, driven by the experience of the subject in its relationship with the environment and its caregivers, filtered through the lens of *emotional* experience. Since so much of the intense early foundations of emotional experience are undifferentiated for the infant, the fine-tuning of how feeling-driven experiences are registered and represented so that one need can be differentiated from another, and met appropriately, relies then on the evolution of ideas, ideational representations, which turn raw affects and feelings into what Solms elegantly calls "mental solids",[20] these being cognitive representations of what a feeling means and how to act on it for a remedy. In a social vacuum in which other humans were not required, then it is conceivable that *communication* of such ideas that represent feeling states (and needs) might remain unnecessary, and that language may not have evolved to communicate more effectively what ideas are representing what internal states. Obviously, communicating needs, which feelings represent, is highly efficient since, as I mentioned, needs *must* be met in the external world. But a complex organism, such as a human, requires a method to represent feeling states to the self, to develop ideational representations or ideas that enable internal states to be efficiently represented. This appears to be what cognition offers the mental apparatus – a mechanism to represent in an ideational way inner feeling states that drive homeostatic remedy in the pursuance of continuance rather than entropy.

This hierarchy of the evolution of the mental apparatus also then suggests that inner feeling states precede cognition and are never fully abandoned in the service of the organism. Without feeling states remaining the master and cognition the slave, our ability to efficiently navigate breaches to homeostasis in its various manifestations would become impaired. Feelings come first, in both an evolutionary sense of infantile development, but also in our adult lives. Cognition takes on the mantle of these 'mental solids' or what Freud calls "object-presentations",[21] that being ideational representations of what feelings mean in their variations and specificity. To make sense of the constant in-flow of affects, feelings, somatic deviations from homeostasis, and so on, consciousness has to be able to represent these to the ego in order to action appropriately in the external world, where needs *have* to be met. Libidinal cathexis with the person's own self and with external objects in the real world is required to be sustainable and avoid entropic pressures. This libidinal drive takes centre-stage, Freud maintained, in both normal functioning but also especially regarding psychopathology.

In fact, in treatment Freud noted that, "During the work of treatment we have to consider the distribution of the patient's libido; we look for the object-presentations to which it is bound and free it from them, so as to place it at the disposal of the ego".[22] Consciousness helps us take note of, and make meaning of, feeling states and their cognitive representations. Humans take great pride in their rationality and representing apparently rational formulations of everything from parenting styles to geopolitical conflicts. But the individual's choice of ideology or theory is often fickle, changeable though life, and subject to perceptions of subjectively-driven identity – I am *this* identity and I belong to a group that thinks *that*.

This essential quality of the human mind imparts a paradoxical conundrum to intellectual enquiry and pursuit, from which no minds fully escape the gravity of subjectivity, and its influences of sentiment and underlying drives. And since subjectivity is inescapably driven by feelings, emergent from primitive experiences developmentally, and influencing the tone of emotional experiences in later life through the feed-forward process of memory, so too intellectual pursuit struggles to wriggle free of these early clutches. Overcoming the 'gravity' of sentiment takes tremendous intellectual effort which relies on being held up by the evidence. But since evidence itself can be cherry-picked in the pursuance of an emotional agenda, we are never really free of the emotional influences on paradigmatic choices and how we interpret the evidence. Great minds can easily reach diametrically opposite interpretations of the same data. And of course, great minds can easily succumb to sentimental prejudices against their own insights. And to make an added point, great minds can reverse strongly held opinions and theoretical formulations as their lives evolve and their experiences change sentiment.

Let us reflect on one such famous example: Stephen Hawking, the brilliant cosmologist and theoretical physicist, in dialogue with his colleague Thomas Hertog, wrote some years after publishing his now famous work that sold over ten million copies: "I have changed my mind. A Brief History of Time is written from the wrong perspective... A God's-eye view is appropriate for laboratory experiments like particle scattering...".[23] Agreeing with the philosophers, Hertog reports that Hawking conceded, "Our physical theories don't live rent free in a Platonic heaven... Our theories are never fully decoupled from us".[24] In Hawking suggesting we are within the universe, not somehow outside of it, he was of course thinking theoretically but it can be argued that he was also reflecting insightfully that his own issues of sentiment, some unconsciously driven, could and would influence his theoretical enquiries, leanings, and convictions. His colleague Hertog even noted that when Hawking thought something "reasonable", he meant one or other idea he could not quite prove but *felt had* to be right on intuitive grounds and hence wasn't up for discussion".[25] Hawking was perhaps beginning to allow for his own subjectivity, or at least I speculate this to be so, to influence his apparently pure rational view, going so far as to communicate to Hertog that there was a need to "start from the surface of our observations", since the "history of the universe depends on the question you ask".[26]

In my view, this reflects the 'leakage' of the unconscious determinant of apparently rational exposition, allowing emotional influences into scientific questions and its answers. Hawking had, like everybody, feelings about the world, at least some of which were based on his personal circumstance and struggle. He became increasingly convicted of the need to build a model of the cosmos that dispensed with the God's-eye view and instead construct a cosmology anew from a worm's-eye view. Using quantum physics and fluctuation, built upon a Darwinian-type model of cosmic evolution, enabled

Hawking to dispense with a Beginning for the universe and hence also the need for a Creator, or at least some form of intelligent design, that cosmologists eternally wrestle with.

At last, Hertog relates, Hawking wrote him that, "I have always had a good *feeling* about the no-boundary proposal".[27] He adds that, according to Hawking, in this quantum universe, "observership is at the centre of the action", suggesting that subjectivity and the feelings that give it form and content, are at the centre of his intellectual (ideational) construction. It is, truly, a bottom-up perspective, coinciding with Solms' neuroscientific rendering of the inversion of the cortical and the id-driven homeostatic drives; the cortical being in service of the feeling, in other words. Paraphrasing Einstein on the blunder of his cosmological constant, Hawking himself commented that looking at his no-boundary genesis from a causal bottom-up perspective was his "biggest mistake" – whereas top-down cosmology turns the riddle of intelligent design upside down because the universe engineers its own biofriendliness. There is no need for a Creator, replacing it instead with the view that the universe is a quantum entity that is self-creating and self-organising. "The theory holds", writes Hertog about Hawking's final theory, "that if there is an answer to the great question of existence, it is to be found within this world, not in a structure of absolutes beyond it".[28]

These interesting developments in one of science's great minds raises several issues. Could it be that Stephen Hawking's about-turn on his theoretical convictions in later life emerged from his angry determination to refute the existence of a God that could have inflicted such cruelty on his life? In 2011, narrating the first episode of the American television series Curiosity on the Discovery Channel, Hawking commented: "We are each free to believe what we want and it is my view that the simplest explanation is there is no God. No one created the universe and no one directs our fate." It is understandable that he felt cynical about life, adding, "This leads me to a profound realization", he said. "There is probably no heaven, and no afterlife either. We have this one life to appreciate the grand design of the universe, and for that, I am extremely grateful".[29]

This 'view', no doubt, expressed his feelings about life as we know it – but armed with his likely personal disillusionment and suffering, and the anger that invariably flows from such experience because technically it must, he seemed determined to find a scientific refutation for the need for an initial Creator in cosmic evolution. If Einstein's theory of Relativity was correct, it suggested there was a beginning to the universe. The biblical Genesis in its theological narrative has *always* held out that there was a beginning, from which all of the universe emerged, but science had not conceded this view until the 20th Century. Ancient theological commentaries such as Nahmanides, had claimed that all the energy and matter of the universe had been contained in something infinitely small, all concentrated within a speck of space that was the entire universe, and as the universe expanded from the size of the "initial minuscule space",[30] the primordial substanceless substance changed into matter, and with it the flow of time, and from which all matter and energy emerged. Nahmanides had written that, "In the beginning, from total and absolutely nothing, the Creator brought forth a substance so thin it had no corporeality, but that substanceless substance could take on form. This was the only physical creation. Now this creation was a very small point and from this all things that ever were or will be formed…".[31]

Such a view seemed utterly preposterous. Until recently. For how could all the energy and matter of the universe be contained and constrained in a tiny space? This apparent delusional fantasy of theologians was corroborated by science in the 20th century, which until recently held out that the universe had no beginning and was static and eternal, and energy and solid matter were separate entities. If the universe had a beginning, and the initial singularity experienced an inexplicable and one-time event of the initial dramatic expansion (the so-called Big Bang), the question is obviously raised, and the implication presents itself, that something or someone had to initiate this sudden expansion. This Creator-factor, let us call it, would likely have irritated a great scientist determined to dispense with the idea for the need of a Creator, and hence pursued his conviction theoretically in his later life of the origin of the universe having no beginning. This required finding a way to dispense with the notion of a Creator. Accordingly, Hawking postulated an evolutionary cauldron, with the laws of the universe themselves subject to a Darwinian-type process, which could have had many outcomes, only one of which was the laws of physics as we now know them in the current universe.

So, two paradigmatic problems presented for Hawking – firstly, his personal sentiment and experience led him to disbelieve in the possibility of a creator, so he had to find an alternative explanation and did so – but such feelings, we might suggest, led to rational scientific theory. Secondly, he reversed his previously held scientific convictions from his famous *A Brief History of Time* [32] book to argue instead for a beginning that never was – a theoretical exposition suggesting there never was a need for a beginning to the universe because the universal laws and time itself cycled through evolutionary processes. This theoretical turnaround is an example of how rationality can be a fickle and changeable substance, as the sands of subjectivity shift through emotional experience.

Now, the reader may already be scratching his or her head as to what the genesis of cosmic laws and creation, the theological exegesis of Genesis and a Creator, and the genesis of symptoms and psychopathology in neuropsychoanalysis have to do with each other?

The essential point I wish to make from the outset, is that sentiment (that is, feelings, experiences, unconscious memories and such) can override and even determine rational insights, even by great thinkers, and especially when cultural paradigms threaten to shift. This is not surprising, since ideas about things, ideation, 'mentalisation' all follow the undifferentiated raw world of primitive impulses, urges, and homeostatic demands that create for the infant the challenges of making meaning out of its primitive state of *meaninglessness*. In psychoanalysis, it is my view that the most significant of Freud's great discoveries has been sidelined, or at least backgrounded, including by Freud himself – put, we might suggest, into a latent state in its role in the genesis of symptoms and psychopathology. Freud was a brilliant scientist with tremendous powers of observation, who valued the importance of evidence, even small and apparently insignificant bits of it. So too was Einstein in thinking about everyday things that most people simply assume as a given, despite the great value he placed on intuition, deduction, and imagination in science, commenting that sometimes theoretical development relies on more than a summation of data, like the compilation of a classified catalogue, which by no means embraces the whole of the actual process, "for it slurs over the important part played by intuition and deductive thought in the development of an exact science".[33] Such intuition enables creative imagination to take great strides in thinking but therein also lies the rub – for intuition and deductive thought are influenced by these same emotional and often unconscious factors.

It is my view that Freud's brilliant insights enabled the greatest breakthroughs on the nature of the human mind in history and yet he too succumbed to the dictates of sentiment. His incisive observations penetrated the depths of the unknowns and the mysterious nature of everything from dreams to the neurobiology of thoughts and feeling, from why groups fight to why couples love. His great breakthrough was to understand the seminal role that the libidinal drive played in driving forward life, attachments, and psychic construction, as does life energy push development in all biological life. So too, he discovered, this drive played a key role in the genesis of symptoms and psychopathology, the neuroses, as he called it. He noted early on in his researches that, "During the interval between the experiences of those impressions and their reproduction (or rather, the reinforcement of the libidinal impulses which proceed from them), not only the somatic sexual apparatus but the psychical apparatus as well has undergone an important development; and thus, it is that the influence of these earlier sexual experiences now leads to an abnormal psychical reaction, and psycho-pathological structures come into existence."[34]

He further noted at this point in his career that, "I can do no more in these brief hints than mention the chief factors on which the theory of the psychoneuroses is based: the deferred nature of the effect and the infantile state of the sexual apparatus and of the mental instrument." Freud conceded that to reach a true understanding of the mechanism by which the psychoneuroses and psychological disorders come about, "a more extended exposition would be necessary".[35]

As we now know, this 'extended exposition' came in the form of many great works over the years and decades that followed this point, but which always remaining incomplete, even by his own reckoning, given the available biological and neuroscientific knowledge at the time. The principle of mental functioning rooted in the libidinal and sexual components proved exceptionally insightful but whilst Freud was not wrong, he remained only partially right. Later in this career he sought to remedy the latter half, and did so brilliantly in his treatise on *Beyond the Pleasure Principle*, wherein he solidly introduced the role of the aggressive drive in tensioning against the libidinal one, and managed to complete the missing links in his theory on homeostasis and conservation, a dialectical tension of all living matter throughout evolution. It was a masterstroke of theoretical insight, brilliantly argued, elegantly formulated, and completed the missing elements in his libido theory.

And yet, Freud maintained his adhesion to his earlier breakthroughs in which the libidinal drive played *the* most significant role, rather than *a* significant role, leaving the questions related to evolution, homeostasis, and aggression not fully explored. In his bold theoretical steps addressing these issues in his seminal work on *Beyond the Pleasure Principle*, Freud recognised and described the duality of the human psyche, and the role of the aggressive drive in tensioning against the life drive, but, I suggest, benignly *refused* to relinquish his initial paradigmatic insights and the sentimental adhesion he had to them. The later work made scientific sense, but his sentiment clung somewhat to the initial paradigms and so the primacy of the role of the aggressive drive in the genesis of symptoms and psychopathology remained backgrounded in the old view, despite its central clinical role.

Like Einstein's and Hawking's *feelings* about the world, they drove their theories in directions at times in contradiction to the evidence, finding ideas and constructing them, including through the manipulation of the maths that, like the ideation of the psyche, is used to represent concept rather than create concept. Mathematical reduction enables the theoretical constructs of deduction and intuition that Einstein touted[36] to become represented into what Solms would call 'mental solids' in the individual.[37] Sentiment, feelings, subjective experience require the mind to turn raw and unprocessed experience into something that makes sense, meaning, and can *represent* the undifferentiated affect and intuition in a form that becomes intelligible. *This* feeling means *that* experience, a specific one different from any other need, and satisfaction of *that* need can be remedied through *this* differentiation. Food hunger feels different from air hunger and requires an entirely different remedy to meet the need and survive, for example. Intellectual pursuits do not escape this human requirement, that when a scientific *intuition* emerges to examine a theoretical or conceptual conundrum, these feelings require transformation into a representational language, that being a form of ideation or ideas that can be communicated about what is felt and intuited. I am, of course, not suggesting that evidence does not modify hypotheses in science but that hypotheses are invariably influenced by emotional experience and life scripts from which the intellectual elements flow. Great intellectual breakthroughs both benefit and often suffer from this intuition/ feeling-driven process. Did Freud suffer the inhibition of his emotional marriage to the dominance of his libido theory?

Clinical work with the symptoms and syndromes of the mind repeatedly and consistently seem to demonstrate the centrality of the aggressive drive in their genesis. Yet, most therapeutic approaches rely on empathic attunement and what often-times emerge as 'empathic collusions' with the 'victim' within the patient and their suffering. But symptoms are a manifestation of dysregulation being responded to in ways that are invariably suggestive of the 'villain' within – that being, the restorative drive aiming to fulfil its function as the immune system of the mind and in the process activating all the complexities that come from the way the mental apparatus manages itself. Equally important, it also addresses how the mind manages its attachments and the frustrations that emanate from them. Such is the challenge of the human psyche – ambivalence of feeling, the strangely pesky problem that uniquely afflicts the human species. We shall have much more to say about these matters through the various chapters that seek to drill deeper into the various psychopathologies, to centralise the aggressive drive in their formation and aetiology, but I want to earmark the point that, as Kinet points out, how as early as the end of pregnancy, relational and affective patterns are recorded in implicit memory. He explains how this domain of implicit memory is unconscious, "not repressed and not recallable through words. The earliest experiences stored there form a structural part of this unconscious and assert their influence in adult life".[38]

But the implicit memory that Kinet refers to, and which is now a familiar descriptor in neuroscience for what Freud called the system Unconscious, comes to form out of an evolutionary requirement for an organism to efficiently navigate a complex world and register states of threat and disequilibrium. Memory, the building blocks of the system unconscious, enables the minimising of, what neuroscientists refer to as prediction-errors, in navigating life to avoid premature entropy.[39] This book aims to take a step forward by reclaiming the theoretical and clinical centrality of the aggressive drive in this aspect of human functioning, and especially in the development of problems with the mind – those maladies of the mental apparatus that plague every one of us from time to time, and which conventional therapeutic approaches do not always resolve as incisively or as expeditiously as treatment could, if the first 50% of Freud's right were completed by the second 50% of Freud's right. As Eissler wrote of Freud's theory of aggression: "Love per se does not gratify: it has to reach its aim, if it wishes to do so. In the same way, true hatred will not come to rest until it has been satisfied."[40] The libidinal is invariably met with the aggressive, since obstacles to satiation must evoke states of dysregulation and hence catalyse the drive aimed at restoring it.

In other words, Freud came to be 100% right, in my view, understanding early that, "This therapy, then, is based on the recognition that unconscious ideas—or better, the unconsciousness of certain mental processes—are the direct cause of the morbid symptoms",[41] and came to emphasise, as we know, the role of the libidinal drive in the aetiology of the neuroses. He added, "Psychoanalytic treatment may in general be conceived of as such an *after-education in overcoming internal resistances. After-education of this kind is, however, in no respect more necessary to nervous patients than in regard to the mental element in their sexual life*".[42] Freud makes no bones about his emphasis on sexuality as the causal factor in psycho-neuroses – stating early on in his career that, "I know that the emphasis which I lay upon the part played by sexuality in creating the psychoneuroses has become generally known"[43] – but he also noted that this was not to be interpreted in a simplistic fashion, since the intra-psychic conflicts within the mind are causal factors in symptoms, as he stated, "The other, no less essential, factor, which is all too readily forgotten, is the neurotic's aversion from sexuality, his incapacity for loving, that feature of the mind which I have called 'repression'. Not until there is a conflict between the two tendencies does nervous illness break out...".[44] In other words, internal conflicts cause symptoms and psychopathology – and the agencies of mind designed to conserve the organisms must be brought to bear on the genesis of its psychical problems.

Resistances are, I will argue, rooted in the drive that Freud tended to neglect, despite his later brilliant insight into its role – namely, the drive designed by nature to conserve and preserve its Markov blanket – using its aggressive capacity for this purpose. But he also came to be only 50% right in his adherence to this centrality of the libidinal drive in the genesis of symptoms and psychopathology. His adherence to cultural paradigms, like Einstein and Hawking, perhaps prevented him from fully embracing his own discoveries and treatment efficacy has, it seems to me, been compromised as a result.

The range in treatment for what is regarded as therapeutically optimal varies considerably from five sessions a week to once per month. Whether a clinician practices five-times-weekly traditional psychoanalysis or a weekly or bimonthly therapy of various forms, invariably the centrality of libidinally driven understanding predominates, and where the aggressive drive is recognised, it is often as a secondary victimhood in the patient's experience of trauma, loss, struggle, etc. Oftentimes, symptoms are understood as illnesses in themselves, void of origin and aetiology, emergent like a disease that is caught and treated and gotten rid of. This vanishing trick can, of course, be partially successful and is usually helped by therapeutic interventions. But the internal unconscious spring from which the drives emanate, and in which memory is stored and activated, if left unresolved, also leaves intact the source of disruption to homeostasis that subjectivity encoded through experience exerts its ongoing effects.

The paradigm requires a shift, baked into the mentation of most therapeutic interventions. Empathy is of course central to all such endeavours and may even be regarded as the curative factor, that being the relationship between therapist and patient, rather than the particular technical and theoretical preferences the clinician might hold. The rigorous debates between so-called Kleinians and Freudians, for example, or behaviourists versus more psychodynamically oriented approaches, often suggest that technical preferences are not the only, or even the main ingredient of clinical success and outcome. In my view, the reason for this may be less about theoretical leanings and more about how the aggressive drive is understood and processed, for therein lies the pathway to symptoms and their alleviation.

Any system must juggle the balance between growth, adaptability, and change to environmental challenges versus their inbuilt character that requires conservation. This eternal organic struggle between adaptation and conservation is built in from the advent of organic life billions of years ago and wends its way through all the layers of organic complexity. Whether you are a virus or an elephant, maintaining your character and avoiding entropy is the immanent and most fundamental of tasks – to maintain homeostatic parameters and continue to persist in the form of which you are made. Energetically, the system will strive to first preserve through conservation since preservation is far more energy-efficient than is change, then adapt to form new methods to manage survival if required, doing all they can, as the Nobel Prize winning geneticist Sir Paul Nurse put it, to "display a sense of purpose: an imperative to persist, to stay alive and to reproduce, come what may".[45] Deviations from homeostasis *require* a restorative response to limit entropic pressures. Disruptions from within or without the organism will require the activation of a restorative response and it is this response that, down the line, appears to be so causal in the genesis of symptoms and psychopathology.

I am, of course, jumping the gun in asserting a position I have yet to verify. This book aims to do so, to drill deeper into the various psychopathologies we deal with daily in our consulting rooms, to illustrate the centrality of the aggressive drive in the clinical work we do. For, treatment efficacy is premised on this emphasis; that the disruption to homeostasis psychically will invariably lead to an activation of a conservative-restorative response, and it is this response that finds a pathway through the regressive layers of the psyche's memory systems to navigate its response. The resultant problem is in how these pathways manifest depending on the layers of memory encoded through the subjectivity of early experience. Moreover, this book aims to challenge the legacy of Freud's prevailing paradigm in which the locus of pathology is centralised in the libidinal drive rather than the aggressive one, and which appears to me to be the logical and clinical extension of Freud's later discoveries. He had noted that he had a direct investment in treatment paradigms, noting, "it is because I have allowed myself to be influenced by purely subjective motives. Because of the part I have played in founding this therapy, I feel a personal obligation to devote myself to closer investigation of it and to the development of its technique".[46] The unconscious exerts its forces upon the processes of treatment, no matter the paradigm used, "for you can convince yourselves theoretically that the somatic and emotional effect of an impulse that has become conscious can never be so powerful as that of an unconscious one. It is only by the application of our highest mental functions, which are bound up with consciousness, that we can control all our impulses."[47]

In other words, the psyche is always in contention with itself; more accurately, two primal tensions are invariably in-play, like with all living organisms, between an adaptive libidinally driven drive promoting evolutionary variation and a conservative one preserving the organism from change and challenge to its identity. Freud brilliantly identified the influence of the former drive in his earlier theories;[48] brilliantly identified the latter drive in his later theories;[49] but for sentimental reasons, it appears that he clung tenaciously to his earlier theoretical investment and disallowed himself to embrace the implications of the next steps in his theoretical development, following the path from which his later discoveries led.

As mentioned earlier, like many brilliant conquistadors of new terrain, their own emotional biases, sentiment, and cultural views, the *zeitgeist* in which they find themselves, can also obscure their ability to turn the intuitions, deductions, and sheer brilliance of imagination and observation into the 'mental solids'[50] that science ultimately requires. Freud entreated his colleagues of the time, "Let me end upon this defensive note. And let us hope that your interest in psychotherapy, when freed from every hostile prejudice, may lend us support in our endeavour to achieve success in treating even severe cases of psychoneurosis";[51] and whilst recognising clearly the multi-determined nature of symptoms and psychopathology, maintained that "better insight shows that the essence of these illnesses lies solely in a disturbance of the organism's sexual processes".[52]

Such treatment success depends more, I aim to show, on the aggressive drive than on the "sexual processes", the libidinal one, this latter drive to which most therapeutic techniques and interventions owe their formulations to this day, and cling tenaciously, as Freud did, to its centrality in the genesis of symptoms and psychopathology, noting as he did that, "we discover that the patient's symptoms constitute his sexual activity".[53] However, the libidinal drive is itself a disruptor of homeostasis, as Freud noted, and hence triggers the requirement to restore it – this being the function of the aggressive drive whose job description through evolution has become the guardian of stasis, including to internal promptings that disrupt it. If, as Kinet puts it, "Consciousness is affective. Full stop",[54] this does suggest that we become aware of the internal promptings through registering feelings that represent needs, such as libidinal and other homeostatic needs. Solms, too, does not centralise the sexual instincts as the sole driver of psychopathology, pushing instead for the notion that all (biological and psychobiological) systems must resist entropic pressures by maintaining their identity within the biological parameters for that identity. In other words, as Kinet says, "All self-organising systems (ourselves included) have one all-important task in common: to persist".[55]

But there is a caveat which I think has contributed to the muddying of the clinical waters and the conundrum we also face: the aggressive drive operates by stealth, remains latent and in the background unless provoked into response, like the somatic immune system. And to be fair to Freud, this capacity of the aggressive drive to operate in the background, unannounced as it were, is unlike the libidinal drive and its homeostatic pressures, which *must* announce themselves to fulfil their function of avoiding entropic pressures – they must make a demand upon the mind for work because of their relationship to the body,[56] or they would prove ineffective for their task of maintaining homeostatic parameters. The paradox of the aggressive drive makes its role in the genesis of symptoms that bit more vexing, and hence tends to leave it receding into the background of therapeutic formations and interventions. And yet, as I aim to show, the aggressive drive is central. Dealing with it head on improves therapeutic efficacy and outcomes.

As mentioned in the beginning of this introduction, Freud wrote to his colleague Georg Groddeck around the time of his monumental shift in theory, lamenting narrow-mindedness and fanatics, writing, in a self-deprecating tone, "Perhaps the latest little work of mine that has just appeared, *Beyond the Pleasure Principle*, will change my image in your eyes a little".[57] This "little work" represents in my view one of the most significant and monumental shifts in the history of science.

I cannot help but wonder if Freud minimised this part of his work, albeit perhaps a little tongue-in-cheek, because it violated his baked-in view of the mind and symptoms as deviations and conflicts driven by sexuality? Ultimately, I have to concur with Rossella Valdrè's comments in her book on the death drive, when she alludes indirectly to the nature of paradigmatic stickiness, the Velcro-effect with which even the greats are afflicted. And this should come as no surprise, since as current neuroscience reveals, affects precede and underlies cognition,[58] so what we feel about matters influences how we think about them. She is right in suggesting that few other concepts in psychoanalysis have caused such a stir, and yet perhaps none has constituted a breakthrough, such as Freud's so-called watershed publication of 1920, "which changed psychoanalytic theory and the way we conceive humankind",[59] she wrote. As mentioned previously, other authors, such as Jon Mills, have also lamented this 'cultural' condition in psychoanalysis, that sometimes tends to view the death drive as fanciful nonsense, "an artefact of imagination". There is so much negativity, he laments, noting that the "force of the negative is so prevalent in psychoanalytic practice that it becomes perplexing why the death drive would remain a questionable tenet among psychoanalysts today". I agree with his sentiment that "the proponents against the death drive simply do not grasp the inherent complexity, non-concretisation, antireductionism, and nonlinearity of what Freud has to offer us" and like Mills and Valdrè must posit firmly the notions that the death drive is Freud's "greatest theoretical contribution to understanding the dynamics of the unconscious mind",[60] and that aggression plays an essential role in all its aspects.

Perhaps Freud's own ambivalence to the concept, and fears of its biological grounding, influenced his followers since, and in-bred a resistance to this central concept. Despite Freud's brilliant insights into the dual nature of the psychical condition, as emergent as it is from all principles in nature and the advent of living matter, and as confirmed later in neuroscience around such concepts as free energy, homeostasis, memory, and preservation, amongst others, retains his adherence to the pleasure principle and the primacy of the libidinal in the genesis of mind and its deviations. I must add here, that it is not only psychoanalysts and post-Freudians that have struggled with the concept of aggression and the death drive but also neuroscientists. Key figures in the field of neuropsychoanalysis, such as Solms, argue that there is no requirement for a separate death drive concept and that there are not two but several drives. Particularly in Chapter 2, but peppered throughout the text, I will tackle both these issues in greater depth – for whilst a thousand pennies have dropped through Solms' work, two important points diverge. I will deal with the question of a multiplicity of drives versus two primary drives, and also argue for the essential role of the death drive as a 'barometric mechanism' that mediates between the drives through the sensation of frustration, a key but neglected concept in Freudian theory, and which suggests that dispensing with Freud's notion of the death drive is not possible.

But for those who accept the death drive, Valdrè writes, the contest is not only between drives one or many, or between the primacy of pleasure or conservation, but between paradigms old and new. "Given that two years earlier he admits that not everything in the psyche tends to pleasure, this may seem like a step backwards, but that is not the case: until the end, Freud always gives *Lust* dominion, and the hereafter of *Lustprinzip* is always a limit, a margin, something that extends beyond." Valdrè adds to this point that in her view, "Freud never renounces his own paradigm based on the *pleasure principle*; what exceeds it will emerge as a limit or paradox of pleasure, not as something that will trample over it completely, break it, defeat it. Freud always holds the pleasure principle as his fundamental interpretative rule: the beyond – Eros and Thanatos – always appear huddled between the lines. But we have seen Lust's ambiguity…".[61]

What Valdrè suggests here is that the pleasure principle, *Lustprinzip,* which is homeostatic, retains its dominance in Freud's mind – the libidinal drive remains ascendant, primary, overarching in its role through development.

Symptoms and psychopathology do not emerge because of the primacy of the death drive and its aggressive derivatives but from the libidinal. At one level this is suggesting that homeostasis remains unidimensional – at another, dual-dimensional. Freud, partly in any effect, turns his back on his greatest breakthrough: the central role that the death drive and its derivatives play in the maladies of mind, the relationship between the drives, and what it is that bridges them. This is where a paradigm shift more in line with current scientific development in both biology, neuroscience, and psychoanalysis is warranted, not refuting Freud's insights but in fact placing them in their proper place as the key driver of symptoms in and of the human mind.

I trust the reader will journey with me through various adjoining themes to make this case for centralising this conservative drive in the aetiology of mental problems and their corrections through psychotherapeutic treatments, for which this shift has significant implications.

Notes

1 Freud, S. (1920) Letter from Sigmund Freud to Georg Groddeck, November 28, 1920. *The Meaning of Illness: Selected Psychoanalytic Writings Including his Correspondence with Sigmund Freud* 105:56.
2 Brian, D. (1996) *Einstein: A Life.* New York: John Wiley & Sons, p.175.
3 Brian, D. (1996) *Einstein: A Life.* New York: John Wiley & Sons, p.194 (italics mine).
4 Brian, D. (1996) *Einstein: A Life.* New York: John Wiley & Sons, p.194.
5 The Big Bang Theory was a picturesque term playfully coined during a 1949 BBC radio broadcast by the astronomer Fred Hoyle, who was a proponent of the steady state universe and remained so until his death in 2001. Perhaps another example of how sentiment can obscure reason, despite the evidence. See also, http s://en.wikipedia.org/wiki/Georges_Lemaître
6 In the original: Annales de la Société Scientifique de Bruxelles.
7 In the original: "Un Univers homogène de masse constante et de rayon croissant rendant compte de la vitesse radiale des nébuleuses extragalactiques".
8 Hertog, T. (2023) *On the Origin of Time: Stephen Hawking's Final Theory.* London: Torva, Penguin, p.53.
9 Hertog, T. (2023) *On the Origin of Time: Stephen Hawking's Final Theory.* London: Torva, Penguin, p.53.
10 See, for example, Schroeder, G. (1997) *The Science of God: The Convergence of Scientific and Biblical Wisdom.* New York/ London: The Free Press.
11 In the original: "Vos calculs sont corrects, mais votre physique est abominable".
12 https://en.wikipedia.org/wiki/Georges_Lemaître
13 Hertog, T. (2023) *On the Origin of Time: Stephen Hawking's Final Theory.* London: Torva, Penguin, p.56.
14 Brian, D. (1996) *Einstein: A Life.* New York: John Wiley & Sons, p.195.
15 Hertog, T. (2023) *On the Origin of Time: Stephen Hawking's Final Theory.* London: Torva, Penguin, p.22.
16 Hertog, T. (2023) *On the Origin of Time: Stephen Hawking's Final Theory.* London: Torva, Penguin, p.22.
17 Solms, M. (2013) The conscious Id. *Neuropsychoanalysis*, 15, 5–19.

18 Solms, M. (2021) *The Hidden Spring: A Journey into the Source of Consciousness.* London: Profile Books, p. 168.
19 Solms, M. (2021) *The Hidden Spring: A Journey into the Source of Consciousness.* London: Profile Books, p. 176.
20 "The answer to our question, 'What does cortex contribute to consciousness?', then, is this: it contributes representational memory space. This enables cortex to *stabilise* the objects of perception, which in turn creates potential for detailed and synchronised processing of perceptual images. This contribution derives from the unrivalled capacity of cortex for *representational* forms of memory (in all of its varieties, both short and long-term). Based on this capacity, cortex transforms the fleeting, wavelike states of brainstem activation into 'mental solids.' It generates *objects.* Freud called them 'object-presentations' (which, ironically, predominate in what he called the "system unconscious")". Solms, M. (2013), p.12, The Conscious Id, *Neuropsychoanalysis,* 2013, 15 (1).
21 "The object-presentation itself is once again a complex of associations made up of the greatest variety of visual, acoustic, tactile, kinaesthetic and other presentations. Philosophy tells us that an object-presentation consists in nothing more than this—that the appearance of there being a 'thing' to whose various 'attributes' these sense-impressions bear witness is merely due to the fact that, in enumerating the sense-impressions which we have received from an object, we also assume the possibility of there being a large number of further impressions in the same chain of associations". Freud, S. (1915) The Unconscious. *The Standard Edition of the Complete Psychological Works of Sigmund Freud* 14:159–215, p.213.
22 Freud, S. (1917) A Difficulty in the Path of Psycho-Analysis. *The Standard Edition of the Complete Psychological Works of Sigmund Freud* 17:135–144, p.139.
23 Hertog, T. (2023) *On the Origin of Time: Stephen Hawking's Final Theory.* London: Torva, Penguin, p.168.
24 Hertog, T. (2023) *On the Origin of Time: Stephen Hawking's Final Theory.* London: Torva, Penguin, p.172.
25 Hertog, T. (2023) *On the Origin of Time: Stephen Hawking's Final Theory.* London: Torva, Penguin, p.174.
26 Hertog, T. (2023) *On the Origin of Time: Stephen Hawking's Final Theory.* London: Torva, Penguin, p.175.
27 Hertog, T. (2023) *On the Origin of Time: Stephen Hawking's Final Theory.* London: Torva, Penguin, p.201 (italics mine).
28 Hertog, T. (2023) *On the Origin of Time: Stephen Hawking's Final Theory.* London: Torva, Penguin, p.258.
29 https://en.wikipedia.org/wiki/Stephen_Hawking
30 Schroeder, G. (1997) *The Science of God: The Convergence of Scientific and Biblical Wisdom.* New York: The Free Press, p.56.
31 Schroeder, G. (1997) *The Science of God: The Convergence of Scientific and Biblical Wisdom.* New York: The Free Press, p.177.
32 Hawking, S.W. (1988) *A Brief History of Time: From the Big Bang to Black Holes.* London: Bantam Dell.
33 Einstein, A. (1995) *Relativity.* New York. Prometheus Books, p. 123.
34 Freud, S. (1898) Sexuality in the Aetiology of the Neuroses. *The Standard Edition of the Complete Psychological Works of Sigmund Freud* 3:259–285, p.281.
35 Freud, S. (1898) Sexuality in the Aetiology of the Neuroses. *The Standard Edition of the Complete Psychological Works of Sigmund Freud* 3:259–285, p.281.
36 Einstein made the point that sometimes theoretical development relies on more than a summation of data, like the compilation of a classified catalogue, for this by no means embraces the whole of the actual process; "for it slurs over the

important part played by intuition and deductive thought in the development of an exact science". Einstein, A. (1995) *Relativity*. New York. Prometheus Books, p. 123.

37   "The answer to our question, 'What does cortex contribute to consciousness?', then, is this: it contributes representational memory space. This enables cortex to *stabilise* the objects of perception, which in turn creates potential for detailed and synchronised processing of perceptual images. This contribution derives from the unrivalled capacity of cortex for *representational* forms of memory (in all of its varieties, both short and long-term). Based on this capacity, cortex transforms the fleeting, wavelike states of brainstem activation into 'mental solids.' It generates *objects*. Freud called them 'object-presentations' (which, ironically, predominate in what he called the 'system unconscious')." Solms, M. (2013) p 12, The Conscious Id, *Neuropsychoanalysis*, 2013, 15 (1).

38   Kinet, M. (2024) *The Spirit of the Drive in Psychoanalysis*. London/ New York: Routledge, p. 32.

39   "In the language of contemporary computational neuroscience, the fundamental task of the ego is to make *predictions*—to make predictions as to how it can meet its multiple needs in the world. (Predictions are action plans.) Next, its task is to periodically *update* those predictions, on the basis of ongoing experience. This is Freud's 'reality principle.' In the language of computational neuroscience, therefore, the ego is regulated by the 'prediction error.' It updates its predictions whenever they do not work—that is, when they *fail* to regulate the id's needs". In Solms, M. (2017) What is "the unconscious," and where is it located in the brain? A neuropsychoanalytic perspective. *Annals of the New York Academy of Sciences, 1406*, 90–97.

40   Eissler, K. R. (1971) Death Drive, Ambivalence, and Narcissism. *Psychoanalytic Study of the Child* 26:25–78, p.72.

41   Freud, S. (1905) On Psychotherapy (1905 [1904]). *The Standard Edition of the Complete Psychological Works of Sigmund Freud* 7:255–268, pp.259–260, p.266.

42   Freud, S. (1905) On Psychotherapy (1905 [1904]). *The Standard Edition of the Complete Psychological Works of Sigmund Freud* 7:255–268, pp.259–260, p.267.

43   Freud, S. (1905) On Psychotherapy (1905 [1904]). *The Standard Edition of the Complete Psychological Works of Sigmund Freud* 7:255–268, pp.259–260, p.267.

44   Freud, S. (1905) On Psychotherapy (1905 [1904]). *The Standard Edition of the Complete Psychological Works of Sigmund Freud* 7:255–268, pp.259–260, p.267.

45   Nurse, P. (2020) *What is Life?* Oxford: David Fickling Books, p. 20.

46   Freud, S. (1905) On Psychotherapy (1905 [1904]). *The Standard Edition of the Complete Psychological Works of Sigmund Freud* 7:255–268, pp.259–260.

47   Freud, S. (1905) On Psychotherapy (1905 [1904]). *The Standard Edition of the Complete Psychological Works of Sigmund Freud* 7:255–268, p.266.

48   For example, Freud, S. (1905) Three Essays on the Theory of Sexuality (1905). *The Standard Edition of the Complete Psychological Works of Sigmund Freud* 7:123–246.

49   Freud, S. (1920) Beyond the Pleasure Principle. *The Standard Edition of the Complete Psychological Works of Sigmund Freud* 18:1–64.

50   To borrow Solms' description of the function of cognition and the higher cortical structures of the brain.

51   Freud, S. (1905) On Psychotherapy (1905 [1904]). *The Standard Edition of the Complete Psychological Works of Sigmund Freud* 7:255–268, p.268.

52   Freud, S. (1906) My Views on the Part Played by Sexuality in the Aetiology of the Neuroses (1906 [1905]). *The Standard Edition of the Complete Psychological Works of Sigmund Freud* 7:269–279, p.279.

53 Freud, S. (1906) My Views on the Part Played by Sexuality in the Aetiology of the Neuroses (1906 [1905]). *The Standard Edition of the Complete Psychological Works of Sigmund Freud* 7:269–279, p.278.
54 Kinet, M (2024) *The Spirit of the Drive in Psychoanalysis.* London/ New York: Routledge, p. 74.
55 Kinet, M (2024) *The Spirit of the Drive in Psychoanalysis.* London/ New York: Routledge, p. 77.
56 Freud, S. (1915) *Instincts & Their Vicissitudes,* The Standard Edition of the Complete Psychological Works of Sigmund Freud 14, 109–140, p.122.
57 Freud, S. (1920) Letter from Sigmund Freud to Georg Groddeck, November 28, 1920. *The Meaning of Illness: Selected Psychoanalytic Writings Including his Correspondence with Sigmund Freud* 105:56.
58 See Solms, M. (2021) *The Hidden Spring: A Journey into the Source of Consciousness.* London: Profile Books, for the neuroscience on this matter.
59 Valdrè, R. (2025) *The Death Drive: A Contemporary Introduction.* New York/ London: Routledge, p.87.
60 Mills, J. (2006) Reflections on the Death Drive. *Psychoanalytic Psychology*, 23(2), 373–382, p.377.
61 Valdrè, R. (2025) *The Death Drive: A Contemporary Introduction.* New York/ London: Routledge, p.39. Valdrè, R. (2019) Psychoanalytic Reflections on the Freudian Death Drive in Theory, the Clinic and Art. New York/ London: Routledge.

Chapter 1

The Character of Symptoms
What is a Symptom?

Universally, in both professional and lay discourse, the term 'signs and symptoms' is used to describe states of illness. Whilst *signs* reflect observable deviations from normative, such as a rash or broken bone, *symptoms* often require self-report, reflecting how a person feels in general, or about something specific in their mind-body system. The Oxford Dictionary defines a symptom as "a physical or mental feature which is regarded as indicating a condition of disease, particularly such a feature that is apparent to the patient".[1] Such a definition is not uncommon – describing conditions in which some state of disequilibrium, out of normative bounds, presents itself. More accurately, we might suggest that a state of '*dis*-ease', rather than disease, represents deviation from an organism's normative state. Whilst some deviations from a normative state may be objectively measurable, such as heart rate or body temperature, in the mental sphere there is often no objective measure to accurately define the nature of a deviation from stasis, or even if there is one at all. A rise in temperature or heart rate may reflect infection in the body – but equally, may signal an anxiety state. Or, for that matter, these 'symptoms' may reflect sexual arousal. Without the patient's subjective report, we would remain unclear as to the meaning of such deviations.

If these 'symptoms' reflected arousal, the subject would not necessarily regard them as deviation from stasis outside the norm. They may even be regarded as welcome visitors that bring pleasure to consciousness. If these same symptoms reflected anxiety, the subject may report them as unwelcome and hence deviations from homeostasis, an unwelcome intrusion, whose mental response might be aimed at alleviating this state and restoring stasis. We might also suggest, of course, that if such symptoms reflected sexual arousal that is *unwelcome* to the person, if the sexual tensions were manifesting in a time, place, or onto a person that the subject regarded as unwelcome, then these libidinal "breakers of the peace"[2] as Freud called them, may be regarded as unwelcome intrusions into stasis, against which some mental response would be required. Defending against these intrusive affects, in some individual form, would therefore require mental manoeuvres that

DOI: 10.4324/9781003628972-2

would enable that individual subjectivity to restore their perception of what stasis *represents* to them, by in some way discharging, repressing, or channelling these affects along another path.

At the outset, therefore, we can see that what appears on the face of it to be a simple defining feature of a symptom, a condition of dis-ease or a deviation from stasis, becomes murkier as we probe deeper into it. Freud made the point that a symptom, "actually denotes the presence of some pathological process.... when a function has undergone some unusual change or when a new phenomenon has arisen out of it."[3] He elaborates that a symptom is:

> a sign of, and a substitute for, an instinctual satisfaction which has remained in abeyance; it is a consequence of the process of repression. Repression proceeds from the ego when the latter—it may be at the behest of the superego—refuses to associate itself with an instinctual cathexis which has been aroused in the id. The ego is able by means of repression to keep the idea which is the vehicle of the reprehensible impulse from becoming conscious. Analysis shows that the idea often persists as an unconscious formation.[4]

In other words, what cannot be permitted into conscious awareness or manifest expression, can find a cathexis elsewhere, be bound or discharged in another way, assisted by repression or other defensive processes that re-route the impulse to a different destination, so to speak. What we also notice, is that Freud places libidinal drives at the centre of psychic conflicts and hence also of symptom-formation. The psychic wrestling with libidinal promptings and libidinal transformations is placed central in the genesis of mental symptoms. For psychoanalysis, these libidinal promptings – that is, sexuality, plays an outsized role in the psychopathologies of the consulting room and of everyday life (see, for example, Freud's paper on the Psychopathology of Everyday Life[5]), and as Freud noted in a letter to Dr M Fürst in 1907, "I regard the psychosexual constitution and certain noxae of sexual life as the most important causes of the neurotic disorders that are so common."[6]

Since energy cannot be ablated or negated, it must, by the laws of physics, find a transformation of some fashion, along some other pathway or into some other manifestation, like a 'symptom'. But also implied in this process, is that the mental apparatus must first interpret deviation from stasis *as* deviation. As mentioned, a sexual prompting, for example, may or may not be interpreted as a welcome or unwelcome visitor, intrusion and disruptive (unpleasurable) or enhancing and welcome (pleasurable). Whilst both states may be deviation from stasis, only the former will create the potential for symptom-formation. Deviation from homeostasis, may therefore be regarded as having an element of subjectivity embedded, an interpretation of the valenced charge of the prompting – whether, to put it broadly, it is interpreted as negative or positive.

However, it may seem as if we are diving in prematurely into the psychic realm and relating the nature of symptoms to the internal conflicts between different agencies of the mental apparatus, and whilst this may be a true reflection, jumps the gun with regard to the phenomenon of symptom-formation that needs deeper elaboration. We might happily suggest that a symptom is simply a deviation from normal, from homeostasis. But if a symptom simply reflects a deviation from homeostasis, we are required to define both the nature of this deviation and the nature of homeostasis, as it applies to any simple system, but equally to the emergent extraordinary complexity of the human psyche.

Homeostasis and Its Deviations

Any system must be able to define itself as 'something' in order to interpret for itself a deviation from that 'something'. Whilst sub-systems in the body may each have their own identifying features, such as a liver knows it is not a kidney and hence defines for itself a different set of parameters, these organs, like their constituent components from the sub-cellular up, also need to define themselves as organs of the *human* body, not those of a polar bear or frog, for the latter would require a different set of homeostatic parameters.

The emergence of complex systems also requires that every element of the billions of elements making up the human body require a set of identity markers, an identifying 'knowledge', that enables this identity to emerge. A human body needs to define itself as different from a canine body, and homeostatic regulation of temperature, for example, is achieved not through panting but through sweating or shivering. But this internal set of identity markers, linked to genetic memory (a topic to which we shall return later) is also accompanied by an identity that this is not just *a* body but a body with a distinct set of subjective parameters that define it and not only a set of objective parameters. A body is not just a body or mechanised 'thing' but inhabited by a subject to whom the somatic experience can be claimed. This body is *my* body, not just *a* body, would be a truism claimed by any individual. Subjectivity then plays a key role in registering the state of the subject's object (that is, its own body) and being the mechanism through consciousness of registering the feeling states that enable conscious *qualia* to orchestrate the *homeostatic work* [7] required to keep living. As Kinet remarks in his citation of Damasio and Solms' neuroscientific work, that "emotions play a key role in our practical reasoning. They are necessary to go over our options, right our choices and make decisions".[8] The implication of this feature of human life, is that physiology and somatic functioning have both objective and subjective parameters defining it, implicating forms of memory and knowledge for both of these parameters.

Significant deviations from homeostasis must invariably threaten any living system or sub-system. But to know what a deviation is for that system requires some form of 'knowledge', identity, and memory to enable parameters to be set and for registering when parameters are stressed beyond homeostasis. We could broadly suggest that any deviation from homeostasis must elicit an indicator of a response aimed at guiding a restoration towards equilibrium, or broadly some sort of 'symptom', even if a remedy is readily available, such as shivering in response to cold, to indicate that there has been a deviation from optimum thermo-stasis.

As such, where the concept of a symptom starts out implying a 'pathological deviation from normal', we run into a muddle when beginning to deconstruct what is regarded as normal, especially from the vantage point of any biological system, from the simplest to the most aggregate, emergent, and complex. Whilst it seems a stretch to suggest that simple systems have subjectivity, such a stretch is only true in the sentient conscious sense of the concept, since even simple systems are required to view themselves in relation to their environments according to their nature and the dictates of their own memory. In simpler systems, of course, memory is information encoded through the system's genetics. A gene is, after all, information encoded and this endows all biological systems with a form of non-sentient memory. At this biological level, even simple organisms or cells require a form of innate subjectivity to fulfil their natural obligation of preservation. This notion suggests that all biological systems are subject to a self-organising principle in the laws of nature, through which a Markov blanket is applied, a theoretical construct in physics suggesting that all systems coalesce to form self-organising systems and once organised will strive to preserve that system and resist entropy. Biologically, the information contained in the memory of genes dictates the direction any self-organising entity should take to both define itself and henceforth also preserve itself. Resistance to entropy must play a central role in any organism's capacity to prolong its existence and find a natural path to its 'encoded' end – this is the essence of what Freud termed the death-drive, an in-built mechanism that must guide every biological entity towards its natural pre-programmed end and resist premature threats that threaten entropy.

"It is as though", argues Freud, "the life of the organism moved with a vacillating rhythm. One group of instincts rushes forward so as to reach the final aim of life as swiftly as possible; but when a particular stage in the advance has been reached, the other group jerks back to a certain point to make a fresh start and so prolong the journey".[9] Hence, as Freud suggested, "everything living dies for internal reasons - becomes inorganic once again - then we shall be compelled to say that 'the aim of all life is death' and looking backwards, that 'inanimate things existed before living ones'".[10] In contrast to the life drive and its energetic promptings, are the conservative instincts whose aim is to preserve and assure that any living organisms shall follow its own path to death, and as Freud puts it "to ward off any possible ways of returning to inorganic existence other than those which are immanent in the organism itself".[11]

Genetic Identity Mutable or Immutable?

The memory encoded in genes appears to provide a blueprint from which biological systems can give expression to the information contained in this *driver* [12] of identity. But any self-organising system, or identity, also faces two fundamental challenges in navigating the exigencies of the environment. The tension between conservation or adaptation underlies all living agency, and as Darwin exposed, faces all living matter. Finally, it emerges at the pinnacle of the evolutionary process of variation, in the psychic realm of the human mental apparatus. As Freud identified, this is achieved though the psychic drives of eros/ libidinal (creative and procreative) in constant tension with the death-drive (which strives to conserve and protect the self-identity) through life, achieving ultimate stasis through its natural pre-programmed route to entropy, rather than premature entropy.

But if the genetic blue-print was immutable, any species or even individual within a species would have no essential mechanism to adapt to environmental impingements and challenges and fulfil the evolutionary imperative for what Darwin called 'variation'.

"Natural selection acts", says Darwin, "by the preservation and accumulation of variations, which are beneficial under the organic and inorganic conditions to which each creature is exposed at all periods of life. The ultimate result is that each creature tends to become more and more improved in relation to its conditions. This improvement inevitably leads to the gradual advancement of the organisation of the greater number of living beings throughout the world".[13]

Modern science has demonstrated that without epigenetic phenomena, the ability of genes to be switched on and off in response to the pressures for adaptation, would limit a species from evolving, which is a requirement for the survival of any species. Genes are not immutable blueprints but a form of living information-memory that guides a species' development, such memory being encoded not in the abstract but in a real relationship to the environment in which it finds itself. In this sense, epigenetics suggests that in some sense genes mediate the relationship between an organism and its environment, an implication of Darwinian evolution that has significance in understanding symptom-formation in more complex systems, especially that of the human psyche.

Memory, in this objective sense, guides future development and serves a *feed-forward* process for a species. But if the environment has changed, only those species that adapt to it will survive the evolutionary pressures, particularly aversive ones, as noted by Eric Kandel. Kandel's Nobel Prize winning research into the epigenetic capacity of organisms to create new neurological circuits that encode aversive stimuli, suggests that adaptation is a capacity built into biology from the ground up. This also suggests that genetic memory mediates, to some extent, the process of adaptation, and that emergent memory in psychic systems may have a function too of mediating the internal and external relationship. For a system to survive it must define itself, and also interpret the environment it finds itself in, so as to respond to it. In this sense, even simple organisms have an in-built subjectivity, a sensory lens through which it defines itself in order to preserve itself from premature entropy. Kandel makes the point that genes are capable of a certain capacity for mutation, for the alleles to be switched on and off in response to the environment, suggesting that genes have a capacity to adapt and, in this sense, also fulfil the Darwinian imperative that adaptability leads to survival. On the other hand, genetic inflexibility to environmental challenges increases risk for entropy.

It may be obvious that I am conflating two forms of memory – that of the species and that of the individual organism. I am also conflating the memory of the ages transmitted through millennia of evolution versus the memory acquired through recent and direct individual experience. Both forms of memory serve a *feed-forward* process, as Solms identifies the neurology of id mechanisms in the human psyche, which is to make for greater efficiency in how any organism can navigate its environment and adapt to the demands of environmental complexity and its constant shifts and changes. But genetic memory works its magic in the background, giving rise to extraordinary complexity in the evolutionary process, since as the biochemist Nick Lane tells us, genes enable adaptation, and notes that "genes are almost infinitely permissive: anything that can happen will happen".[14]

The human psyche invites a deep complexity, not reducible to the sum of its parts, nor equatable with simple biological systems. Nonetheless, we can feel confident in noting that even the most complex higher order systems carry the essential qualities of their simpler biological heritage. Humans rise above, but are never free of their primitive drives. Homeostatic imperatives dictate the terms of biological survival within narrow parameters and keep constrained all animals' capacity for hubris, since deviation from the narrow zone of optimum functioning that genetic memory determines, keep all organisms tucked into their evolutionary niche. Humans, of course, have some capacity to temporarily suspend natural constraints through mechanical ingenuity or intellect, but in any event, such latitude buys experience but not a freedom from the constraints of nature's dictates. But there is one exception to this rule of nature, and that is regards to the mechanism of aggression as a human drive. Aggression can be scaled in the human species, unlike all other species constrained by their inherent limitations of tooth and claw. Not even a lion can really rule the jungle beyond its natural limitations. Kurt Eissler made an interesting comment about this, suggesting,

But man's aggression, just because it is directed by narcissism and ambivalence, constitutes a supreme danger to man and culture. It has been said that the lion and its potential prey are able to mingle peacefully together so long as the lion is satiated. With the first signs of the lion's need for food, however, its prospective victims disperse in a hurry. Here we observe aggression wisely distributed, limited to the area where it belongs—namely, self-preservation.[15]

Humans can annihilate themselves as a species through the fusion of intellect with aggression and the capacity to harness nature to this end. Humans can create weapons of mass destruction in a manner than no other species can. This capacity also centralises the aggressive drive in how humans preserve themselves, and how this drive centralises itself in the genesis of symptoms in the human psyche, a topic we will later explore in detail.

If memory encoded in an organism's genetic makeup dictates the terms of its nature, this memory also dictates the parameters for what is homeostatic and sustenance-promoting and what trends it towards premature entropy. In other words, genes communicate to an organism its parameters for survival and these leave little wriggle-room for deviation from stasis, at least not without cost. Homeostatic mechanisms are cost-sensitive, including for memory. As Solms asks rhetorically, why do more to achieve less when one can do less to achieve more? The 'predictive brain' (of memory) is revealed neuroscientifically to be 'lazy', at least over the long term, "vigilant for every opportunity to achieve more by doing less".[16]

This makes intuitive sense, of course. Why would any intelligent biological system spend more energy to achieve less if it can achieve more by doing less? This inherent biological 'laziness' is a simple issue of resource effectiveness in a resource-shy and resource-competitive world. But this is only true for biological parameters, and to a large extent depends on relatively objective criteria for these homeostatic parameters to be set and met. The human psyche does not lend itself to simple reductionism. The emergent complexity of the mental apparatus takes the element of 'biological subjectivity' into a stratospheric level of 'psychological subjectivity', from which personal memory roots itself and garners for itself the lion's share of influence. In fact, I venture to say that both objective and subjective memory forms the bedrock of human survival. Without both these forms of memory, genetic encoding and the psychological and neurological encoding of personal experience, human survival would be short and brutish. Deviations from homeostasis transcend any objective measure and, in many senses, cannot be generalised at any level beyond the simplest of emotional descriptions. Loss tends to generate sadness, injury tends to generate aggression, love tends to generate the bitter-sweet machinations of ambivalence inherent to every human attachment. But these are sweeping and broad descriptions that do little to properly represent any individual and their internal worlds. If it did, psychoanalysis and psychotherapy would be a redundant method of treatment.

Homeostasis and Subjectivity

In the complexity of the human mind, individual memory is deeply conflated with subjectivity, taking centre stage in how memory gets encoded for an individualised *feed-forward* capability, and from which deviations from individual homeostatic parameters are set. The mind has to represent itself *to* itself using templates carved into the early formation of psychic experience. This principle is well established in psychology and neuroscience, that early experience plays an outsized role in the mind's formation. The question of why this should be so relies on the single most important mechanism that humans rely on to ascertain deviation from both biological and psychological homeostatic parameters – that of drives and feelings. It relates to Freud's definition of a drive, and concurring with Solms' modern neuroscientific views,[17] which he defined as "the psychical representative of the stimuli originating from within the organism and reaching the mind, as a measure of the demand made upon the mind for work in consequence of its connection with the body".[18] Feelings represent to consciousness when deviations from homeostasis are prompting. If you *feel* hungry, you take remedial action to restore equilibrium – perhaps you find food. A drive can therefore be partially understood as a remediator of states of disequilibrium, and the most effective mechanism for doing so in a complex three-dimensional and ever-changing world. In a simple and unchanging world, there is no need for the evolution of feelings since simple reflexes can achieve what is required to avoid entropy, like a goldfish opening its mouth to ingest food. But if a human fails to drop food in the bowl, that same goldfish has no internal resources available to create alternative remedies. Even in humans, it seems straightforward – you *feel* hunger and you eat.

So, whilst feelings represent a complex mechanism to register and respond to states of both physiological and psychical disequilibrium, we could also say that consciousness is the slave to memory and serves its purpose. Freud made the point that "consciousness arises instead of a memory trace",[19] the ego representing the thin layer of 'mental skin', like the skin surface of the body that separates the somatic internal from the external, and must do the bidding of the internal world by registering and interfacing with external stimuli, submitting to the internal world what this surface registers in the external world. But also, the internal world is governed by memory, since memory is the foundation of conservation, its bedrock, by recording states of threat and sources of disequilibrium that must be responded to in a feed-forward process to ensure a more effective resistance to entropy. Hence, we might say that *consciousness is the servant to memory*, interpreting the world and reporting it to the system unconscious, testing the world against older reference points stored for this purpose. Whilst fulfilling a need appears straightforward, in humans it is never quite so.

Associations and Links

Complex psychic systems, such as consciousness and the system Unconscious, give rise to the ability to form associative links. In humans, the signals from body to psyche are never so straightforward as they might appear in more primitive organisms. For example, whilst food may represent something generalisable to the human species, it is also filtered through an *associative* process, in which experiences of oral impulses and satiation, gastric satisfaction or disturbance, and all the emotional connections that an infant will register as it navigates the early psychosexual focus on the mouth and oral region and its experiences at the breast will colour how that apparently physiological response is registered. Freud's remarkable insight into the emergence of psychic structures from somatic foci through early psychosexual development form, as he put it, "the prototype of a process which, in the form of identification, is later to play such an important psychological part",[20] demonstrates how psychic systems, including the defences and defensive systems that an individual develops, are formed through subjective experience and interpretation of such experience from the outset of life.[21] Whilst oral foci are universal in human mental development, and its developmental unfolding common across individuals, this is only partially true at the broadest of developmental levels. We could, by way of analogy, accurately describe the features of the human face in universal terms but this would be a grossly inadequate representation of the finer details and difference to which the infinite variety of facial features presents in reality.

In mental development, always, there is also an "I" from the outset having somatic experiences, informing the infant how the world is *through its own lens* and creating mental representations of this world. This subjective perspective on the world is both internal and external since in the early stage of development there is little to differentiate these two. Impingements from within or without present as threats to equilibrium to an infant, from which a response is required to restore it. Crying is the only significant mechanism an infant has to *induce* a response from the environment upon which is depends to restore equilibrium when needs are pressing and not being met. This striving for homeostasis is powerful and one which we can see represents conservation of the self, and is hence why Freud thought of the death drive, as he named it, as a conservative drive, supplementing the life drive when needs are being frustrated. But this drive for conservation is constantly tensioned against the drive for growth and adaptation, to attach and bond and create new states of developmental achievement, which are in the interests of meeting needs to maintain life. This muddle will make more sense in Chapter 2, when we address the relationship of these drives with each other and the bridge between them.

This libidinal drive or life drive (Eros) can, as we shall discuss later, also represent a 'breaker of the peace', one against which conservation is in constant tension. Like all organic life, this tension appears to have been present from the outset of living matter, governing the Darwinian principle of an evolutionary imperative when an organism faces environmental change or challenge. It must adapt or risk entropy, but such adaptation being governed from its perspective. An eagle adapting to temperature changes in the environment will be different to that of a fish or human. Both species, and individual, subjectivity seems to govern the two drives of all living matter, that any organism is required to experience the world though its own lens and from its own perspective.

This subjectivity is central in the mental life of humans, and appears to be present from the very outset of an individual's life. There is an emergent *subject* at home in the somatic experience of embodiment coming into life, and hence this subject is making interpretations of such experience from the outset. The way somatic foci emerge as representations in the psyche of the infant become increasingly individual and nuanced through both the temperamental and circumstantial lenses, that is, through both an internal nature and the complexities of its personal environment. Homeostatic demands are therefore both innate at basic levels but filtered through the individual's own psychic interpretations. An infant whose gastric system after an easy birth is settled and an easy responsive supply of milk and maternal supplies is present will have a different experience to one who might have struggled at birth, suffer reflux or colic, have a breast that is undersupplied, or a mother unable to respond to her infant adequately, or in a "good enough" manner, as Winnicott would suggest. So, the subjectivity of how deviation from homeostasis gets interpreted will be influenced by three elements: the internal world of the infant and its temperament, the external environment and its responsiveness, and the phenomenon of *time*. I will deal with the first two points later but first a deviation into the concept of time and its influence on what I will call psychogenesis.

Time and Psychogenesis

Development unfolds according to the forward thrust of time that governs all of the cosmic elements, both organic and inorganic. The inexorable arrow of time flows forward from the outset of cosmic evolution and which in psychic development *pushes* life's developmental thrust in a forward direction. This push creates its own inner tension since all attempts to achieve homeostasis are short-lived and temporary. Perhaps if it could, the infant would stop time when in a state of balance and homeostasis – that is to say, when all its physical and psychological needs are met – and revert back to the state of two billion years of evolutionary bliss-in-stasis when it could remain alive without the pressures to evolve. The biochemist Nick Lane laments these paradoxes in the very first flushes of life itself: "Since the first complex eukaryotic cells arose", he writes, "some 1.5 to 2 billion years ago, we have had warfare, terror, murder and bloodshed: nature, red in tooth and claw. But in the preceding aeons, we had 2 billion years of peace and symbiosis, bacterial love...".[22] In other words, Lane argues, "only rarely is natural selection actually a force for change. Most commonly, it opposes change, purging variation from the peaks of an adaptive landscape. Only when that landscape undergoes some kind of seismic shift does selection promote change rather than stasis".[23]

But alas, species-memory encoded genetically assumes that growth and adaptation, the creative-procreative libidinal thrust of life takes precedent in the development of living things and there is no room for permanent homeostasis – firstly, because the environment is complex and ever-changing and stasis in the face of change leads to entropy; but also, because the internal world of a complex organism requires constant and complex manoeuvring to meet both homeostatic demands but also, according to Darwinian evolutionary principles, enable better adaptation and survival when homeostatic manoeuvres are inadequate or fail. Interestingly, according to physicists such as Stephen Hawking in his later work on cosmic evolution, suggest that time itself, and the physical laws as we know them, was itself born though an evolutionary process in the immediate aftermath of cosmic expansion.[24] Time drives forward and is affected by quantum variation and randomness, making future events unpredictable and in some senses random. This principle also can be seen to govern the libidinal push of psychic development and its inexorable forward flow.

The psyche cannot stay in a conservative state for long without internal promptings pressing it into some form of momentum to engage with the environment to satisfy a need, or to succumb to the gradual pressures of intrinsic development. Internal to the mechanism of both somatic and psychic life is a forward push toward development that appears present from the outset of living matter, as Nick Lane suggests that as he reflects on his depiction of the origins of life finds himself also using the term *drive*, since he says, "there isn't a better word" to capture the idea that it is not passive chemistry "but it is *forced*, pushed, driven by the continuous flux of carbon, energy, protons. These reactions *need* to happen...".[25] Freud noted too that there is a drive in organic life that thrusts forward, and in his work on Beyond the Pleasure Principle wrote of the drives that "push forward towards progress and the production of new forms",[26] this libidinal thrust emerging too in the tensions of the psyche and these 'breakers of the peace' internal to the organism.

Tensioned against this libidinal drive is one towards stasis, aimed at protecting the organism from impingements and representing its identity in the environment. More accurately, when needs are not met by the promptings of the libidinal drive, excess energy and arousal follows, which requires remedy.

The conservative death drive activates in response to such frustration and utilises aggression, proportional to its experience of threat, in the service of restoration of this excess arousal. At the risk of spurious parallels, it is interesting to note that the forward push of time and the forward push of organic development both carry an intrinsic forward *drive* and that this forward drive is unidirectional, heading towards a horizon in the future. This intrinsic force in and of nature seems to be one key characteristic of the libidinal psychic drive too, which Freud identified and emphasised in the genesis of psychopathology. Science concurs with this force of nature, and the forward thrust of time in both cosmic terms and the advent of organic life.

We might suggest that the forward thrust of energy in organic life, and from its outset as the biochemists tell us, underpins all living matter in increasing complexity, as complex life evolves from simpler forms, since complexity appears to confer the advantage of adaptability to threats and change, to move, to manipulate, and ultimately to think and plan. Ideation evolves from more primitive needs; it does not seem to lead them as we wish to believe. This concurs with a Darwinian perspective that embedded in both cosmic and biological evolution is a drive to evolve. We could ask any organism why not first 'choose' the path of entropy? And *prima facie* this would not be an entirely trite suggestion. Life, from the outset and through its complexity, *is* a struggle. Why struggle to survive and adapt when peace awaits the choice of entropic rest? We could also suggest that on the balance of it, entropic rest would be a more sensible choice than struggling for existence and the associated resource expenditure that goes with sustaining life. Is it not, simply, too difficult and costly?

The answer that returns on us is yes, the economics of survival do not make sense when nature will generally do more for less rather than less for more. Why labour against the odds to prolong a pithy and transient existence which at first blush seems so pointless? Inadequate as it is, the only answer we have to this muddle of existence, outside of a theological one, is that for some reason we cannot be certain of, there is an intrinsic quality to the flow of time, invented at the beginning of time, that prompts cosmic energy in a forward direction; but so too, as the inorganic evolved into the organic, and electron gradients gave way to self-organising simple structures that could replicate, the advent of a forward and irresistible thrust to drive-development found its way into a form of life drive that eventually brought us to human Eros and the powerful and inexorable drive to both survive, push forward, and evolve through adaptation.

However, as mentioned earlier, this forward push to development does not find itself unopposed. Any organism must also be able to define itself, have a genetic and individual perspective that gives it its character in the world, its Markov blanket that enables an entity to self-organise and maintain a cohesive identity in the face of ongoing threats to its existence. Evolving without a means to protect and preserve the identity doing the evolving would invariably lead to an imposed and unchosen entropy.

The Death Drive and Conservation

The drive to preserve and conserve is also present from the outset of life and it is reasonable to infer that without this mechanism, a form of somatic and mental immune system, life could not endure. Its parallel in the complex mental apparatus of humans is a drive in opposition to the life drive and its forward thrust of time and development, that being the conservative drive, a form of an immune system, operating in the mental realm, whose aim is the maintenance or homeostasis or a return to homeostasis when equilibrium is disrupted and needs are not being adequately fulfilled. Although Freud called this the death drive, it is, perhaps, a misnomer of sorts since he did not mean there is a forward *drive* towards death but rather an instinctual and intrinsic mechanism in the mind that strives to prolong the journey of living towards its own natural and circuitous path, to a return to homeostasis according to the elements that are in-built and pre-programmed to the organism itself (its species genetic memory) – to, as he put it, "ward off any possible ways of returning to inorganic existence other than those which are immanent in the organism itself".[27] Conservation and preservation find their representative in the form of the death drive, a mental duality of drives emergent from the somatic experiences to which an infant is subject.

But this contra-distinction that tensions against the thrust of the life drive suggests also that there is a contrary pull against the forward thrust of life, a drive to go backwards and hold steady what 'was'. This backward drive psychoanalysis and neuroscience has linked to memory since memory represents the core mechanism to register threats to homeostasis and provide a feed-forward system to efficiently navigate the fulfilment of life's needs and the threats to their fulfilment. Regression in the service of the ego, as Freud noted, indicates a going back in time to more effectively ward off threats and dangers going forward in time. Solms speaks to this point that the neuroscience of the mind suggests that the brain (and its psyche) cannot rediscover the world afresh with each new engagement but must have an energy-efficient way of navigating complexity by accessing old reference points psychically to guide future responses. The old adage that 'what's past is past' is not entirely accurate, for it references the forward thrust of time, indeed, and in this sense is partially true – but it fails to account for the necessity of having a mechanism to go backwards in time in order to go forwards in time, even for primitive organisms whose behaviour is often governed by 'instinct' – that is, genetic memory rather than personal memory. But complex beings require both elements to survive – and personal memory through the lens of subjectivity is a requirement to encode experience in the memory of the unconscious system.

Regression and the Backward March of Time

Regression serves preservation by enabling the mind to go back to previous sources of injury and check new encounters against these previous reference points. The mind can go back in time *as if* the history being referenced is in the present. This great discovery of Freud demonstrates the significance of the unconscious in storing and encoding life's experiences through the lens of subjectivity, which can be currently referenced to better enable preservation going forward. Aversive life experiences, in particular, find themselves neurologically encoded into permanent neural circuitry through epigenetic facility, as Kandel's research demonstrated.[28] It makes sense that aversive impingements that threaten the integrity of an organism and violate the parameters for homeostatic regulation will require encoding as a form of future inoculation. Of course, the parameters for homeostatic regulation will differ for different biological systems, organs, or complex animals. The thermodynamics of a whale differ from that of a giraffe yet both will have encoded their own particular parameters for what is acceptable in a normal range. Humans are not constrained by their biology to quite the same extent, in that emergent mental structures in their complexity accent the degree of subjectivity that colours human parameters.

Feelings represent more than signals of homeostatic imbalance in the soma but also of psychological imbalance, impingements in the mental realm that hurt and threaten the integrity of the 'narcissistic envelope'.[29] Perception, based on the influences of the regressive pull into old reference points of memory, takes on the lion's share of significance. Early aversive experience, the valence of it being inversely proportional to the reversal of time, imbuing the earlier the experience with the greater of emotional impact. This is because the proportionality of experience is more total the earlier it occurs. A pin prick or hunger-pang in adulthood will represent a small part of psychic experience but the same impingement for a one-hour old neonate will represent almost the totality of its experience, a novel and aversive moment that may represent not a brief discomfort but an existential threat, that if left unsoothed by its mother may embed neurologically as a memory trace to be future-referenced under the pull of later regression.

This emergent template of subjectivity will have a major influence on subjectivity through the mechanism of regression and its returning to old encoded interpreted imprints. Regression is thus about going backwards in time to enable more effective navigation of the future in a complex and demanding external world. The future forward drive of time and psychic development is the master of development but recruits the templates of history to interpret life going forward. This well-established concept in psychoanalysis and neuroscience adds significant complexity to how homeostatic parameters are determined. Since, beyond the simpler homeostatic needs of the body and its physiology, lies a complex set of ongoing interpretations about the world, subjectively imprinted and encoded, which makes deviations from homeostasis significantly more nuanced and complex.

In essence, symptoms represent deviations from homeostatic parameters but whilst those parameters of the body are more objectively determined, those of the mind are subjectively driven and suffer all the convolutions, embellishments, and associative influences that subjectivity of experience confers. Impingements in life for one person may not represent a deviation from stasis, whilst for another it may be the trigger for the onset of minor or major symptoms. If an individual loves flying, getting aboard an aeroplane would likely represent something quite different from someone who is anxious about flying and which may trigger the onset of panic attacks or generalised anxiety. What determines these parameters we will address in more detail later but for the moment I hope the reader can accept that the interpretation of life, filtered through the lens of unconscious subjectivity and history, will influence how parameters are set or breached for the advent of psychological symptoms. The genesis of psychopathological symptoms will, in large measure, be influenced by the unconscious associations from which they originate – ideation encoded in memory systems that give personal meaning to the subjective place in an often bewildering and initially meaningless world.

A symptom can be thought of as representing a deviation from homeostasis of both objective somatic and subjective parameters, the former encoded in the memory of genes and the latter in individual memory, influenced by perception of experience. But also, important to note, is that deviations from homeostasis represent a threat that requires a response to restore such deviation – a way of meeting needs and when this is failing, the activating of an immune response – at times in the somatic realm and at times in the psychical one. This also suggests then, and I will elaborate on this as we go along, that there cannot be symptoms without the activation of the aggressive drive whose function is restoration, whenever there are deviations from stasis, and that this drive, in fact, plays the central role in their genesis. It is this central thesis that I aim to develop through the course of this book.

Notes

1 https://www.google.com/search?client=safari&rls=en&sxsrf=AB5stBgjr0EXFKQ4S4
   xetyS6ZlMLXi3Hdg:1689922024812&q=symptoms&si=ACFMAn8_M7eJwStsnxy
   YBiM9Eo6iElQQ8rwi1canCMovEy5zcpdbPlh2FC8iI0aVOyaT0Oty2JPc1x74Pcy
   QoB4bD2jJjiWW0Lzp4pnOfTFPmU-sG65sNlE=&expnd=1&sa=X&ved=2ahUK
   EwiNr_KPmp-AAxXXgVwKHV6sCw4Q2v4IegQIGxA_&biw=1728&bih=977&d
   pr=2
2 Freud, (1920) Beyond the Pleasure Principle. *On Metapsychology: The Theory of Psychoanalysis*. London: Penguin, p. 337.

3 Freud, S. (1926) Inhibitions, Symptoms and Anxiety. *The Standard Edition of the Complete Psychological Works of Sigmund Freud* 20:75–176, p.87.
4 Freud, S. (1926) Inhibitions, Symptoms and Anxiety. *The Standard Edition of the Complete Psychological Works of Sigmund Freud* 20:75–176, p.91.
5 Freud, S. (1901) The Psychopathology of Everyday Life: Forgetting, Slips of the Tongue, Bungled Actions, Superstitions and Errors (1901) *The Standard Edition of the Complete Psychological Works of Sigmund Freud* 6:vii–296.
6 Freud, S. (1907) The Sexual Enlightenment of Children (An Open Letter to Dr. M. Fürst). *The Standard Edition of the Complete Psychological Works of Sigmund Freud* 9:129–140, p.131.
7 Homeostatic demands of any sort require work. At times, this is mental work, at times somatic, at times conscious and at times this work goes on in the background totally out of conscious awareness. For example, the body uses water to enable hydration which provides the chemical components for cellular work. Mostly, this is happening out of awareness. But should the body require action to remedy a shortfall in available resources, then *feelings* of thirst will notify consciousness that a state of disequilibrium is emerging which requires the subject to find water. At both levels, work is required by both body and mind to maintain or restore stasis. Failure to do this work leads to increasing risk of entropy.
8 Kinet, M. (2024) *The Spirit of the Drive in Psychoanalysis*. London: Routledge.
9 Freud, S. (1920) Beyond the Pleasure Principle. *On Metapsychology: The Theory of Psychoanalysis*. London: Penguin, p. 313.
10 Freud, S. (1920) Beyond the Pleasure Principle. *On Metapsychology: The Theory of Psychoanalysis*. London: Penguin, p. 311.
11 Freud, S. (1920) Beyond the Pleasure Principle. *On Metapsychology: The Theory of Psychoanalysis*. London: Penguin, p. 311.
12 Nick Lane, the biologist, makes the point that as he reflects on his depiction of the origins of life finds himself also using the term *drive*, as does Freud, since he says, "there isn't a better word" to capture the idea that it is not passive chemistry "but it is *forced*, pushed, driven by the continuous flux of carbon, energy, protons. These reactions *need* to happen..." – see Lane, N. (2016) *The Vital Question: Why is Life the Way it Is?* London: Profile Books, p.135.
13 Darwin, C. (2003) *The Origin of Species: By Means of Natural Selection of the Preservation of Favoured Races in the Struggle for Life*. New York: Signet Classic, p.124.
14 Lane, N. (2016) *The Vital Question: Why is Life the Way it Is?* London: Profile Books, p.289.
15 Eissler, K. R. (1971) Death Drive, Ambivalence, and Narcissism. *Psychoanalytic Study of the Child* 26:25–78, p.55.
16 Solms, M. (2021) *The Hidden Spring: A Journey to the Source of Consciousness*. London: Profile Books, p. 176.
17 See Solms, M. (2017) What is "the unconscious," and where is it located in the brain? A neuropsychoanalytic perspective. *New York Academy of Sciences* 1406 (2017) 90–97, 2017.
18 Freud, S. (1915) Instincts and Their Vicissitudes *The Standard Edition of the Complete Psychological Works of Sigmund Freud 14*,109–140, p.122.
19 Freud, S. (1920) Beyond the Pleasure Principle. *The Standard Edition of the Complete Psychological Works of Sigmund Freud* 18:1–64, p.25.
20 Freud, S. (1905) Three Essays on the Theory of Sexuality (1905) *The Standard Edition of the Complete Psychological Works of Sigmund Freud* 7:123–246, p.98.
21 "The first of these is the oral or, as it might be called, cannibalistic pregenital sexual organisation. Here sexual activity has not yet been separated from the

ingestion of food; nor are opposite currents within the activity differentiated. The object of both activities is the same; the sexual aim consists in the incorporation of the object—the prototype of a process which, in the form of identification, is later to play such an important psychological part. A relic of this constructed phase of organisation, which is forced upon our notice by pathology, may be seen in thumb-sucking, in which the sexual activity, detached from the nutritive activity, has substituted for the extraneous object one situated in the subject's own body", Freud, S. (1905) Three Essays on the Theory of Sexuality. *The Standard Edition of the Complete Psychological Works of Sigmund Freud* 7:123–246, p.98.

22 Lane, N. (2016) *The Vital Question: Why is Life the Way it Is?* London: Profile Books, p. 157.
23 Lane, N. (2016) *The Vital Question: Why is Life the Way it Is?* London: Profile Books, p. 196.
24 See Hertog, T. (2023) *On the Origin of Time Stephen Hawking's Final Theory.* London: Torva, Penguin.
25 Lane, N. (2016) *The Vital Question: Why is Life the Way it Is?* London: Profile Books, p.135.
26 Freud, S. (1920) Beyond the pleasure principle. *On Metapsychology: The Theory of Psychoanalysis.* London: Penguin, p. 309.
27 Freud, S. (1920) Beyond the Pleasure Principle. *On Metapsychology: The Theory of Psychoanalysis.* London: Penguin, p. 311.
28 Kandel, E. (2006) *In Search of Memory: The Emergence of a New Science of Mind.* New York: WW Norton & Co.
29 See for example, Solan (p. 197), in Solan, R. (1999) The Interaction between self and others: A Different Perspective on Narcissism. *Psychoanalytic Study of the Child* 54, 193–215.

Chapter 2

The Multiplicity of Subjectivity
The Dialectic of Subjectivity

Somatic memory is driven by the almost infinite variability and permutational power of the genome and is bottom up, so to say – we don't decide whether we get blue or brown eye colour or end up greying early. Whilst epigenetics would decry such a simplification of genetic variability, since genes have a striking capacity for adaptation and variation for both individual and species, it is broadly true that species memory has a power in dictating the forward development of a human being. Psychoanalysis has long suggested that the effects of the environment, and the complex nuances of maternal, parental, and family dynamics influence how the psyche evolves during early development. But psychoanalysis and neuroscience has also long suggested that from the get-go of life the infant is expressing its subjectivity and interpreting its experiences according to prior ones and its own somatic realities and its impingements and sensitivities.

We might say that the system unconscious of the psyche is extremely personal and tends to formulate itself in an endless dialectical engagement between the inner and outer worlds. From the outset, there is an "I" having experiences of the world, as *meaningless* [1] and primitive as these might initially be. The world impinges on an infant which invites its interpretations of these impingements and what they say about the world in which it finds itself. Since inner and outer are poorly differentiated in the early months of life, somatic impingements or external ones create the potential for mistrust, those being *affect-driven* conclusions about the world. But nonetheless, the agency of the infant demands it make interpretations and *create* meaning out of meaningless mental states. Ideation emerges to formulated primitive conclusions about the object-world from which the psyche can encode such experience and learn the lessons of its world to navigate forward. If the world is disorganised or frustrating for whatever reason, poor maternal attunement and the consequent frustration, or because the infant struggles with reflux which causes pain, it may conclude, for example, that it better not attach because the world on whom it depends is also a source of 'poison' and discomfort, and so concludes that it is better to not trust than to trust, with the challenges that real dependency fosters for an infant deciding, as it were, not to trust its attachments.

DOI: 10.4324/9781003628972-3

The notion of a *dialectical* relationship with the environment is a more accurate description of early subjectivity. But this depiction of the filter of subjectivity through which the world is experienced, interpreted, and acted on, is also an inadequate depiction of the psyche in the world. There may be an "I" experiencing the world, and encoding it in memory, but is it true to say that there is one "I"? Is the mind a monolithic whole that differentiates itself from the other in and of the world? Simply put, Freud's brilliant insights and discoveries uncovered more than one subjectivity in the human mind, that in reality there is not one subjectivity but a mind with competing and conflicting agendas. The forward push of libidinal energy conjures up all manner of need and fantasy, including desires of, and for the parental object. But simultaneously, there are currents placing obstacles and taboos in the path of their fulfilment, stirring up frustrations and losses, guilts and inhibitions. This suggests the mind can both know and not know itself simultaneously, be conscious of one striving whilst suffering the machinations of other component defences trying to neutralise or inhibit these urges, impulses, and wishes. In fact, so much of the problems humans struggle with are rooted in cathexes and counter-cathexes of innate strivings, particularly libidinally charged strivings, some of which are directed at external objects and some at the individual's own body and its needs. "Experience goes on to show that a psychical element (for instance, an idea) is not as a rule conscious for a protracted length of time. On the contrary, a state of consciousness is characteristically very transitory; an idea that is conscious now is no longer so a moment later, although it can become so again under certain conditions that are easily brought about", Freud wrote.[2]

Already in his early work on Hysteria and the aetiology of the neuroses, Freud noticed the competing and often conflicting parts to the human mind, with internal desires, wishes, and longings originating in childhood development meeting counter-trends in the form of repression that seeks to neutralise, divert, or simply repress those longings and wishes. The libidinal push to cathect (with objects) appears to meet with a powerful counter-cathexis in some individuals, with desire competing with taboo, for example, to negotiate some form of compromise-formation. Although, in individuals who become symptomatic, some in childhood and some later in life, these tensions and psychic conflicts are exaggerated, the inner conflicts of the mind remain universal and intrinsic to all human development. For example, one of the great discoveries of Freud was of the oedipal complex of childhood psychosexual development, what he referred to as the "shibboleth" in psychoanalysis,[3] in which the desire of children to take pride of place in the lives of their opposite sex parent is met with powerful prohibitions (against incest) and the associated anxieties that competing for this place with the same sex parent. These challenges of anxiety, albeit different for boys and girls, are universal and unavoidable and drive inner conflicts between the desire and yearning (the libidinal cathexis) that meets up against the counter-cathexis of the equally powerful and universal incest-taboo. Internal psychic conflict is, for better or worse, an inherent part of human mental development.

The Multiplicity of Subjectivities

This fascinating tendency of the human mind appears unique amongst the species. As best we can observe, no other organism suffers from the complexity of internal conflicts, or is caught in the muddle of multiple internal voices. Whilst such mechanisms as flight-fight appear common through evolution, humans are uniquely endowed with the capacity to evaluate flight-fight responses through a filter of historical associations. These associations are embedded in personal memory and how such memory was encoded. The intra-punitive mechanism that humans suffer, that of guilt and conscience, for example, does not seem to afflict lower organisms. A lion does not feel guilty after a kill. Nor does a Zebra suffer the ambivalence of its attachments. As Freud quipped in letters to Marie Bonaparte written a few years before his death, "Dogs love their friends and bite their enemies, quite unlike people, who are incapable of pure love and always have to mix love and hate",[4] that is, to suffer the pain and complexity of ambivalence.

This reminds us that intra-psychic conflict is hardwired into human development and the human mental apparatus in a fashion unique amongst the biological species. Even primates appear less tormented by mental conflicts or conscience, less hamstrung by the burden of mixed feelings. Human psychic complexity struggles from the outset with internal tensions and conflicts out of which, suggests psychoanalysis, symptoms are born. The reason Freud centralised sexuality in the genesis of neuroses is that the libidinal drive renders helpless any attempts to neutralise its intense and immensely powerful thrust, since, without it, the evolutionary push to survival, attachment, procreativity might have been dilute, weak, and invariably the indicator of biological demise in the evolutionary processes. But human sexuality suffers the restrictions of the libidinal drive in evolution too: the genetic and psychic inhibition against incest. In fact, it could be argued that the taboo against murder of one's own parent is lower than the taboo against having sex with one's parent. Matricide, for example, may seems horrendous and rare despite murderous feelings being normative and common, but incestuous desires are universal and in-built to psychosexual development in childhood and engenders all manner of complicated yearnings and counter-measures in the form of various defensive manoeuvres and repression.

Even further back in development, before the oedipal drama takes hold at around three years of age, the infant struggles with the slings and arrows of its feelings to its primary attachment, the love and hate of the maternal object, since it is she upon whom dependency is critical to survival. The maternal object represents love and security when bonding goes well and needs are well satiated, but also represents the frustrations and threats to psychic stability and equilibrium, and intensely negative feelings can be stirred in response to these perceived maternal failures. It is as if the infant is occupied by various internal selves, one that hates and one that loves, one that strives to attach and one that strives for individuation.[5] As Mahler notes, "Through maturation of the ego apparatuses—and facilitated by the flux of developmental energy — a relatively rapid, yet orderly process of separation-individuation takes place in the second year of life".[6] These tensions are never lost to the human mind, even in adulthood, and the pain of losses and longings pepper all humanity all the time all of their lives. The internal conflicts are encoded into memory, so that layers of later development are never free from these influences.

If symptom states represent deviations from stasis, but mixed feelings are so endemic to human development, and unconscious conflicts between different parts of the mind so ubiquitous, we are left to ponder how deviations from homeostasis can be fairly represented? Which part of the mental apparatus' inner voices, so to speak, could be associated with stasis and which deviations from it? At first blush, psychoanalysis would argue that this conundrum is a non-sequitur, since it has long been understood that the human psyche is capable of compromise-formations, creating a balancing act of different internal tensions, many unconscious, through which conflicts can then be navigated. Wrote Freud about dream life: "What becomes conscious in such cases is a compromise between the intentions of one agency and the demands of the other. Repression—relaxation of the censorship—the formation of a compromise, this is the fundamental pattern for the generation not only of dreams but of many other psychopathological structures...".[7] But later, added that whereas dream work provided the initial impetus for understanding symptoms, he came to see that although previously psychoanalysis had only been concerned with solving pathological phenomena, that in order to explain them it had often been "driven into making assumptions whose comprehensiveness was out of all proportion to the importance of the actual material under consideration". But when it came to dreams, he noted, it was no longer dealing with a pathological symptom, but with a phenomenon of normal mental life that might occur in any healthy person.

Dealing with the link to symptom formation, Freud posited the ideas that,

> If dreams turned out to be constructed like symptoms, if their explanation required the same assumptions—the repression of impulses, substitutive formation, compromise-formation, the dividing of the conscious and the unconscious into various psychical systems—then psycho-analysis was no longer an auxiliary science in the field of psychopathology, it was rather the starting-point of a new and deeper science of the mind which would be equally indispensable for the understanding of the normal.[8]

Freud had thus observed that psychical conflicts between the differences agencies of the mind are imbedded deeply in the structure of normal human functioning. The three primal agencies of mind that Freud designated to capture this concept was what he termed the ego, super-ego and id. The ego is a technical mental barrier between the internal and external worlds, one that operated much like the surface of the skin of the body. The id (the "It" in German) is characterised as the source of the impulse world, but in neuroscientific terms, the fountain of consciousness, as Solms explains it, a 'fountain' essentially for homeostatic regulation. The superego, emergent as a branch of the aggressive drive that turns inwards and serves as a self-regulating, guilt-induing function, this intra-punitive mechanism serving to regulate primal and unbridled instinct originating in the id.

We never escape internal conflict, and, in a sense, this gives rise to the peculiar characteristic of human functioning that there are different subjectivities operating within the mental apparatus and that the mind can both know itself and not know itself simultaneously. The individual is invariably wrestling internally between one part of the mind and another, and Freud emphasised that the pathway of the life drive (or libidinal drive) from the outset of life played an extraordinary role in the genesis of both normal human development and deviation from it. Psychoanalysis has long recognised the inner conflicts between these different agencies of the mental apparatus, and the tensions that govern competing needs between the unbridled and rambunctious 'greed' of id impulses against the harsh regulations of the super-ego. But this idea of different agencies of the psyche in tension and conflict, carries a deeper dimension that fuels this structural tension. This is the dual-drive nature of the mind – the essential drives of sexuality and aggression that Freud elegantly discovered as the governors of mental life. Important to note, is that for Freud, sexuality carries primacy since this energetic push presents from the outset of life, and forges the adaptive capacity of all organic beings in the evolutionary imperative that Darwin identified.[9] Without this powerful prompting, life would be short and brutish. But this drive is met with another, whose purpose is to maintain, conserve, and protect the organism from the impingements of the environment, making the aggressive drive function as the immune system of the mental apparatus that I identified in my previous book.[10]

So, these two primal and primary energetic drives also tension against each other, the one striving to enable (epi)genetic variation and adaptation and the other to maintain and conserve by expending less energy to achieve more, if at all possible, as a principle of efficient organic functioning. As Solms points out, that for example, the 'predictive brain' is revealed neuroscientifically to be 'lazy', at least over the long term, "vigilant for every opportunity to achieve more by doing less"[11]. This makes intuitive sense, of course, that any organic system survives best by being efficient and energetically economical.

So, conflict is imbedded *in* the human psyche from the get-go, even before the structural agencies of the mind that Freud's 'topographical' model identified are fully formed in later infancy and early childhood. But these intrapsychic conflicts, for Freud, invariably centred around how psychosexual foci and their challenges were navigated and the emergent defensive constellations either largely resolve or become stuck, fixated when the infant fails to adequately migrate through the requisite developmental phase. These defensive constellations are *emergent*, a brilliant insight that Freud noted governed mental life, that the conduits of the soma give rise to an experience of literal 'polymorphism', or what he termed 'polymorphous perversity',[12] with somatic foci at different development stages of infancy governing the nature of the defensive systems that can emerge in the psychic realm. The body is an unending source of pleasurable (and unpleasurable) sensations. If, for example, the early infant in their first-year experiences its psychogenic focus around feeding, the mouth, tongue, swallowing, gastrointestinal tract becomes the central somatic experience of the infant. Denial (closing of the mouth and excluding the outer world from inner reality), incorporation or introjection (the taking in and swallowing) or projection (the ejection of the inner into the outer) become mental representations of somatic foci and when poorly navigated can lead to these mechanisms becoming fixated, as aversive experiences get encoded in early memory for later effective retrieval. Memory encoding of aversive experience will determine which mental constellations and its defences are returned to repeatedly. These occur according to the dictates of the repetition compulsion and the need neurobiologically to return to and retrieve aversive associations in the interests of restoring equilibrium by referencing the past in the service of the future.

Psychosexuality and Its Centrality

We can readily see why Freud came to regard the sexual drive as occupying a dominant part of the genesis of psychopathology and neuroses, and being the essential driver of all the key early psychosexual phases of development, from pre-genital to genital sexuality. "In the Oedipus complex", he wrote, "the libido was seen to be attached to the image of the parental figures. But earlier there was a period in which there were no such objects. There followed from this fact the concept (of fundamental importance for the libido theory) of a state in which the subject's libido filled his own ego and had that for its object. This state could be called *narcissism* or self-love."

But this observation that libidinal drives are inset from the outset of life and that a self-preservatory mechanism had to exist in a portion of that libido directed at the self, consolidated Freud's theory at that time that this life drive was ceaseless during the natural course of a life cycle. He added, that a "moment's reflection showed that this state never completely ceases. All through the subject's life his ego remains the great reservoir of his libido, from which object-cathexes are sent out and into which the libido can stream back again from the objects. Thus, narcissistic libido is constantly being transformed into object-libido, and *vice versa*."[13]

A key element of the libido theory was not that infants experience genital sexuality but that their bodies both generate and absorb sensations and sensory foci which give rise to representations in the psyche,[14] since the "analysis of the perversions and psychoneuroses has shown us that this sexual excitation is derived not from the so-called sexual parts alone, but from all the bodily organs." Accordingly, Freud suggested at the time that "It should be the task of a libido theory of neurotic and psychotic disorders to express all the observed phenomena and inferred processes in terms of the economics of the libido".[15] More and more, this took hold of Freud's imagination and empirical work, leading him to suggest: "For I was then already aiming at a libido theory of the neuroses, which was to explain all neurotic and psychotic phenomena as proceeding from abnormal vicissitudes of the libido, that is, as diversions from its normal employment".[16] The libidinal drive thus appeared to drive all development and psychological organisation, from the outset of life, and as the biological sciences would later verify, drove life from the very outset of its advent. Energy gradients drive the animate, and appear to have been present from the outset of the animate. Life, from the beginning, is characterised first by a chemical and later emergent psychical drive, contained in every living cell and in the complex emergences of multicellular life, and ultimately in the vicissitudes of instinctual and emotional life. Particular somatic experiences take centre stage at various ages through which the world is experienced.

For the individual infant, making *efficient* meaning out of these initially *meaningless* experiences means that the infant must form mental representations of these experiences. They must create ideational impressions, albeit primitive ones, that 'explain' the nature of the feelings it is having, since these promptings have the essential aim of restoring homeostasis when it is disrupted, in response to both external and internal impingements. It must interpret and encode experience meaningfully if such memory is to be used *efficiently* in a *feedforward* manner, as Solms describes it, to fulfil the predictions of earlier memory in navigating life forward.[17] As Solms writes, "In other words, when a need propels us into the world, we do not discover the world afresh with each new cycle. It activates a set of predictions about the likely sensory consequences of our actions, based upon past experience of how to meet the selected need in the prevailing circumstances".[18] This point is central to understanding the function of memory in serving both drives in the direction of homeostasis, and is a point I will return to throughout the book.

There are somatic experiences that promote feelings of what Freud called 'unpleasure', this unpleasure being a form of information, evoking the need for remedy. However, homeostatic needs, as they become felt, are initially in life amorphous, meaningless, primordial, and require some form of ideation to emerge (cortically) that can represent these feelings to the self – to make 'mental solids'[19] out of diffuse feelings that enable their differentiation. Not all needs are the same, *feel* the same (and this is crucial in understanding the role feelings play in homeostatic rendering), or require the same remedy. Thirst, for example, has a very different requirement to choking, or being too cold, or experiencing sexual tension. In infancy, such ideational representation is primitive and, one might suggest, chaotic and only becomes more meaningful through the mediation of the maternal mind and the mirroring and metabolising she affords her infant. The drive to live is fostered by the powerful urge to bond, since without bonding the infant's health and life would be seriously and entropically compromised. Life's most important guard against premature entropy in infancy is the presence of a caring, loving maternal object, attuned to the physical and emotional needs of her infant in all its mixed feelings that emerge.[20]

I indicate mixed feelings since even a well-attuned mother, in Winnicott's terms a 'good-enough' mother, will fail her infant by her inability to create perfect stasis and comfort for her baby, or to be perfectly attuned. Frustration and failure are inevitable, in fact imbedded in early life, and whilst the life drive promotes bonding in the service of its sustainability, so too feelings of frustration and failure are inevitable. Disruptions to the libidinal drive and the bonding (love) it induces, create mixed feelings, ambivalences that are early seeds for the feelings of love and hate that define themselves more clearly through psychic maturation in the life cycle. We could say that whilst one part of the psyche speaks of the deepest love when content, another speaks of the darkest hate when not.

Minds in Contest

On the face of it, this claim appears preposterous – that different minds inhabit one mind, that there are divergent internal voices speaking of different things, and invariably simultaneously. This multiplicity of subjectivities occupying one mental apparatus pits the drives against each other, libidinal and aggressive (about which I will have much more to say later), but also the different forming agencies of the mind. Put differently, the human psyche finds itself perpetually in conflict, not only with the external world but with its own internal states and feelings, and by extension, the central objects that inhabit its world, especially its mother, upon whom it depends both physically and mentally for her interventions, ministrations, and mediations. The mutuality of this bond, this love we might say, is so central to human survival and health that without it, all manner of problems threatens for later life. This intense and requisite life force, so central to sustaining life itself, underscores the libido theory that Freud came to attribute great importance in the centrality of human development. Also, understandably, this drive seemed to predominate in later sexuality and especially as genital sexuality took primacy at puberty during the second wave of the di-phasic developmental nature of human sexuality that Freud identified. "Over and over again we find", he wrote, "when we are able to trace instinctual impulses back, that they reveal themselves as derivatives of Eros".[21]

In this regard, Freud noted, "that the neuroses arise in the main from a conflict between the ego and the sexual instinct, and that the forms which the neuroses assume retain the imprint of the course of development followed by the libido—and by the ego".[22] However, Freud also stressed through his theoretical work that the conflicts within the psyche and between the different agencies of the psyche are also a normative process in all mental functioning: "The importance in the causation of illness which must be ascribed to *quantity* of libido is in satisfactory agreement with two main theses of the theory of the neuroses to which psychoanalysis has led us: first, the thesis that the neuroses are derived from the conflict between the ego and the libido, and secondly, the discovery that there is no *qualitative* distinction between the determinants of health and those of neurosis" and that, on the contrary, healthy people have to contend with the same tasks of mastering their libido. But, Freud says, "they have simply succeeded better in them".[23]

This is important, since it suggests that neurotic disturbance and psychopathology are not a qualitatively distinct set of parameters which afflict the unwell and distinguish such patients from the well. With physical diseases it may often be said that one person has it and another simply does not. But in psychic terms, rather, the unwell can be said to be a continuum of the well, perturbations *in-extremis* of defences and process of psychic conflict attributable to all human minds, "as proceeding from abnormal vicissitudes of the libido, that is, as diversions from its normal employment."[24]

The reader will note that conflicts derived from disturbances in the quantity and quality of libidinal cathexes underlie neurotic, psychotic and normal development. Some of that libidinal drive is attached to the infant's own ego in the service of self-preservation, without which the pressure to meet needs might be severely compromised. Libidinal promptings drive this process, from the mitochondria of cells and its electron gradients to the multiplicity of complex emergent organ systems, the drive to maintain and preserve life appears central to its maintenance. But with the tendency to conflicts between the love and hate of the mind in relation to its objects, and also the inner tensions between different agencies of the mental apparatus, it is as if the human psyche is wracked by a multiplicity of subjectivities driven primarily and powerfully by the drive to sustain cohesion of the self in the face of constant challenges to both stasis and inevitably to existential longevity of the Self *itself*.

Eros therefore appears to dominate life since this force of energy in the human mind has roots in the advent of living matter itself. The human infant has to struggle to both evolve and conserve itself, subject to the laws of nature that Darwin and later biologists identified, suggesting that the struggle for life is beset by variation and adaptation versus conservation and self-preservation. This balancing act of life in all forms, suggests that without adequate conservation, identity of any self-organising system would become too diffuse and lead to entropy. On the other hand, every living thing is challenged by pressures from an evolving environment, and those that can adapt to change through what Darwin called variation, that being (epi) genetic changes, survive better and those that resist change through inadequate variation also suffer heightened risk for entropy. Life is a fine dance between these strains, a balancing act in which only those that manage to tread the fine line make it through the generations.

In the human infant, Freud wrote, "At the very beginning, all the libido is accumulated in the id, while the ego is still in process of formation or is still feeble. The id sends part of this libido out into erotic object-cathexes, whereupon the ego, now grown stronger, tries to get hold of this object-libido and to force itself on the id as a love-object. The narcissism of the ego is thus a secondary one, which has been withdrawn from objects".[25] Erotogenic zones emerge through this process of libidinal cathexes in which parts of the infant's own body, most dominant at any particular phase of development, will become cathected with libidinal energy and in this dialectic of somatic sensation and need becoming an 'object' of focus. In this process, relatedness is set up in a back-and-forth fashion, between the forming and rudimentary ego of the infant and its body part in-focus. Hence, these somatic zones or parts become imbued with libidinal or erotogenic energy, the foundation then of mental representations and psychic ideation as the infant makes meaning of rudimentary experiences and sensations and applies ideational representations to them. This process is less abstract than this sounds: What the mouth or upper gestatory tract can do, for example, forms the mental representation of closing, opening, ingesting and incorporating, ejecting, and so forth. These mental representations become the mental prototypes of projection, introjection, denial and so forth that characterises early oral defences in the first phase of mental development. The relationship between somatic and mental experience forges itself in this dialectic process to consolidate early memory representations of how to both interpret and navigate life forward, in the primary interests of homeostasis and preservation.

This process presents us with challenges, since it implies that the encoding of memory traces is subjective from the outset, that there is an "I" experiencing and interpreting the environment unconstrained by any objective version of the same. Homeostatic deviation in the mental sphere therefore presents as deviation from subjective interpretation of the body in relation to the world around it, through a rudimentary ego unable to strictly differentiate internal and external worlds. Symptoms are therefore built-upon deviations from subjective interpretations of homeostasis, influences, we would suggest, by the myriads of environmental and temperamental factors in play for the infant. Freud's observations were ground-breaking but his libido theory was not the final word on psychic tensions or the manner in which the psyche protects itself. Indeed, libido directed at the self is in play as a self-preservatory mechanism (and has to be) but Freud also came to recognise that the tension of the psyche was rooted in the tension of all living mater – something deeper predated the evolutionary advent of the mental apparatus. Against this force of life, the drive (libidinal) that promotes adaptation and variation and is therefore inherently creative and procreative, is tensioned a conservative mechanism aimed at preserving an organism's Markov blanket and 'narcissistic' identity at both personal and species levels.

But if the body utilises an immune system (and of course, other regulatory systems) to preserve itself from entropic threats when impingements threaten it, what does the mental apparatus utilise for this emergent purpose, when disequilibrium prevails and variational free energy is increasing in the direction of entropy? This question imposed itself between Freud's earlier dominant model of libido and its self-preservative elements and his later realisations of the incompleteness of this model. In his theoretical developments he wrote strongly that: "Lastly, I cannot conclude the present work, which is once again only a fragment of a larger whole, without foreshadowing the two chief theses towards the establishment of which the libido theory of the neuroses and psychoses is advancing: namely, that the neuroses arise in the main from a conflict between the ego and the sexual instinct, and that the forms which the neuroses assume retain the imprint of the course of development followed by the libido—and by the ego".[26] As we can see, by this stage of his work, Freud had certainly pinned his colours to the mast, and was convinced that the aetiology of mental disorders, the origin of symptoms, was in disturbances within the mental apparatus in relation to the sexual drive.

Borrowing from biology, Freud grappled with the question of what I call mental immunity, since the question of what services or drives this *conservation* system remained elusive and incomplete, especially in a context in which the intriguing and paradoxical qualities of human aggression appeared to serve no evolutionary purpose and hence violates the science in this regard. This conservative drive appeared to utilise some form of aggression to mediate deviations from homeostasis when needs are not being met and the arrow of homeostasis is heading in the wrong direction, and whose aim Freud noted was the restoration of an earlier state that existed prior to an impingement-causing deviation from stasis. To remedy the instability of his earlier theoretical model, and to account for homeostatic requirements, Freud later settled on a more dualistic model of mind in which the primary forces of life (eros or libidinal) and what he termed the death-drive (aggressive), wrestle with each other and complement each other from the outset of both animate and complex mental life. In other words, Freud's more mature model, formulated in his brilliant thesis *Beyond the Pleasure Principle*, [27] tapped into this duality that the biosciences also note is present in all living matter – two forces in opposition, a conservative drive and a life drive operating at both physical and mental levels.

Beyond the Pleasure Principle

As mentioned above, Freud had noticed and emphasised the sexual drive in the genesis of symptoms and neurotic disorders, over and over. To remind the reader, how in a letter to a Dr M. Fürst, he wrote that he came to regard the psychosexual constitution and certain noxae of sexual life as the most important causes of the neurotic disorders that are so common, adding, "My Three Essays on the Theory of Sexuality, too, where I have described the way in which the sexual instinct is compounded and the disturbances which may occur in its development into the function of sexuality…"[28] are at the root of neurotic conflicts and their consequent disorders. Already, in 1898, he had begun to engage deeply with this concept, noting how, "A dim knowledge of the overwhelming importance of sexual factors in the production of neuroses (a knowledge which I am trying to capture afresh for science) seems never to have been lost in the consciousness of laymen",[29] and he never seemed to shift away from this emphasis, albeit for good reasons we shall continue to explore, and which links to current neuroscientific approaches from some quarters that also emphasise life-drive neurological circuits and mechanisms in the pursuit of homeostatic bounds, a debate I shall return to shortly.

The tensions of the psyche in managing the complex conflicts of sexual wishes and promptings, fantasies and enactments, driven by what he identified as the pleasure principle, the promotion of pleasure and the avoidance of unpleasure, governed the 'pressures' from within the mind and body and the way that guilt, repression, and other mental manoeuvres lay at the foundation of psychic tensions. From the outset, managing these tensions was a challenge for the infant and as they matured through oedipal awareness, so the advent of gender identity and the associated cross-gender same-gender tensions and rivalries added complexities to the parental *imagos* that would come to govern post-pubescent sexuality and genital adult sexuality.

But Freud retained an intellectual niggle that challenged the neatness of his libido theory. In particular, when Fechner brought to attention the notion of what today we may refer to as homeostatic deviation, pleasure and unpleasure "as having a psycho-physical relation to conditions of stability and instability",[30] Freud had framed this as "the mental apparatus endeavours to keep the quantity of excitation present in it as low as possible or at least to keep it constant".[31] Freud's acknowledgement of a limitation of the pleasure principle led to his making the point that:

> This latter hypothesis is only another way of stating the pleasure principle; for if the work of the mental apparatus is directed towards keeping

the quantity of excitation low, then anything that is calculated to increase that quantity is bound to be felt as adverse to the functioning of the apparatus, that is as unpleasurable. The pleasure principle follows from the principle of constancy: actually, the latter principle was inferred from the facts which forced us to adopt the pleasure principle.[32]

The essence of the concept that homeostatic deviations too far from normal parameters of constancy will yield unpleasure, also suggests that a mechanism is required to register and respond to such deviations. In this regard, a 'conscious' layer that served to differentiate the outer from the inner worlds would be required to limit the bombardment of stimuli against the mental apparatus but also, it would require a method of storing information to better navigate environmental complexity.

The memory of the unconscious also cannot simply be a store of unfiltered stimuli since the economics of the mind as well as its efficiency would not tolerate an endless and unfiltered storage of raw data. Rather, the psyche must interpret and encode the endless streams of data in a fashion that is relevant and useful, according to the subjectivity of the individual psyche doing the experiencing. Hence, subjective interpretation of experience may be said to trigger from the outset of life, following birth, at which point there is an outer and inner world that requires navigation and differentiation, a state that does not exist in utero. As Kinet puts it, "What appears in consciousness, after all, are not direct, unprocessed signals from the periphery but predictive inferences from the memory traces of those signals and their consequences. Our perceptions of the here and now are guided by predictions derived mainly from long-term memory"[33] but in the interests of guiding the future, in the present.

Also, in the mix, Freud noted that the psyche has a tendency to return repeatedly to old traumata, experiences interpreted by the infant to be outside of their homeostatic parameters, influenced, no-doubt, by a host of elements including temperament, maternal attunement, somatic balance, nutrition, and a host of other influencing variables. Essentially, those experiences that might reflect poorly on maintaining a *conservative* position, would likely be encoded as deviations from homeostasis, requiring a response mechanism to remedy such deviations. In future time, when the mind registers a (re-)triggering of old threats to stasis and hence psychic integrity, it can efficiently reference these threats in real-time, and respond accordingly. A current association triggering an old memory of such a threat to stasis will trigger then also a mechanism to restore homeostasis, as subjectivity perceived. Here is, therefore, the significant mechanism that Freud identified for this purpose, one that operates by stealth until activated, which he termed the death-drive, but which is driven by an aggressive process whose effects in the outer world can be deadly even when its aims are benign – that is, the restoration of homeostasis when deviation is increasing through frustration of needs. Put differently, as I mentioned earlier, that Freud noted that there are "component instincts whose function it is to assure that the organism shall follow its own path to death, and to ward off any possible ways of returning to inorganic existence other than those which are immanent in the organism itself".[34] This drive represents a group of instincts which can thus be observed, having "a conservative, or rather retrograde, character corresponding to a compulsion to repeat",[35] whose job is the conservation and preservation of an organisms natural path to death. Two innate drives can thus be seen to emerge: "one constructive or assimilatory and the other destructive or dissimilatory",[36] one striving to create-procreate and promote change and one striving to conserve and maintain the stasis and identity of the self-organising system. Regarding the latter drive, important to remind the reader that the aim of this drive is entirely benign (conservation) but its effects can of course be malignant and destructive to others.[37]

This dualistic view of the psychic drives cements Freud's more mature theoretical discoveries, published even today under the category of 'metapsychology' or 'meta-theory', suggest that the biological and neurosciences had not yet empirically validated such a duality in all life. However, the natural sciences have indeed caught up with Freud's theoretical speculations and in my view serve to validate his bold observations. In all living matter we do observe a pressure to life and 'variation', an epigenetic creativity from which an organism can adapt to change and evolve according to the Darwinian imperative. On the other hand, we observe a conservative tendency, to resist impingement and preserve the 'subjective' identity, what current theorists term the Markov blanket that differentiates self from other.[38] I place subjective in inverted commas because this is not simply about perception in an abstract sense, but the fundamental biological, neurological, and psychological imperative to identify the self as distinct from the environment, without this distinction the risk of entropy increases dramatically. A chimpanzee that thinks it is a bird and can fly will suffer rapid demise as an individual and potentially as a species.

The Death Drive

To say a little more about this mechanism, if feelings and emotional experience give the human mind an advantage in rapid and effective homeostatic regulation through meeting needs and restoring feelings of unpleasure back to pleasure, and this facility is enabled through the ability to encode and record particularly aversive experiences for future *feedforward* reference, then memory is a vital part of the ability to go back in time to be useful to go forward in time. But the layer of conscious perception would be utterly overwhelmed if its job was to hold and navigate sensory data on an ongoing basis. Instead, the unconscious store of experience, filtered through the lens of subjectivity, provides the guide to meeting needs, but also to be a registrar of states of disequilibrium for future use.

But a record of experience, no matter how efficient, is also of little advantage without a mechanism to remediate in the presence of impingements causing states of homeostatic deviation. This led Freud to identify the role of aggression in the preservation of an organism and hence also its conservative character when needs are not being met and/or the individual experiences threat to itself; in other words, when the infant is unable to induce a remedy for deviations from stasis, free energy increases in the direction of entropy, and a 'binding' of this free energy is required. The aggressive drive serves the function of restoring homeostasis in the face of such states of disequilibrium, whether these states originate from the interior of the infant or from its environment, these being largely indistinguishable in the early stages of development when encoding of aversive experience will be heightened and undifferentiated. Interestingly, in line with later neuroscience in which Solms upends some common-held assumptions about consciousness residing in the cortex, places consciousness in the id, in the deeper structures of the brain, in order to fulfil its homeostatic functions effectively. Freud put it that consciousness "communicates to us *feelings from within* not only of pleasure and unpleasure but also of a peculiar tension which in its turn can be either pleasurable or unpleasurable"[39] (italics mine), in his developing the idea of a dual drive theory, an acknowledgement of the homeostatic imperative served by the mental apparatus, and how the internal "breakers of the peace" as well as external threats to equilibrium activate a restorative response.

These speculations of the two drives "seek to solve the riddle of life by supposing that these two instincts were struggling with each other from the very first".[40] All organic matter must, accordingly, have two mechanisms inbuilt which struggle against each other, the one fulfilling the imperative to be able to adapt, evolve (epi)genetically, and procreate in the service of greater unities which protect against entropy (there is strength in identity and numbers), and the other to conserve, preserve, and maintain steady-states in the face of challenges to equilibrium. The death drive, or aggressive drive, utilises aggression for this purpose, and like the immune system of the body seeks to do its work unobtrusively and with a stealth-like quality unless provoked into action. Its aims are benign, therefore, merely the restoration of stasis, but its effects can be lethal, violent, and annihilatory to perceived threats that are regarded as significant. These two drives struggle against each other from the outset of living matter and find their way into higher emergent systems with greater complexity too.

The mental apparatus never escapes these more primitive drives, which wrestle against each other in the complexities of human subjectivity and its deviations in the forms of neuroses and other psychopathologies. Symptoms emerge when this balancing act fails to maintain the tension between the libidinal and conservative drives and their routes through the topographical agencies of the mind. The direction of homeostatic deviation must be as experience is encoded through the lens of subjective experience from the outset, with ideation forming to better describe internally what these somatic and mental states are. Having ideas and words that can distinguish being cold from *having* one enables more efficient response to homeostatic deviations. But ideation is never free from its underlying emotional roots, no matter the complexity of its diversions into ideology or other theories about the self or its environment. The mind has at its disposal these two energetic trends, wrestling with each other in the greater complexities of its emergent systems. Since Eros and its libidinal drives tend to be breakers of the peace and create stimulation that require remedial action, these instincts cannot in themselves always serve this function of remediation. When feelings and affects (libidinally driven) fail to fulfil *their* function of meeting needs that restore homeostasis, the death drive and its aggressive derivatives must activate to bind increasing free energy, moving the infant away from homeostasis, to restore homeostasis. The death drive, with its ability to aggress in the service of restoration, appears to fulfil this function, using memory as its guide to what is experienced and regarded as a deviation or threat, and finding a route to fulfil this function.

The Death Drive in Contention

As I have highlighted, Freud's great breakthrough on the *duality* of drives has forever, and it seems, continues to cause "such a stir".[41] From various angles, analysts and theorists have resisted the concept of the death drive, and his use of the term 'death' as a descriptor, leading to a multitude of misinterpretations and colloquial misrepresentations, despite others regarding it as Freud's "greatest theoretical contribution to understanding the dynamics of the unconscious mind".[42] I don't intend to engage with the many philosophical and theoretical debates around this contentious space, since that would be a book on its own, but I would be remiss to not address current neuroscientific thinking that challenges Freud's dual-drive model from a different and newsworthy angle, and, to boot, from an eminent neuroscientist, who makes the claim that "there is no death drive at work in the mind".[43] Solms argues the point that "there is no need to invoke the existence of a separate "death" drive that serves the Nirvana principle[44]; it is served by the "life" drives *and it represents their ideal state*".[45] The 'ideal state' can be thought of, in this sense, as a form of a quiescent state, one in which homeostatic demands have achieved perfect balance and there is no immediate demand upon the mind for work. In other words, life drive mechanisms can *by themselves*, accordingly, service and achieve the imperative to strive for, and achieve homeostasis. Solms writes about this as such:

> What all of this means, at bottom, is that drive pressure (affective arousal) must be minimised, and the way we do this is by generating the best

predictions we can as to how we might reduce the pressure by meeting our needs in the world. This is the great task of learning from experience. Let me be as clear as possible, since this is so fundamental: drive is a measure of the expected free energy in the mind, energy that must be deployed in effective work, work that requires learning. Learning, in turn, entails improving the system's predictive model of its self-in-the-world, and this is the ground-zero origin of *representation*. [46]

However, as I will argue below, Solms' interpretation suggests that life drive mechanisms are capable of achieving the goal of the "ideal state", which often, for internal and external reasons, they are not. It is seldom that life-drive pressures to meet our various needs occur without *frustration*, of at least some of them, some of the time. Most of the time, we are making the best of a bad lot, a homeostatic 'approximation'. Rarely, in real life, is anything we strive for not accompanied also by some frustrations. Metaphorically, every meal has to be sourced, prepared, cooked, and cleaned after. The moments of blissful satiation are few by comparison, and even these moments are often accompanied by gastric distention and wind. It is true, that, at bottom, "drive pressure (affective arousal) must be minimised",[47] says Solms. Yet, we simply cannot meet all needs all of the time. Invariably, one need gets triaged against another, so that we may have to sacrifice our oedipal desires to avoid the taboo of incest, or the retaliation of a competing parent; we cannot always meet our needs for love or novel sex at the same time we stay married or have to work! That is to say, that *frustration* as a concept is omnipresent in life's demands for psychological work. *Frustration* creates a sensation (an experience of sorts) that indicates free energy is increasing and that needs are not being fully met or not being met at all. Freud himself wrote of free and bound energy from early in his career and never abandoned the concepts.[48] The question must be asked: can the life drive and its neurobiological systems remedy this problem alone? As arousal increases due to uncertainty, says Solms, we must "*learn* how to minimise arousal",[49] or put differently, strive to reduce increasing free energy; the life drive and its mechanisms cannot continue trying to meet irreconcilable needs or 'banging its head against a brick wall', as the risks in the direction of entropy would become compelling. And of course, the whole corpus of psychoanalysis rests on the findings that most of the causes of neuroses and psychopathology is rooted in infancy when the infant is helpless to remedy their frustrations, except through crying (an aggressive *inducing* mechanism rooted in the death drive) or mental defences that do the job when even this proves ineffective.

It would seem that the mental apparatus requires another drive to mobilise when this phenomenon of frustration of needs and increasing free energy is current (real-world exogenous frustration per se *or* because of irreconcilable and competing endogenous needs). This task, Freud argued, is delegated to the aggressive drive in its various manifestations, and the associated defence mechanisms the subject uses based on their past early experiences, when defences mobilised to bind free energy but have become 'fixated', automatised in memory as a result. Freud's dual drive theory accounts for the work of the death drive/ aggression not in the service of meeting needs directly, but of binding free energy when feeling-driven needs are not met. It accounts also for the perversion of the aggressive drive in the "promiscuous" form that Anna Freud identifies.[50]

I will explore these issues in more detail below but first must point out a second and equally important point in contention – which Panksepp identifies neurologically, and Solms employs in his writings, to dispute the notion of the *two* Freudian drives, claiming on the neurological evidence that there is a *multiplicity* of drives – some of which are somatic/ bodily and seven of which are emotional.

When getting into the ring with a scientific Mike Tyson, it behoves one to tread with great respect and caution, and I intent to do so here. My only comfort in challenging two of Solms' assumptions is that I have Freud in my corner. In reviewing Solms' 'revision of drive theory', there is much to agree with, based on modern neuroscience and Freud's own injunctions to future generations to challenge his theories based on newer evidence from science and biology. Neuroscientists such as Damasio,[51] Panksepp,[52] and Solms[53] have done so to great neuroscientific benefit. There are, however, the two points of departure to question, which drive some 'revisions of the revision' to posit, and hopefully also a remedy for my disagreements. The first point of departure, I have dealt with above and will deal with it further shortly. The second one I will deal with below.

In Solms' paper revising Freud's classical drive theory[54] he both updates Freud's classical drive theory and diverges from it in several significant ways, basing his arguments on current researches and insights into the brain and its connection to mind. As mentioned, this is a task for which Freud would certainly have expressed his approval, and did so in the seminal work formulating the dual drive theory. I will briefly highlight Solms' points of revision, basing his reformulation on authors such as Panksepp and others, and indicate those which are not in contention and those which are.

A Multiplicity of Drives?

Solms argues that firstly, drives are conscious and are the source of consciousness. This is hard to refute, especially given his insights and evidence espoused elegantly in his latest book.[55] Of course, infantile consciousness is not of the kind that emerges later in human development, as cognitive capacity develops to enable ideational representations to form, that create meaning out of emotionally *meaningless* states, but the essential point brings current science into alignment with Freud's initial formulations. Secondly,

Solms argues that drive energy is equated with variational free energy, the implication being that as we move away from homeostatic settling points free energy increases, which also moves the subject in the direction of entropy. If the subject cannot respond to *feelings* as they become conscious, which indicate deviations from homeostasis, and through this perform the action/work required to meet the specific needs that would return to viable bounds, then the risks for mental and somatic morbidity and mortality increases.

In infancy, this function is expressed though crying (and variations of niggling, fussing, protesting etc.), an *inductive* mechanism rooted in the aggressive drive. This point of variational free energy is important, which despite being correct in my view, also provides one of the challenges I will shortly suggest below to Solms' revision. Thirdly, based on Panksepp's researches and formulations, Solms suggests there are not two but many drives, seven on which may be described as "emotional" as opposed to "bodily" drives. This revision is based on the brain circuits that are correlated with particular emotional states and affects that drive behaviour.

There is no refuting of these neurological circuits here but the question must be asked: are these separate drives or are they circuits or mechanisms that still serve the two fundamental drives that Freud identified? I will elaborate further on this and add a new dimension that speaks to the bridge between what I maintain are branches of the same tree. All the circuits Panksepp identifies are 'organs of the same body', not separate *drives*. Fourthly, Solms suggests that all drives are self-preservative and preservative of the species, that is, "all drives are homeostatic"[56], and serve a homeostatic function which moves the individual *subject* away from unpleasure and towards pleasure, in the service of preservation. There can be little disputing that homeostatic pressures govern the mind in service of the body, and that even emotional drives, and not only bodily ones, serve this purpose.[57] As a result, Solms concludes there is no death drive.

On this latter point, I part ways with the implication that because all drives are homeostatic and anti-entropic this obviates the need for a conservative mechanism to activate when needs are *not* met, free energy increases as a result, *frustration* increases, and a second mechanism becomes a requirement to step in and bind this excess free energy. Without this, how do we explain the well-recognised concept of defence mechanisms? Fifthly, Solms suggests that the great task of development is to learn how to meet conflicting needs and multiple drive demands. Here, too, there can be little to refute – except to add that by the time learning becomes effective, the infant has already experienced a multitude of challenges that have endlessly frustrated it, which required binding, and fixated (became automatised) in memory (both implicit and explicit) through early defence mechanisms, as a result.

So, in short, yes, drives are conscious or become so. Yes, drive energy is equated with variational free energy and is therefore associated with homeostatic requirements and are preservative and anti-entropic. However, the multiple circuits (or mechanisms) that Solms and Panksepp identify to achieve this end are serving the continuance of life, biological persistence against the pressures of premature entropy. That is, they serve the life drive, much like the different biological systems of the body, such as the respiratory system, the cardiovascular system, the nervous system, etc. are all systems or mechanisms designed to fulfil the needs of the body in pursuance of the drive to keep living: they are parts of the whole and serve the different bodily requirements to maintain life. All the neurological 'drives' that Panksepp identifies surely exist, based on the evidence, but they are tasked with maintaining life requirements, of promoting the life drive, Eros, and serving libidinal needs towards this end. Are they each a separate drive? Or mechanisms/ circuits/ systems that cover the various requirements to maintain life and promote it? Hence, are they servants to the life drive, or competitors for it? This is not a merely semantic challenge but conceptually important. I will shortly further elaborate this duality and the relationship they have to each other. But first, a tour through these mechanisms.

Panksepp identifies seven neurological emotional drives or circuits, which I will briefly outline to make this point. These "emotional drives", which he capitalises to distinguish them from colloquial use, can be reliably elicited by electrical or (specific) chemical stimulation and are shared across the evolutionary ladder with all mammals, "from mice to men",[58] as Solms puts it. The seven emotional 'drives' consist of SEEKING, LUST, RAGE, PLAY, FEAR, PANIC-GRIEF, and CARE,[59] and for the most part can be understood by the descriptors he has awarded these 'drives'. They do what these labels suggest they do. From an evolutionary perspective, we can suggest that each of these mechanisms or systems of, and in the brain have developed to facilitate the requirements and pressures of life, for each one has as its task to create the necessary attributes for the furthering of the *push* of the life drive in complex organisms. As humans, this complexity is considerable and these emotional mechanisms have evolved to better achieve the result of sustaining life by promoting affects and their behavioural manifestations. Lust, seeking and foraging, the impulse to care for offspring, to bond in ways that promote love and attachment, to express a powerful sexual drive through lust that facilitates the creative/ procreative requirement for evolutionary continuance. All these mechanisms can be viewed not as separate drives but as branches of the life drive, and the libidinal requirements to maintain the individual and their offspring in the interests of the species too, *serving* their master of Eros and the libidinal branches that enable this life requirement. These branches of the same primary tree are serving the grand master of homeostasis in the pursuance of life drive requirements, which is, fundamentally, to persist.

If this is true, that the two fundamental primary drives remain intact in a dual-drive model of the mental apparatus, as Freud had suggested, we are

challenged then to explicate how these streams connect, what their relationship is to each other, their bridge. We know from Freud that these two forces
have tensioned against each other from the outset of life, and carry the features of cosmic and biological life in general, suggesting the tensions of self-
organising/ self-preservation versus diffusion or entropy. In humans, we
notice another omnipresent phenomenon in and of mental life, which we
commonly refer to as *frustration*, and yet it is a phenomenon that is most
difficult to explicate theoretically. What is this sensation of *frustration* that is
so ubiquitous to the lived experience of human life?

The Bridge Between the Drives

Frustration is unlikely to be found in the brain in any mechanistic sense, and
yet in mental life this all-too familiar *experience* plays a constant and significant role, one so central to the drives and yet poorly represented in the
literature as a concept, except interestingly by Freud himself, who saw frustration as directly linked to the onset of mental problems but located this
squarely around sexuality. Some writings have linked frustration with
aggression but it still remains background as a concept. Yet, it appears to me
that this subjectively driven psychical experience offers us a key to making
sense of the bridge between the drives.

Freud wrote, that, "Frustration has a pathogenic effect because it dams up
libido, and so submits the subject to a test as to how long he can tolerate this
increase in psychical tension and as to what methods he will adopt for dealing with it. *There are only two possibilities for remaining healthy when there is
a persistent frustration of satisfaction in the real world.* The first is by transforming the psychical tension into active energy which remains directed
towards the external world and eventually extorts a real satisfaction of the
libido from it. The second is by renouncing libidinal satisfaction, sublimating
the dammed-up libido and turning it to the attainment of aims which are no
longer erotic and which escape frustration".[60]

In other words, life drive pressures can keep going, continue to press for
fulfilment by amplifying the drive until they reach a dead-end, as it were, in
which need satisfaction-through-drive cannot be fulfilled, or simply, that
need-fulfilment violates an internal taboo or mental conflict. The term frustration (*versagung*) is one Freud came to use to describe both sources, a more
embracing concept,[61] covering both kinds of internal and external obstacles
to satisfaction of a need. Frustration must then activate subjective dispositional factors, such as defence mechanisms, in its service. Defences are
required to bind increasing free arousal. "The immediate effect of frustration
lies in its bringing into play the dispositional factors which have hitherto
been inoperative",[62] writes Freud. Such defensive manoeuvres are rooted in
the quest for conservation and preservation, making the best of a bad lot by
binding excess arousal with whatever available *mental* means are present to

the infant/ baby and which via the repetition compulsion will have a tendency to be revisited throughout life. In other words, writes Freud, "the libido may thenceforward move on a backward course; it may follow the path of regression along infantile lines, and strive after aims that correspond with them". Increasing intensity of frustration triggers regression, setting in motion old mechanisms for preservation. He adds:

> If these strivings, which are incompatible with the subject's present-day individuality, acquire enough intensity, a conflict must result between them and the other portion of his personality, which has maintained its relation to reality. This conflict is resolved by the formation of symptoms, and is followed by the onset of manifest illness. The fact that the whole process *originated from frustration* in the real world is reflected in the resulting event that the symptoms, in which the ground of reality is reached once more, represent substitutive satisfactions.[63]

The experience of *frustration* signals that the affects and feelings that are in pursuance of the life drive, in their quest to maintain the pleasure-principle (that being homeostatic parameters in their viable bounds), are failing to meet expectations of the mental work being done (this includes crying in infancy to induce a response from the maternal object with a view to remedy of states of disequilibrium). When needs are not being met in the interests of restoring homeostasis, *frustration* increases, this being the subjective representative of increasing free energy, which is moving the *subject* outside of their perceived viable bounds and in the direction of "uncertainty"[64] and entropy. As Freud noted, "The unsatisfied and dammed-up libido (that is, life drive pressures) can once again open up paths to regression and kindle the same conflicts which we have demonstrated in the case of absolute external frustration. We are reminded in this way that the quantitative factor should not be left out of account in any consideration of the precipitating causes of illness".[65] The quantitative factor suggests an increase in *drive pressure* beyond subjective capacity to reduce it through directly meeting the need. Many experiences in this direction are not life-threatening from a somatic point of view – such as having a heart broken in love is not the same as having a cardiac arrest – but life's challenges introduce into experience situations that increase surprise, unpredictability, and free energy – unexpected states that push experience in the direction of entropy.

Solms articulates this problem in different terms, but which essentially describes the same phenomenon. "This brings us to the crux of the matter", he says. "The difference between the sensory states that are *predicted* by the system's internal states to flow from its active states and the sensory states that *actually* flow from them must be minimised. This difference is called 'surprisal.' Put simply: the system must avoid surprising (unexpected) states if it is going to survive. This is the mechanism of homeostasis all over again".[66]

In other words, when "surprisal" increases and "prediction errors" based on memory increase, so uncertainty and free energy increases, and the arrow of homeostasis is going in the wrong direction. Subjective needs are not being adequately met. In a similar way that the feeling of hate is a subjective *conscious* experience reflecting an otherwise latent aggressive drive, so *frustration* signals consciously to the subject that needs are not being met and free energy/ unpredictability is increasing. This phenomenon, of life-drive mechanisms failing to fulfil their function, failing to fulfil need-requirements, failing to ensure predictable outcomes, suggests that with increasing free energy another mechanism is required to bind this excess energy, to cathect it, in the interests of restoring mental homeostasis. It is surely a compromise-formation, since often the needs remain unmet and yet mental dysregulation finds a return to a form of a quiescent state. The excess arousal through frustration is 'mopped up', as it were, reduced, despite inadequate real-world remedy of needs being met.

To return to Solms' point, the question that must be asked: what happens when the mental work of life-drive demands and learning to meet them is failing? Solms adds, "The gap between the predicted sensory states of a self-organising system and its actual states, over a given period of time, is measured as its free energy. Because increasing free energy is an existential threat to the system, the system must minimise the *expected* free energy. And this, it appears, is the fundamental mechanism of drive. Drive is a (quantifiable) measure of the demand made upon the system for *more effective* work",[67] or as Valdrè puts it citing Freud, to aim for "a reduction or annulment of unpleasure..."[68] in the service of homeostasis.

The point about "*effective*" work, is also an implicit theoretical concession that mental work is not always effective, that often in life the real world is a never-ending source of frustrated or incompatible needs. The fall-out from this requires a mechanism to manage it, to reverse the direction of the arrow of free energy and entropy. What all this essentially means, and I want to repeat Solms' point, that since drive pressure (affective arousal) must be minimised, the way we do this is by generating the best predictions we can as to how we might reduce the pressure by meeting our needs in the world. This is the great task of learning from experience. "Let me be as clear as possible" he writes, "since this is so fundamental: drive is a measure of the expected free energy in the mind, energy that must be deployed in *effective* work, work that requires learning. Learning, in turn, entails improving the system's predictive model of its self-in-the-world, and this is the ground-zero origin of *representation*".[69]

Once again, let me emphasise the notion that *effective* work is required to meet needs. That is, when life drive mechanisms are failing, another mechanism is required to bind free energy. But the life drive cannot remediate its own frustrations except through trying different courses of action, or amplifying its efforts and eventually, as Freud put it, "extorts a real satisfaction of the libido"[70] from the external world. This is not always possible, especially in the helpless states of infancy, creating the imperative for another mechanism to manage excess or increasing arousal. It is the conservative drive, the death drive, that is tasked with this role of binding increasing free energy and reducing it to a manageable level of 'excitation', "to keep the quantity of excitation present in it as low as possible or at least to keep it constant".[71] In other words, Freud makes the point that,

> This latter hypothesis is only another way of stating the pleasure principle; for if the work of the mental apparatus is directed towards keeping the quantity of excitation low, then anything that is calculated to increase that quantity is bound to be felt as adverse to the functioning of the apparatus, that is as unpleasurable.[72]

In neuroscientific terms, we must trend in the direction of homeostatic parameters, not away from them, at least over time. This means the mental apparatus is never in a fully quiescent state, of course, because the complex demands of the mind-body system are perpetual, but the requirement to approximate it, to move in the direction of stasis, remains an ongoing imperative. When this is not being achieved, in real time as it were, disequilibrium creates increasing arousal in a negative direction, a precursor to *frustration*.

To put this essential point differently: Life-drive needs, and the feelings that come to represent them, can only prompt in one direction, along the path of doing the work required to fulfil *specific* needs, but cannot on their own do anything to remediate frustration when this mission is incomplete, except to continue to prompt and push feelings in that direction of which the need is directed. But this cannot continue indefinitely, and nor does it invariably solve the problem. Sometimes, in fact, often, a real satisfaction of the libido cannot be "extorted"; it leaves exposed no remedy to reverse the direction of increasing arousal/ free energy.

The presumption error that Solms makes, I believe, is that needs get met when feelings 'announce' them to consciousness, and prompt the work required for their fulfilment. This imperative is not in contention. But, most often, the route to this fulfilment of needs is not plain sailing. Needs are often not *fully* met, not met at all, or conflicting agencies of the mind obscure any remedy for needs to be met – especially the classical neurotic internal psychic conflicts of infancy and childhood, which are often irreconcilable. For an example, the infant hating and wanting to destroy the bad breast/ frustrating mother that the infant also depends upon and needs for survival, can be an irreconcilable conflict. Hence, for example, the attachment needs that drive CARE and attachment relate to PANIC-GRIEF when separation is promoted, including through the infant's own felt and phantasised RAGE. Or, the impossible resolution of the oedipal complex where the phantasy and the reality can and should never coincide. The question must then be repeated: when needs are not met, what then? What mechanism provides a mental remedy when this free energy and arousal is rising? And this is pertinent especially considering that *most* of a person's mental life is forged in the furnace of early development, the first few years in fact, where the infant is utterly helpless to meet any of their own needs. Frustration abounds!

Increasing free energy tends to correlate with a rising sensation of *frustration*, which appears to be the signal to the psyche to achieve a binding by whatever means are available; to reverse the direction of increasing arousal and frustration, back in the direction of a bound (cathected) state where a return to a perceived quiescence is possible. Of course, much of the time, in humans, this is a mental state, a compromise, that creates automatised repetitions through the same learning that Solms mentions for meeting life-drive needs. So too, as Nobel Prize winning neuroscientist Eric Kandel points out, and is well noted in psychoanalysis, negative or aversive experiences get encoded too, stored in memory for later feedforward use.[73] Here, we note the aggressive drive activating to step in and do the work required in the direction of conservation, to get back to psychological and biological integrity through binding rising free energy. The use of the defence mechanisms of infancy, encoded in personal history and hence subjectively driven, can be used to achieve such a binding, a mental mechanism that finds a compromise-formation to obviate the satisfaction of the need in the real world and simultaneously resist mental fragmentation that would follow without excess arousal being brought under control. These mechanisms which are so central to psychopathology, will be explored further in the various chapters below.

Mediated by Frustration

James Strachey, the editor of the Standard Edition of Freud's works, pointed out that Freud came to regard 'frustration' as a significant feature of mental life and as a "principal precipitating cause of neurosis" which "became one of the most commonly used weapons in Freud's clinical armory, and it recurs in many of his later writings".[74] It may be said that the life-drive uses various neurological systems and circuits to *push* its agenda, from the outset of life and through the timeline of human development. Whilst Freud strongly linked life drive pressures to libidinal ones of a direct sexual nature, stating, for example, that "a comparative study of the determining causes of falling ill leads to a result which can be expressed in a formula: these people fall ill in one way or another of frustration, when reality prevents them from satisfying their sexual wishes".[75] But of course, life-drive pressures are not always of a direct sexual nature in the genital sense – even when they are of a *libidinal* nature – that is, driven by life-drive promptings and needs. Freud does concede that "people fall ill of a neurosis if they are deprived of the possibility of satisfying their *libido*—that they fall ill owing to 'frustration', as I put it— and that their symptoms are precisely a substitute for their frustrated satis- faction".[76] In this sense, libido is a more general expression of life-drive pressures which aim for satisfaction of needs in general, for the purpose of returning to stasis and the subject's viable settling points. This latter point is simply to state the obvious, that whereas some homeostatic settling points are non-negotiable and objective, such as thermoregulation, others of an emotional nature become much more subjective and hence much wider in what would be regarded as viable bounds.

I am sure we can all agree, as Solms suggests, that all *feelings* are homeo- static-inclined, and must be consciously felt, but at the same time not all *drives* are consciously felt. The life drive, having much more contact with our internal perception, gives rise to affects and feelings. Life drives and their feelings are felt because they have so much more contact with our internal perception, "as breakers of peace and constantly producing tensions whose release is felt as pleasure"[77] (that is, prompting in the direction of home- ostasis), writes Freud, and are hence themselves disruptors – they disrupt mental homeostasis to serve somatic homeostasis – think thirst, hunger, or sexual arousal. Whether of a bodily or emotional nature, feelings therefore prompt remedial action to fulfil needs that move *the subject* in the direction of viable bounds.

But the less manifest drive is less felt – the death drive doing its work "unobtrusively",[78] as Freud noted. When needs are frustrated and the work required is either impossible to solve (think the oedipus complex) or get fru- strated for other reasons, the subjective and conscious valence of *frustration* serves as a bridge between the two fundamental drives and seems to stimu- late aggression into a more manifest form, but in the service of, and with the aim of, restoration and conservation, of binding. When needs are prompting through the conscious experience of feelings, it is an indication that home- ostasis is being challenged from interoceptive or exteroceptive sources, and with these deviations free energy is increasing, which must be reduced or eliminated to resist entropic pressures. Invariably, says Freud, "I find a por- tion of frustration operating alongside of a portion of incapacity to adapt to the demands of reality; inhibition in development, which coincides, of course, with inflexibility of fixations, has to be reckoned with in all of them...".[79] Here again we can link Freud's concept of libidinally driven life drive pres- sures meeting limited solutions and resolution in the real world – hence, *frustration* increases proportionally to the perception or experience of the rising of arousal and hence free energy. In this sense, we could say that free energy in the mental apparatus has a subjective element, based on early experience.

Doing the mental work required to meet needs reduces or eliminates free energy and returns the individual to homeostasis, or a quiescent state, in which tension has been reduced or eliminated, at least temporarily. This can be thought of as a state of "Nirvana", to use Low's concept,[80] but this Nirvana principle is a fleeting island in time before endogenous or exogenous stirrings prompt needs again. As needs get frustrated and cannot be fulfilled, allowing free energy to keep increasing, this becomes proportionally related to the *experience of frustration*, frustration being the bridge from the life drive, a signal to the aggressive/death drive to step in and perform a binding using available defences. The former function is the prompting of greater measures to overcome the obstacles to satiation of the need – but this on its own moves the individual in one direction only – when what becomes required is to move the individual back.

Preferably, I would call it a *sensation* of frustration, since it is driven by a feeling-of, rather than ideation, and appears to be *experienced* as a sensation that needs are *being* frustrated in real-time; it is variable, not binary, as there appears to be a quantitative measure that correlates increasing frustration with increasing mobilisation of the aggressive drive. Freud put it the other way around, that "fixation of the libido and frustration—are represented in such a manner that if there is more of the one there is less of the other",[81] but of course, where there are impediments to satisfying libidinal needs there will be a direct increase of frustration, which must then be bound. We could perhaps call this 'sensation of frustration' an in-built *barometric sensor*, one that picks up on a change in the internal atmosphere of the mind-body system when there is increasing disequilibrium to unmet needs, and those invisible changes in the interior atmosphere of the mind-body system activate a mechanism to address this unwelcome trend.

Conservation and Fixation

This task of binding free energy falls to the conservative mechanisms of the mental system, of its 'immune' system – which activates aggression through regression, revisiting in memory those earlier defences that served to bind free energy in infancy and reduce it to manageable levels of relative quiescence. There is no other mechanism to achieve this benign aim. As I will discuss later in more detail, this is what defences are for – early mental mechanisms working in conjunction with the body (as emergent representatives of somatic experience), mobilised by frustrations as free energy is increasing, to reduce tensions to a *manageable* level, and these become encoded in implicit or explicit memories that form to feedforward. As defences, these mechanisms can and do become automatised ('fixated' in analytical language). Memory must encode to automatise and reduce prediction surprise for life-drive needs, but it also must encode aversive events, frustrations that mobilise the aggressive drive in its quest for restoration and conservation. These too can become automatised and hence 'perverse' – "promiscuous" in Anna Freud's terminology, directed at many objects: but their true quest is preservation of the subject's own identity, their Markov blanket, through such regression to earlier defences.

If there are two principal drives, their relationship to each other must be made clear. What is the bridge between the two basic drives? *Mediated by frustration*, the life drive's failure to meet needs activates the aggressive drive. This duality emerges out of all evolutionary trends, from the cosmic expansion and the forward flow of time prompting self-organising versus diffusion or entropy of matter and energy, to biological tensions between (epigenetic) variation versus conservation. Cosmic and biological life is invariably a tension between forces. The mental apparatus presents us with no exception.

It is interesting to consider that this compellingly ubiquitous and universal daily experience of *frustration* as an experience of the human mind is hardly written about as a central concept – except by Freud. Yet, the bridge between the human drives appears to be mediated by this central experience, representing the conscious experience that the work being done by the mind to move it towards 'pleasure' is failing. This is unlikely to be represented in concrete mechanistic terms in the brain and yet it is a compellingly important part of it, serving as a proportional indicator and remediator of life-drive promptings failing, with the degree of frustration being inversely proportional to the degree of this failure. Decreasing satisfaction of needs met, correlates with an increasing free energy and threat of entropy, mediated by *frustration*, that signals this *trend* to activate or mobilise the death drive, to regress to previously encoded automatisms (defences) tasked to bind or decrease this trend, in the interests of conservation and a return to homeostasis, via the best available compromise-formation. This manoeuvre enables a reduction for the subject of free energy and a return to a semblance of *perceived* stasis and quiescence.

The shift from drives being preservative and hence homeostatic and anti-entropic, which Solms identifies I believe correctly, does not necessarily equate to a singularity of drive theory, that being the life drive, or the notion that Panksepp's identification of multiple brain circuits suggest these are multiple separate drives. Rather, these various brain circuits and branches serve this fundamental premise of living, of Eros, and in fact all biological life on earth. The life drive, Eros, would underpin Solms' revision of drive theory in which the underlying circuits or mechanisms of the brain that Panksepp identifies *push* affects and feelings to the surface of mentalisation, with a view to remedial action in the real world, where needs must be met. However, and this is key, needs are not always met, and certainly not always fully met. *Frustration* invariably accompanies this partial success, or even failure of life-drive libidinal pressures, and appears to be the mental mechanism that mediates to steer the psyche away from needlessly and fruitlessly trying to continue to meet needs that cannot be met, instead mobilising the aggressive drive to find a way to bind this excess free energy.

We could say that if needs were always met once feelings identified increasing free energy and a move away from homeostasis towards entropy, then I would agree that there would be no need for a death drive or even a conservative mechanism beyond the rage circuit whose function is self-preservation through hierarchical competition for resources or for adaptive predatory gain. But alas, organic life, and especially human life, is fraught with failures, frustrations and impossible dilemmas, such as those of the infant hating the frustrating breast it also depends upon, or the oedipal phase of psychosexual development wherein desire and phantasy can never be met in reality. *Frustration* mediates the link between the two fundamental drives that Freud identified in his dual-drive theory and, I suggest, strengthens the case for both the death drive and its relationship to the life drive rather than weakens it. As Valdrè suggests: "The Freudian death drive offers us one of the best, if not the only, hypothesis able to explain in psychoanalytic terms this paradoxical thrust of the human being",[82] and based on the neuroscience of today, and the neuroscience of Freud's thinking, an excellent confluence.

Since this is such an important point, I wish to distil its essence into one sentence: it is not the fulfilment of homeostatic needs that leads to symptoms and psychopathology in humans; it is the *frustration* of need-fulfilment and its effects that leads to symptoms and psychopathology.

Life drive needs do not in themselves lead to symptoms – death drive mobilisation leads to symptoms. In the form of an equation, we could say simply, that from the outset of life: the aggressive drive is directly proportional to increasing frustration of need-fulfilment.

Or, put differently: aggression is directly proportional to rising free energy and, mediated by frustration, inversely proportional to meeting homeostatic needs and their subjectively-perceived settling points. The mobilisation of the death drive and its constituent processes (such as defences and regression to them) is thus directly proportional to the subjective barometric experience of *frustration*, that signals the arrow of entropy is moving in the wrong direction away from homeostasis.

At this juncture, we could conclude our point that aggression fulfils this function of homeostatic restoration when the libidinal one fails to meet needs, or other impingements threaten, and little more would need to be said. It may be true that a RAGE circuit can be neurologically identifiable, but is not experienced by the individual subject in one form - and as Panksepp acknowledges, "to the best of our meagre knowledge, most of these complex feelings, just like our jealousies, resentments, and hatreds, are not instinctual primary-process potentials of the ancient emotional part of the mammalian brain". What Freud termed the death drive is not a reductionistic variant of the notion of a rage circuit in the brain, but a complex set of psychical elements whose job description presents in various forms. Is there a need for a separate death drive concept? I hope to show through the remaining chapters that the answer that returns to us is 'yes'. There are two principle drives: one life and one death. Unfortunately, remediation is not so simple for humans and the complexity of the psyche, struggling with itself from the outset, and not only against the outside world.[83]

Notes

1 I deal with this notion of the early infant turning the *meaningless* into meaning in my book *Unlocking the Nature of Human Aggression* (2023), Routledge, related in different terms by Bion characterising this process as the turning of Beta into Alpha elements, or what neuroscientists like Solms calls 'mental solids' – cognitive representations of raw affects.

2 Freud, S. (1923) The Ego and the Id. *The Standard Edition of the Complete Psychological Works of Sigmund Freud* 19:1–66, p.14.

3 Freud, S. (1905) Three Essays on the Theory of Sexuality. *The Standard Edition of the Complete Psychological Works of Sigmund Freud* 7:123–246.

4 Cited in Sacks, A. (2008) The Therapeutic Use of Pets in Private Practice. *British Journal of Psychotherapy* 24:501–521, p.501.

5 Mahler writes, "In this sense, I would propose to distinguish, within the phase of primary narcissism—a Freudian concept to which I find it most useful to adhere—two sub-phases: during the first few weeks of extrauterine life, a stage of absolute primary narcissism, which is marked by the infant's lack of awareness of a mothering agent. This stage I have termed 'normal autism,' as discussed above. In the other, the symbiotic stage proper (beginning around the third month)—while primary narcissism still prevails, it is not such an absolute primary narcissism, inasmuch as the infant begins dimly to perceive need satisfaction as coming from a need-satisfying part object—albeit still from within the orbit of his omnipotent symbiotic dual unity with a mothering agency, toward which he turns libidinally". In Mahler, M. S. (1967) On Human Symbiosis and the Vicissitudes of Individuation. *Journal of the American Psychoanalytic Association* 15:740–763, p.743.

6 Mahler, M. S. (1967) On Human Symbiosis and the Vicissitudes of Individuation. *Journal of the American Psychoanalytic Association* 15:740–763, p.752.

7 Freud, S. (1901) On Dreams. *The Standard Edition of the Complete Psychological Works of Sigmund Freud* 5:629–686, p. 676.

8 Freud, S. (1925) An Autobiographical Study. *The Standard Edition of the Complete Psychological Works of Sigmund Freud* 20:1–74, p. 47.

9 Darwin, C. (2003) *The Origin of Species: By Means of Natural Selection of the Preservation of Favoured Races in the Struggle for Life.* New York: Signet Classic.

10 Perkel, A. (2023) *Unlocking the Nature of Human Aggression: A Psychoanalytic and Neuroscientific Approach.* London: Routledge.

11 Solms, M. (2021) *The Hidden Spring: A Journey to the Source of Consciousness.* London: Profile Books, p. 176.

12 Freud, S. (1905) Three Essays on the Theory of Sexuality (1905). *The Standard Edition of the Complete Psychological Works of Sigmund Freud* 7:123–246.

13 Freud, S. (1925) An Autobiographical Study. *The Standard Edition of the Complete Psychological Works of Sigmund Freud* 20:1–74, p. 56.

14 We have defined the concept of libido as a quantitatively variable force which could serve as a measure of processes and transformations occurring in the field of sexual excitation. We distinguish this libido in respect of its special origin from the energy which must be supposed to underlie mental processes in general, and we thus also attribute a qualitative character to it. In thus distinguishing between libidinal and other forms of psychical energy we are giving expression to the

presumption that the sexual processes occurring in the organism are distinguished from the nutritive processes by a special chemistry. The analysis of the perversions and psychoneuroses has shown us that this sexual excitation is derived not from the so-called sexual parts alone, but from all the bodily organs. We thus reach the idea of a quantity of libido, to the mental representation of which we give the name of 'ego-libido', and whose production, increase or diminution, distribution and displacement should afford us possibilities for explaining the psychosexual phenomena observed. Freud, S. (1905) Three Essays on the Theory of Sexuality. *The Standard Edition of the Complete Psychological Works of Sigmund Freud* 7:123–246, p. 217.

15 Freud, S. (1905) Three Essays on the Theory of Sexuality. *The Standard Edition of the Complete Psychological Works of Sigmund Freud* 7:123–246, p.218.

16 Freud, S. (1914) On the History of the Psycho-Analytic Movement. *The Standard Edition of the Complete Psychological Works of Sigmund Freud* 14:1–66, p.29.

17 Solms, points out, that "… long-term memories serve the future. Once the midbrain decisions triangle has evaluated the compressed feedback flowing in from previous action, what it activates is an expanded *feedforward* process which unfolds in reverse direction, through the forebrain's memory systems, generating an *expected context* for the selected motor sequence. This is the product of all our learning. In other words, when a need propels us into the world, *we do not discover the world afresh with each new cycle.* It activates a set of predictions about the likely sensory consequences of our actions, based upon past experience of how to meet the selected need in the prevailing circumstances". Solms, M. (2021). *The Hidden Spring: A Journey to the Source of Consciousness.* London: Profile Books.

18 Solms, M. (2021) *The Hidden Spring: A Journey to the Source of Consciousness.* London: Profile Books, p. 141.

19 Solms, M. (2021). *The Hidden Spring: A Journey to the Source of Consciousness.* London: Profile Books.

20 See for example, Donald Winnicott (1975). *Through Paediatrics to Psychoanalysis, Collected Papers.* London: Hogarth Press; Winnicott, D. W. (1965) The Maturational Processes and the Facilitating Environment. *Studies in the Theory of Emotional Development* 64:1–11. However, many writers have since corroborated the essential function of a warm and attuned maternal presence in both psychological and neurobiological development.

21 Freud, S. (1923) The Ego and the Id. *The Standard Edition of the Complete Psychological Works of Sigmund Freud* 19:1–66, p. 46.

22 Freud, S. (1911) Psycho-Analytic Notes on an Autobiographical Account of a Case of Paranoia (Dementia Paranoides). *The Standard Edition of the Complete Psychological Works of Sigmund Freud* 12:1–82, p. 79.

23 Freud, S. (1912) Types of Onset of Neurosis. *The Standard Edition of the Complete Psychological Works of Sigmund Freud* 12:227–238, pp 236–237.

24 Freud, S. (1914) On the History of the Psycho-Analytic Movement. *The Standard Edition of the Complete Psychological Works of Sigmund Freud* 14:1–66, p.67.

25 Freud, S. (1923) The Ego and the Id. *The Standard Edition of the Complete Psychological Works of Sigmund Freud* 19:1–66, p. 46.

26 Freud, S. (1911) Psycho-Analytic Notes on an Autobiographical Account of a Case of Paranoia (Dementia Paranoides). *The Standard Edition of the Complete Psychological Works of Sigmund Freud* 12:1–82, p.79.

27 Freud, S. (1920) Beyond the Pleasure Principle. *The Standard Edition of the Complete Psychological Works of Sigmund Freud* 18:1–64.

28 Freud, S. (1907) The Sexual Enlightenment of Children (An Open Letter to Dr. M. Fürst). *The Standard Edition of the Complete Psychological Works of Sigmund Freud* 9:129–140, p.131.
29 Freud, S. (1898) Sexuality in the Aetiology of the Neuroses. *The Standard Edition of the Complete Psychological Works of Sigmund Freud* 3:259–285.
30 Freud, S. (1920) Beyond the Pleasure Principle. *The Standard Edition of the Complete Psychological Works of Sigmund Freud* 18:1–64, p.8.
31 Freud, S. (1920) Beyond the Pleasure Principle. *The Standard Edition of the Complete Psychological Works of Sigmund Freud* 18:1–64, p.8.
32 Freud, S. (1920) Beyond the Pleasure Principle. *The Standard Edition of the Complete Psychological Works of Sigmund Freud* 18:1–64, p.9.
33 Kinet, M. (2024) *The Spirit of the Drive in Neuropsychoanalysis*. London/ New York: Routledge.
34 Freud, S. (1920) Beyond the Pleasure Principle. *The Standard Edition of the Complete Psychological Works of Sigmund Freud* 18:1–64, p.39.
35 Freud, S. (1920) Beyond the Pleasure Principle. *The Standard Edition of the Complete Psychological Works of Sigmund Freud* 18:1–64, p.39.
36 Freud, S. (1920) Beyond the Pleasure Principle. *The Standard Edition of the Complete Psychological Works of Sigmund Freud* 18:1–64, p.39.
37 I give a thorough treatment of this distinction in my earlier book, Perkel, A. (2023) *Unlocking the Nature of Human Aggression: A Psychoanalytic and Neuroscientific Approach*. London/ New York: Routledge.
38 See Solms' book for a wonderful treatment of these links: Solms, M. (2021) *The Hidden Spring: A Journey to the Source of Consciousness*. London: Profile Books.
39 Freud, S. (1920) Beyond the Pleasure Principle. *The Standard Edition of the Complete Psychological Works of Sigmund Freud* 18:1–64, p.63.
40 Freud, S. (1920) Beyond the Pleasure Principle. *The Standard Edition of the Complete Psychological Works of Sigmund Freud* 18:1–64, p.60.
41 Valdrè, R. (2025) *The Death Drive: A Contemporary Introduction*. New York/ London: Routledge, p.87.
42 Mills, J. (2006) Reflections on the Death Drive. *Psychoanalytic Psychology*, 23(2), 373–382, pp.373–374, p.377.
43 Solms, M. (2021) Revision of Drive Theory. *Journal of the American Psychoanalytic Association* 69(6), 1033–1091, p.1033. https://doi.org/10.1177/00030651211057041.
44 The notion of the 'Nirvana principle' is a concept Freud borrowed from Barbara Low, see Freud, S. (1920) Beyond the Pleasure Principle. *The Standard Edition of the Complete Psychological Works of Sigmund Freud* 18:1–64, p.39. The concept really refers to a condition in which all active states come to rest in perfect homeostasis and there are no impingement from within or without the organism making demands for work, and in which tensions are reduced or even eliminated.
45 Solms, M. (2021) Revision of Drive Theory. *Journal of the American Psychoanalytic Association*, 69(6), 1033–1091, p.1054. https://doi.org/10.1177/00030651211057041
46 Solms, M. (2021) Revision of Drive Theory. *Journal of the American Psychoanalytic Association* 69(6), 1033–1091, p.1060. https://doi.org/10.1177/00030651211057041.
47 Solms, M. (2021) Revision of Drive Theory. *Journal of the American Psychoanalytic Association* 69(6), 1033–1091, p.1060. https://doi.org/10.1177/00030651211057041.
48 See, for example, the footnote 10 in Valdrè, R. (2025) *The Death Drive: A Contemporary Introduction*. New York/ London: Routledge, p.16.
49 Solms, M. (2021) Revision of Drive Theory. *Journal of the American Psychoanalytic Association* 69(6), 1033–1091, p.1060. https://doi.org/10.1177/00030651211057041.

50 Freud, A. (1949) Aggression in Relation to Emotional Development; Normal and Pathological. *Psychoanalytic Study of the Child 3*, 37–42.

51 Damasio, A. (2018) *The Strange Order of Things: Life, Feeling, and the Making of Cultures.* London: Penguin Random House.

52 Panksepp, J. & Biven, L. (2012) *The Archaeology of Mind: Neuroevolutionary Origins of Human Emotions.* New York: Norton.

53 Solms, M. (2021) Revision of Drive Theory. *Journal of the American Psychoanalytic Association* 69(6), 1033–1091. https://doi.org/10.1177/00030651211057041.

54 Solms, M. (2021) Revision of Drive Theory. *Journal of the American Psychoanalytic Association* 69(6), 1033–1091. https://doi.org/10.1177/00030651211057041

55 Solms, M. (2021) *The Hidden Spring: A Journey to the Source of Consciousness.* London: Profile Books.

56 Solms, M. (2021) Revision of Drive Theory. *Journal of the American Psychoanalytic Association,* 69(6), 1033–1091, p.1062. https://doi.org/10.1177/00030651211057041.

57 Panksepp distinguishes between bodily and emotional drives – but all essentially aim to maintain the subject within its viable bounds of 'pleasure' and away from unpleasure – that is, towards homeostasis rather than away from it.

58 Solms, M. (2021) Revision of Drive Theory. *Journal of the American Psychoanalytic Association* 69(6), 1033–1091, p.1064. https://doi.org/10.1177/00030651211057041.

59 Panksepp, J. & Biven, L. (2012) *The Archaeology of Mind: Neuroevolutionary Origins of Human Emotions.* New York: Norton. As Solms explains, Panksepp put his terms for the drives in full capitals, to distinguish them from colloquial usage – that is, to indicate that he was talking about whole biological systems, not only the feelings. In Solms, M. (2021) Revision of Drive Theory. *Journal of the American Psychoanalytic Association,* 69(6), 1033–1091, p.1064. https://doi.org/10.1177/00030651211057041.

60 Freud, S. (1912) Types of Onset of Neurosis. *The Standard Edition of the Complete Psychological Works of Sigmund Freud* 12:227–238, p. 232. Italics mine.

61 Freud, S. (1912) Types of Onset of Neurosis. *The Standard Edition of the Complete Psychological Works of Sigmund Freud* 12:227–238, p. 230. Versagung means 'failure' (of a need) through denial of fulfilment because of depriving the self through an inner obstacle or through an outer obstacle – both lead to frustration.

62 Freud, S. (1912) Types of Onset of Neurosis. *The Standard Edition of the Complete Psychological Works of Sigmund Freud* 12:227–238, p.232.

63 Freud, S. (1912) Types of Onset of Neurosis. *The Standard Edition of the Complete Psychological Works of Sigmund Freud* 12:227–238, p.232. Italics mine.

64 As Solms explains it, referencing Pfaff (2005): "increasing arousal is the same thing as increasing information-processing; the more *uncertain* an animal is, the more aroused it becomes. The converse of arousal, in a sense, is habituation. Therefore, the essential task of mental life (of what we psychoanalysts call 'ego development') is to *learn* how to minimize arousal". Solms, M. (2021) Revision of Drive Theory. *Journal of the American Psychoanalytic Association* 69(6), 1033–1091, p.1060. https://doi.org/10.1177/00030651211057041.

65 Freud, S. (1912) Types of Onset of Neurosis. *The Standard Edition of the Complete Psychological Works of Sigmund Freud* 12:227–238, p.236 (brackets mine).

66 Solms, M. (2021) Revision of Drive Theory. *Journal of the American Psychoanalytic Association* 69(6), 1033–1091, p.1059. https://doi.org/10.1177/00030651211057041.

67 Solms, M. (2021) Revision of Drive Theory. *Journal of the American Psychoanalytic Association*, 69(6), 1033–1091, p.1059. https://doi.org/10.1177/00030651211057041.
68 Valdrè, R. (2025) *The Death Drive: A Contemporary Introduction*. New York/London: Routledge, p.20.
69 Solms, M. (2021) Revision of Drive Theory. *Journal of the American Psycho-analytic Association*, 69(6), 1033–1091, p.1060. https://doi.org/10.1177/00030651211057041; italics mine.
70 Freud, S. (1912) Types of Onset of Neurosis. *The Standard Edition of the Complete Psychological Works of Sigmund Freud* 12:227–238, p. 232.
71 Freud, S. (1920) Beyond the Pleasure Principle. *The Standard Edition of the Complete Psychological Works of Sigmund Freud* 18:1–64, p.9.
72 Freud, S. (1920) Beyond the Pleasure Principle. *The Standard Edition of the Complete Psychological Works of Sigmund Freud* 18:1–64, p.9.
73 Kandel, E. (2006) *In Search of Memory: The Emergence of a New Science of Mind*. New York: WW Norton & Co.
74 Freud, S. (1912) Types of Onset of Neurosis. *The Standard Edition of the Complete Psychological Works of Sigmund Freud* 12:227–238, p.229.
75 Freud, S. (1917) Introductory Lectures on Psycho-Analysis. *The Standard Edition of the Complete Psychological Works of Sigmund Freud* 16:241–463, p.300.
76 Freud, S. (1917) Introductory Lectures on Psycho-Analysis. *The Standard Edition of the Complete Psychological Works of Sigmund Freud* 16:241–463, p.345.
77 Freud, S. (1920) Beyond the Pleasure Principle. *The Standard Edition of the Complete Psychological Works of Sigmund Freud* 18:1–64, p.63.
78 Freud, S. (1920) Beyond the Pleasure Principle. *The Standard Edition of the Complete Psychological Works of Sigmund Freud* 18:1–64, p.63.
79 Freud, S. (1912) Types of Onset of Neurosis. *The Standard Edition of the Complete Psychological Works of Sigmund Freud* 12:227–238, p.237.
80 Freud, S. (1920) Beyond the Pleasure Principle. *The Standard Edition of the Complete Psychological Works of Sigmund Freud* 18:1–64, p.56.
81 Freud, S. (1912) Types of Onset of Neurosis. *The Standard Edition of the Complete Psychological Works of Sigmund Freud* 12:227–238, p.347.
82 Valdrè, R. (2025) *The Death Drive: A Contemporary Introduction*. New York/London: Routledge, p.3.
83 Panksepp, J. & Biven, L. (2012) The Archaeology of Mind: Neuroevolutionary Origins of Human Emotions. New York: Norton, p.161.

Chapter 3

The Ascendance of Libido and Psychic Conflicts

The Enemies Within

It would be a simple matter if, as with more primitive organisms, the conflicts between the life and death drives flowed in the manner we observe. If life were simpler for the human construction, we would vanquish our enemies and go home to eat! But what if the enemy is within? What if the enemies we seek to vanquish are instinctual promptings or agencies of mind within ourselves? What if, wracked by inescapable ambivalence, we were doomed to struggle with ourselves and our objects, both in the outer world and as we represent these objects within our own psyches?

Unfortunately, the human mind is blessed, and some may suggest cursed, by the inner nature of conflicting feelings, of ambivalence, of love and hate to the same objects. Moreover, it is doomed to wrestle with an internal mechanism that is intra-punitive, namely the superego or conscience. Not only that, but we have instinctual promptings that strive to defy taboos and which require counter-measures to prevent the enactments of such taboos. Time and evolution have cast certain human impulses into this category of 'taboo', building into development mechanisms to inhibit specific impulses for the risk they pose to species and individual adaptation. Genetic variation is compromised by poor cross-over of genetic material and the great advantage that procreative sex bestows, enabling the combining of genetic material in the interests of long-term species preservation. At a species level, the bio-chemist Nick Lane points out that sex, that is the ability of complex organisms to combine their DNA, enables deviant cells to be sidelined in the course of evolution, a mechanism to ensure viability. Cellular and DNA cloning seems like an easier option for reproduction but according to the biochemists would lead to extinction as genetic flaws reproduce.[1] In other words, over time, genetic in-breeding creates genetic weakness and so successful genetic code embeds in itself those taboos that inhibit libidinally driven impulses and phantasies towards familial love objects. And yet, most libidinal impulses are directed at precisely such familial objects. These first love objects in life are also those prohibited from enactments of what we might call 'impure love'. So, in the first instance, the embodied nature of human love both invites and simultaneously prohibits certain impulses and

DOI: 10.4324/9781003628972-4

wishes, originating both from the love of a child and we might observe from and to the love also of the mother and later the father.[2] Internal conflicts therefore inhabit the psyche and rage in the child from the outset. These inner conflicts are universally inescapable in humans.

But the simultaneous striving for, and prohibition of 'impure' love being a feature of the internal conflicts and machinations of the mind also link to the frustrations of the love-object in much less conscious ways. The pre-oedipal infant must find ways to manage its unbridled love and adaptive benefits of bonding and secure attachment to its mother but also the inevitable feelings of frustration and consequent moments of hate that characterise the ambivalent nature of human bonding. In fact, we observe that the greater the bond and the love, so too the greater the propensity for hate. This complicated feature of human bonding, suggests that those who are closest and most meaningful in a life are also those with the greatest power to initiate hurt and psychic injury, especially the mother in whom so much of the infant's mental energy and investment is made. Defaults at this early level carry great valence since the dependency is so significant and the scope of the infant's world so narrow. Affective experience is hence also intense and disproportionate.

The internal machinations and conflicts that plague the human psyche can therefore be seen to be drawn from two domains: the one, the mixed feelings and ambivalences embedded in attachment – the love and hate; but also, it would seem that the different agencies of the mental apparatus are in conflict with each other – the id is regulated by the ego, repression mounts a response to the uncontrolled expression of affects and impulses, and later in development with the advent of the superego, the "heir to the oedipal complex", as Freud noted, conflicts between the id and superego as they wrestle for unbridled enactments tensioning against the conscience and restrictive intra-punitive regulations of guilt and its inhibiting tendencies. Freud observed:

> It has justly been said that the Oedipus complex is the nuclear complex of the neuroses, and constitutes the essential part of their content. It represents the peak of infantile sexuality, which, through its after-effects, exercises a decisive influence on the sexuality of adults. Every new arrival on this planet is faced by the task of mastering the Oedipus complex; anyone who fails to do so falls a victim to neurosis. With the progress of psycho-analytic studies the importance of the Oedipus complex has become more and more clearly evident; its recognition has become the shibboleth that distinguishes the adherents of psychoanalysis from its opponents.[3]

The love and hate are subjective experiences of feeling states. On the one hand, they reflect the core underlying drive of libidinal strivings for attachment and greater unities, and on the other, the frustration-driven hate, the *subjective feeling* of the conservative latent aggressive drive becoming activated. The internal conflicts between the different agencies of the mind would seem to operate in a different fashion, separate from these fundamental internal drives. This is only true in part, for agencies of the mind also evolve from and are governed by these underlying drives. Or put differently, the agencies of the mind require energy to drive their function, and despite fulfilling a topographical function by giving structure to the mental apparatus, are nought without the underlying energetic drives. The id may be a seething cauldron of unbridled impulses, "which contains the passions"[4] and as Freud notes, that "object-cathexes proceed from the id, which feels erotic trends as needs",[5] but these are still *energetic* promptings of the libidinal force that underpins the life drive. Without the primitive free-flowing impulses of the libidinal drive there would be no id agency, the id being as "the great reservoir of libido"[6] from which form and ideation must still emerge to create meaning for and as these libidinal promptings attach to love-objects in the infant's life.

The ego forms over time, from which an emergent "I" of consciousness develops. "It is to this ego that consciousness is attached", says Freud, "the ego controls the approaches to motility—that is, to the discharge of excitations into the external world; it is the mental agency which supervises all its own constituent processes…".[7] It represents the interface between the internal and external worlds. Neuroscience debates whether the actual *seat* of consciousness resides in the ego (and the higher cortical structures of the brain), since it can be argued according to the function of consciousness which is a sophisticated homeostatic regulator, that the seat of consciousness emerges from the id itself, the internal mechanisms of brain regulation,[8] leading to a paradoxical observation: Solms argues that, "the conclusion is inescapable: *consciousness is generated in the id*, and the ego is fundamentally unconscious".[9]

Neuroscientists such as Solms make a strong and pioneering case for this notion, that consciousness is not a simple derivative of higher cortical function but has its origins in the affective 'feel' of deep brainstem promptings. Freud does acknowledge that, "All perceptions which are received from without (sense-perceptions) and from within—what we call sensations and feelings—are Cs. (conscious) from the start",[10] but he did wrestle with the function of consciousness as an agency of mind and appeared to locate it in the cortex, which was normative for the scientific understandings of his day. The question he asks about mental energy seeking discharge is, "Do they advance to the surface, which causes consciousness to be generated? Or does consciousness make its way to them?".[11] This conundrum is never fully resolved by Freud, but certainly the more recent neuroscientific views of the id are that it serves the function of bringing somatic requirements to the mind in order that the mind can both make meaning of raw feelings and serve its homeostatic function of restoring stasis when deviations from stasis occur.

The superego, or ego-ideal, is a structure that emerges as an internal regulator, not in the homeostatic sense of consciousness and its relation to the id, but as a form of a moral interlocutor between unbridled drives and the social environment. One can, of course, see its value in promoting familial and social cohesion in groups in the interests of a human imperative to survive. However, this agency of the mind is formed from a branch of the aggressive drive, turning inwards as an intra-punitive device to regulate incestuous impulses through identification with the paternal competitor. This mechanism we can describe, as Freud does, as one which he asks, is how and why does the superego develop such extraordinary harshness and severity towards the ego? Turning to depression as a point of departure, he pointed out that we find that the excessively strong super-ego "which has obtained a hold upon consciousness rages against the ego with merciless violence, as if it had taken possession of the whole of the sadism available in the person concerned". Following his view of sadism, he argues that we should say that the destructive component had entrenched itself in the super-ego and turned against the ego. "What is now holding sway in the super-ego is, as it were, a pure culture of the death instinct, and in fact it often enough succeeds in driving the ego into death, if the latter does not fend off its tyrant in time by the change round into mania".[12]

We will have more to say about this superego mechanism in Chapter 6 on depression, but for now want to note the connections between deep brain and mind structures, consciousness and its function, aggression, the environment, internal agencies of mind, and so on.

Agencies of Mind

Nonetheless, Freud's formulation with the available neuroscientific knowledge at the time, recognised the role of consciousness as linking to both id and ego agencies. It suggests that libidinal energy drives forward from primitive parts of the brain in order to promote the ability to navigate internal perceptions springing from the body system, and, of course, their fulfilment (or frustration) in the external environment. This point is important to remind ourselves, since it is in the external environment where invariably needs *have* to be met.[13] But also, the drive whose function it is to *action* homeostatic imbalances in order to achieve a restoration of stasis, as subjectively experienced by the organism, relies on the *feelings* of aggression to surface from their stealth-like latent state in order for an organism to remediate disequilibrium caused by impingements.

So, the id is like the well-spring of consciousness in that from its depths arises the bubbling currents of both streams of sensual and affectional affect. The super-ego is an intra-punitive agency which, although can be seen as a structure of the mind, is fuelled by aggressive energies turned against the individual's own ego. Aggression against the self ultimately feeds the suicidal impulse in some mental states, when sufficiently bloated as in depression, rather than an outward homicidal impulse that characterises the psycho-pathic psyche whose aggression is all turned outwards towards the object with none left in reserve that is turned against the self, in the form of a conscience that can regulate it. In balance, superego function places inhibi-tions on the unbridled impulses seeking discharge which find themselves bound by the ego prior to discharge, in adhering to the dictates of the super-ego and the constraints of external reality.

Said Freud: "...we see this same ego as a poor creature owing service to three masters and consequently menaced by three dangers: from the external world, from the libido of the id, and from the severity of the super-ego".[14] All three structures of the mind are 'enlivened' as it were by the energetic flow of libidinal or aggressive energies serving the ultimate master of evolu-tion. In fact, we may again say that all organic life is premised on this tussle between the imperative to form greater unities through creative and pro-creative strivings in the interests of adaptation to an unpredictable and changing world, and the need to maintain and conserve identity to ward off threats to homeostasis and therefore entropy. Nonetheless, survival of a complex organism relies on complex navigation in multiple dimensions: namely, that different energetic flows enliven and hence become managed by the competing agencies of the mental apparatus that Freud so deftly identi-fied. These agencies in conflict with each other suggest a multiplicity of sub-jectivities within the self-identity of an individual, each one striving to fulfil its function in the most efficient possible way and to best effect.

This would be all well except that we have ignored one key factor: namely, that of *time*. Like time itself, development can only move forward, in fact *drives* forward inexorably, along paths carved out through the memory of genes and billions of years of organic evolution. With the forward pressures of time, an individual too must evolve through psychogenesis – yet also retain its character within the species, and its memory of individual experi-ence, to better navigate and preserve itself. A person's subjectivity influencing early development, fixated there for reasons of some previously experienced adversity, compete with later versions of the adult in an adult world, yet retain the templates of early development and its adversities, *as subjectively experienced* at the time. Fixation (of personal memory) for the purposes of adaptation invites regression to these reference points, to better *forward-*navigate complex environments. So, too, as difference agencies of the mind tension and conflict, there emerge different subjectivities rooted in both pre-sent, and paradoxically, the past that belongs to this present. At times, old subjectivities, or parts of mind, must be privileged by the psyche so that efficient navigation of new challenges can be better achieved. Old and new compete against the internal struggles of the day and the tensions of gratification versus inhibition, or at least regulation of these impulses reaching the surface of the mental skin, the ego, as it strives to promote satiation and homeostasis.

Freud grapples with these contradictory elements: "It would be possible to picture the id as under the domination of the mute but powerful death instincts, which desire to be at peace and (prompted by the pleasure principle) to put Eros, the mischief-maker, to rest; but perhaps that might be to undervalue the part played by Eros".[15] Indeed, we can empathise with Freud's hesitation, since both libidinal and aggressive drives emerge from primitive structures of the brain and its emergent psyche, wrestling with each other from the outset an individual life. This well-spring of instincts and drives not only flow *through* the agencies of mind (id, ego, super-ego) but are instrumental in *creating* these agencies. Without the aggressive drive, for example, there could be no super-ego formation since without a tributary of the aggressive drive flowing back against the ego as an intra-punitive trend, there would not be this system forming or operating. But at the same time, the death drive is more than a simple brain circuit of rage (which Panksepp identifies), as with more primitive species – it also has ascendant barometric and binding properties, these qualities being irreducible to one function.

Without the prompting of libidinal impulses pressing for discharge, for example, there would be no necessity for a surface skin to mediate between the external and internal environments, since free-flowing impulses would require no binding into cathexes. It is true that the role of the ego is more than this would suggest, enabling also a separation barrier that defines self-identity, the Markov blanket of the organism *in relation to its external world*. Nonetheless, the function of the ego without instinctual promptings and drives would be considerably changed. And of course, without the energetic drives originating from the id as a direct consequence of its relationship to the body and its function of both driving life forward as well as protecting and conserving itself, suggests that the id is also like a bridge between soma and psyche through which the energetic drives of life flow, from electron gradients, to the mitochondria of cells, and upwards into complex cellular and organ systems. The psychic structures of the mental apparatus are not, after all, anatomical structures but emergent ones. Without energetic drives, they could scarcely exist.

So, two primary energetic drives retain their place as the vanguard of the mental apparatus through which its various agencies are both born and enlivened, on a continuous basis. But we can also observe that these drives are in tension since they fulfil opposing but complimentary requirements genetically – the one group of instincts "rushes forward so as to reach the final aim of life as swiftly as possible; but when a particular stage in the advance has been reached, the other group jerks back to a certain point to make a fresh start and so prolong the journey".[16] The one drive pushes forward for individual life needs and species variation whilst the other must bind excess and retard energy that is heading in the wrong direction (as we discussed in Chapter 2). What became known as the life and death drives underpin, also, as the biologists suggest, the *push* of the emergence and constraints of living matter, and the emergent psyche too, infusing it with the energetic trends of its more primitive roots in evolution. Lane makes the point that as he reflects on his depiction of the origins of life finds himself also using the term *drive*, since he says, "there isn't a better word" to capture the idea that it is not passive chemistry "but it is *forced*, pushed, driven by the continuous flux of carbon, energy, protons. These reactions *need* to happen…".[17] Without these energies, the structures of the mind could not form, any more than without cellular mitochondria or electron energy gradients cellular life and hence complex biological systems could not exist either. The energetic drivers of life, both physical and mental, are essential toward understanding how structures form and are enlivened.

But also, it enables us to recognise that as Freud observed in complex mental life, we are never free of the conflicts and tensions of these two id drives of the mental apparatus, and of the different organs of the mind. Since the superego, for example, had evolved to regulate some of the impulses of earlier developmental phases, and acts to enable the power of the incest-taboo, this still reflects a branch of the aggressive drive turned back against the unbridled impulses of the id, requesting the mediation of the ego in its function to recognise both internal promptings and the constraints of the external world, and find manoeuvres that can accomplish what Freud termed a compromise-formation, a balancing act that achieves what it can with the variables available but invariably at some or other cost – making the best of a bad lot, so to speak.

The trouble emerges when the comprise reached at the time these sorts of cathexes-anticathexes were set up, continue to exert its influence in current circumstances based on old versions of available options. Regression to a six-month old phase of life to navigate adult tensions based on earlier fixations cease to be optimal in later conditions, when other options and pathways are possible. But as we have mentioned, Freud emphasises the libidinal elements as key in the genesis of symptoms, "substitutive satisfactions for unfulfilled sexual wishes", he says. "In the course of our analytic work, we have discovered to our surprise that perhaps every neurosis conceals a quota of unconscious sense of guilt, which in its turn fortifies the symptoms by making use of them as a punishment".[18] Freud adds to this point that, "When an instinctual trend undergoes repression, *its libidinal elements are turned into symptoms*, and its aggressive components into a sense of guilt. Even if this proposition is only an average approximation to the truth, it is worthy of our interest".[19]

An Average Approximation

As we can see, deep down Freud recognised that his emphasis on sexuality as the driver of *symptom-formation* was an "approximation",[20] and was straining against both the evidence and the theoretical imperative to explain how then the aggressive drive, in his more mature dual-drive theory, would link to symptom-formation. He had noted that the super-ego, both essential in its protection if individual morality and the incest-taboo at the end of the oedipal period, and the social world in which the individual is required to survive, was formed out of a branch of the aggressive drive. He wrote that aggressiveness is introjected, internalized, in point of fact, sent back to where it came from – that is, it is directed towards his own ego. "There it is taken over by a portion of the ego, which sets itself over against the rest of the ego as super-ego, and which now, in the form of 'conscience', is ready to put into action against the ego the same harsh aggressiveness that the ego would have liked to satisfy upon other, extraneous individuals." Enlivened by this branch of the drive, leads to the "tension between the harsh super-ego and the ego that is subjected to it, is called by us the sense of guilt; it expresses itself as a need for punishment."[21]

As we can see, the inner tension of the psyche between ego and super-ego, or these agencies and the instinctual promptings of the id, are driven by libidinal and aggressive trends flowing first outward, with a branch of the aggressive drive turning back inward against the ego. This comes to represent a mature form of internal regulation that also facilitates adaptation in groups and serves the interests of a branch of the libidinal drive. That is, the libidinal drive can be said to have two components: one which seeks a procreative rendering of genetic variation and has an intimate connection to the psychic and somatic interior of the *individual* (induces feelings of arousal and attraction to others), and a second branch which seeks to engage in greater unities as a creation of group identity and which enables differentiation and identification of self-identity from other out-groups. This potential tension also puts the individual need to *pair* sexually, and the collective interest (which resists separation of identity that pairing creates) into contest. The latter in some manner seeks to avoid the sexual component of pairing because it creates separation from the collective, in the interests of maintaining communal cohesion.

To elaborate on this tension: Erotic promptings, as we know, create all manner of mischief in groups, from promoting envious attacks by others seeking the same prize, to all the emotional complexities that come from the striving to give expression to, and satiate sexual cravings. In some respects, the satisfaction of sexual longings and the protections and maintenance of group cohesion are at odds with each other, and the one or the other must suffer the constraints of inhibition. The super-ego fulfils the inhibitive function for the family and social group by intra-punitively, and aggressively judging these impulses as taboo, or at least necessary of inhibition and forcing back their flow. In this sense, without some form of inhibition, these impulses would flow outwards and find uninhibited expression, as we see with lower animals for whom public displays of sexual promptings invite no inhibition or self-recrimination, no shame or internal regulation. But in humans, there is a remarkably powerful tendency toward inhibition, regulation of unbounded free-flowing libidinal energy in ways that scarcely seem to allow for its expression, except under very curated circumstances of mutual consent, careful conditions of social discourse, and, of course, privacy.

We could say that there are two streams of libidinal energies: one that drives the individual to 'take for itself' the fulfilment of the internal promptings and satisfy them, and the other that strives to coalescence in greater attachments through groups and group identities, and which must preserve these by inhibiting the sexual aim. Marriage and marital rituals, present in all cultures, appear to be a compromise-formation in themselves, which deftly navigate the tension between the self and sexual expression with all its provocations to the external world, and its place in a cohesive community, assisting to hold both conflicting dimensions together. If John Lyly was correct, the old saying that 'all is fair in love and war'[22] reminds us that human love and sexual life is a complex and conflictual affair, which stirs up profound destructive feelings too, of envy and betrayals, losses and longings. What the heart longs for, so too breaks it. Sexuality can almost be considered the most creative of forces that produces life and yet can also be one of the most destructive ones of all. The crossing of the sexual line, even when entirely consensual, appears to represent a quantum jump into another dimension, in which all manner of feelings of warmth and goodness, but often more so of anxiety, loss, rage, envy, and consternations of all sorts emerge. The cross-over from fantasy and flirtation into sexual enactment invariably stirs all manner of deep feeling, in both the couple and their community, even when no emotional investment is planned for the encounter.

For reasons that are not altogether obvious, this transition from desire (especially lust) to fulfilment of desire has the power to stir many feelings and associations, many of which turn destructive and painful. It is strange that Nature's gift of sexuality can be both so fulfilling and euphoria-inducing and simultaneously so painful and destructive. The taking for the self of sexual satisfaction whilst intensely private is also usually not only so – and indicates to communities of friends, family, and others something of great significance. As Freud puts it: "To put it in other words, the development of the individual seems to us to be a product of the interaction between two urges, the urge towards happiness, which we usually call 'egoistic', and the urge towards union with others in the community, which we call 'altruistic'".[23]

This paradox of private and public tensions applies to few other things, at least so intensely, and seems to represent the separation from the collective, when a couple pairs themselves sexually. This separation through pairing both fulfils and simultaneously violates the drive to coalesce into greater unities through genetic variation via copulation. How so? When two individuals join in sexual union, they are separating themselves from the collective in what we might call a 'conspiracy of love and sensuality', and this is in itself an evocative and potentially threatening step for the collective. And yet, the collective requires it for reproduction. "Sexual intercourse has been associated in the strongest possible way with prohibitions; lawful and permissible intercourse is not, therefore, felt to be the same thing"[24] – wrote Freud, indicating the complexity and paradox with which this powerful and essential driver of humanity runs into social and emotional difficulties.

So, as I mentioned earlier, we might conjecture that the libidinal drive seems to split into two streams: the one into a striving towards greater unities in order to expand the Markov blanket of identity differentiating self from other, and facilitating survival through greater numbers and belonging; the other, a striving to pair off with *an* Other and separate from the collective in order to fulfil the evolutionary drive for genetic variation. Eros and its two streams are never, however, as we shall explore further below, occurring in a vacuum – these 'breakers of the peace' disrupt homeostasis by their presence and so they cannot escape the activation in response of that mechanism designated the role of being the 'guardian of the peace', namely, the aggressive drive.

One could say therefore that the universal ceremony of marriage represents a compromise-formation of the ambiguous space between the conservative protection of the community and its Markov blanket of identity, and the libidinal imperative of evolution through procreation. The condonation of the community group enables the fulfilment of both elements of the libidinal drive – to greater unities requiring conservation and the variation that succumbs to fulfilment of the pairing and separation of the couple from the community in fulfilling sexual longings at the personal level. To repeat Freud's point, this requires the navigation of an urge towards happiness, which we can call 'egoistic', and an urge towards union with others in the community, which we can call 'altruistic'.[25] Perhaps, we could also surmise, that in addition to the marital rituals which enable the separation from, and the simultaneous communal ownership of the couple, we also note the 'deflowering' rituals so common in most cultures, in which it seems that sex and erotic life is enabled through the private separation of the couple immediately after the marital ceremony and their apparently consummating the marriage, whilst the community waits outside to celebrate the event and claim its communal ownership. In some cultures, this public-private compromise is symbolic (the couple spends a few minutes in a separate room whilst the parents or spiritual leaders wait outside), and in other cultures this affair is more concrete (such as displaying a sheet with a blood stain on it to symbolise the 'deflowering'). This navigates the complex threats that separation poses for a couple from their community whilst enabling private sexuality with communal ownership.

As mentioned, therefore, we can note that these two streams of libido can come into conflict, the one stream striving for group cohesion and the other for pairing that separates from the group. This separation is wrought with all its accompanying potentials for evocative negative responses and associations, taboos and envies, longings and losses. A marital ritual navigates this ambiguity: co-opts the group into the couple and the couple into the group. A compromise meets both needs of the libidinal imperative – for group adhesion and identity, and for variation through procreation. When this compromise is breached, through infidelity for example, all manner of personal and group sanction and aggression can be triggered. The reality of crossing the sexual line is that it is like a quantum jump into another dimension, which stirs up all manner of feelings of hostility, envy, contempt, judgement, sanction, and other negative responses, that strive to balance the interests of the procreative drive against the collective interest. Unbridled expression of sexuality has destructive results often, and threatens the fabric of a community collective by rousing hostilities when erotic enactments, or even suggestions thereof, cross the divide and boundaries of what is socially sanctioned. In both personal individual and social senses, the enactment of sexual drives, the breaking of the peace, rouses the potential for deep hostilities at both levels. To remind the reader, Freud commented that, "neurotic symptoms are, in their essence, substitutive satisfactions for unfulfilled sexual wishes". He remarked how, in the course of analytic work, "we have discovered to our surprise that perhaps every neurosis conceals a quota of unconscious sense of guilt, which in its turn fortifies the symptoms by making use of them as a punishment".[26] The power of the sexual drive tends, as it must, to unsettle equilibrium and thereby also activate the conservative drive and its aggressive derivatives, often at both individual and collective levels.

"Since civilisation obeys an internal erotic impulsion which causes human beings to unite in a closely-knit group, it can only achieve this aim through an ever-increasing reinforcement of the sense of guilt",[27] wrote Freud, suggesting that the power of unbridled libido is kept in check by the activation of both external and internal sanction through derivatives of the aggressive drive – the internal one being that branch of the aggressive drive creating super-ego function and its guilt derivative, and the other through external sanction through aggressive disapprovals or social, cultural, or religious blow-back. Hence, Freud noted that, "If civilisation is a necessary course of development from the family to humanity as a whole, then—as a result of the inborn conflict arising from ambivalence, of the eternal struggle between the trends of love and death—there is inextricably bound up with it an increase of the sense of guilt, which will perhaps reach heights that the individual finds hard to tolerate".[28]

As we again see, Freud continued throughout his career to locate the genesis of symptoms in the libidinal stream, even when the evidence from his own theories were pointing increasingly in the direction of the disruptive consequences of the sexual drive and its capacity to activate the conservative/

aggressive drive. If libidinal promptings were allowed to flow without internal censure, we could surely judge that no psychological symptoms would accrue. In such circumstances, why would they? There is no conflict between energetic drives nor the agencies of the mind that emerge to regulate such matters. Libidinal promptings cause symptoms, in this case, because they bump up against an aggressive internal agency forcing back this wave of energetic "breakers of the peace", and does its job well if the balance between satisfaction and group cohesion is maintained. When it is not, such as when the super-ego function becomes bloated, such as in depression (a topic to which we will return later), the level of aggression against the self becomes skewed and suffocates entirely the flow of eros. Suffocated thus, libidinal energy becomes impoverished and depleted, giving rise to the familiar symptoms of depression we note of loss of energy, libido, interest, etc. But as we can see, it is not the flow of libidinal energy that is somehow lost at source, since this can never occur in living beings, but this intra-punitive aggression that, being activated *in response to such promptings*, generates problems in psychic function. Withdrawal of libido does not lead to depression – aggression introjected against the own ego, setting up merciless attacks against the individual's own self, is what does. Freud understood this function but clung to his early model of libidinal ascendance in the genesis of such symptoms, noting that libido has a key role: "This transformation is a function of the psychical conflict under pressure of which the symptom had to be formed",[29] he asserted, referring to the vestiges of earlier frustrations.

I use this example simply to illustrate the ease with which the appropriate causal sequence can get inverted. Some may argue that this is a simplification which reflects later oedipal and post-oedipal development. But let us step back into earlier developmental phases to make the same point. We also note that Freud's formulation of the super-ego evolving from a branch of the aggressive stream turning back against one's own ego emerges at the end of the oedipal period, around five years of age, through identification (with the potential adult aggressor) – but as I have already mentioned in my previous book, the first worldly action of the new-born infant is a cry, an act of the aggressive drive signalling a violation of homeostasis through being born, expelled from an environment in which the drive for homeostasis is at a premium.

Pre-Oedipality in Ascendance

From the outset of life, time drives development and psychogenesis forward. Each developmental phase from birth on moves in a drive-forward direction, pushed inexorably in a teleological programme of unfolding. This process is accompanied by both somatic and mental developments. The mental appears to form as emergent systems based on the experience of the infant and the psychosexual foci that characterise these phases. In fact, we should say with greater accuracy that what emerges are mechanisms to manage states of disequilibrium with what somatic and mental tools are available to the infant at the time. This suggests that the various defences that characterise human development and are relied on through life, and to which the mind returns repeatedly, are mechanisms aimed at maintaining or restoring homeostasis when there are internal or external threats to it.

However, this begs the question: what are these psychical defences defending against, exactly? Invariably, we observe that defences emerge to protect against increasing states of disequilibrium caused by impingements from within or without the infant. Defences are, to put it differently, mechanisms whose job it is to restore a form of stasis *as it evolves through the life cycle,* [30] when libidinally driven needs are being frustrated and arousal is increasing; defences must, therefore, be able to bind increasing free energy when no other methods of remedy are available. In infancy, few remedies are available to bind excess arousal when needs are frustrated – crying as an inducing mechanism being its main toolkit – but this is not always able to achieve its task – and so auxiliary mental mechanisms based on available means must be used. 'Available means' are those mental representations available to the somatic foci current at the infant's age and stage of development.

We also know that the drives govern homeostasis: the life drive activating the seeking of need-fulfilment, and the conservative-aggressive death drive aimed at regulating excess states that threaten it. We can fairly suggest that psychical defences are linked to the aggressive drive and operate in its service – activate when arousal, driven by frustration, is increasing. All mental defences are, therefore, methods for responding to and restoring (binding) states of disequilibrium, from the vantage point of the individual in question, influenced by that individual's subjective perceptions (albeit primitive) of their experiences. Since sexuality and the libidinal drive prompt disequilibrium in the pursuit of fulfilling needs, as mentioned, by being itself a breaker of the peace and a driver of change, it invariably activates defensive manoeuvres when such needs are frustrated or cannot be fulfilled. Hence, for example, we note the guilt, anxiety, or other states that Freud referenced as resulting from the libidinal drive. His link of the sexual stream with symptom states does not fully account for his own observations that the main reason it leads to symptoms is because it activates counter-measures aimed at balancing the two drives and avoiding the consequences of unbridled sexuality and libidinally driven frustrations in individual and social life. I will list these defences and how they operate later but first, we need to backtrack to establish how defences emerge in the first place as mechanisms to represent states of disequilibrium; a brief overview of early development.

Emergent Defences

In the earliest phases of life, the infant finds itself expelled from an environment rich and perfect in its homeostasis. The womb provides for every conceivable need and no aggressive response can exist to calibrate impingements since there are none. But once emergent into the world, there is no such homeostasis in play. On the contrary, every conceivable discomfort from cold to hunger to loneliness makes its presence felt and all manner of challenge to homeostatic familiarity, prompting the infant to have to make meaning out of its states of *meaninglessness*. Maternal attunement facilitates this but invariably only imperfectly and cannot be fully relied upon. Rather, the infant must develop its own mechanisms to defend against states of disruption, from its own perspective and temperament, and according to the available means given its age.

This reality enabled Freud to see that each development phase carried its own psychosexual foci on the erotogenic zones in vogue at each age. This is another way of observing that the libidinal drive not only attaches to the external object (of the breast and mother, for example) but also to the infant's own body and its sensations. In the first year, this is dominated by an oral focus, in which the mouth, lips, tongue, swallowing and the gastrointestinal tract are central to the infant's first months of life. It cannot do much physically, but it can close its mouth, swallow or ingest, or spit out or posit the contents and expel them from the inner world into the outer world. Frustrations and discomforts of all sorts must be dealt with through these mechanisms and their psychic representatives that are emerging as these somatic experiences take shape. Without them, homeostatic regulation would remain primitive and ineffective in a complex environment. Closing the mouth mentally represents to the infant that it can create a separation barrier between its internal and the external world, symbolising that by doing so, the outer world no longer having access to the inner world, ceases to influence its reality. Such denial of reality is associated with later psychotic states in which reality is denied. Oral ejection places the inner contents of consciousness into the outer world, the roots of a projective mechanism in which what was internal becomes attributed to the external. Introjection describes the taking in, the turning inwards and incorporating into the self-contents of experience, the prototype for introjection, the turning in of emotion, associated with depression in later life dynamics.

Later in development, from approximately ages one year to three years, the infant discovers its bowels, and a shift in consciousness of its somatic zone and ability to be aware of defecation and controlling it through expelling or withholding faeces. Hence, Freud identified an anal focus to development in which various mechanisms emerge: reaction-formation (turning an impulse into its opposite), displacement, sublimation, isolation, and so on. And still later, from age three, we see the emergence of a phallic focus in which awareness of the genitalia becomes conscious, alongside urethral sensations that draw a child's hands to them through the need for sensation-relief. In addition, together with these somatic shifts, and perhaps driven by them, we note alongside these sensations also a greater attachment to the opposite-sex parent in this oedipal phase. These attachments invite contentious mental processes such as rivalries and competition, a most significant one being, as Freud identified it, castration anxieties that both trigger for the girl, and bring to an end for the boy, this oedipal phase through his identification with the aggressor, in the form of the threat from the father. Sublimation follows during phallic development since libidinal impulses can find their cathexes onto alternative symbolic pathways, such as channelling libido into art, sport, or even ideation.

This elaboration, as an example, suggests that libidinal energy powers development, the way the biochemists describe the push of the biological energy of electron gradients and the mitochondria of cells that power development in a singularly forward direction. It is understandable that the power of this libidinal thrust in life gave Freud good reason to centralise it in his formulations and discoveries, and to note that invariably sexual conflicts informed psychopathology and its symptoms and the neuroses he observed clinically. It also informed the way the sexual drive channelled some libido into the self, a self-preservatory mechanism that Freud regarded as "the libidinal complement to the egoism of the instinct of self-preservation, a measure of which can be attributed to every living creature"[31] – and which consolidated the pleasure-principle as the central driver of both healthy development and deviations from it.

However, as we shall discuss further in the next chapter, this was, and remains now, only part of the story. In his later development, Freud's formulation of his dual-drive theory brilliantly rooted itself in evolutionary and biological development in animate life, suggesting, as I have mentioned, there are two forces in play countering each other from the outset – one driving the organism forward but another whose primal aim was to conserve the organism and maintain its identity in the face of impingement and pressures to change. The aggressive drive, we can note, is activated when *any* challenge to homeostasis is present – but the degree and form of its mobilisation will depend on how needs are met (or frustrated) and/or threats navigated, as we discussed in Chapter 2.

What is also clear, is that such disruptors can be either external or internal, and that when disruption is present this drive is unavoidably activated from its latent state into a more manifest one. From the outset of the infant's life and its expulsion from the perfect homeostasis of the womb, activations and disruptions proliferate from both external and internal causes. We might say therefore, that the aggressive drive some of the time 'whispers' and at other times 'shouts forth' from its silent, dark, and stealthy cave, depending on the degree of frustration of needs, with the psychical immune system activating in response to changes in homeostasis, even when the disruptor is internal, and even good, such as sexual desire. Also, since external threats, including emotional ones that drive self-identity or esteem downward, for example, violate the need to minimise surprisal and hence free energy in the service of homeostasis, aggression will activate in a restorative response.

Nonetheless, despite his later discoveries of the dual-drive nature of the mental system, Freud appeared to remain wedded to his paradigm of the primacy of sexuality in the genesis of symptoms, and noted that, as I mentioned previously, his regard for the psychosexual constitution as the most important causes of neurotic disorders[32] with the essence of mental illnesses lying solely in a disturbance of the organism's 'sexual processes'.[33] It is thus fair to suggest that Freud remained theoretically ambivalent even after his seminal work in *Beyond the Pleasure Principle* appeared to demonstrate that the sexual drive is itself a disruptor of homeostasis and would therefore activate the restorative drive, one whose defences emerge as a servant of the biological requirement to minimise variable free energy and bind it when it is increasing.

Never at rest, the life drive sets alight the need to keep moving developmentally according to the forward thrust of time and psychogenesis, and the need to find attachment in later life for the purpose of release of sexual tension. Already in childhood, urethral sensations give rise to guilt, as Freud noted in his discussion on masturbation,[34] but these sensations activated by libidinal pressures also create disruption and through such disruption is manifest many psychic conflicts, including guilt. Since we know that guilt is also a branch of the aggressive drive, it becomes unavoidable to recognise that sexual disruptors, by definition and by mechanism, activate the 'awareness' of the inner-guardian's role in detecting, combatting, and restoring threats to homeostasis, which sexuality is, especially when discharge of sexual tension is not readily available. Sexuality may have a causal link in neurotic outcomes and psychic conflicts, but it is only in the first part of the process that this is so; actually, the effect this stream has on activating the aggressive drive can be seen to be central in psychic disturbance and the genesis of symptoms.

It is to these pathways that I wish to venture in the next chapters.

Notes

1 Lane, N. (2016). *The Vital Question: Why is Life the Way it Is?* London: Profile Books.
2 The onset of gender differentiation becomes marked during the oedipal phase from around three to five years of age, according to psychoanalysis, in which Freud notes that boys and girls follow a different path in the development of their sensual current – see, for example, Freud, S. (1924) The Dissolution of the Oedipus Complex. *The Standard Edition of the Complete Psychological Works of Sigmund Freud* 19:171–180.

3 Freud, S. (1905) Three Essays on the Theory of Sexuality. *The Standard Edition of the Complete Psychological Works of Sigmund Freud* 7:123–246, p.226.
4 Freud, S. (1923) The Ego and the Id. *The Standard Edition of the Complete Psychological Works of Sigmund Freud* 19:1–66, p.25.
5 Freud, S. (1923) The Ego and the Id. *The Standard Edition of the Complete Psychological Works of Sigmund Freud* 19:1–66, p.30.
6 Freud, S. (1923) The Ego and the Id. *The Standard Edition of the Complete Psychological Works of Sigmund Freud* 19:1–66, p.30.
7 Freud, S. (1923) The Ego and the Id. *The Standard Edition of the Complete Psychological Works of Sigmund Freud* 19:1–66, p.17.
8 Solms argues in his paper on the conscious id that emotional or affective representations of experience may be represented to consciousness through higher level cortical structures in the brain, but ultimately, consciousness emerges from internal brain structures that generate sensory experiences of dysregulation. "The classical conception is turned on its head. Consciousness is not generated in the cortex; it is generated in the brainstem. Moreover, consciousness is not inherently perceptual; it is inherently affective. And in its primary manifestations, it has less to do with cognition than with instinct. In terms of the parallels drawn in Section 2, the conclusion is inescapable: *consciousness is generated in the id*, and the ego is fundamentally unconscious. This has massive implications for our conceptualisation of the ego and all that flows from it, such as our theories of psychopathology and clinical technique. It was, after all, the essence of the "talking cure" that words, being ego memory-traces derived from external perception and therefore capable of consciousness, must be attached to the deeper processes of the mind (which are unconscious in themselves) before they can be known by the subject". Solms, M. (2013) The Conscious Id, *Neuropsychoanalysis*, 15 (1), p.7.
9 Solms, M. (2013) The Conscious Id, *Neuropsychoanalysis*, 15 (1), p.7.
10 Freud, S. (1923) The Ego and the Id. *The Standard Edition of the Complete Psychological Works of Sigmund Freud* 19:1–66, p.19.
11 Freud, S. (1923) The Ego and the Id. *The Standard Edition of the Complete Psychological Works of Sigmund Freud* 19:1–66, p.19.
12 Freud, S. (1923) The Ego and the Id. *The Standard Edition of the Complete Psychological Works of Sigmund Freud* 19:1–66, p.53.
13 The exception to this rule is with substance abuse, a topic for a later chapter.
14 Freud, S. (1923) The Ego and the Id. *The Standard Edition of the Complete Psychological Works of Sigmund Freud* 19:1–66, p.56.
15 Freud, S. (1923) The Ego and the Id. *The Standard Edition of the Complete Psychological Works of Sigmund Freud* 19:1–66, p.59.
16 Freud, S. (1920) Beyond the Pleasure Principle. *The Standard Edition of the Complete Psychological Works of Sigmund Freud* 18:1–64, p.41.
17 Lane, N. (2016) *The Vital Question: Why is Life the Way it Is?* London: Profile Books, p.135.
18 Freud, S. (1930) Civilisation and its Discontents. *The Standard Edition of the Complete Psychological Works of Sigmund Freud* 21:57–146, p.139.
19 Freud, S. (1930) Civilisation and its Discontents. *The Standard Edition of the Complete Psychological Works of Sigmund Freud* 21:57–146, p.139 (italics mine).
20 Freud, S. (1930) Civilisation and its Discontents. *The Standard Edition of the Complete Psychological Works of Sigmund Freud* 21:57–146, p.139 (italics mine).
21 Freud, S. (1930) Civilisation and its Discontents. *The Standard Edition of the Complete Psychological Works of Sigmund Freud* 21:57–146, p.123.
22 See John Lyly, *Euphues: The Anatomy of Wit*. London: Gabriel Cawood.

23 Freud, S. (1930) Civilisation and its Discontents. *The Standard Edition of the Complete Psychological Works of Sigmund Freud* 21:57–146, p.123.

24 Freud, S. (1918) The Taboo of Virginity (Contributions to the Psychology of Love III). *The Standard Edition of the Complete Psychological Works of Sigmund Freud* 11:191–208.

25 Freud, S. (1930) Civilisation and its Discontents. *The Standard Edition of the Complete Psychological Works of Sigmund Freud* 21:57–146, p.140.

26 Freud, S. (1930) Civilisation and its Discontents. *The Standard Edition of the Complete Psychological Works of Sigmund Freud* 21:57–146, p.139.

27 Freud, S. (1930) Civilisation and its Discontents. *The Standard Edition of the Complete Psychological Works of Sigmund Freud* 21:57–146, p.133.

28 Freud, S. (1930) Civilisation and its Discontents. *The Standard Edition of the Complete Psychological Works of Sigmund Freud* 21:57–146, p.133.

29 Freud, S. The Paths to the Formation of Symptoms. In Freud, S. (1917) Introductory Lectures on Psycho-Analysis. *The Standard Edition of the Complete Psychological Works of Sigmund Freud* 16:241–463, p.366.

30 Homeostatic parameters of any sort change through the life span. The thermal, nutritional or sexual needs of a six-day old infant will differ markedly from that same infant as a sixteen-year-old adolescent.

31 Freud, S. (1914) On Narcissism: An Introduction. The Standard Edition of the Complete Psychological Works of Sigmund Freud 14:67–102, p.66.

32 Freud, S. (1907) The Sexual Enlightenment of Children (An Open Letter to Dr. M. Fürst). *The Standard Edition of the Complete Psychological Works of Sigmund Freud* 9:129–140, p.131.

33 Freud, S. (1906) My Views on the Part Played by Sexuality in the Aetiology of the Neuroses (1906 [1905]). *The Standard Edition of the Complete Psychological Works of Sigmund Freud* 7:269–279, p.279.

34 Freud, S. (1912) Contributions to a Discussion on Masturbation. *The Standard Edition of the Complete Psychological Works of Sigmund Freud* 12:239–254. See also the chapter on this topic in a later section of this book for greater elaboration of this point.

Chapter 4

Masturbation: Somatic Self-engagement

A Region Interpolated

Masturbation is a useful starting point for illuminating the central role of the aggressive drive since it sits at the intersection of the somatic and psychic, the conscious and the unconscious, the unbridled and the inhibited. Furthermore, it activates both conscious and unconscious elements. Whilst somatic sensations are omnipresent, breakers of the peace and constantly producing tensions whose release is felt as pleasure,[1] the aggressive drive has a latent character, which does its work unobtrusively,[2] and is not consciously felt until activated beyond a quantitative threshold, much like the immune system of the body. Self-engagement begins in infancy, the discovery that the somatic zone carries many sensations that are pleasurable and which make demands upon the mind through the requirement to engage with them. When babies reach oedipal age at around three years of age, and their erotogenic focus moves to the genitals, various associative processes are set up which serve to disrupt the child's equilibrium. We are not here, of course, talking of ejaculatory or orgasmic relief in the post-pubescent sense, but rather of urethral sensations that induce the need to touch the self genitally and which, if neutral to the psyche, would pass as insignificant and no more of interest than the scratching of an itch. But to the outside world, a child's masturbation is never viewed entirely without discomfort. Further, to the child themselves, this focus of consciousness is never neutral in its significance, and even more so in adolescence where some elements of guilt present itself, a 'masturbatory guilt' that invariably accompanies the experience of pleasure and release. This is, of course, normal. "We have long known that the same complexes and conflicts are to be looked for, too, in all normal and healthy people. In fact, we have grown accustomed to attributing to every civilised human being a certain amount of repression of perverse impulses, a certain amount of anal erotism, of homosexuality and so on, as well as a piece of father-complex and mother-complex and of other complexes besides".[3]

We notice that somatic self-engagement even in childhood is never entirely free of associated feelings and a cascade of mental events, some of which are experienced as feelings of guilt, anxiety, depression, and associative processes

DOI: 10.4324/9781003628972-5

related to both conscious and unconscious elements. Masturbation is, of course, not one thing, since somatic self-engagement in infancy and childhood scarcely resembles that of puberty or adulthood, in either its processes, mental effects, or outcomes. Freud noted that he "divided masturbation according to the subject's age into (1) masturbation in infants, which includes all auto-erotic activities serving the purpose of sexual satisfaction, (2) masturbation in children, which arises directly out of the preceding kind and has already become fixed to certain erotogenic zones, and (3) masturbation at puberty, which is either continuous with childhood masturbation or is separated from it by the period of latency".[4]

The use of phantasy is primitive and unconscious in childhood yet usually fully conscious in the second phase of psychosexual development in adolescence and adulthood. It also has a beginning, a middle, and an end – a *process* that we might deem teleological, whereas in children there is no such thing, merely the intermittent promptings of sensations that trigger an action from the child and then recede again as if they had never presented. It is also generally done in public in childhood and in private in puberty, except in the transitional space between childhood and the onset of puberty when masturbation may exhibit characteristics of both phases, in the form of group masturbation or games of the like. These soon pass and give way to the privacy of both fantasy and its physical expression through the *process* masturbation of the adolescent and adult phase. But these processes, at all ages, are never free of psychic associations and conflicts, triggering feelings that require some form of expression or defence. Freud wrote that:

> We must keep in mind the significance which masturbation acquires as a carrying into effect of phantasy—that half-way region interpolated between life in accordance with the pleasure principle and life in accordance with the reality principle; and we must remember how masturbation makes it possible to bring about sexual developments and sublimations in phantasy, which are nevertheless not advances but injurious compromises.[5]

Injurious compromises? This is an interesting turn of phrase since it captures the link between disruption and a conservative pull-back, as he adds that the "cruel component of the sexual instinct" develops in childhood even more independently of the sexual activities that are attached to erotogenic zones. "Cruelty in general comes easily to the childish nature", he observes, "since the obstacle that brings the instinct for mastery to a halt at another person's pain—namely a capacity for pity—is developed relatively late."[6]

These elements of cruelty in children, and their attraction to the darkest of human nature in their love for stories and films that capture the most evil of inclinations, puzzled Freud in the early years of his work, lamenting "The fundamental psychological analysis of this instinct has, as we know, not yet been satisfactorily achieved".[7] It is indeed a puzzling phenomenon that children exhibit tendencies of utmost callousness, at times sadistic in its unwashed innocence, with words or hands or telling it like it is, there is often no 'pulling of the punches' and obliviousness to the effects they can have on hurting another's feelings. Adult socialisation tries to temper this directness, but the attraction to the darkest elements of life is never fully lost. Freud wondered if this element of cruelty arose "from the instinct for mastery and appears at a period of sexual life at which the genitals have not yet taken over their later role",[8] but in his later work on the death drive came to recognise the duality of the drives from the outset of living matter and of an individual life and the function of aggression underlying the 'cruelty' of children, which flexes itself in defence of the child's identity and perceived interests.

In Response To

It seems obvious, on reflection, that the somatic zone represents an unending source of sensations and demands, both pleasurable and unpleasurable. Somatic sensations and the feelings that accompany them, invariably represent the drive that, to remind the reader, Freud described as a "the psychical representative of the stimuli originating from within the organism and reaching the mind, as a measure of the demand made upon the mind for work in consequence of its connection with the body",[9] some of these sensations and feelings being pleasant and some unpleasant. At times, the line between the two is fine, such as the unpleasant need to urinate and the pleasant sensation of voiding, or the gritty pangs of hunger and the pleasant sensation of satiation, so long as satiation is not extreme. Some of these sensory promptings have a direct link to maintaining homeostasis and require little by way of explanation, such as thirst or thermoregulation. Some appear in childhood, however, that seems to have little bearing on homeostatic demands of the body, such as genital sensations, and even when they reappear at the onset of puberty in the second wave of psychosexual development can be said to have such a relation, since the buildup of sexual tension and the requirement for its release forms part of the fulfilment of the libidinal imperative in evolution. So, individual sexual tensions are encoded into the genetic memory of the species, notwithstanding the complexity of interfacing the individual, couple, and community requirements, sometimes in conflict and tension with each other, as discussed above.

In childhood, during the Oedipal phase between approximately three and five years of age, we observe the tendency of children to develop a focus on their genitals, both their own and that of others and the 'doctor-doctor' games so universally common at this age reflects the curiosity that is prompted by sensations arising from this phallic psychosexual zone. At this age, children appear to experience urethral sensations in the genital zone that wax and wane for no apparent reason of any immediate biological value, and yet prompt with enough power to require the child's attention. The genital fiddling amongst both biological sexes shows itself without consciousness or shame, even when exhibited in full view of others in their orbit. Sometimes, the most public of places in no way inhibits this activity without adult feed-back or distraction serving the purpose. This form of biological prodding and the somatic self-engagement it prompts is unconscious in that the child's innocence at this age shows no significant realisation initially of the sig-nificance of the behaviour. It brings to the fore the way somatic promptings driven by libidinal pressures that in the moment appear to have no biological value or importance, yet induce a behaviour to manage the sensations. This management of these breakers of the peace, originating from within the somatic zone of the child, may set off cascades of disturbance which Freud identified, including later anxieties and guilt.

If we place the optic of Freud's later dual-drive theory on top of his earlier theory of sexuality and the primacy of the pleasure-principle, never fully abandoned by him (which makes sense if we hold the lens of equivalence between the concept of pleasure-unpleasure to homeostasis), we quickly notice that the issue is not only the psychosexual promptings from the somatic zone and their pathways but also the effects these have on disrupting stasis. Guilt and anxiety are by-products of deviations from homeostasis and activate a restorative mechanism, namely the conservative drive. This contest between the libidinal and conservative drives is often symmetrical and metabolised without undue effects but when the anxiety or guilt is greater, fixations and subsequent symptoms can develop, which we will discuss further in the chapter on sexual dysfunction in adulthood.

The self-engagement of children with their genital zones during the oedipal period, signals something different to other sensations, and although these associative elements may be unconscious, come to be connected with mean-ings that are far from neutral. It is a puzzling phenomenon that the depth of emotional significance of the genital zone carries such significance from so young, carrying with it the capacity to generate anxieties, guilt, and other powerful associative processes. The libidinal drive, when cathecting with the genital zone, is never neutral in the manner of its activations. Part of the reason for this, is that it is also associated with phantasies of alliances and attachments with the opposite sex parent in whom libidinal investments get made. Such oedipal longings are never free of the rivalries that come from having to compete within this symbolic triangulation, and the incorporation of the father into the mother-infant dyad. This tendency invites feelings of rivalry and hostility, and the anxieties that can be activated from such ambivalences and conflicting sentiments – to both have and be rid of the rival parent simultaneously. These 'family romances', as Freud referred to them, are full of complexities, ambiguities, and psychical tensions that have to be navigated through development, noting that, "If anyone is inclined to turn away in horror from this depravity of the childish heart or feels tempted, indeed, to dispute the possibility of such things, he should observe that these works of fiction, which seem so full of hostility, are none of them really so badly intended, and that they still preserve, under a slight disguise, the child's original affection for his parents".[10]

In later sexual life from puberty on, sexuality is never free from these powerful associative elements and the enactment of sexual longings invariably carry the import of early childhood "imagos",[11] these being representations of parental figures. Crossing the sexual line, even in adulthood, is never free of feelings, fantasies, and consequences that generate intense ambivalences of longing, and love, hate and dejection. When the line is crossed, expectations are invariably created which sometimes lead to lifetime memories with emotional content. Expectations and disappointments abound in this space, and the amplification and power of what sex signifies to the human condition suggests its power as a disruptor is considerable. Sexual drives and yearnings are disruptors in many ways and at many levels, and the significance of refraining or crossing the sexual line poses interesting theoretical challenges. Even in the innocence of childhood development, the awakening of genital sensations disrupts homeostasis and represents a disruptor from within. At times, external stimuli and attractions trigger the arousal response, evoking a cascade of wishes, longings, and desires *for another object*, even when that external object is a complete stranger. Somatic promptings in infancy do not require an object during the phallic phase, although feelings are often bound up with the primary objects in the child's life, the proprioceptive urethral and genital sensations do not always appear correlated with these internal parental imagos but emerge randomly for some biological reasons, although we can deduce that these sensations may become attached to objects, particularly in the form of castration anxieties or because of sanction from adults.

In post-pubescent sexuality, however, there is invariably an object external to the self that demands cathexis. Erotic desires stimulated by exposure to external objects is more often than not bound to activate desires that cannot be fulfilled. Emotional needs for attachment that are unfulfilled lead to loneliness and the longing for connection, also a branch of the libidinal push for attachment. Libidinal promptings for both erotic and emotional longings, or what Freud referred to as the sensual and the affectional currents,[12] creates many opportunities for loss, frustration, and invariably hence the activation of the aggressive drive. We notice that erotic life in adults is often a fusion of the drives, and it begs the question as to why erotic life in adults is often a fusion of aggressive and libidinal elements, since the disruptor effects of the libidinal are so intense, necessitating all manner of defence in the interests of their management.

The inability to fulfil those longings, probably more often than it is possible, evokes frustrations that themselves require discharge to recalibrate and restore. At other times these libidinal and somatic pressures wax and wane at their own behest, evoking mental and physical responses that generate qualia or *feelings*. As we have established, any disruption to homeostasis requires a restorative response and even positive sensations that prompt for homeostatic re-regulation and are only unpleasurable to the extent that they are unfulfilled for extended periods, unlike thirst or hunger which are sensations of unpleasure and require more immediate fulfilment to restore homeostasis. This leads us to consider that sensations either pleasurable or unpleasurable can be breakers of the peace and any such disruptor of stasis will activate an immune response from the mental apparatus to restore equilibrium, since the intrusion of desire, phantasy, and disruption meets up with the constraints and taboos of the social and familial environment. This is the ongoing tension that characterises the two principle drives of the human mind-body system.

Psychic Dysregulation and Its Associations

The difference between animals and humans, rests in the associative capacity humans demonstrate, and the cascade of mental representations, that this triggers. A dog or a chimpanzee appears to hump another, or attempt to, and walks away without any apparent feelings, guilt, anxiety or conscious awareness. Or these animals defecate, usually publicly, and appear to show no signs of discomfort or consciousness. But humans from the outset of life have feelings that require meaning to be made from early states of *meaninglessness*, and mental representations form that constitute the ideation that come to represent otherwise meaningless emotional states. These ideas register at unconscious and conscious levels since ideational representation enables more efficient action to reregulate imbalances. But this mechanism also creates the room for ideational representations to form in memory that fixate unconsciously and form templates of subjective meaning through which the world is experienced. Governed by the repetition compulsion, there is a return to embedded memory as a form of efficient feed-forward navigation of complex demands in a complex world. But this memory in humans is scarcely an objective representation of reality – always coloured by subjective experience that interprets the world in ways that are uniquely individual. In fact, Freud made the observation that "we arrive at a knowledge of the infantile experiences to which the libido is fixated and out of which the symptoms are made. Well, the surprise lies in the fact that these scenes from infancy are not always true. Indeed, they are not true in the majority of cases, and in a few of them they are the direct opposite of the historical truth".[13]

The oedipal stage of life represents a bifurcation of the affectional and sensual currents, with boys and girls forming attachments that must navigate the complexity of maintaining affectional bonds to the same-sex parent whilst also 'suffering' the flushes of romantic phantasy for the opposite sex parent. These positive feelings and promptings are never free of some disruption. If triangulation is embedded in the oedipal drama, rivalries, feelings of envy, and anxieties of punitive sanction infiltrate the innocent space. This dialectic in which feelings trigger associations and associations in turn trigger feelings, creates a complex set of psychic activations for the child, wrestling between love and longing and loss, or the threats of sanction in the rivalries that are constituted psychically. Whilst nothing external may have changed, the developmental pressures within the mind of the child do create change and with it challenges to stasis.

For humans, homeostatic demands are not only biological but emerge into the mental realm in which feelings require attention and mental associations can have a life in themselves. Psychic conflicts abound in the human mind, partly as a result of the in-built tendency to suffer ambivalences. The closer an attachment, the greater the emotional investment and hence the greater the risk of emotional loss. I could suggest that *there is no greater hate than for those to whom we have the greatest love*. This peculiarity of human ambivalence leads me to suggest that invariably *where love lands, hate lurks*. Love unrequited, or at least perceived of as unrequited, or in some way perceived as reciprocated but in unequal measure, leads invariably to the activation of the psychical immune response, whether in the phantasies of childhood or the realities of adult attachments. What Freud observed in this regard was that, here it bumps into the obstacles that have been erected in the meantime by the barrier against incest, making efforts to pass on from these objects which are unsuitable in reality, and find a way as soon as possible to other, extraneous objects with which a real sexual life may be carried on. "These new objects will still be chosen on the model (imago) of the infantile ones, but in the course of time they will attract to themselves the affection that was tied to the earlier ones".[14]

At times, libidinal pressures are aroused not only by familial attachments but by a stranger with whom no emotional attachment or history is apparent, at least on the face of it. Attractions in adulthood are never free of the associations of childhood and the parental imagos that populate psychic memory. Pure sensual arousal unrequited can, particularly in damaged individuals, activate an aggressive and debasing response since attraction or love unrequited constitutes, by definition, a narcissistic injury. Love and attraction that is unrequited hurts feelings. In some individuals that hurt will activate aggression that turns to violence, a mechanism to restore internally. I suggest 'by definition', since added to this point, unrequited libidinal investment signals an experience of loss, and loss is activating of injury to the self. This does not suggest that all people will enact or retaliate for these feelings, since, in some, the perception of injury is mild and in those with early narcissistic dysregulation unresolved it can be severe, activating either implosive or explosive affects.

At other times, the unrequited love of emotional attachments in whom a great deal of affective store is placed and to whom a great deal of libidinal energy is cathected, leads to a deep sense of injury. Parental figures and their love and approval, if missing, represents an asymmetry in libidinal cathexis *from the subjective vantage of the child* and this asymmetry triggers the indignity of love lost, self-esteem tarnished, trust diminished. It is no surprise that these losses activate dysregulation and deviations from homeostasis, triggering a need for a restorative mechanism. Aggressive activations must, unless restricted, occur.

I suggest 'unless restricted' since this is an oxymoron – the aggressive drive cannot be ablated but can find alternative pathways through which to manifest. For example, "The phenomena of conscience, however, lead us to infer that the destructiveness which returns from the external world is also taken up by the super-ego, without any such transformation, and increases its sadism against the ego".[15] Sadism against the ego is, of course, a form of aggression against the ego. Guilt, prompted by libidinal yearnings, for example, can turn aggression against the ego in the form of guilt. It is invariably too easy to empathise with the heavy burden a person with guilt carries, as if they are too hard on themselves and feel bad about themselves – suggestive of a victim experience. But this fails to identify the persecutor within, that guilt is really aggression against the self, a branch of the aggressive drive turned inwards, and hence reflects an internal perpetrator. This introjection reflects a defence rooted in early oral dynamics and its mental prototypes, that ripens in the form of super-ego development as a mental agency at the end of the Oedipal period at around five years of age.

Both libidinal and aggressive drives emerge through the developmental layers of time's forward push and the gene code's determination. These phases *have* to happen. But the subjective experience of how they do is no simple matter, since many layers of interpretation and experience from within and from without impact how these energetic drives resolve or fixate in personal memory. Since very early homeostasis tends to be binary, the infant feels good or not, it may assist in understanding why borderline states emerge in the early stages of infancy as Klein identified. Homeostatic *differentiation* only emerges with a little advance in age, after the first few months of birth. The psychological defence of 'splitting', primitive as it may be, makes more sense if the homeostatic differentiation is as yet undifferentiated and operates in an on-off fashion, or what Freud would refer to as pleasure-unpleasure. Differentiation of different homeostatic states and their imbalances only emerge over the next few months post-partum where the infant comes to be able to know one form of imbalance from another, such as knowing the difference between hunger, thirst, or cold, or knowing that loneliness is different from cramp. But in the earliest stages, homeostatic parameters are undifferentiated and binary, on or off, regulated or dysregulated.

The Psychosexual Matrix and Its Defences

It is, however, a misrepresentation to suggest that there is one manifestation of the aggressive drive. Counter-measures are invoked against libidinal promptings depending on the age and stage of an infant in its development. The aggressive drive manifests immediately after birth in the form of the first cry of an infant signalling its first experience of a breach to homeostasis, triggering the immune response of the infant's mental agency aimed at a restoration of homeostasis. I mentioned above that the aggressive drive that ripens in the form of the super-ego at around five years of age has earlier roots. If the aggressive drive activates immediately after birth in response to the rupture of intra-uterine homeostasis, it obviously cannot manifest with developed guilt and its ideational representation (since the early infant has no words or even ideas of any formed sort). Rather, this immune response must utilise whatever mental representations are available to the infant at the developmental stage in which it finds itself. A one-day old infant, for example, cannot get mobile, or express coherent demands, or represent itself either to itself or the external world, beyond primitive homeostatic demands that crying aims to remedy by *inducing* a response from the environment and restoring a binary version of homeostasis that is either good or not-good. Gradations of comfort are not very nuanced in these early stages, unlike an adult, for example, where homeostatic demands are inordinately varied, subtle, and complex.

However, if the infant must rely on whatever mental representations are available to it to intervene in deviations from homeostasis and its restorations, it limits its optionality to those somatic zones that are represented to the infant. In the first year of life, the mental representations are focused on the erotogenic zone of the lips, mouth, throat, and upper digestive tract. Reflexes of sucking, swallowing, positing, and vomiting, for example, centralise the zones to which libidinal energy cathects and enables representations of the world to form according to these representations. Biological imperatives drive these somatic mechanisms into action but the emergent mental energy that is libidinal *drives* cathexes with these associative processes and the agencies of mind. Mental representations of the only available mechanisms to regulate and re-regulate from states of disequilibrium allow the infant to close or open its mouth, to incorporate or take in contents of the outer world to its inner world, and to eject these same contents, that is, put what is internal *into* the external. These representations become extensions of the aggressive drives' task of restoration of stasis, and form the prototypes of denial, introjection, and projection respectively.

Whilst confusing, in that Freud suggests the driver for erotogenic zones that focuses these mechanisms is in the libidinal drive, which of course it is, but which tells only part of the story and describes only part of the process. The missing part is the counter-cathexes that are set up by the primitive defences whose aim is restoration of equilibrium, these defence mechanisms not only being associated with the libidinal drive but with the death-drive, the aggressive drives' immune system aiming at re-regulation. The internal conflicts of these two drives are present from the outset, tensioning against each other in their attempts to both drive growth and survival and maintain the subjective identity of the infant's Markov blanket and the nature of this self-regulating system, but to also strive to counter the forward-drive of development and its disruptive elements (including, for example, hunger or thirst, which promotes development and survival but breaks the peace by dysregulating the infant). The mental representations of this aggressive drive root themselves in whatever available systems are present at the age of the infant, and these evolve through the different psychosexual stages that Freud so brilliantly identified.

Feelings as Amorphous Homeostatic Information

The link between mind and body remains one of the most complex and quizzical of problems on psychology and neuroscience. In his day, Freud addressed this link by suggesting as we know that the concept of an instinct (drive) is thus one of those lying on the frontier between the mental and the physical. But he added, that the simplest and likeliest assumption as to the nature of instincts "would seem to be that in itself an instinct is without quality, and, so far as mental life is concerned, is only to be regarded as a measure of the demand made upon the mind for work. What distinguishes the instincts from one another and endows them with specific qualities is their relation to their somatic sources and to their aims. The source of an instinct (drive) is a process of excitation occurring in an organ and the immediate aim of the instinct lies in the removal of this organic stimulus".[16]

Freud recognised the tension required organically of an instinct that is paradoxical – it serves to 'break the peace', that is to drive mental dis-equilibrium, with the aim of restoring somatic equilibrium of some sort. It is thus both a driver of disequilibrium with the aim of also discharging or reducing tension. But Freud at this stage remained unclear of the mechanisms available to do so, except through the release of the energy. In his later work, however, he established the duality of the drives, and how these link into what biology and physics have since established in organic life. The discharge of tension is not simply a passive process, which Freud's original formulation implied, but an active one driven by the conservative mechanism of the mental apparatus, its immune system.[17] Any disruption to stasis, including from within the infant's own body, must catalyse an *active* restorative response, using the representations or defences, available.

We might say that a defence is a particular pathway of the aggressive drive manifesting at each developmental phase. If the mind is effectively a homeostatic mechanism driven by feeling states[18] that become encoded in ideational representations, in order to fashion meaning for greater efficiency and to automatise, and since this mind is regulated by two primary drives, we would have to concede that for every disruptive shift from the libidinal drive must also be a counter-move aimed at restoring stasis. This contest is the essential stuff of living matter, homeostasis being at first entirely undifferentiated and binary in human infants, leading to primitive splitting mechanisms of good *or* bad, associated with states of pleasure *or* unpleasure. The infant is in a state of unpleasure or pleasure, good or bad, driven by what we might term love and attachment versus primitive feelings of aggression and hate, the latter manifesting in expressed discontents, crying, niggling, fussing, and in extreme moments inconsolable screaming. We could say that feelings are a form of amorphous homeostatic *information* whose aim is to guide re-regulation from dysregulation and maintain an appropriate developmental trajectory. Only with time, does the amorphous become better differentiated, so that one need is different from another.

Early development is exponentially rapid and in the first months after birth a great deal of subjectively filtered developmental evolution occurs. Differentiation becomes possible and the early undifferentiated state becomes increasingly differentiated, *meaningless* states gradually become more meaningful. The infant 'hatches' from its autistic shell, as Mahler describes it,[19] focuses, increasingly responds to various cues in the environment, and is able to move from a state of being almost entirely unconscious and reflex-driven, to a state of developmental subjectivity. Mental representations of somatic experiences have already imprinted but are also open to modification, if encoded memory is subject to attunement and maternal responsiveness that can undo these potential fixations. Information encoded in memory through feeling states of experience can be modified but this does not invariably happen spontaneously, even when homeostasis is repaired, unless the aversive disruption is perceived of as brief. Extended disruption that is aversive, such as leaving a baby to cry for prolonged periods, may become encoded in long-term memory,[20] which even when nondeclarative (cannot be declared to cognitive and consciousness later in life),[21] will exert an influence on later psychological function and perception. Since crying in infancy is an offshoot of the aggressive drive whose aim is restoration of states of disequilibrium, left unchecked and ineffective, will require it to find some pathway to a form of resolution, even when such resolution represents an imperfect compromise, given available means. This must recruit a mental representative pathway that is open to the infant at its developmental stage, which can become fixated and be returned to repeatedly via regression in later years.

I will return to these mechanisms later, but to remind the reader that we often interpret an infant's crying as associated with distress signals – the infant is in need and we feel sorry for the infant as 'victim' in distress. But this is only half the story – since such a state (of dysregulation) is also triggering an *inducive* mechanism that, driven by the conservative-aggressive drive, is attempting to force (induce) a response from the environment to restore homeostasis or pleasure. Aggression is in the mix of distress and disequilibrium, the response required systemically to restore stasis when needs are not being adequately met. Whilst we don't socially associate crying with aggression, the mechanism for this is rooted in this homeostatic drive. We could fairly rename the death drive as a 'homeostatic drive' whose ultimate aim is a quiescent state, driven by what Freud called the principle of constancy.[22] The requirement for defences to evolve in the mental apparatus is driven by the need to down-regulate what is too up-regulated and up-regulate what is too down-regulated, towards a mean of age-appropriate developmental homeostasis.

Beyond Libidinality

As development evolves, differentiation improves, and the infant can begin to distinguish different states of dysregulation and different sources for these eros-driven internal breakers of the peace. Gradually, awareness dawns as different erotogenic zones are brought online mentally and the infant can cathect with these pathways. Somatic differentiation is accompanied by mental differentiation, the ability of the infant to identify the source and location of one part of sensory experience from another, and over time determine the internal from external. Initially, this is undifferentiated and pain from outside or inside the body is as if it is the same impingement disrupting stasis. In the oral phase, ejecting what is unpalatable to appease impingements that are leading to gastric fullness, for example, leads to the prototype of ejecting/projecting into the external world what is unpalatable in the internal one. Introjection is the taking in to the self for the purposes of appeasing gastric promptings such as hunger. Or denial enables the rejection of the external world through closing of the mouth and creating a barrier against external impingements. These somatic mechanisms lead to emergent mental processes, representing these somatic experiences in the form of primitive ideation, becoming associated with these binders of increasing arousal.

As development prompts the infant's growth, the anal focus emerges, as Freud noted, with its accompanying possibilities for the homeostatic drive to do its work of regulation. Control of the bowel and the retention, expulsion, or sanitising of the dirty into clean enables new possibilities to emerge for regulation. Once again, anal-retentiveness, anal-expulsiveness, reaction-formation, sublimation, undoing, and isolation surface as differentiated possibilities. These defences rooted in surfacing control and autonomy, allow the child to exert its will against both internal and external pressures. As we know, toddler tantrums can be intense as the aggressive drive increasingly surfaces into the mental apparatus and forms representations that permeate mobility and action, agency that was not there when the infant lacked mobility and the 'power' to exert control. This also allows direct conscious control of anal sphincter-function and this erotogenic focus gives rise to its own mental representations, with, for example, obsessive-compulsive disorder (OCD) type features rooted in these defences. But the outpouring of anal-sadistic urges onto an object gave pause for Freud to wonder whether, "Is it not plausible to suppose that this sadism is in fact a death instinct which, under the influence of the narcissistic libido, has been forced away from the ego and has consequently only emerged in relation to the object?"[23] Once again, we can note the preservative drive seems to underpin the defensive manoeuvre of hostile impulses.

At around three to five years of age, Freud described the advent of the oedi-pal phase in which genital awareness emerges and gender differentiation becomes more conscious – boys and girls discover they are different and issues of 'having' or 'not-having' a penis and external genitalia evoke various mental reactions, including envy and the effects of this in relation to the phantasies of intimacy with the opposite-sex parent. These promptings also engender anxiety for boys as competition with the father becomes apparent, as the phase reaches its crescendo and as Freud put it, the oedipal complex is "not simply repressed, it is literally smashed to pieces by the shock of threatened castration. Its libi-dinal cathexes are abandoned, desexualised and in part sublimated"[24] through the internalisation into the superego function and the identification with the aggressor as a defence again the threat of castration by the superior male.

However, perception of loss or envy of the other, or the threat of castra-tion, are powerful threats to stasis and hence all require an immune response psychically. Whilst Freud is correct that libidinal promptings catalyse a defensive response, it is the response that is catalysed that produces symp-toms. He noted: "By an 'instinct' is provisionally to be understood the psy-chical representative of an endosomatic, continuously flowing source of stimulation, as contrasted with a 'stimulus', which is set up by single excita-tions coming from without."[25] This 'continuous flowing source of excitation' is driven by the libidinal imperative to *push* life forward developmentally in addition to its function as a homeostatic regulator. By contrast, in his work *Beyond the Pleasure Principle*, Freud drew on Fechner's work on 'con-stancy',[26] suggesting that organic substances must be governed by homeo-static mechanisms to preserve it from entropy, since extremes in any direction will violate the self-organising principle, we understand now from the biolo-gical and physical sciences. Freud wrote: "Moreover, a more detailed discus-sion will show that the tendency which we thus attribute to the mental apparatus is subsumed as a special case under Fechner's principle of the 'tendency towards stability', to which he has brought the feelings of pleasure and unpleasure into relation".[27] Solms makes the point too that in modern neuroscientific terms, homeostatic mechanisms predominate in emergent systems, from the micro to the macro, as a regulator of deviations from what is biological optimal, regulating those "billions of little homeostats wrapped in their Markov blankets".[28]

The reader will notice that these powerful promptings of the libidinal drive and its tendency to cathect through various erotogenic zones during different phases of development are never alone. These drives are invariably 'managed' or regulated through counter-cathexes, the conservative drive that gets activated, which aims to reduce excitation to manageable, minimal, or even neutral levels; the mental apparatus "being first and foremost a device designed for mastering excitations which would otherwise be felt as distressing or would have pathogenic effects", as Freud wrote.[29] The important concept here is not only that defences emerge as mental representations of somatic foci in these phases, but that the libidinal pushes to meet needs through development are met with the internal requirement to reduce excitation through a homeostatic mechanism when frustration is increasing, "the task of mastering or binding excitations",[30] whose aim is "to keep the quantity of excitation present in it as low as possible or at least to keep it constant".[31] However, the question of why some individuals require greater defensive reactions to similar promptings and why they might choose a particular emphasis or pathway for this depends on a host of temperamental, internal and external factors which make libidinal promptings fixate because of some inhibition or taboo or because arousal has exceeded the infant's capacity for tolerance.

Freud argued that when the ego has succeeded in defending itself against a dangerous instinctual impulse, as for example by the mechanism of repression, it has "inhibited and inflicted damage upon that portion of the id but has at the same time also given it a bit of independence and renounced a bit of its own sovereignty". This follows from the nature of repression, "which is, at bottom, an attempt at 'flight'. The repressed material is now 'outlawed', excluded from the great organisation of the ego, subject only to the laws which prevail in the domain of the unconscious".[32]

Freud makes the added point that, the pathogenic importance of this phenomenon accrues from the fact that most of the instinctual demands of this infantile sexuality "are treated as dangers and guarded against by the ego, so that the sexual impulses of puberty, which should be ego-compatible, are in danger of succumbing to the attraction exerted by their infantile prototypes and of following them into repression. It is here that we come upon the most definite aetiology of the neuroses. It is noteworthy that early contact with the demands of sexuality has the same effect upon the ego as premature contact with the environment".[33]

This statement "treated as dangers" in the above quote, captures both the point that libidinal promptings induce disequilibrium that require restoration whether in childhood pre-latency or in adolescence, wherein the sexual promptings may present more maturely in the form of manifest sexuality. How, we might ask, can something so positive, such as sexual promptings, be experienced by the mind as disruptive or dysregulating, hence activating an internal aggressive response mechanism whose job is homeostatic restoration?

Dysregulation must meet with a homeostatic response and we might suggest that this aggressive response is activated no matter the source of disruption to stasis – but the pathway for its manifestation will vary depending on the internal or external barriers or taboos that might prevail. Freud amplifies this conundrum, suggesting that the psychological factor is to be found in an 'imperfection' of the psychic apparatus which is connected with its differentiation into ego and id and hence to the influence of the environment. "By reason of the dangers which reality offers, the ego is compelled to adopt an attitude of defence towards certain instinctual impulses in the id, to treat them as dangers", he notes. But as we know the ego cannot protect itself against internal instinctual dangers as it can against a piece of reality external to it. Given its intimate connection to the id, the ego is able to stave off an instinctual danger only by putting restrictions upon its own organisation and "by tolerating symptom formation as a substitute for its crippling of the instinct. If then the press of the repudiated instinct is renewed, there result for the ego all the difficulties which we know as neurotic suffering".[34]

In this statement "by tolerating symptom formation as a substitute...", we notice the link between threat (the danger) originating from either the outside or from the id in the form of the libidinal drive, and a state of emergent disruption to homeostasis, necessitating a restorative response. But further, and in his latest writings, Freud became clearer in moving away from his pleasure-principle model of symptom-formation and of sexuality being the key source of neuroses, into theoretically recognising that libido *prompts* – but that this is not the full story. He wrote that his previous assumptions of the direct transforming of libido into anxiety had now changed. "If we do take it into consideration", he declared, "we have several possibilities to differentiate. In the case of anxiety which the ego instigates as a signal, this transformation does not enter in, and thus plays no part in any of the danger situations which impel the ego to initiate a repression".[35]

Put differently, anxiety is a *signal state* activated through situations of danger to the ego, such danger emanating from both internal and external sources, and to which the response of the ego is not significantly different, except that against internal dangers an effective response is mounted through the instigation of strategies of defence available to the infant developmentally, or through fixation and regression of a return to older states and its defences. Infantile defences are activated even in adulthood in response to similar threats to the ego through the mechanisms of the repetition compulsion, fixation, and regression to these points of fixation. If libidinal promptings meet up with either internal threats (guilt) or external ones in the form of inhibitions or taboos, the aggressive drive must register and react to this perception of threat or danger. It is, of course, an artificial distinction since internal dangers must have interfaced historically with external ones to be registered and encoded as a danger, even when in infancy this danger is the threat of loss of the love-object through aggressive impulses in response to frustrations. Freud noted, "It is the part of this archaic heritage having to do with object loss which alone has utility for man. If such childhood phobias become fixed, grow more intense, and persist into a later period of life, analysis demonstrates that their content has become connected with instinctual demands, has become the representative of internal dangers also".[36]

Nonetheless, it is fair to distinguish objective-realistic threats that signal potential harm from internally represented and cathected ones associated with more symbolic representations held in personal memory.

Freud's Theoretical Misstep?

I am aware that some of these points will seem repetitious to some readers but nonetheless I want to distil a few essential issues here to crystalise their essence before delving into clinical syndromes and treatment in more detail in the next chapters. As I have argued, Freud was not unaware of the need to move beyond the pleasure principle, which emphasised the role of libido and sexual drive in both normal psychogenesis and the genesis of symptoms, and his dual-drive theory formulated in *Beyond the Pleasure Principle* represents a major turning point in psychoanalysis. But, as I have also argued, Freud, like Einstein, and many of his followers since, seemed to remain wedded to his own intuitive conceptions and struggled to embrace the full implications of his work, which effectively implied his model of the genesis of symptoms and psychopathology be turned on its head. He recognised, and in fact utilised, Fechner's theory on constancy (homeostasis) to reconceptualise his model of mind, and as later history would bear out, was correct in understanding the imperative for self-organising systems to both strive for and simultaneously resist evolution, wrestling from the "outset of living matter" with the push for time-development and the "pull-back" required to protect any organism from the excess of the life drive.

The dual-drive theory concords well with more recent discoveries and formulations in the neurosciences and in particular the mechanisms required for living organisms to read and respond to states of somatic disequilibrium by registering such states through feelings, activating a response that aims at restoration and a return to stasis.[37] And yet despite Freud's brilliant foresight, he persisted in his emphasis on sexuality and eros, framing the self-preservative drive in his earlier works as a portion of narcissistic libido turned or cathected with the ego, and later on never fully relinquishing this concept. In his earlier work he had conceptualised this idea and evolved beyond it, subsequently coming closer to the idea of libido invested in the ego and recognised that a portion of the 'ego drives' is of a libidinal character and has taken the subject's own ego as its object. "These narcissistic self-preservative drives had thenceforward to be counted among the libidinal sexual drives".[38] He conceded that later the opposition between the ego drives and the sexual drives was transformed into one between the ego drives and the object drives, both of a libidinal nature. "But in its place a fresh opposition appeared between the libidinal (ego and object) drives and others", he declared, "which must be presumed to be present in the ego and which may perhaps actually be observed in the destructive drives. Our speculations have transformed this opposition into one between the life drives (Eros) and the death drives".[39]

This reconceptualisation was significant. But despite this concession, Freud wrestled with the prominence of libidinal and life-drive elements in the genesis of psychopathology. The id was the source of these internal pressures, and accords well with Solms' view of brainstem structures being the source of conscious feelings, whose role is essentially in the service of homeostasis. Freud described this agency of mind as follows, but if Solms wrote this description, I imagine we would be at home with the neuroscientific rendering of the source of affects and conscious feelings, bringing into awareness deviations from stasis and the rising of free energy: "We approach the id with analogies: we call it a chaos, a cauldron full of seething excitations. We picture it as being open at its end to somatic influences, and as there taking up into itself instinctual needs which find their psychical expression in it, but we cannot say in what substratum. It is filled with energy reaching it from the instincts, but it has no organisation, produces no collective will, but only a striving to bring about the satisfaction of the instinctual needs subject to the observance of the pleasure principle"[40] – that being homeostasis – promptings from within the brainstem structures to alert the mind about deviations from stasis and driving remedial steps.

Freud argued that this id played a powerful role in psychic functioning: "The economic or, if you prefer, the quantitative factor, which is intimately linked to the pleasure principle, dominates all its processes. Instinctual cathexes seeking discharge—that, in our view, is all there is in the id".[41] Symptoms are therefore generated because, for example, "...anxiety serves the purposes of self-preservation and is a signal of a new danger"; it arises from libidinal pressures that have in some way become 'unemployable' and unable to extort a remedy from the environment, but "it also arises during the process of repression; it is replaced by the formation of a symptom, is, as it were, psychically bound...".[42] He later reiterated the primacy of libidinal elements in both healthy and pathological functioning, suggesting that in the course of this long-drawn-out development several phases of preliminary organisation can be recognised and "also how this history of the sexual function explains its aberrations and atrophies...".[43]

Moreover, it is not only symptoms but character itself that emerges from the pressures of libido: "During our studies of the pregenital phases of the libido we have also gained a few fresh insights into the formation of character".[44] Freud fully acknowledged the duality of the drives, noting, "And now the instincts that we believe in divide themselves into two groups— the erotic instincts, which seek to combine more and more living substance into ever greater unities, and the death instincts, which oppose this effort and lead what is living back into an inorganic state".[45] This development was theoretically significant and yet despite this acknowledgement, Freud never seemed at rest in maintaining the dominance of the sexual instincts and their role in the genesis of neuroses or symptoms more generally, stating quite emphatically that the aggressive instincts are never alone but always alloyed with the erotic ones. "These latter have much to mitigate and much to avert under the conditions of the civilisation which mankind has created".[46] Indeed, this dialectic is crucial in the bridge between the two primary drives that signals movement towards or away from rising free energy.

Of course, the conditions of civilisation that mankind has created can also be understood inverted, as the conditions of the instincts which have created mankind, from the outset, originating as early as life began. Today, as civilised creatures, we still grapple with our primitive nature, tensioning the two drives against each other in a perpetual struggle for homeostasis. Individual and species preservation must dominate the landscape through the tension of these drives to avert the greater risk of entropy in the greater picture of the economics of life.

Regarding grappling with our nature, I trust the reader will have some forbearance in my liberal quoting of Freud, and also of my tendency to repeat concepts in places, like a theoretical repetition-compulsion, but my aim in so doing is not to bore the reader or assume any compromise in memory, but to contextualise these complexities and muddles in the different theoretical locations that require them, recognising that for some readers the material is more familiar than for others, with the aim of working these threads into the multifaceted tapestry that the mind is. I have quoted Freud's writing at length to give a taste of his inner machinations, and both his giant theoretical steps and calculations, and his paradigms that were so revolutionary and yet also incomplete in certain respects. It goes without saying that the very concept of the death drive and its role and manifestations is also *quintessential* Freud, and hence he warrants pride of place in considering the concept and those that surround it. I trust, also, that the weaving of modern neuroscience enables an updating that consolidates and refines drive theory, and the death drive concept, and its central role in symptom formation and hence the implications this has for clinical work.

In the next chapters, I aim to go deeper into various symptoms and psychopathologies to attempt to demonstrate this tension between the libidinal and conservative drives, and its role on the formation of symptoms and psychopathology. I will begin with one of the most universal and ubiquitous of human experiences.

Notes

1 Freud, S. (1920) Beyond the Pleasure Principle. On Metapsychology: The Theory of Psychoanalysis. London: Penguin, p. 337.
2 Freud, S. (1920) Beyond the Pleasure Principle. *On Metapsychology: The Theory of Psychoanalysis.* London: Penguin, p. 337.
3 Freud, S. (1912) Contributions to a Discussion on Masturbation. *The Standard Edition of the Complete Psychological Works of Sigmund Freud* 12:239–254, p.249.
4 Freud, S. (1912) Contributions to a Discussion on Masturbation. *The Standard Edition of the Complete Psychological Works of Sigmund Freud* 12:239–254, p.246.
5 Freud, S. (1912) Contributions to a Discussion on Masturbation. *The Standard Edition of the Complete Psychological Works of Sigmund Freud* 12:239–254, p.252.
6 Freud, S. (1905) Three Essays on the Theory of Sexuality. *The Standard Edition of the Complete Psychological Works of Sigmund Freud* 7:123–246. pp192–193.
7 Freud, S. (1905) Three Essays on the Theory of Sexuality. *The Standard Edition of the Complete Psychological Works of Sigmund Freud* 7:123–246. p.193.
8 Freud, S. (1905) Three Essays on the Theory of Sexuality. *The Standard Edition of the Complete Psychological Works of Sigmund Freud* 7:123–246. p.193.
9 Freud, S. (1915) Instincts & Their Vicissitudes. The Standard Edition of the Complete Psychological Works of Sigmund Freud 14:109–140, p.122.
10 Freud, S. (1909) Family Romances. *The Standard Edition of the Complete Psychological Works of Sigmund Freud* 9:235–242, p.240.
11 Writes Freud: "Normally it departs more and more from the original parental figures; it becomes, so to say, more impersonal. Nor must it be forgotten that a child has a different estimate of its parents at different periods of its life. At the time at which the Oedipus complex gives place to the super-ego they are something quite magnificent; but later they lose much of this. Identifications then come about with these later parents as well, and indeed they regularly make important contributions to the formation of character; but in that case they only affect the ego, they no longer influence the super-ego, which has been determined by the earliest parental imagos". Freud, S. (1933) New Introductory Lectures On Psycho-Analysis. *The Standard Edition of the Complete Psychological Works of Sigmund Freud* 22:1–182, p.64; see also Freud, S. (1924) The Economic Problem of Masochism. *The Standard Edition of the Complete Psychological Works of Sigmund Freud* 19:155–170, p.168.
12 Freud, S. (1912) On the Universal Tendency to Debasement in the Sphere of Love (Contributions to the Psychology of Love II). *The Standard Edition of the Complete Psychological Works of Sigmund Freud* 11:177–190, pp.183–184.
13 Freud, S. (1917) The Paths to the Formation of Symptoms. In Freud, S. (1917) Introductory Lectures on Psycho-Analysis. *The Standard Edition of the Complete Psychological Works of Sigmund Freud* 16:241–463, p.367.
14 Freud, S. (1912) On the Universal Tendency to Debasement in the Sphere of Love (Contributions to the Psychology of Love II). *The Standard Edition of the Complete Psychological Works of Sigmund Freud* 11:177–190, p.181.
15 Freud, S. (1924) The Economic Problem of Masochism. *The Standard Edition of the Complete Psychological Works of Sigmund Freud* 19:155–170, p.170.

16 Freud, S. (1905) Three Essays on the Theory of Sexuality (1905). *The Standard Edition of the Complete Psychological Works of Sigmund Freud* 7:123–246, p.168 (brackets mine).
17 See my book Perkel, A. (2023) *Unlocking the Nature of Human Aggression: A Psychoanalytic and Neuroscientific Approach.* London: Routledge, for a greater construction of this notion.
18 See Solms, M. (2021) *The Hidden Spring: A Journey to the Source of Consciousness.* London: Profile Books.
19 Mahler, M. Pine, F. & Bergman, A. (1975) *The Psychological Birth of the Human Infant: Symbiosis and Individuation.* New York: Basic Books.
20 See Eric Kandel's Nobel Prize winning pioneering work on memory: Kandel, E. (2006) *In Search of Memory: The Emergence of a New Science of Mind.* New York: WW Norton & Co.
21 See Solms, M. (2021) *The Hidden Spring: A Journey to the Source of Consciousness.* London: Profile Books.
22 Freud, S. (1920) Beyond the Pleasure Principle. *The Standard Edition of the Complete Psychological Works of Sigmund Freud* 18:1–64, p.38.
23 Freud, S. (1920) Beyond the Pleasure Principle. *The Standard Edition of the Complete Psychological Works of Sigmund Freud* 18:1–64, p.54.
24 Freud, S. (1925) Some Psychical Consequences of the Anatomical Distinction between the Sexes. *The Standard Edition of the Complete Psychological Works of Sigmund Freud* 19:241–258, p.257.
25 Freud, S. (1905) Three Essays on the Theory of Sexuality (1905). *The Standard Edition of the Complete Psychological Works of Sigmund Freud* 7:123–246, p.168.
26 Fechner's statement is to be found contained in a small work, *Einige Ideen zur Schöpfungs-und Entwick-lungsgeschichte der Organismen*, 1873 (Part XI, Supplement, 94), and reads as follows: "In so far as conscious impulses always have some relation to pleasure or unpleasure, pleasure and unpleasure too can be regarded as having a psycho-physical relation to conditions of stability and instability. This provides a basis for a hypothesis into which I propose to enter in greater detail elsewhere. According to this hypothesis, every psycho-physical motion rising above the threshold of consciousness is attended by pleasure in proportion as, beyond a certain limit, it approximates to complete stability, and is attended by unpleasure in proportion as, beyond a certain limit, it deviates from complete stability; while between the two limits, which may be described as qualitative thresholds of pleasure and unpleasure, there is a certain margin of aesthetic indifference....". Cited in Freud, S. (1920) Beyond the Pleasure Principle. *The Standard Edition of the Complete Psychological Works of Sigmund Freud* 18:1–64, pp.8–9.
27 Freud, S. (1920) Beyond the Pleasure Principle. *The Standard Edition of the Complete Psychological Works of Sigmund Freud* 18:1–64, p.8.
28 Solms, M. (2021) *The Hidden Spring*: A Journey to the Source of Consciousness. London: Profile Books, p. 165.
29 Freud, S. (1914) On Narcissism: An Introduction. The Standard Edition of the Complete Psychological Works of Sigmund Freud 14:67–102, p.79.
30 Freud, S. (1920) Beyond the Pleasure Principle. *The Standard Edition of the Complete Psychological Works of Sigmund Freud* 18:1–64, p.36.
31 Freud, S. (1920) Beyond the Pleasure Principle. *The Standard Edition of the Complete Psychological Works of Sigmund Freud* 18:1–64, p.9.
32 Freud, S. (1936) Inhibitions, Symptoms and Anxiety. *Psychoanalytic Quarterly* 5:415–443, p.424.
33 Freud, S. (1936) Inhibitions, Symptoms and Anxiety. *Psychoanalytic Quarterly* 5:415–443, p.426.

34 Freud, S. (1936) Inhibitions, Symptoms and Anxiety. *Psychoanalytic Quarterly* 5:415–443, p.427.
35 Freud, S. (1936) Inhibitions, Symptoms and Anxiety. *Psychoanalytic Quarterly* 5:415–443, pp.434–434.
36 Freud, S. (1936) Inhibitions, Symptoms and Anxiety. *Psychoanalytic Quarterly* 5:415–443, p.439.
37 For example, Solms, M. (2021) *The Hidden Spring: A Journey to the Source of Consciousness.* London: Profile Books.
38 Freud, S. (2015) Beyond the Pleasure Principle. *Psychoanalysis and History* 17:151–204, p.200.
39 Freud, S. (2015) Beyond the Pleasure Principle. *Psychoanalysis and History* 17:151–204, p.200.
40 Freud, S. (1933) New Introductory Lectures On Psycho-Analysis. *The Standard Edition of the Complete Psychological Works of Sigmund Freud* 22:1–182, pp.73–74.
41 Freud, S. (1933) New Introductory Lectures On Psycho-Analysis. *The Standard Edition of the Complete Psychological Works of Sigmund Freud* 22:1–182, p.74.
42 Freud, S. (1933) New Introductory Lectures On Psycho-Analysis. *The Standard Edition of the Complete Psychological Works of Sigmund Freud* 22:1–182, pp 84–85.
43 Freud, S. (1933) New Introductory Lectures On Psycho-Analysis. *The Standard Edition of the Complete Psychological Works of Sigmund Freud* 22:1–182, p.98.
44 Freud, S. (1933) New Introductory Lectures On Psycho-Analysis. *The Standard Edition of the Complete Psychological Works of Sigmund Freud* 22:1–182, p.102.
45 Freud, S. (1933) New Introductory Lectures On Psycho-Analysis. *The Standard Edition of the Complete Psychological Works of Sigmund Freud* 22:1–182, p.107.
46 Freud, S. (1933) New Introductory Lectures On Psycho-Analysis. *The Standard Edition of the Complete Psychological Works of Sigmund Freud* 22:1–182, p.111.

Chapter 5

Anxiety
Diagnosis or Signal State?

Psychiatrists and psychologists diagnose anxiety every day, in one form or another. But anxiety is no more a diagnosis than is suggesting that someone with pain or having a temperature makes their diagnosis 'pain' or being 'pyrexial'. Such a 'diagnosis' would be a mere description of a symptom, that is essentially meaningless and of no value in treatment. It leaves no understanding of the 'why'. Pain or being pyrexial are 'signals' that something deeper pathogenic or disruptive to somatic homeostasis is occurring, which requires remedy. The pain, or the raised temperature, is merely a symptom of a deeper dysregulation that requires understanding and intervention. Likewise, with anxiety, the path that is triggering the anxiety must be understood to appropriately treat the underlying cause. In this chapter, I wish to address what these pathways to the signal state of anxiety might be.

In the previous chapters I have hinted at the function of anxiety as a *signal state*, of some threat to equilibrium. At times such a threat emanates from external sources, such as a mugger on a mountain path or being jilted in love. At other times, the source is purely internal, and often without any clear conscious cause. Such a threat that can originate from within, can do so from the body or from the mind. It is a peculiar characteristic of anxiety that its function in registering threats and signalling them to the ego makes little differentiation between those threats originating outside of the ego from this emanating from within the psyche itself. This appears unique amongst the species and counter-intuitive that the mental apparatus can see itself as the enemy, mounting an immune response to itself when something unconscious prompts disruption. It is as if the line between adaptive and maladaptive appears too thin to be any use in promoting health. Yet, anxiety is ubiquitous to the human condition and serves a deeper purpose as a signalling mechanism that the self is under threat of disruption.

It would seem obvious that where a threat originates from the external environment, a fear response is triggered, suggesting to the individual that a disruptor to equilibrium is pending. We might regard an external threat as objective, viewed from any perspective. A rock rolling down a hill towards a hiker would be suggestive of an accelerated risk toward entropy, unless a

DOI: 10.4324/9781003628972-6

cascade of stress hormones signals a need for remedial action. We would all agree that this represents an objective threat and the fear or anxiety triggered by such a threat is both justifiable and appropriate. But let us assume this hiker began to have panic attacks following the event and presented in a consulting room with what is now an anxiety disorder. We would be forgiven for being sympathetic to the shock, counsel that the anxiety is a response to a trauma, and his thoughts about finding the world an unsafe place were understandable.

But here we are at risk for falling into a conceptual trap – since the evaluation of a threat must be filtered through ideational evaluation held in memory. In other words, to know where you are and what that thing rolling down the hill is must reference memory and all that goes into its encoding from the past, for future reference. To make Solms' point, which I will repeat in the book in different contexts to remind ourselves of this central aspect of memory becoming automatised in both positive life drive but also 'negative' death drive forms:

> ... long-term memories serve the future. Once the midbrain decisions triangle has evaluated the compressed feedback flowing in from previous action, what it activates is an expanded *feedforward* process which unfolds in reverse direction, through the forebrain's memory systems, generating an *expected context* for the selected motor sequence. This is the product of all our learning. In other words, when a need propels us into the world, *we do not discover the world afresh with each new cycle.* It activates a set of predictions about the likely sensory consequences of our actions, based upon past experience of how to meet the selected need in the prevailing circumstances.[1]

Risk-evaluation can thus never truly be objective, since the conscious evaluation of such a pending impingement must be filtered through the layers of psychic memory, some of which, perhaps all of which, is tainted by personal history. If the outside 'objective' observer knew that the hiker had a history of being nearly killed in an avalanche as a child, it would shift how their reaction was perceived and how their internal associations would register and respond to this precipitating event. A psychologist might take a slightly deeper look and suggest that the current anxiety was understandable because the precipitating event and its shock had reawakened a previous trauma and the anxiety and feelings of unsafety were understandable. The patient has been a victim of a threatened trauma reawakening an old trauma perhaps long 'forgotten'. Some 'working through' would be in order and there the matter might rest.

But let us delve further: since what if we uncovered that this hiker not only survived an early childhood avalanche, but his father was killed in the same event. Our insight into their psychological reaction would shift again. The patient struggles with unresolved grief as well as the direct trauma that must have mobilised an intense response at the time to the traumatic precipitant. Therapeutic work might require the working through of trauma, loss, and the associated complications of mixed feelings that loss invariably activates. A good clinician would recognise these layers and assist the patient to deal with the loss, grief, guilt, and perhaps even anger at his father's being taken from him at such a young age. Some 'working through' would be in order and there the matter might rest.

But let us delve further: now, what if we uncover that the hiker had been feeling hostile to his father for pushing him to walk on the mountain as a four-year-old, when the tragic accident occurred, at an age when he was more inclined to spend that time in front of the fire with his mother, to whom he was at that age oedipally attached, rather than struggle to keep up with his athletic father who had a tendency to expect his son to be a 'little man' and take on the challenge of the elements. Perhaps this little boy felt some guilt at his hostile impulses to his father, and his resentments for both the pressures and discomforts of performance. Perhaps also, he had held some unconscious rivalry with his father, as boys of that age do, in his attachment for his mother and the 'romantic' phantasies he held for her at that age, and the wish that his father would 'go away', which may have led to guilt that his wish had manifest in reality. A good psychodynamic clinician might recognise the complexity of ambivalence in this boy's attachments and the manner in which normal developmental resolutions of the oedipal drama were short-circuited by the tragedy, leading to now deeply buried and repressed feelings and wishes, no longer consciously recalled and yet exerting a deep influence on his current mental state. A good therapist would be able to uncover the unconscious elements in this clinical presentation, enabling a working through at a deeper level. Now, we find, the anxiety is not simply a signal of impending entropy and a mental response to it, but contains internal associative elements, uniquely subjective in the patient's personal history, which are contributing to the current clinical presentation. Some 'working through' would be in order and there the matter might rest.

But what if we delved even a little deeper, and discovered that during his first year of life, the patient struggled with gastric reflux that created disruption to the breast-feeding regimen, led to maternal fatigue, sleep dysregulation, and some post-partum dysthymic symptoms, which disrupted his own infantile attachment to the breast during the early oral phase of his development. He screamed repeatedly after feeds, took two to three hours to be settled by constant rocking, eventually succumbing to sleep from sheer exhaustion. As mentioned before, we can understand that infantile crying represents an aggressive-drive response in infancy, aimed at *inducing* [2] a response from the environment to remedy disruptions to homeostasis, but in this case proved ineffective, despite the mother's well-meant but vain attempts to reregulate her baby. Put differently, from the outset our patient struggled with his rage and its futility in remedying his constant states of dis-equilibrium. Eventually, out of desperation and on the well-meant (but entirely misguided) advice of nurses at her local clinic, she took home the notion that 'all babies cry' and that she should avoid spoiling her baby and rather let him learn to self-sooth and cry himself to sleep. The mother attempted this for two weeks, eventually giving up when he continued to protest and scream, returning to her attempts to soothe her baby, and getting medication from her GP to ease her depression. Eventually, after six months, the baby settled and the relationship between mother and baby improved. A good analyst would of course understand these unconscious associations, and assist the patient to work through these deeper layers of experience.

But here we encounter a problem to this clinical intent: whilst much of the patient's memories remained unconscious but eventually made accessible through analysis, the *earliest* of this patient's memories were held uncon-sciously but in a *non-declarative* [3] state – these primitive memories cannot be 'declared' to consciousness since they are pre-cognitive, formed of primitive ideational representations as yet without meaning, and hence contained with emotional associations inaccessible to words-representations. And yet, as Kinet discusses, these imprints or primitive memories exert a significant and outsized role in future development, especially given how early these imprints are formed. Kinet captures this well, noting that as early as the end of preg-nancy, relational and affective patterns are recorded in implicit memory, unconsciously stored, but not repressed in the conventional psychoanalytic sense of a defence, and hence not recallable through words. He asserts that, the earliest experiences are stored there to form a structural part of the unconscious and powerfully and permanently assert their influence on adult life, influencing "later relationships' depth and emotional colour. And yet treatment requires a 'working-through' if healing is to be achieved in a ther-apeutic context that invariably relies on words and word-representations",[4] a paradox we will deal with in Chapter 11 on treatment implications.

Vinegar is to Wine?

Anxiety represents a signal state,[5] as mentioned, but as we can see through the layers, tells us only half the story about the distress and trauma. What of the other half? The other half is about the activation of the conservative drive whose aim is to register states of homeostatic deviation and strive for restoration of homeostasis when threat is pending or actualising from that individual's subjectivity. None of the clinical interventions above have addressed this part of the mental response.

But I am here again putting the cart before the horse. This cascade of layers suggests a number of elements that we have not yet covered. There is no *objective* measure for anxiety since all experience must be filtered through the lens of subjectivity. All subjectivity aims to maintain the Self in relation to its environment in the interests of self-preservation. The mechanisms used for this preservation is two-fold, relying on two inter-linked mental processes: namely, memory and aggression.

Memory, I have suggested, is a registrar of states of disequilibrium and aggression its remediator[6] – and I should add, is activated when life drive needs are failing. Obviously, life drive needs also become automatised to efficiently meet needs when they can. But when not, aggression mobilises to remediate. The layers and tapestry of experiences, and of traumatic disequilibrium from infancy, will have influenced the patient's responses in our example above. Early disruptions to homeostasis lead to the registration of neurologically encoded memories,[7] non-declarative but nonetheless encoded, in a feed-forward process that is constantly referenced through other mechanisms: regression, subjectivity, and the repetition compulsion. Our patient is revisiting older layers of *his* psyche according to associations and their links being triggered by a current event. These associations are not simply of threat, but of primary objects in his life that have affected outcomes of development, catalysed rage, evoked guilt, set in motion a series of emotional reactions premised on their valence of early experience and which hidden below layers of defence are creating symptoms in the present, some of which appear on the surface disproportionate to the activating event.

Yet, struggling again with the implications of his own discoveries, Freud seemed to hold fast to his original formulations in places, and according to James Strachey, the Editor of the volume on anxiety, noted Freud adding a footnote to the fourth edition of his *Three Essays:* "'One of the most important results of psycho-analytic research is this discovery that neurotic anxiety arises out of libido, that it is a transformation of it, and that it is thus related to it in the same kind of way as vinegar is to wine.'"[8] As discussed, this sentiment peppered much of his writings despite noting in his later paper on anxiety that, "He no longer regarded anxiety as transformed libido, but as a reaction on a particular model to situations of danger",[9] and yet as Strachey quoting Freud, "that it was very possible that in the case of the anxiety neurosis 'what finds discharge in the generating of anxiety is precisely the surplus of unutilised libido'", he was nonetheless moving in the direction of anxiety as response to perceptions of threat from both external and internal sources, noting that in a passage near the end of his discussion of anxiety in Lecture XXXII of his New Introductory Lectures, "he wrote that in the anxiety neurosis, too, the appearance of anxiety was a reaction to a traumatic situation: 'we shall no longer maintain that it is the libido itself that is turned into anxiety in such cases'".[10] Through his writing, we see, that Freud grappled with the nature of symptom formation in more general ways, suggesting, "A symptom, like a dream, represents something as fulfilled: a satisfaction in the infantile manner. But by means of extreme condensation that satisfaction can be compressed into a single sensation or innervation, and by means of extreme displacement it can be restricted to one small detail of the entire libidinal complex".[11] Symptoms were, in this analysis, a by-product of "the libidinal satisfaction whose presence we suspect and which is invariably confirmed".[12] Symptoms are, in general, compromise-formations of libidinal promptings bumping into the constraints of internal and external realities.

This begs the question whether what Freud identified as 'objective' anxiety (that is, originating in the external rather than internal environment and more associated with a fear response) can ever be free of the subjective lens through which experience of any sort of perceived. Infants born temperamentally more sensitive might experience disequilibrium with greater intensity, eliciting a greater emotional response, and hence encoding such a perceived experience in memory carrying greater valence as a result and, in turn, influencing later stages of development and the longings and losses that invariably pepper these developmental psychic layers. It is undeniable that some threats emanate from external sources, from outside the body and outside the mental apparatus and some from within.

This distinction between internally driven neurotic anxiety derived from unconscious conflicts, and that from external sources is important and relevant. But in reality, there is never a neat separation between these elements. Research is clear that temperament in infancy or perceptions of control in adulthood, mediates the impact of external traumata and can mitigate or amplify them through a lens of subjectivity, how an experience is perceived and then encoded. Are snails good to eat and a delicacy, or a source of disgust and dysregulation when presented on your dinner plate? And, if you are one of those that finds snails good to eat, how about when presented on your breakfast plate rather than your dinner plate? As Freud noted, citing Bleuler, "All neurotics, and many others besides, take exception to the fact that '*inter urinas et faeces nascimur* [we are born between urine and faeces]'"[13] – the line between desire and disgust can be narrow indeed! External pressures of all sorts are mediated through the lens of subjectivity and hence must invariably be linked to intra-psychic filters, and the conflicts and the residues of unconscious associations that are triggered, between the agencies of mind but also through the tension of ambivalence (for the object).

Differentiation and Non-differentiation

It may seem that two different, but related, elements are in play when psychic injury threatens. In the first place, needs that are unfulfilled timeously may feel like a threat to the infant's integrity, and libidinal promptings for attachment, as a route to need-fulfilment, are invariably associated with some frustrations and failures. Two elements become triggered in the resultant cascade: the agencies of mind conflict with each other, so that ego function (albeit primitive in the first months) attempts to reconcile reality with need, but in the process, both driven by and resulting from the two primary drives, conflicting energies emerge. The roots of ambivalence can be seen in this conflict. These two intersecting elements provide the ground for mental tensions and conflicts, that activate both states of disequilibrium and a deviation from homeostasis, but also trigger thereto a restorative response in the form of the conservative-aggressive drive. How the latter behaves and finds its routes will have an effect on whether anxiety manifests. The tendency of the psyche to treat sources of disequilibrium in an undifferentiated manner in the early stages of life, diffusing external and internal sources of impingement as if they were the same, is never fully lost to the mental apparatus.

Whilst the infant does of course come to recognise sources of discomfort originating from within its own body as separate from those originating from outside sources, and differentiation of this sort must clearly manifest through development in order to enable the individual organism to navigate the environment, it is also true that subjectivity-filtered memory must be activated in response to *both* sources of impingement. Since memory is tied together with a drive response that can restore stasis when memory signals a need or a threat, we can assume that differentiation of internal and external sources is never fully achieved. Objective stimuli are never truly objective since they must be filtered through the associative elements activated through memory. Regression, in other words, is never far behind any state of disequilibrium, bar the proviso that the degree of emotional activation may vary, depending on the level of threat perceived or the intensity of emotional associations that are triggered. Highly differentiated states are still under the influence of ancient personal history through the influence of regression to previously encoded experiences, so that even impingements originating from external sources will activate internal associations. "They create a substitute, then, for the frustrated satisfaction by means of a regression of the libido to earlier times, with which a return to earlier developmental stages of object-choice or of the organization is inseparably bound up",[14] wrote Freud.

It is also true that what Freud termed 'neurotic anxiety'[15] or 'super-ego anxiety'[16] might originate from within the mental apparatus, since phantasies and libidinal promptings are also sourced from instinctual drives that *push* energetic forces within the psyche and prompt attachment and the feelings required for attachment, in both the interests of preserving individual life as an infant-child, but also preserving the Markov blanket endemic to the species, through procreative-adaptive tendencies. These "breakers of the peace" flow like a spring from within the depths and prompt both immediate gratification from within the id (and associated brainstem structures), but also long-term satiation of deeper desires for bonding, children, and ultimate quiescence when life follows its natural course, destined to return to dust at the end of an organism's natural days. In this sense, when these impulses conflict with external inhibitions, prohibitions, or taboos, they serve up a representation of danger to the psyche that is effectively no different from threats emanating from the exterior. Psychically, threats originating from the interior or the exterior will activate a response aimed at psychic restoration of homeostasis and a return to quiescence.

It is worth repeating that perceptions of threat must be based on some reference to memory and its associations, since evaluation of what is a threat must also be regulated by the principle of economics and the efficient use of energy. It would serve little purpose if innocuous triggers were reacted to as if they were mortal threats, since this would be anathema to an evolutionary advantage. The need to achieve more by doing less systemically, in the pursuit of homeostasis, is embedded in all organic systems, since energetic efficiency enables an evolutionary advantage over organisms that are energetically inefficient, as Solms points out, for example, that the 'predictive brain' is revealed neuroscientifically to be 'lazy', at least over the long term, "vigilant for every opportunity to achieve more by doing less".[17] As mentioned, the mechanism for the purpose of homeostatic restoration when the psyche is under threat of some sort, is the conservative drive that utilises aggression in some form to respond to an impingement or state of disequilibrium, even those created when needs are frustrated. So, in later writings, Freud began to backtrack on his original formulations and conviction of anxiety being linked to transformed libido, asserting,

> It is no use denying the fact, though it is not pleasant to recall it, that I have on many occasions asserted that in repression the instinctual representative is distorted, displaced, and so on, while the libido belonging to the instinctual impulse is transformed into anxiety. But now an examination of phobias, which should be best able to provide confirmatory evidence, fails to bear out my assertion; it seems, rather, to contradict it directly.[18]

The problem with anxiety emerges when the ego's differentiation of internal from external threats to stasis is diffuse. This can trigger a reaction to the (perceived) threat, based on encoded memory of experience, but in the absence of concrete remedial action to remedy the source of disequilibrium. If concrete measures can be enacted to defuse the source of imbalance, anxiety would have no necessary place. But in the absence of concrete remedy, particularly if the source of threat is internal and unconscious, so too anxiety will manifest since the restorative response remains ineffective as "no flight can avail against it".[19] As Freud noted, "An instinct, on the other hand, never operates as a force giving a *momentary* impact but always as a constant one. Moreover, since it impinges not from without but from within the organism, no flight can avail against it".[20]

What is the mental apparatus to do in the face of a threat that is constant, derives from within the apparatus, presses for fulfilment in the face of the constraints of both external reality and internal prohibitions? It must compromise,[21] find pathways that both satisfy the need without violating taboos or threats, through displacements or other effective defensive man-oeuvres that dominate that individual subjectivity's mental landscape and experience. Moreover, the psyche must muster a restorative response to the con-stant flow of needs, phantasies, feelings that unsettle the mind and invariably can be only partially fulfilled, hence triggering in its wake the conservative drive. This aggressive response, not aimed at an external source, can take aim at an internal source and activate defensive manoeuvres. In theory, the mental apparatus can never face states of deviation from stasis without a restorative response being activated, this response finding a regressive path through the subjective associative mechanisms of memory and its link to earlier experience and encoded defences.

Anxiety is, therefore, not only about the stress of the 'victim' within the psyche but also the response of the internal 'perpetrator' to it. If this link is as strong as this might suggest, we could say that anxiety is married to the conservative drive, being activated in response to threats to stasis. There is a quantitative element to this suggestion, in that the level of anxiety must therefore be proportional to the level of threat. However, we know from clinical evidence that, mostly, anxiety is not in any consistent manner pro-portional to the level of threat. Someone who is phobic about stepping on the cracks on the pavement, or has panic attacks in response to a benign or unknown trigger, is not reacting proportionally, since, objectively, there is often little or even no actual threat. An open space for an agoraphobic, or a closed one for someone claustrophobic, has no objective valence as a threat except as filtered through an individual's subjective associations that uncon-sciously represent some memory trace encoded to represent some source of threat. Even in the normal course of life, the anxieties that plague us at night are seldom proportional to problem solving them during the day. This places subjectivity in a centrally deterministic place in how humans perceive and decode stimuli that are *interpreted* to be threatening and hence also in the generation of anxiety as a signal response to it. Whilst real threat emanating from the outside of the psyche, that is in the external environment, will elicit a fear response, what Freud thought of as 'objective anxiety', such fear is never entirely free of internal associations through which encoded memory informs how to interpret the exter-nal threat and react to it. The mind must evaluate a response drawn from encoded memory associations, how best to respond efficiently to the threat, in neu-roscientific terms to automatise as best it can by making predictions based on past experience, to minimise the risk of entropic failure to whatever course of response and action is chosen. Remember, that basing future predictions and response is based invariably on past experience of unpleasure, much of which derives from infancy whence affective intensity and perceived threat is greatest, and yet also meaningless for the infant. Accordingly, Freud reminds us:

> So far, we have had no occasion to regard realistic anxiety in any differ-ent light from neurotic anxiety. We know what the distinction is. A real

danger is a danger which threatens a person from an external object, and a neurotic danger is one which threatens him from an instinctual demand. In so far as the instinctual demand is something real, his neurotic anxiety, too, can be admitted to have a realistic basis. We have seen that the reason why there seems to be an especially close connection between anxiety and neurosis is that the ego defends itself against an instinctual danger with the help of the anxiety reaction just as it does against an external real danger, but that this line of defensive activity eventuates in a neurosis owing to an imperfection of the mental apparatus.[22]

Freud recognised that his earlier theories of anxiety as transformed libido did not fully explain its nature or source. Testing himself against his earlier theories, reflected, "But I must admit that I thought I was giving more than a mere description. I believed I had put my finger on a metapsychological process of direct transformation of libido into anxiety. I can now no longer maintain this view. And, indeed, I found it impossible at the time to explain how a transformation of that kind was carried out".[23] His later dual-drive theory pointed the way, since once the recognition of the aggressive drive acting as a counter-weight to any breakers to homeostasis became clearer, the central role of the aggressive drive in the genesis of anxiety began to take a more central role in the genesis of symptoms in general.

The Psychosexual Matrix

So far, we have a picture emerging of the tension between libidinal promptings and a conservative reaction aimed at restoration of homeostasis. If we take this deeper, it would be remiss to theoretically regard 'neurotic' internal libidinal promptings or external '*Realgefahr*' ('real danger')[24] on the one hand, and aggression as neatly dichotomised into two equal but opposing psychic streams. The complexity of human subjectivity simply does not allow for it. Rather, we notice through clinical work that individual pathways for both these streams emerge over time and fixate at various developmental stages, depending on the mix of personal and perhaps endogenous factors. The puzzle invariably remains as to how two or more siblings reared in the same broad environment end up with such different personalities, neuroses, and psychic pathways for their instinctual drives.

But such is the nature of subjectivity that it demonstrates exquisite complexity and nuance in how an infant interprets their environment and encodes memory traces based on these 'interpretations'. The fixation points of early development show that when the conservative drive is activated, it must utilise what means are available for its 'remedial intervention'. A three-day old infant cannot swing a club in its defence nor even fire its mother from her maternal job when she proves frustrating. But it can fuss or scream, both expressions of the conservative/ aggressive drive. It can also utilise its mouth to give expression to this drive – closing its mouth, spitting or ejecting contents, incorporating or swallowing contents, and in this fashion, enable a form of remedy through inducing a response from the (maternal) environment. An overt verbal expression of "no", for example, which may be available to an older anal-stage toddler, is only available to a younger infant through ejection, biting, closing of the mouth and so on, which enables the infant to exert agency over the dictates of the failures and frustrations of the environment.

These somatic expressions create *mental representations* and enable these mental representations to form a life-of-their-own quality which can represent the somatic in response to sources of disequilibrium through the years of later development, a "transformation is a function of the psychical conflict under pressure of which the symptom had to be formed".[25] This mental efficiency means that the infant does not have to invent anew each time it is confronted by frustration but can react through reversion to memory encoded as to how to respond going forward. Thus, economic efficiency in the service of homeostasis links to Freud's notion of regression, to use Ernst Kris' phrasing, 'in the service of the ego'[26], to which earlier points of reference *must* be revisited to fulfil the function of memory as the storage of prior impingements that unsettle the mind-body system, and as mentioned before, to automatise predictions to minimise surprise. Almost as soon as experience begins in life, memory traces are being laid down to register sources and states of disequilibrium for future use, both in the service of the libidinal drive (how to meet needs efficiently) but also in the service of the death drive (how to bind excess free energy when arousal and frustration is increasing). As Freud noted that reality can be persistent even though the libido is ready to take another object in place of the one that has been refused to it, then it will be compelled to take the path of regression and revert back to previously encoded automatisms, striving to find satisfaction "either in one of the organisations which it has already outgrown or from one of the objects which it has earlier abandoned. The libido is lured into the path of regression by the fixation which it has left behind it at these points in its development".[27]

But what use is memory without a response mechanism to remedy the deviation from stasis? It is like a house alarm without an armed response is just background noise. Hence, evolution has enabled early deviation from stasis to meet with a response aimed at restoration when needs cannot be fulfilled by the libidinal push. In humans, the aggressive drive plays this role, but offers no binary solution, like a light that is on or off. Rather, activation of the drive meets up with limitation from external parameters, the infant's own somatic limitations according to age and stage, and the internal conflicts and taboos that might limit expression of destructive feelings for fear of damaging or destroying the object upon whom the infant depends. The compromise-formations that each psyche renders for itself will depend on the many nuanced variables that are in play for that subjectivity, at the time, and in their context. Anxiety may manifest when the activation of this drive represents a threat to self or others against which no flight can avail, and yet a state of disequilibrium prevails that *requires* a remedial response or action.

Through available pathways, given the age and stage and the somatic correlates in use, mechanisms may manifest through which the aggressive response is being repressed, sublimated, constrained, or diluted. Perhaps, we might suggest, that any activation of a state of change from stasis, whether through libidinal pressures or external impingements, must activate this drive, which if it could do its work unobstructed by internal or external constraints, would cause no symptoms.[28] But such an idealised scenario is never possible, since ambivalence, love and hate for the same object, is the blessing and curse of humanity.

Variations and Obsessive-Compulsive Disorder

There is not one form of anxiety. Since the aggressive response must channel itself through the available somatic and mental means available to the infant or developing child, it must recruit those mental representations that are current in development. An early oral-stage child in the first months of life has no conscious awareness of its anal sphincter or control over its mechanism. It can exert control over its mouth, swallowing, spitting and so on but not over toilet functions. However, later in development as the child enters the anal phase from about one to three years of age, its ability to control anal functions develops, enabling mental representations to form of the contents of the bowel and its pushing out or holding in. Retention or expulsion gains some control through the will of the child, who can use their emotional frustrations through this mechanism, and giving rise to the mental defences that accompany this stage. Defences such as reaction-formation, isolation, and undoing represent the relationship of the child to both faecal matter and their mental representation of it, alongside the ability to control whether such faecal matter disappeared through withholding it, expelling it not only into but *onto* the world, or turning it opposite so that mental representations of 'dirty' are disguised by 'clean'.

In obsessive-compulsive disorders, regression to these fixation points dictate the nature of the defences utilised in the disorder. The separation of affect and ideation leading to obsessional thinking, the defence of 'undoing' leading to compulsions such as hand-washing or constant ritualised enactments, are attempts to ward off or undo the impulse that threatens emergence. Rooted in the infantile stage of development, the rage response, so intense in the anal stage of toddlerhood, becomes managed through these available mechanisms. On the face of these examples, we might see no aggression at all. Ritualised hand-washing or distressing obsessions present with no inner experience of aggression nor usually any outward manifestation of it. This separation of the deeper impulse from manifest awareness is rooted in the infantile attempts to utilise available mechanisms to restore stasis during periods of disruption to it, with this aggressive drive channelling through these available mechanisms. A toddler attempting to exert control bumping into sufficient frustration will utilise the anal sphincter as a *psychical* representation of the intense rage that can well up at that stage of development. Through anal retention and withholding or expulsion this rage response can create a pathway through which impulses and affects can find a compromise, neither destroying nor preserving the attachments that might be perceived as the source of the frustration. Of course, faecal matter can also represent psychic phantasy and the 'bad' that can be represented when it becomes visible outside of the body. Many children may feel haunted, disgusted, frightened by the faecal matter that appears in the potty or toilet after them, and this matter extracts symbolic valence from the child's psyche. The expelled matter comes to represent inner mental contents too, phantasies and feelings, both powerful and persecutory.

I will not dwell on these elements since they are well represented in the psychoanalytic literature. The point I make here is that mental representations during this anal phase, for example, become fixated and give rise to adult disorders of anxiety such as OCD because the defences associated with the anal phase and its functions encode into memory for later regressive access when the ability to metabolise the rage response is exceeded, and recruits somatic zones available at the time, and its mental representations, to manage the activation of the aggressive drive, and channel it into these available defence mechanisms. The libidinal promptings *pushing* the child's needs are met with resistances from both external and internal sources, that *require* a compromise. Sometimes this compromise is adequate and resolves the tension and sometimes it does not, leading to developmental fixations that will be referred back to in personal memory as part of the efficiency of memory's *feed-forward* process. But memory does not appear to define itself quite so neatly, since earlier fixations carry through into later development and both influence the emergence of later defences but also, we see, that later defences can supersede earlier ones, so that this supersession dominates the floor to which regressive moments revert. The dominance of some defences in the psychosexual matrix of development represent points of significant fixation that took the infant-child beyond their capacity to metabolise the aggressive activations, leading to a dominant fixation in their psyche, from which their defensive system then emerges to manage life going forward.

In phobias, as another example, a substitute object takes the place of a hidden impulse, projected into the external elements. In Freud's case study of Little Hans, he later noted that, "But the *affect* of anxiety, which was the essence of the phobia, came, not from the process of repression, not from the libidinal cathexes of the repressed impulses, but from the repressing agency itself. The anxiety belonging to the animal phobias was an untransformed fear of castration. It was therefore a realistic fear, a fear of a danger which was actually impending or was judged to be a real one".[29]

Freud later recognised the inverted nature of his earlier hypotheses around anxiety, and lamented his early position, to remind the reader, "It is no use denying the fact, though it is not pleasant to recall it, that ... the libido belonging to the instinctual impulse is transformed into anxiety. But now an examination of phobias, which should be best able to provide confirmatory evidence, fails to bear out my assertion; it seems, rather, to contradict it directly".[30]

The notion that the anxiety was reflecting some perceptions of danger took its place, "I believed I had put my finger on a metapsychological process of direct transformation of libido into anxiety. I can now no longer maintain this view".[31] In the famous case of Little Hans, the fear of castration emerges oedipally under the spell of libidinal promptings for his mother, a normal process eliciting fear since it also evokes the threat of competition and rivalry with the opposing parent, in this case his father. The threat of castration dominates the psychical representations during this phase and represents a danger, albeit a projected one, from an external source. Of course, no father would enact such a terrible punishment on his son and this universal fear of paternal retaliation occupies a symbolic place in the mind of every boy navigating this stage of development.

The libidinal promptings I am describing (in this case during the oedipal stage), therefore disrupt stasis and in the process also create a threat. The line between this threat emanating from the inside or outside of the mental apparatus invariably remains diffuse, since the intra-psychic source of the threat does not differentiate itself from the outside object onto whom this threat is projected. The psyche *interprets* this threat as if it were objective and real, and hence activates the conservative drive in its defence. But where does this aggression-in-defence go if the threat emanates from intra-psychic sources against which no flight *or fight* can avail against it? It must represent a threat that cannot be combated effectively since no manoeuvres in the real world would address it. The *signal* of this dysregulation is the anxiety state displaced in the case of phobias onto an external but neutral stimulus, "that phobias have the character of a projection in that they replace an internal, instinctual danger by an external, perceptual one".[32] It is worth nothing that projection is an oral defence brought into the service of later anal defences, in which isolation, undoing, and reaction-formations abound, and yet triggered by even later oedipal longings in which the defence of displacement can dominate.

This matrix of defences all attach themselves to the activation of the conservative drive, mobilising in response to the subjective perception of injury and threat (to homeostasis). Freud had begun to fully recognise the limited explanatory power of rooting anxiety (and other symptoms) solely as responses to libidinal pressures and distortions. Rather, the dual-drive theory suggested that aggression and the conservative drive lay at its root and that its activation from any source would generate a signal state if that energy could not be adequately discharged in the normal course towards restoring homeostasis, "the theory that anxiety is only an affective signal and that no alteration has taken place in the economic situation",[33] that is, the requirement to achieve lots with little expenditure of energy, the brain being, as mentioned, "vigilant for every opportunity to achieve more by doing less".[34] I might add that anxiety, Freud conceded, is "a reaction to a situation of danger",[35] that danger is perceived through the lens of individual subjectivity, and reacted to accordingly. In fact, Freud concluded strongly that "(w)e cannot find that anxiety has any function other than that of being a signal for the avoidance of a danger-situation"[36] and that "my present conception of anxiety as a signal given by the ego in order to affect the pleasure-unpleasure agency does away with the necessity of considering the economic factor".[37] Of course, if anxiety was not felt consciously it would serve little purpose, and hence must recruit the ego in its service. Anxiety in this regard, cannot emanate directly from the id or even from an intra-punitive super-ego, because it must be registered consciously to fulfil its role of alerting the psyche to situations of symbolic, pending, or actual danger or threat. Freud conceded that: "Anxiety is an affective state and as such can, of course, only be felt by the ego. The id cannot have anxiety as the ego can; for it is not an organisation and cannot make a judgement about situations of danger".[38] Rather, the id can be a source of endless impulses and stirrings, the fountain of libidinal promptings pushing the organism along its developmental path, activating affects and conscious feelings pointing at needs.

These stirrings and affects from the id are the source of homeostatic regulation, and according to Solms, consciousness itself.[39] *Consciousness emerges in an evolutionary sense to represent to the interior what it needs to maintain itself in relation to the exterior,* and as Freud proposed, "consciousness emerges instead of a memory trace".[40] Perhaps in more current terms, Solms describes neuroscientifically, that "consciousness registers the state of the subject, not of the object world. The sentient subject is first and foremost an affective subject. Only then can it experience perceptual and cognitive representations".[41] It is, in other words, the interface of the psychic skin between the inner and outer world. Consciousness enables impressions of the interior somatic world to form, representing it in its tremendous complexity, and feeding information to the ego that allows it to regulate, express, and sometimes fulfil those emergent needs *in the service of homeostatic regulation.*

But why then would such stirrings, whose agenda and purpose are noble and necessary, become represented to the ego as a danger that requires the activation of anxiety? This surely makes little sense that nature would put itself into conflict with itself? Alas, this unique feature of the mental apparatus of humans suggests that in both the complexity and the freedom such complexity enables in choice and transcendence, humans come into conflict with themselves and their own intra-psychic worlds constantly. Needs, desires, and wishes are always in contention with reality and the constraints of the external world. Humans are also blessed (and cursed) with the capacity for ambivalence, love and hate for the same object, and longings and desires for objects that are also taboo makes for a conflictual mix of needs. The desire to both destroy the object when frustrated bumps up against the need to preserve the object upon whom the infant depends. Later, the desire for the object that emerges oedipally, bumps up against the reality of competition with a larger and more powerful (parental) rival but also the powerful prohibition that is hardwired into the human psyche making sexual incest a greater taboo than matricide or patricide.

Civilisation is built on group cohesion, and group cohesion upon the regulation of boundaries and restrictions on incestuous enactments. Conflict is thus inherent to the human psyche from the outset of life, seeding the proliferation of mental tensions as needs, feelings, and impulses prompt against the reality-principle and the restrictions of both social, familial, and internal dynamics. Anxiety signals to the organism that these conflicts and compromises are not being well managed. Dangers lurk in the external environment but so too when promptings in the internal environment require satiation *through* these needs being met in the external environment, as needs usually do require, then the distinction between the internal and external becomes thinned and auxiliary mechanisms of projection must define the emotional valence and significance of the promptings. The threat becomes indistinguishable, as real from the inner as if they were from the outer. Freud noted this point as key to the genesis of anxiety, writing at the end of his paper on anxiety, that in view of the dangers of external reality, the ego is obliged to guard against certain internal instinctual impulses in the id and to treat them as dangers. But it obviously cannot protect itself from internal instinctual dangers as effectively as it can from some piece of reality that is not part of itself. "Intimately bound up with the id as it is", Freud tells us, "it can only fend off an instinctual danger by restricting its own organisation and by acquiescing *in the formation of symptoms* in exchange for having impaired the instinct. If the rejected instinct renews its attack, the ego is overtaken by all those difficulties which are known to us as neurotic ailments".[42]

In other words, psychical conflicts underpin the genesis of various forms of anxiety, but can take different pathways and find different compromise solutions to its conundrums, but are a form of 'attack' against the ego, which requires an aggressive activation. Their manifestation can also take different symptom forms.

Panic

Phobias and obsessional neuroses are specific in their presentation and provide a certain predictability to the onset of the anxiety. If certain triggers are created or avoided, the phobic stimulus will not have any real effect. If the hands can get washed or the locks checked, the compulsions satiate the pending anxiety and prevent its emergence. The danger, so to speak, is averted psychically. Panic attacks, however, present a different set of clinical and theoretical challenges. This form of anxiety appears random, intense, incapacitating, and usually entirely unpredictable, and it is with difficulty that obvious triggers are identified in treatment. In fact, to the contrary, in many cases of panic disorder the attack occurs when the patient is quite relaxed, going on holiday, or sitting in a restaurant having a meal. This unpredictability presents a peculiar challenge since identifying the perception of danger that we must assume underlies the attack, means probing only into the unconscious association presenting at the time of the attack.

Since the threat may appear quire diffuse, non-specific, and often entirely symbolic psychically, we can make the speculative link to some state intrapsychic associative process that has been activated, often through benign or symbolic triggers entirely unconscious to the patient. These attacks are also not characterised by a graded input of anxiety as if the perceived threat or danger lurks over time, more typical of the phobias or obsessive-compulsive disorders, but by a sudden, usually unexpected rupture of the repressive layer that normally enables some control over the breakthrough of such feelings, and sends the patient into a profound flight-fight response in which physiological parameters are activated *in-extremis*. Cardio-vascular, pulmonary, neurological, hormonal, and other response cascades are activated, as if the danger is annihilatory and existentially threatening. Often, such cases present to the emergency rooms of local hospitals with suspected cardiac distress, given the degree to which such physical symptoms present as convincing of some physical event. The sudden and dramatic burst of panic symptoms in this acute form represent to the mental apparatus that some imminent threat has presented itself, and threatens to break through the barrier that has been utilised to keep dangerous impulses below the threshold of consciousness.

Other mechanisms that may be used in OCD disorders, such as displacement onto other objects, or reaction-formations, are not in use, often because the rage response derives from earlier developmental phases during which such creative 'partnering' is not yet possible. Repression is relied on heavily to neutralise this intra-psychic threat, but under sufficient pressure of association, this fails. What this means, is that the associative chain of mental links has been triggered by a stimulus that overwhelms the primitive mechanisms of denial and repression, activating affects that were previously *held* in check.

But what are these impulses? Whilst sexual ones may of course be in the mix, they are only disruptive or even dangerous from a psychic point of view because invariably sexual longings are unable to be met and generate frustrations, or bump into taboos that invite the phantasy of retaliation from the environment. Hence, such promptings represent the risk of psychic danger as the conservative drive rumbles into life, as the breakers of the peace disrupt equilibrium, creating an internal danger. Repression in the early stages of life does a wonderful job of containing aggressive impulses in the service of preserving the infant's love-objects and its extreme dependency needs. But in later life, when this primitive mechanism fails under the pressures of reality, associative referencing to old memories occurs and the affects connected with them. The breakthrough, or at least threatened breakthrough, of this unconscious disruption suggests danger to the mental apparatus, a signal of overwhelming threat. The sudden dramatic burst of anxiety and its symptoms represent a response to this dynamic at play. Panic disorder is therefore triggered by internal threat that prompts the aggressive drive into action against such internal associations but against which no flight can avail. The libidinal impulse may underly the psychic conundrum, but it is the aggressive drive immobile, paralysed, that breaks through repression and triggers the danger.

Post Traumatic Stress Disorder

The syndrome we have come to associate with trauma was originally observed in the First World War when troops exhibited severe symptoms of what was termed "shell-shock",[43] whereby, as Freud wrote, "the condition of the tr. N. (traumatic neurosis) seems to be that the soul had no time to recur to this protection and is [overrun] taken by the trauma unprepared".[44] This syndrome, initially thought to be associated with acute brain injury, was later understood as a psychological reaction to severe trauma, which Freud noted, suggesting that "(a)part from this, the war neuroses are only traumatic neuroses, which, as we know, occur in peace-time too after frightening experiences or severe accidents, without any reference to a conflict in the ego".[45] Freud later conceded: "But the traumatic neuroses of peace-time have always been regarded as the most refractory material of all in this respect; so that the emergence of the war neuroses could not introduce any new factor into the situation that already existed".[46] Added to this concession, he remarked: "The traumatic neuroses of peace will also fit into the scheme as soon as a successful outcome has been reached of our investigations into the relations which undoubtedly exist between fright, anxiety and narcissistic libido".[47]

In this form of anxiety, the threat is not of a purely internal nature and the triggers are never benign, as is usually the case with phobias, or other neurotic anxiety states. With PTSD, overwhelming impingements across all the senses, representative of an existential and annihilatory threat-potential, triggers a massive immune response in the mental realm. Freud had suggested, "In traumatic and war neuroses the human ego is defending itself from a danger which threatens it from without or which is embodied in a shape assumed by the ego itself. In the transference neuroses of peace, the enemy from which the ego is defending itself is actually the libido, whose demands seem to it to be menacing. In both cases the ego is afraid of being damaged—in the latter case by the libido and in the former by external violence".[48]

When such an external and overwhelming threat prevails, a "realgefahr",[49] there *must* be a massive upsurge in the conservative drive to meet this threat, such a threat being by any *objective* measure a threat to the integrity and continued drive-to-life of the individual. This objective challenge to homeostasis is not only in one or two dimensions of shifts to equilibrium, but a global and total challenge to the stasis of life itself – an acceleration of entropy rather than the natural genetically encoded path "of returning to inorganic existence other than those which are immanent in the organism itself".[50] Trauma, writes Kinet, represents a "sudden stimulus increase that overwhelms the mental apparatus, which cannot comprehend or 'contain it'",[51] or in different terms, cannot be mentalised and digested, given the overflow of emotional stimuli, because in "the absence of a representation, the mental device cannot bind or channel it" – leaving free energy engulfing the *subject* and threatening disintegration and entropy.[52] I italicise 'subject' to highlight the interpretative element in trauma, and that trauma is only trauma as perceived and experienced through the individual's own lens. A toy gun must be differentiated from a real gun to create a real threat, and this relies on interpretation through previous experience encoded in both implicit (non-declarative) and explicit (declarative) memory.

It may be true that in some instances the threat may not be to take life itself (such as in rape), but this reality is often only known after the fact. Moreover, rape represents a degree of violation that impairs self-hood and the Markov blanket that preserves a sense of self and self-cohesion. The loss of control through degradation, violation, and debasement is so severe and disempowering, as to represent a loss of psychological agency and life, a psychical death, as it were. Not surprising that PTSD is commonly associated with this form of violence too. In essence, when the mental apparatus cannot shield itself from impingement or reduce the scale of dysregulation, we arrive at a point of trauma. Freud described this process as occurring when any excitations from outside which are powerful enough to break through the protective shield. He characterised the concept of trauma as necessarily implying a connection of this kind, with a breach in an otherwise efficacious barrier against stimuli. "Such an event as an external trauma is bound to provoke a disturbance on a large scale in the functioning of the organism's energy and to set in motion every possible defensive measure."[53]

In such cases of severe and overwhelming threat to homeostasis, both somatic and psychological, the massive immune response that would follow its natural course of fighting back remains immobilised. Put in more neuroscientific terms, Kinet notes that "...entropy increases with the increased randomness of the possible outcomes",[54] and when faced with existentially threatening outcomes over which no control is exerted, the perceptions of entropic demise loom large, against which a restorative response is required, since "(a)ll self-organising systems (ourselves included) have one all-important task in common: to persist".[55] Kinet adds that as living agents required to adapt, we "must have limited states and limit the long-term average of surprises to counteract the tendency for disorder/ dissolution/ entropy to increase. Surprise relies on predictions of sensations and these predictions rely on an internally generated worldview... For self-organising systems (living ones included) to exist, they must resist entropy by minimising free energy",[56] which is a striving of all systems to be economical in energy expenditure. Prediction error through surprise must be minimised to lead to the most "error-free prediction machine possible" (that's us), since the free-energy principle states "that survival is striving to avoid being too surprised by the future", since "knowing what might happen is a good survival strategy".[57]

This minimising surprise in the real world, avoiding unsafety, devolves essentially to the function of the aggressive drive when free energy is increasing through danger – tasked to minimise free-energy, strive for homeostasis through binding excess arousal, and through reliance on memory encoded subjectively, create control over outcomes – which as Kinet points out that, "(o)ur perceptions of the here and now are guided by predictions derived mainly from long-term memory".[58] Traumatic situations challenge this intrinsic requirement to minimise error through prediction based on the past but feeding-forward. Traumatic situations *maximise* possibilities, *remove* prediction and increase prediction error, *increase* dramatically energy expenditure rather than reduce it (violating the economics of the mental system), and increase the possibility of system failure and survival error – that is, in our case, organic entropy.

These are significant points regarding trauma, since the inbuilt mechanism designed to provide all the intrinsic 'solutions' to nasty surprises, the aggressive drive, becomes either overwhelmed or immobilised, the former in natural disasters and the latter when faced with the threat of violence. In the presence of a "sudden stimulus increase" that overwhelms the mental apparatus, which cannot comprehend or 'contain' it", then free energy "engulfs the subject"[59] and threatens entropy. This is the heart of trauma – the stimulus shield is breached "because the excitations are too great to be captured and psychically bound..."[60] – and so "severe trauma unleashes the death-drive..."[61] whose function is to attempt to restore homeostasis and psychic-organismic continuation. I want to remind the reader that the term "subject", as in 'engulfs the subject' is apt, since between the internal and external psychic reality lies the subjective encoding and of memory, and although trauma is usually categorised as an experience outside the normal range for anyone, we do recognise the elements that mediate subjective experience in both reactivity and managing post-trauma. Not everyone suffers the same effects in the same ways or at the same levels. Different perceptions of control over outcomes – that is, different perceptions of how surprisal can be minimised through control of outcomes – can mitigate or accentuate trauma.

This simultaneous upsurge in the aggressive drive in response to threat, meeting up against a simultaneous immobilisation of the same response, triggers a dissociation, emotional paralysis, and other symptoms. The surge of the aggressive drive rendered ineffectual does not mean the rapid escalation of energy is eradicated through immobilisation. The emotional energy must find a pathway to manifest itself and this generates the cascade of symptoms and their often-paradoxical presentation in PTSD. High-arousal states require discharge and mobilisation but in cases of extreme threat, the high arousal is met with paralysis whereby the choice to immobilise (that is, compliance or submission) presents a better route to survival than does fighting back. The heightened 'nervous' posture of the central nervous system (CNS), representing a mobilisation against threat, remains held in memory since discharge is impossible at the source of the threat, even after the threat has passed in actuality. The irritability and often aggressive leakage in PTSD speak to this heightened state of constant disequilibrium that has not become normalised. Associative elements also appear to imbed themselves with PTSD, but these associative elements seem less about intrapsychic associations 'of old' and more associated with the source of the trauma, the sight, smell, or sound of the 'perpetrating' stimulus.

Once again, we become aware of the representations that a traumatic source has on the psyche, in re-triggering the cascade of stress and mobilisation when an apparently neutral trigger presents itself but which to the patient is associated with the original impingement or attack. The trigger in PTSD is usually significantly less symbolic than in neurotic anxieties, and will usually have a real and direct connection to the original trauma as it presents in the outer world. A real external trigger, rather than a symbolic one, will often serve to activate the trauma response, or at least some parts of it, through symptoms like the dissociative elements or startle response. Dissociation is a common characteristic of trauma, since the simultaneous mobilisation and immobilisation of the aggressive response leads to the only feasible compromise-formation in this internal stalemate, which is to 'step out' of the irresolvable conflict and psychically distantiate. In the aftermath, however, irritability and leaking aggression is a common complaint of PTSD sufferers, leading often to social isolation as a precaution against feared enactments that could hurt loved ones. The use of substances to ease this unresolved aggressive response is also common, an attempt at palliation of an illness that can feel subjectively unresolvable.

Do these points that the aggressive drive underpins anxiety states concur equally across the different manifest anxiety syndromes and states we witness clinically? In essence, the answer seems to be yes, that in all cases anxiety is generated by the signalling to the ego of a pending danger or threat to homeostasis, that at some stage of infantile development has required the conservative drive to rear itself up and flex its muscle against the prompting which threatens it. These breakers of the peace usually emerge from internal sources because of their relation to external sources, since needs and threats from the inside are met in the outside world and the objects therein comply or threaten against their expression or satiation. But with some anxiety states, like PTSD, the objective threat may have no direct associations to internal conflicts, or at least, renders them secondary, rather than the primary source of danger. Of course, subjectivity may mediate these elements, and perceptions of control, even over events that some may regard as helpless, can mitigate the threat and its effects. If a person feels enabled to take action against the pending tsunami, for instance, and by so doing survives through their agency, it is quite possible that this perception of empowerment and agency can mitigate the effects of real dangers and objective threats.

Notes

1 Solms, M. (2021) *The Hidden Spring: A Journey to the Source of Consciousness.* London: Profile Books, p. 141.
2 Inducing is, of course, a forceful process, and hence can be understood as a derivative of the aggressive drive whose aim is the restoration of homeostasis through mobilising the adult care-giver to read and respond, something the infant is helpless to do for itself.
3 See, for example, Solms, M. (2021) *The Hidden Spring: A Journey to the Source of Consciousness.* London: Profile Books, p. 32, 112–113, etc for a fuller exposition of this aspect of implicit memory and how it differs from explicit or declarative memory.
4 Kinet, M. (2024) *The Spirit of the Drive in Psychoanalysis.* Routledge: London/ New York.
5 See Freud, S. (1926) Inhibitions, Symptoms and Anxiety. *The Standard Edition of the Complete Psychological Works of Sigmund Freud* 20:75–176, p.138.
6 See my book *Unlocking the Nature of Human Aggression: A Psychoanalytic and Neuroscientific Approach.* Routledge: New York/ London, p.28.
7 See Eric Kandel, *In Search of Memory*: The Emergence of a New Science of Mind. New York: WW Norton & Co.
8 Freud, S. (1926) Inhibitions, Symptoms and Anxiety. *The Standard Edition of the Complete Psychological Works of Sigmund Freud* 20:75–176, p.79.
9 Freud, S. (1926) Inhibitions, Symptoms and Anxiety. *The Standard Edition of the Complete Psychological Works of Sigmund Freud* 20:75–176, pp.79–80.
10 Freud, S. (1926) Inhibitions, Symptoms and Anxiety. *The Standard Edition of the Complete Psychological Works of Sigmund Freud* 20:75–176, pp.79–80.
11 Freud, S. (1917) The Paths to the Formation of Symptoms. In Freud, S. (1917) Introductory Lectures on Psycho-Analysis. *The Standard Edition of the Complete Psychological Works of Sigmund Freud* 16:241–463, p.366.
12 Freud, S. (1917) The Paths to the Formation of Symptoms. In Freud, S. (1917) Introductory Lectures on Psycho-Analysis. *The Standard Edition of the Complete Psychological Works of Sigmund Freud* 16:241–463, p.367.
13 Freud, S. (1930) Civilisation and its Discontents. *The Standard Edition of the Complete Psychological Works of Sigmund Freud* 21:57–146, p.105.

14 Freud, S. (1917) Introductory Lectures on Psycho-Analysis. *The Standard Edition of the Complete Psychological Works of Sigmund Freud* 16:241–463, p. 365.
15 Freud, S. (1926) Inhibitions, Symptoms and Anxiety. *The Standard Edition of the Complete Psychological Works of Sigmund Freud* 20:75–176, p.162.
16 Freud, S. (1926) Inhibitions, Symptoms and Anxiety. *The Standard Edition of the Complete Psychological Works of Sigmund Freud* 20:75–176, p.115–116.
17 Solms, M. (2021) *The Hidden Spring: A Journey to the Source of Consciousness*. London: Profile Books, p. 176.
18 Freud, S. (1926) Inhibitions, Symptoms and Anxiety. *The Standard Edition of the Complete Psychological Works of Sigmund Freud* 20:75–176, p.109.
19 Freud, S. (1915) Instincts and their Vicissitudes. *The Standard Edition of the Complete Psychological Works of Sigmund Freud* 14:109–140, p.118.
20 Freud, S. (1915) Instincts and their Vicissitudes. *The Standard Edition of the Complete Psychological Works of Sigmund Freud* 14:109–140, p.118.
21 Freud, S. (1917) Introductory Lectures on Psycho-Analysis. *The Standard Edition of the Complete Psychological Works of Sigmund Freud* 16:241–463, p.358.
22 Freud, S. (1926) Inhibitions, Symptoms and Anxiety. *The Standard Edition of the Complete Psychological Works of Sigmund Freud* 20:75–176, p.167.
23 Freud, S. (1926) Inhibitions, Symptoms and Anxiety. *The Standard Edition of the Complete Psychological Works of Sigmund Freud* 20:75–176, p.109.
24 Freud, S. (1926) Inhibitions, Symptoms and Anxiety. *The Standard Edition of the Complete Psychological Works of Sigmund Freud* 20:75–176, p.108.
25 Freud, S. (1917) The Paths to the Formation of Symptoms. In Freud, S. (1917) Introductory Lectures on Psycho-Analysis. *The Standard Edition of the Complete Psychological Works of Sigmund Freud* 16:241–463, p.366.
26 See, for example, Danielle Knafo, PhD (2002). Revisiting Ernst Kris's Concept of Regression in the Service of the Ego in Art. *Psychoanalytic Psychology* 19 (1), pp.24–49.
27 Freud, S. (1917) Introductory Lectures on Psycho-Analysis. *The Standard Edition of the Complete Psychological Works of Sigmund Freud* 16:241–463, p.359.
28 "You see, then, that the libido's escape under conditions of conflict is made possible by the presence of fixations. The regressive cathexis of these fixations leads to the circumvention of the repression and to a discharge (or satisfaction) of the libido, subject to the conditions of a compromise being observed. By the roundabout path viá the unconscious and the old fixations, the libido finally succeeds in forcing its way through to real satisfaction—though to one which is extremely restricted and scarcely recognisable as such." In Freud, S. The Paths to the Formation of Symptoms. In Freud, S. (1917) Introductory Lectures on Psycho-Analysis. *The Standard Edition of the Complete Psychological Works of Sigmund Freud* 16:241–463, p.360.
29 Freud, S. (1926) Inhibitions, Symptoms and Anxiety. *The Standard Edition of the Complete Psychological Works of Sigmund Freud* 20:75–176, p.108.
30 Freud, S. (1926) Inhibitions, Symptoms and Anxiety. *The Standard Edition of the Complete Psychological Works of Sigmund Freud* 20:75–176, p.109.
31 Freud, S. (1926) Inhibitions, Symptoms and Anxiety. *The Standard Edition of the Complete Psychological Works of Sigmund Freud* 20:75–176, p.109.
32 Freud, S. (1926) Inhibitions, Symptoms and Anxiety. *The Standard Edition of the Complete Psychological Works of Sigmund Freud* 20:75–176, p.126.
33 Freud, S. (1926) Inhibitions, Symptoms and Anxiety. *The Standard Edition of the Complete Psychological Works of Sigmund Freud* 20:75–176, p.126.
34 Solms, M. (2021) *The Hidden Spring: A Journey to the Source of Consciousness*. London: Profile Books, p. 176.

35 Freud, S. (1926) Inhibitions, Symptoms and Anxiety. *The Standard Edition of the Complete Psychological Works of Sigmund Freud* 20:75–176, p.128.
36 Freud, S. (1926) Inhibitions, Symptoms and Anxiety. *The Standard Edition of the Complete Psychological Works of Sigmund Freud* 20:75–176, p.138.
37 Freud, S. (1926) Inhibitions, Symptoms and Anxiety. *The Standard Edition of the Complete Psychological Works of Sigmund Freud* 20:75–176, p.170.
38 Freud, S. (1926) Inhibitions, Symptoms and Anxiety. *The Standard Edition of the Complete Psychological Works of Sigmund Freud* 20:75–176, p.140.
39 Solms argues that Emotional or affective representations of experience may be represented to consciousness through higher level cortical structures in the brain, but ultimately, consciousness emerges from internal brain structures that generate sensory experiences of dysregulation. "The classical conception is turned on its head. Consciousness is not generated in the cortex; it is generated in the brainstem. Moreover, consciousness is not inherently perceptual; it is inherently affective. And in its primary manifestations, it has less to do with cognition than with instinct. In terms of the parallels drawn in Section 2, the conclusion is inescapable: *consciousness is generated in the id*, and the ego is fundamentally unconscious. This has massive implications for our conceptualisation of the ego and all that flows from it, such as our theories of psychopathology and clinical technique. It was, after all, the essence of the "talking cure" that words, being ego memory-traces derived from external perception and therefore capable of consciousness, must be attached to the deeper processes of the mind (which are unconscious in themselves) before they can be known by the subject".
40 Freud, S. (1920) Beyond the Pleasure Principle. *The Standard Edition of the Complete Psychological Works of Sigmund Freud* 18:1–64, p.25.
41 Solms, M. (2017) What is "the Unconscious", and Where is it Located in the Brain? A Neuropsychoanalytic Perspective. *Annals of the New York Academy of Sciences*, 90–97, p.92.
42 Freud, S. (1926) Inhibitions, Symptoms and Anxiety. *The Standard Edition of the Complete Psychological Works of Sigmund Freud* 20:75–176, p.156 (italics mine).
43 Freud, S. (1956) Memorandum on the Electrical Treatment of War Neurotics (1920). *International Journal of Psychoanalysis* 37:16–18.
44 Freud, S. (1919) Letter from Sigmund Freud to Ernest Jones, February 18, 1919. *The Complete Correspondence of Sigmund Freud and Ernest Jones 1908–1939* 28:333–335, p.334.
45 Freud, S. (1919) Introduction to Psycho-Analysis and the War Neuroses. *The Standard Edition of the Complete Psychological Works of Sigmund Freud* 17:205–216, p.209.
46 Freud, S. (1919) Introduction to Psycho-Analysis and the War Neuroses. *The Standard Edition of the Complete Psychological Works of Sigmund Freud* 17:205–216, p.209.
47 Freud, S. (1919) Introduction to Psycho-Analysis and the War Neuroses. *The Standard Edition of the Complete Psychological Works of Sigmund Freud* 17:205–216, p.210.
48 Freud, S. (1919) Introduction to Psycho-Analysis and the War Neuroses. *The Standard Edition of the Complete Psychological Works of Sigmund Freud* 17:205–216, p.210.
49 Freud, S. (1926) Inhibitions, Symptoms and Anxiety. *The Standard Edition of the Complete Psychological Works of Sigmund Freud* 20:75–176, p.108.
50 Freud, S. (1920) Beyond the Pleasure Principle. On Metapsychology: The Theory of Psychoanalysis. London: Penguin, p. 311.

51 Kinet, M. (2024) *The Spirit of the Drive in Psychoanalysis.* London/ New York: Routledge, p.137.
52 Kinet, M. (2024) *The Spirit of the Drive in Psychoanalysis.* London/ New York: Routledge, pp.136–137.
53 Freud, S. (1920) Beyond the Pleasure Principle. *The Standard Edition of the Complete Psychological Works of Sigmund Freud* 18:1–64, p.29.
54 Kinet, M. (2024) *The Spirit of the Drive in Psychoanalysis.* London/ New York: Routledge, p.77.
55 Kinet, M. (2024) *The Spirit of the Drive in Psychoanalysis.* London/ New York: Routledge, p.77.
56 Kinet, M. (2024) *The Spirit of the Drive in Psychoanalysis.* London/ New York: Routledge, p.78.
57 Kinet, M. (2024) *The Spirit of the Drive in Psychoanalysis.* London/ New York: Routledge, p.78.
58 Kinet, M. (2024) *The Spirit of the Drive in Psychoanalysis.* London/ New York: Routledge, p.75.
59 Kinet, M. (2024) *The Spirit of the Drive in Psychoanalysis.* London/ New York: Routledge, p.136–137.
60 Freud identified these forces in the psychological realm as a "free flowing cathexis that presses on towards discharge and a quiescent cathexis. We may perhaps suspect that the 'binding' of the energy that streams into the mental apparatus consists of a change from a freely flowing into a quiescent state". When the "protective shield against stimuli" that the psyche uses is breached, says Freud, for example in trauma, then the psyche will employ mechanisms to manage these breaches but invariably with some symptoms or consequences. In Freud, S. (1920) Beyond the Pleasure Principle. On Metapsychology: The Theory of Psychoanalysis. London: Penguin, p.303.
61 Kinet, M. (2024) *The Spirit of the Drive in Psychoanalysis.* London/ New York: Routledge, p.126.

Chapter 6

Depression
The Common Cold of Psychopathology

Depression is common, so common that it is sometimes referred to as the 'common cold of psychopathology'.[1] Most people will, at least once in their lifetime, experience some form of moderate to severe depression. Of course, not all depressive episodes are pathological in the true sense or necessarily fulfil all the criteria for a major depressive episode. Freud distinguished between mourning and melancholia to differentiate normal depressive mood from pathological depression. Whether self-remitting or enduring, depression is a painful condition in which loss of pleasure in all things is accompanied by a withdrawal of libidinal investment in both the outer and inner worlds. Energy becomes depleted, cognitive impairment follows suit, with memory and concentration deterioration, and in pathological variants of this state, much normal functioning ceases in the outer world. The somatic complaints that accompany this state include pain, fatigue, and a deep heaviness and weariness, making even small life demands seem heavy and insurmountable, like wading through mental and physical treacle. Guilt and other self-persecutory attacks abound, often to the extent that self-reproach about perceived sins and personal crimes might seem delusional. It is as if there is an "an impoverishment of his ego on a grand scale".[2] Freud's description of this is hard to top:

> The patient represents his ego to us as worthless, incapable of any achievement and morally despicable; he reproaches himself, vilifies himself and expects to be cast out and punished. He abases himself before everyone and commiserates with his own relatives for being connected with anyone so unworthy. He is not of the opinion that a change has taken place in him, but extends his self-criticism back over the past; he declares that he was never any better. This picture of a delusion of (mainly moral) inferiority is completed by sleeplessness and refusal to take nourishment, and—what is psychologically very remarkable—by an overcoming of the instinct which compels every living thing to cling to life.[3]

DOI: 10.4324/9781003628972-7

A feature of depression, albeit a puzzling one, demonstrates repeatedly that those patients for whom the affliction of depression becomes more severe, will attack themselves in every conceivable fashion, feeling worthless and guilty for sins of omission and commission, sometimes impossibly beyond their influence, such as feelings of guilt for starving children on another continent. The marked feature of worthlessness, self-reproach, and impoverishment of the ego from an energetic and vegetative point of view, demonstrates, as I will attempt to posit, an underlying *hostility* to the self, in extreme cases through suicidal ideation, intent, or even action – that is, a grand 'homicidal' attack against their own Self. This extreme form of drive-violence to the self, to the patient's own ego we might say, suggests that a form of intra-punitive attack against the patient's own Self is in process and appears to operate on a hefty scale.

Loss and Longing

It is not overly astute to notice the dogged persistence of a particular theme in mood disorders related to loss. So often, the precipitant for periods of depression appear to derive from some form of experienced loss. Loss of a job, relationship, attachment, actual loss of a love-object, loss of love itself, loss through physical death, or emotional death, like when a love-attachment ends. Actual or symbolic loss is equally real to the subjectivity of the patient, who may suffer the haemorrhage of esteem, trust, dignity, or self – all intangible losses that may exist independently of actual loss or related to it. In fact, so ubiquitous is loss to depression, that one might suggest the two are never un-linked. Underlying all depressive episodes, we notice when we look for it, are *perceptions* or experiences of loss. I suggest perceptions of loss, since at times the outer quality of the person's life might suggest abundance and success with no apparent loss at all. And yet beneath this exterior can lie a world of torment and darkness, in which all the colour of the world has leeched out and, in its wake, left a monochromatic experience dominating the landscape of the patient's life. These perceptions of loss may reside unconsciously, and even where loss has been a more immediate precipitant, melancholic depression invariably reflects a regression to a much earlier and unconscious variant of such loss, as Freud puts it, "regression from object-cathexis to the still narcissistic oral phase of the libido in our characterisation of melancholia".[4]

This point that more severe variants of depression or melancholia must involve regression to an earlier phase of development, to a fixation at this level, begs the question at which level depression seems rooted. One of the key features, or defences we observe in depression falls under the banner of self-attack. Almost all the symptoms we see, impoverishment of the ego, self-reproach, guilt, suicidality, and so on, all suggest that self-attack is a prominent feature of the condition. Self-attack also supposes that there is aggression, that is, the aggressive drive is turned mercilessly against the person's own ego, introjected against the self. This reflects a form of oral incorporation in which the bad is turned into and against the self, as, we often observe, protection of the love-object upon whom the infant depends. If the bad (feelings) are turned inward, the love-object upon whom survival depends, can be protected from these emotional attacks and hence preserved.

This ambivalent mix of love and hate against the same object creates a conundrum for the frustrated infant who must *attack* the source of frustration whilst simultaneously *preserving* its sole source of nourishment and survival. This conundrum of ambivalence can benefit from a compromise-formation in which the hostility and rage is not directed against the love-object but turned back against the infant's own ego, preserving the maternal object in the process. But such an introjected aggression, when revisited later in life, creates a set of problems that can lead to a melancholic problem – a disproportionate intensity of infantile rage turned back against the patient's own ego, enabling us to find, as Freud noted, an insight into the clinical picture: "So we find the key to the clinical picture", he observed, "we perceive that the self-reproaches are reproaches against a loved object which have been shifted away from it on to the patient's own ego".[5]

Early infancy is plagued by the requirement to manage ambivalence, since satiation and frustration are never far apart and when frustration precipitates a state of disequilibrium, so too must manifest a raging at the object perceived to be the source of the 'persecution', of the 'poison', at least when frustration of needs becomes prolonged or the infant's own body is 'attacking' it due to health issues or gastric disturbances. Unfortunately for the infant, the source of poison is invariably also the source of nourishment, which generates a universal and endemic conundrum during this early oral phase of development. The infant is also 'handicapped', as it were, by a limited number of defensive options. Since the oral phase only enables introjection, ejection (projection), or denial as prototypes of somatic foci, the infant must rely on these to manage the ambivalence and its conundrum of increasing arousal (and hence, free energy in the direction of perceived entropy). Attacking the mother or the bad breast that persecutes leaves the infant exposed to annihilation and abandonment without its love-object. So, one compromise to the dilemma is to introject the hate, to turn the aggression inwards through an incorporative manoeuvre. This links to identification which is a preliminary stage of object-choice, "that it is the first way— and one that is expressed in an ambivalent fashion—in which the ego picks out an object. The ego wants to incorporate this object into itself, and, in accordance with the oral or cannibalistic phase of libidinal development in which it is it wants to do so by devouring it".[6]

Incorporation of the object as a means of control, is also accompanied by raw aggression turned in, since this drive must be activated in response to failures and frustration. Deviation from homeostasis must trigger an immune response, leading to frustrations activating the aggressive drive, a portion of which in the infant is introjected into the self, forming the foundation for later melancholic cascades when loss is reactivated in later life.

Hate Against the Ego

We cannot avoid the notice that underlying the conundrums of infancy lie buried deep within development are the dual drives tensioning against each other from the outset. Whilst the life drive presses forward for attachment and bonding in the service of sustaining life, the conservative drive is activating aggression to remediate challenges to stasis. Hate, it might be said, precedes love: "It should be emphasised", writes Valdrè, "that hate is primary and so it appears before love".[7] Although it appears as a logical contradiction, quiescence precedes the advent of life – not only in a philosophical sense but in the cold reality that an infant in-utero experiences a form of 'Nirvana', homeostasis without any requirement to perform any mental work. It is done *for* the infant through biology. But the moment birthing occurs, homeostasis is ruptured and the infant suddenly has to begin the mental task of performing work itself to restore homeostasis. It cannot, of course, do so on its own – but its first cry signals an inducement into the environment, a forceful and aggression-driven mechanism, to 'poke and prod' the environment to do whatever it takes to return the infant to a homeostatic state. This rupture to its perfect state through being born, evokes first and foremost a cry aimed at restoration, but it is driven by the aggressive drive whose aim is restoration. We can therefore say that the first act of the human infant in post-uterine life is one not driven by love and attachment but by the restorative death drive pulling back to a quiescent state. Tensioned against this are the pressures of the life drive springing into activity to meet needs, which are usually not instantly and easily met. What then does the infant have at its disposal to remedy this condition of a new and ongoing stream of impingements and disequilibrium?

Young age goes with primitive mechanisms of defence, and in particular when frustration presents. Winnicott made the point that, "Frustration acts as a seduction away from guilt and fosters a defence mechanism, namely, the direction of love and hate along separate lines".[8] To put this differently, guilt is intra-punitive, a branch of the aggressive drive turned in against the self to protect the love-object. The 'separate lines' speak to the tensioning of the life and death drives in the face of frustration, the *push* factor of life-drive needs and the pull factor of binding free energy by the death drive. Freud addressed this in a different way, suggesting that, "a particular way is adopted of dealing with any internal excitations which produce too great an increase of unpleasure (and lead to *frustration*): there is a tendency to treat them as though they were acting, not from the inside, but from the outside, so that it may be possible to bring the shield against stimuli into operation as a means of defence against them. This is the origin of projection, which is destined to play such a large part in the causation of pathological processes".[9]

The experience of 'unpleasure', that is, a trend away from homeostatic settling points, creates in the infant a pressure to mentally manage the feelings of unpleasure, which in the mental realm give rise to the experience of an undifferentiated 'badness', leading to a primitive feeling of unbridled hate, which must be expelled into the external environment in order to strive for a reduction of internal unpleasure. But what can an infant do to remediate frustration? Precious little – except cry and induce a response from the mother. And this 'precious little' is the nub of an important matter, addressing Solms' revision of drive theory, which suggests there is no need for a death drive (as we dealt with in more detail in Chapter 2). Feelings are homeostatic – they drive work to meet needs to mediate homeostasis – but are not always successful, especially in infancy and early childhood. Primitive hate, although originally directed at internal states of unpleasure from the outset, become encapsulated and expelled as a form of restoration, placing the bad/ unpleasure on the outside against which a shield can be brought. Such projection of the bad, must surely first be fleetingly directed at the infant's own primitive and rudimentary ego for it to be recognised as a disruptor, against which a shield must be brought.

It is thus strange to consider that hate precedes love, aggression and disengagement-undoing precedes the creativity of bonding, unpleasure precedes restoration. Of course, love and attachment are powerful drivers too, but they activate initially as 'remedial' mechanisms to achieve need-requirements in the service of homeostatic restoration, which surely becomes the favoured way to operate in life. But technically, it can be suggested that love and attachment are remedies in the service of meeting infantile needs, neurologically in-built, and that from the outset, hate is first directed momentarily at the self from where the bad-unpleasure seems to arise. From here on, it must find an inner-binding of excess dysregulation and the sensation of an increasing trend of free energy, through projecting outward the bad, and hence hating the maternal object and attacking it through crying, before finding restoration again through her efforts to soothe the baby.

These oscillations of the turning in and the projecting out of the unpleasure, must interface with the need for, and the hate of, the maternal object. The projection of the bad onto and into the maternal, and attacking of her, simultaneously threatens the source of remedy for *frustration*, creating a vacillation of projection and introjection in the service of self-protection and (m)other-protection. Developing the ambivalence of integration of the love and hate, the pleasure and unpleasure, is a developmental achievement, usually, says Klein, at around four months of age.

Klein describes this: "The breast, on which the life and death instincts are projected, is the first object which by introjection is internalised. In this way both instincts find an object to which they attach themselves and thereby by projection and re-introjection the ego is enriched as well as strengthened".[10] Klein further notes, that "the relation to the first object implies its introjection and projection, and thus from the beginning object relations are moulded by an interaction between introjection and projection, between internal and external objects and situations".[11]

One could understand this process as one of the infant's attacks on perceived sources of unpleasure (frustration) and reparation to re-engage care and bonding in the service of life-drive needs and pressures, a cycle of destroy and reconstruct in its relation to the maternal breast. In Panksepp's neuroscientific terms, one could recognise that there is an oscillation between a primitive aggressive response in relation to post-uterine unpleasure, then frustrations not having needs instantly and fully met, triggering the mechanisms of a PANIC-GRIEF response driving attachment, and the requirement to solicit CARE in the service of meeting fundamental needs. The transition from the intra-uterine state of perfect Nirvana to the real world of meeting needs, is a journey through the 'eye of the needle', a quantum leap from one significant state of mental non-work to another in which all the complexities of mental work is suddenly and dramatically thrust to the fore, and from which, from then on, no escape is possible through the life span.

Although initially somatically driven, over time these bodily experiences enable a mental apparatus to form, with representatives in the psychic realm developing to facilitate complex representations and ideation of the somatic world, in its relation to the external world. Whilst the life drive pushes forward, the death drive 'pulls back' to sustain familiarity and conservation. Linking these mechanisms to depression, the topic of this chapter, we note these mechanisms of projection and introjection dominating the mental landscape. I am reminded of Freud noting:

> In melancholia, the occasions which give rise to the illness extend for the most part beyond the clear case of a loss by death, and include all those situations of being slighted, neglected or disappointed, which can import opposed feelings of love and hate into the relationship or reinforce an already existing ambivalence. This conflict due to ambivalence, which sometimes arises more from real experiences, sometimes more from constitutional factors, must not be overlooked among the preconditions of melancholia. If the love for the object—a love which cannot be given up though the object itself is given up—takes refuge in narcissistic identification, then the hate comes into operation on this substitutive object, abusing it, debasing it, making it suffer and deriving sadistic satisfaction from its suffering.[12]

What Freud identifies, and which has become well understood since, is that destructive energies and feelings of hate can be turned upon the patient's own ego as a mechanism to preserve the maternal object upon whom dependency is critical. This is a form of weighing the best options to reduce the arrow of increasing free energy and potential entropy, making the best of a bad lot. "The analysis of melancholia now shows that the ego can kill itself only if, owing to the return of the object-cathexis, it can treat itself as an object—if it is able to direct against itself the hostility which relates to an object and which represents the ego's original reaction to objects in the external world".[13]

Loss has a precipitating power to trigger regression to earlier oral phases of development in which the prominence of introjective mechanisms turns the aggressive drive against the patient's own ego. These aggressive attacks lead to impoverishment of the ego and all the self-denigrating elements that characterise severe depressive states. Suicidality, on the opposite end of the spectrum of homicidality – that is, aggression against the other is turned against the self in the form of aggression against the ego, and homicidal impulses give way to suicidal ones, a by-product of ambivalence that remains unresolved in the unconscious of melancholic patients.

Lubbe's work on depression distils these concepts into the notions that rage against loss and object-love gets introjected, turned in against the patient's own self with the purpose of, amongst other things, disavowing guilt – "guilt in relation to the feared loss of love of the object; guilt relating to ongoing ambivalence; and the specific defence against guilt of turning aggression upon the self".[14] The three key elements of depression, namely loss, ambivalence (towards the object), and the internalisation of the aggressive drive in its attempts at maintaining stasis through preservation of the love object and the infant's dependency upon it, distils essentially into a singular key component of depression, which is the turning of the aggressive drive against the self. Such a defensive manoeuvre leads to all the characteristic symptoms of depression: impoverishment of the ego, anhedonia, loss of libido in both a sexual and life force sense, self-reproach and guilt, fatigue, and so on, all reflections of the immune system of the mental apparatus going into an overdrive state, in which it is now perpetually attacking the self, making depression a form of psychically auto-immune illness in which the preservatory mechanism turns against the self and proceeds to annihilate rather than protect it.

This, psychically speaking, auto-immune element to depression is key to noting the role the aggressive drive plays in the genesis of this condition. Themes of loss, rage at this *experience*, and preservation of the love-object upon whom survival is dependent, and upon whom the fulfilment of the libidinal strivings rest, conjures up primitive guilt, not because super-ego function is yet fully developed, but because the intra-punitive component of the rage turns back against the self in its attempts at object-preservation. It is a psychical compromise in the interests of preservation. One agency of mind puts itself at odds and in conflict with another; namely, id impulses rampage through the mental apparatus seeking fulfilment in the service of eros, whilst this powerful driver meets with frustrations against which it *must* rage, since the source of sustenance produces also the frustration of needs. This 'persecutory' element of the love-object induces the challenge and the curse of ambivalence, the plague of intra-psychic conflict so unique, apparently, to human attachments and the human species. As Freud noted, "In melancholia, accordingly, countless separate struggles are carried on over the object, in which hate and love contend with each other; the one seeks to detach the libido from the object, the other to maintain this position of the libido against the assault".[15]

The Conundrum of Ambivalence

It is a quirk of the human condition that the source of pain and frustration lies buried deep in the source of love and survival. From the outset of its life, the infant must wrestle with its foundation of all the milk of goodness, nourishment, and survival is also the source of frustration, poison, and persecution. The good milk is sometimes sour milk; or more accurately, the good milk and the sour milk are forever intermixed. Humans are doomed to suffer the complexities of this unique feature of mental life: ambivalence. It is a process for which the projective-introjective mechanisms mentioned earlier feature so strongly. Love and hate for the same object reflect these primitive needs to repair disruptions to homeostasis from the outset, then meet life-drive needs, both attacking and protecting the object simultaneously, or at least, in rapid-cycling oscillations. Freud put it that this conflict due to ambivalence, which sometimes arises more from real experiences, sometimes more from constitutional factors, must not be overlooked among the preconditions of melancholia. "If the love for the object—a love which cannot be given up though the object itself is given up—takes refuge in narcissistic identification", he writes, "then the hate comes into operation on this substitutive object, abusing it, debasing it, making it suffer and deriving sadistic satisfaction from its suffering". Let us also keep in mind that the self-tormenting in depression, is in a sense also 'enjoyable', and signifies, Freud argues, just like the corresponding phenomenon in obsessional neurosis, "a satisfaction of trends of sadism and hate which relate to an object, and which have been turned round upon the subject's own self...".[16]

In normal mourning of loss, when an attachment imbued with libidinal cathexis and regarded as carrying value for the patient, leads in pathological states of depression to the unleashing of core oral-stage ambivalence, a wrecking-ball of conflicting feelings that find themselves cornered in the patient's psyche, inducing a cascade in which "so does each single struggle of ambivalence loosen the fixation of the libido to the object by disparaging it, denigrating it and even as it were killing it. It is possible for the process in the Ucs. (Unconscious) to come to an end, either after the fury has spent itself or after the object has been abandoned as valueless".[17]

The homicidal impulse against the (abandoning) love-object, co-mingled with guilt as a primitive in-turning of the aggressive impulse to protect the object upon which there is dependency, leads to a regression to an early stage in which the impulse is turned inwards, against the infant's own ego, in the service of object-preservation. This manoeuvre to preserve the needed love-object, creates the conditions for an effective compromise-formation in which both aggression and preservation of the object can exist side-by-side and sustain both the self and the object; increasing arousal through distress and frustration demands a binding, a cathecting of this excess in the best possible mental manner available to relieve the pressures towards perceived entropy. It works effectively during infancy and this early oral phase. But in later life, when loss precipitates regression to this early unconscious part of development, the turning in of the aggressive feelings, the hate introjected, leads to impoverishment of the ego as relentless and inescapable attacks are processed.

Alas, without the function of ambivalence in humans, we may find ourselves in a kinder world both internal and external. But so too, the complexity of human development would give way to simplicity, and a world in which binaries would prevail over the rich textures of human experience. Ambivalence, as a blessing and a curse, underlies the conundrum of both infantile experience in relation to the love-object, and as a prototype of all subsequent attachments in life, since there is never a possibility of escaping the oscillations of mixed feelings. With investment and affectional or sensual valuation (or sometimes over-valuation) of an object, so too emerges the heightened risk of hurt, love-unrequited, or loss that was not there preceding such an investment. Freud reminds us, that of the three preconditions of depression, namely, loss of the object, ambivalence, and regression of libido into the ego. The first two are also found in the obsessional self-reproaches arising after a death has occurred. "In those cases, it is unquestionably the ambivalence which is the motive force of the conflict, and observation shows that after the conflict has come to an end there is nothing left over in the nature of the triumph of a manic state of mind".[18]

It might be said that ambivalence lies at the core of depressive disorders, and in particular when they turn from normal downward mood to more serious forms of the disorder. The longing prompted by the life drive, to *bond into psychic being*, enables the accrual of mental development, both cognitive and affective. Disruption and dysregulation in this process invariably trigger frustration, loss, and the activation of the aggressive drive attempting to induce restoration through binding free energy with available defensive means. Libidinal strivings, and I don't mean erotic ones, represent the life-drive *push* to forge bonds with love-objects, since these bonds facilitate both survival at the most basic of levels but also *optimal* survival, enabling psychological and cognitive development for the infant to better inter-face with its current and future world. This powerful drive also fuels the later sexual elements that facilitate procreative bonding, sexual pairing that enables the survival of the species too. Bonding and optimal development also facilitates better variation in the evolutionary sense, a more fluid capacity to adapt and respond to the impingements of life, reducing morbidity and mortality, enabling better mating options, and the ability to navigate the complexity of coupling and family life in the future.

But these evolutionary thrusts and their advantages come at a price for humans – we suffer feelings and we suffer ambivalences in all attachments, inescapably and inexorably, since with investment comes the risk of loss, and with loss comes dysregulation and threats to ego-integrity. Loss is painful and egregious and must activate the immune system of the mental apparatus in order for the aggressive drive to fulfil its mandate of restoration and con- servation. However, the price to pay for attacking the source of these dis- ruptions to homeostasis, these inevitable failures in and of attachment, suggests that when options are few, such as in infancy, conservation of the object may take precedent over conservation of the self, a compromise-for- mation that privileges survival over thriving. But the cost of this 'choice' is that preservation of the love-object, who is also the source of the pain/ frus- tration/ disequilibrium must lead to a channelling of the conservative drive (that is, the aggressive mobilisation) along another path. Since the lion's share of early development takes place intensely in the first year, when defensive strategies are few, leads to an introjective tendency in which aggression is turned inwards against the self, to preserve the (maternal) object upon whom dependency is utter and without alternative. Such aggression against the self leads to the impoverishment of the ego, and an energetic denuding associated with many of the symptoms we note in the condition. The bloated superego element, that leads to heightened and some- times delusional guilt, is a branch of the aggressive drive that hives off during the oedipal stage to fuel the human conscience, providing an evolutionary advantage that inhibits patricide in developed species (Freud's speculations about the primal horde come to mind).

The Conundrum of Empathy

Depression seems to invite an empathic note, or at least one of sympathy, for the sufferer. The poor soul is tormented and we feel sorry for this state. At least, in the initial stages of the disorder this is true but as time gathers momentum, this sympathy can often turn to frustration, irritation, and even fury. Forceful injunctions to get up, open the curtains, just *do something!* replaces the first turn southwards in mood and functioning. Exasperation replaces sympathy and with enough time, a subtle fury percolates in the undergrowth of those around the depressed patient. The person may have so much to live for and have many blessings to the outsider, yet struggles to nourish themselves off of any of these blessings or opportunities.

This is not surprising however, given the underlying nature of depressive dynamics. The depressive is in a state of perpetual attack not retreat, vengeance not dependency. The aggressive elements are hidden from view and yet dominant, attacking life itself and the life drive that promotes attachment. The attack on the life drive, Eros, in both the external and internal representations of the object, create the conditions for libidinal shutdown that, immobilised as it is, leads to the inertias associated with the condition. The depressive is attacking life itself. Not suffering its slings and arrows of misfortune, not struggling with the victimhood of loss, for these are merely the precursors for a more important problem – but the unleashing of aggressive energies aimed at protecting the patient from their loss and all that loss represents, but leaving the psychic emphasis on the aggressive thrust which, unconscious as it may be, seems far away from either the patient or those around them.

Therapists too, easily collude with the 'victim' within the patient, their deep suffering. But this does not cure depression, since the aetiology of the condition lies buried in the aggressive drive and its 'violent', often sadistic emotional effects. Put differently, immobilised by the remnants of early history, the aggressive drive cannot do its work properly, serve its immune function for the mental apparatus, and so converts instead to the immense buildup of aggressive energy retained in the mental apparatus and unable to perform the work required by feelings to restore homeostasis. Since feelings are essentially homeostatic, mechanisms of maintaining organismic balance, their mobility is essential for healthy homeostasis. Immobilised, a cascade of imbalance is created over time which in this case converts aggression into self-immolation, denuding essential life energies of their free-flow, and ability to then cathect onto both internal and external love-objects.

This is the conundrum of ambivalence, the mixing of love and hate for the same object that renders human attachments full of complexities. These complexities of attachment appear inescapable; in fact, we could suggest that the greater the investment of libidinal energy in a love-object, the greater the potential for feelings of hate and hostility, since only when there is investment is there also the threat of loss. At times, such loss is at the purely emotive level, that subjective activation through the lens of the individual and their micro-histories, the dissolution of esteem through perceived rejection or neglect; at other times the loss is concrete, death, abandonment, illness – all evocative and a threat to equilibrium, leading to an aggressive activation. Depression is a consequence of this process, but in melancholic states, the regression to early oral fixations reactivates previously unresolved ambivalences, and the crises of ambivalence remain stuck for future referencing, and what Solms' refers to as the *feedforward* process of encoded memory, automatising both life drive needs and old fixated defences too. To remind the reader, that when a need propels us into the world, *we do not discover the world afresh with each new cycle.* Rather, "It activates a set of predictions about the likely sensory consequences of our actions, based upon past experience of how to meet the selected need in the prevailing circumstances".[19]

Put differently, the past is never contained in the past, since it exists only through its storage in memory – and memory always resides in the present as a living mechanism to efficiently guide the organism into its next steps, its future. Memory may have been *encoded* in the past but lives only in the present, through subjectivity and its value-add to sustenance, survival, and the efficient navigation of a complex world. What's past is never past, so far as human memory is concerned. I venture to suggest, in fact, that *there is no such thing as the past*. The past only exists as it is contained in genetic, cultural, or personal memory. With no-one or nothing to hold the past in memory, it ceases to exist, and since memory is subjective, even when contained in the species' or individual's genetic code, since epigenetic variations can only exist through subjective organismic experience, it will guide the future through a personal lens. Memory is also then the bridge between the present and the future, a guide to navigation of the complex physical and emotional environment, and this gives form to the notion of regression that Freud identified, a mechanism to reference the past in memory but as a guide to future action and emotional response (to efficiently automatise), or as Solms puts it, "The purpose of learning is not to maintain records but to generate predictions".[20] Such is its adaptive *intent* and its sometimes maladaptive *effects* when referencing old losses, and psychic injuries impact current mental states, so we can suggest that, as Solms does, that "the main task of memory (i.e., of the ego) is not to make a permanent record of everything it experiences. It is not a passive recording device. Rather, the task of the ego is to learn how to satisfy the demands of the id in the outside world, that is, *how to meet its vital and reproductive needs* there".[21]

Aggression in the Service of the Ego

Aggression '*in the service of* the ego' is a critically important point, since it reminds us that subjectivity underpins the encoding of memory – it is never a neutral record of past events but a system of navigation of present and future events. The activation of the aggressive drive under the pressures of early disequilibrium, trigger memories to encode these states, and the feelings and *predictions* they engender – that is, these memories laid down in implicit storage nonetheless acts to guide future action and is hence returned to repeatedly.

Depression, like other psychopathologies, returns to guide the present according to old losses and old reactions to them – infantile rages recur on adult states through regression, a return of the repressed to guide the present, but sometimes in the misguided way that catalyses symptoms. "Indeed", says Kandel, from a neuroscientific point of view, "after a single exposure to a threat, the amygdala can retain the memory of that threat throughout an organism's entire life".[22] This central role of the unconscious, and the memory traces encoded there, is supported by the finding that, as Solms argues, the "unconscious evaluation of a frightening stimulus precedes conscious, cortical evaluation of fear..."[23] and that this source of conscious experience is bridged through the (subjective) experience registered consciously as *feelings*.

Kandel and Solms concur that regression to old reference points in memory is a deeply subjective and individual process: "For all of us explicit memory makes it possible to leap across space and time and conjure up events and emotional states that have vanished into the past yet somehow continue to live on in our minds." There is a caveat, though, suggests Kandel, that "recalling a memory episodically - no matter how important the memory - is not like simply turning to a photograph in an album. Recall of memory is a creative process. What the brain stores is thought to be only a core memory. *Upon recall, this core memory is then elaborated upon and reconstructed with subtractions, additions, elaborations, and distortions*".[24]

In other words, in depression, there is a regression to, a revisitation of, old and developmentally primitive losses when emotional valences were high and undifferentiated, triggering an aggressive response that turned inwards to protect the love-object, repair the imagined damage done to it, and restore the good-breast to its noble and idealised perch, turning in the bad bits, and reigning hostile affects against the infant's own rudimentary ego. Such self-attack, the introjecting of heightened aggression, is like an autoimmune disease of the mental realm – inflicting harm against the ego, denuding it of supplies, and leaving it impoverished and unwell, with the characteristic symptoms we note in depression. As mentioned about guilt earlier, Lubbe makes the point that, the "superego comes into being as part of the depressive process, developmentally speaking, and its initial function is to invert the mourner's repressed rage towards the lost object by turning it on the self for the express purpose of disavowing guilt... guilt in relation to the feared loss of love of the object; guilt relating to ongoing ambivalence; and the specific defence against guilt of turning aggression upon the self".[25] But important to add, is that these intra-punitive superego attacks are already built upon a more primitive foundation – the turning of the raw aggressive drive, whose aim of restoring homeostasis to a dysregulated infant in the early stages of oral development when only these defences of projection, introjection and denial are available for mental use. The function of managing raw affects, and the aggressive mobilisation in the face of disruption and loss (of homeostasis) in the early months, predisposes to depression in later life.

However, the cure does not lie in addressing the hurt – it lies in the hate. It lies not in ideation or cognition, but the mobilisation of affects contained in implicit memory and only accessible through the working-through processes of psychoanalysis or psychotherapy. This is not only about insight, since, as Solms explains it, some early memory cannot be remembered cognitively: "The best-known subcortical memory systems are the 'emotional' and 'procedural' systems. The crucial thing to note about these systems is that they are nonrepresentational, *nonthinkable* associations; they are 'non-declarative'. This means they are *not subject to updating in working memory*".[26] The implication of this point of the neuroscience is that the emotional imprinting of depression (and, of course, other symptoms) occur prior to cognitive development and ideational representation, which can turn affect into ideation, and so these early oral fixations in the first months and year of development will be revisited in an emotional way. With no direct access to pre-cognitive or non-declarative memory of the early psychical insult, the primitive experience of loss and the aggressive (immune) response to it, will recur in adult states too, as direct affect-driven experience, what Freud calls primary process, in which feelings and drives play such a significant part, and the associated memories are, in fact, "indelible",[27] as Solms put it.

The Cure

As a result of the core dynamics of depression, it becomes clear that we do not cure depression with empathy, something I will say more about in Chapter 11 on treatment. At least, through empathic collusion with the injured part of the patient's psyche we risk losing sight of the key driver of the disorder. It is true that depression is subjectively *painful*, almost physical in its manifestation of a heart gripped by weariness, heaviness, and often somatic pain. Depression is so terribly painful. And this is where treatment often gets stuck – it is a draw for empathic attunement. In response to loss, injury to the psyche *must* conjure an immune response to this dysregulation. The depressed patient's regression to earlier states, where this aggressive outpouring threatened to engineer a much greater loss through its expression than through its introjection, meant that instead of being directed at the source of the injury, this drive became turned inward, directed against a safer object of the infant's own ego, protecting the love-object upon whom all dependency needs were met. The revisiting this ancient mental process in some individuals creates an unconscious *attack* against the self, a violence of sort against the patient's own ego, with all its accompanying symptoms.

Broadly, we could suggest that the outward manifestation of the aggressive drive has become immobilised and hence unable to do its work of restoring homeostasis in response to perceived frustration, loss or injury. The cure is in re-mobilising this drive, facilitating its pathway through consciousness into being cathected and abreacted or catharted against those objects that historically and currently have triggered the conservative drive into an action it cannot perform, psychological work it must do, but which it cannot for reasons of this ancient personal history.

Notes

1 DOI:10.15761/ADCN.1000124 - https://www.oatext.com/depression-a-comm on-cold-of-mental-disorders.php#:~:text=Depression- A common cold of mental disorders; Also, Goodwin, G.M. (2008) Major Depression is Sometimes Descri-bed as the Common Cold of Psychiatry. *Journal of Psychopharmacology* Sep; 22(7 Suppl):3. doi: 10.1177/0269881108094716.
2 Freud, S. (1917) Mourning and Melancholia. *The Standard Edition of the Com-plete Psychological Works of Sigmund Freud* 14:237–258, p.246.
3 Freud, S. (1917) Mourning and Melancholia. *The Standard Edition of the Com-plete Psychological Works of Sigmund Freud* 14:237–258, p.246.
4 Freud, S. (1917) Mourning and Melancholia. *The Standard Edition of the Com-plete Psychological Works of Sigmund Freud* 14:237–258, p.250.
5 Freud, S. (1917) Mourning and Melancholia. *The Standard Edition of the Com-plete Psychological Works of Sigmund Freud* 14:237–258, p.248.
6 Freud, S. (1917) Mourning and Melancholia. *The Standard Edition of the Com-plete Psychological Works of Sigmund Freud* 14:237–258, pp.249–250.
7 Valdrè, R. (2025) *The Death Drive: A Contemporary Introduction.* New York/ London: Routledge, p.7.
8 Winnicott, D. W. (1975) Chapter XVI. Aggression in Relation to Emotional Development [1950–5]. *Through Paediatrics to Psycho-Analysis* 100:204–218, p.207.
9 Freud, S. (1920) Beyond the Pleasure Principle. *The Standard Edition of the Complete Psychological Works of Sigmund Freud* 18:1–64, p.29 (brackets mine).
10 Klein, M. (1958) On the Development of Mental Functioning. *International Journal of Psychoanalysis* 39:84–90, p.89.
11 Klein, M. (1946) Notes on Some Schizoid Mechanisms. *International Journal of Psychoanalysis* 27:99–110, p.99.
12 Freud, S. (1917) Mourning and Melancholia. *The Standard Edition of the Com-plete Psychological Works of Sigmund Freud* 14:237–258, pp.249–251.
13 Freud, S. (1917) Mourning and Melancholia. *The Standard Edition of the Com-plete Psychological Works of Sigmund Freud* 14:237–258, pp.249–252.
14 Lubbe, T. (2011) *Object Relations in Depression: A Return to Theory.* London: Routledge, p. 17.
15 Freud, S. (1917) Mourning and Melancholia. *The Standard Edition of the Com-plete Psychological Works of Sigmund Freud* 14:237–258, p.256.
16 Freud, S. (1917) Mourning and Melancholia. *The Standard Edition of the Com-plete Psychological Works of Sigmund Freud* 14:237–258, p.251.
17 Freud, S. (1917) Mourning and Melancholia. *The Standard Edition of the Com-plete Psychological Works of Sigmund Freud* 14:237–258, p.257.
18 Freud, S. (1917) Mourning and Melancholia. *The Standard Edition of the Com-plete Psychological Works of Sigmund Freud* 14:237–258, p.258.
19 Solms, M. (2021) *The Hidden Spring: A Journey to the Source of Consciousness.* London: Profile Books, p. 141.
20 Solms, M. (2015) Reconsolidation: Turning Memory into Consciousness. *Beha-vioural and Brain Sciences* 38:e24. doi: 10.1017/S0140525X14000296.

21 Solms, M. (2017) What is "the Unconscious," and Where is it Located in the Brain? A Neuropsychoanalytic Perspective. *Annals of the New York Academy of Sciences*, 1406, 90–97, doi: 10.1111/nyas.13437, p.93.

22 Kandel, E. (2006) *In Search of Memory: The Emergence of a New Science of Mind*. New York: WW Norton & Co, p.343.

23 Kandel, E. (2006) *In Search of Memory: The Emergence of a New Science of Mind*. New York: WW Norton & Co, p.344.

24 Kandel, E. (2006) *In Search of Memory: The Emergence of a New Science of Mind*. New York: WW Norton & Co, p.281 (italics mine).

25 Lubbe, T. (2011) *Object Relations in Depression: A Return to Theory*. London: Routledge, p. 17.

26 Solms, M. (2017) What is "the Unconscious," and Where is it Located in the Brain? A Neuropsychoanalytic Perspective. *Annals of the New York Academy of Sciences*, 1406, 90–97, doi: 10.1111/nyas.13437, p.94.

27 Solms, M. (2017) What is "the Unconscious," and Where is it Located in the Brain? A Neuropsychoanalytic Perspective. *Annals of the New York Academy of Sciences*, 1406, 90–97, doi: 10.1111/nyas.13437, p.94.

Chapter 7

Sexual Dysfunction

Where the Rubber Meets the Road

As mentioned before, the libidinal drive occupied a central place in Freud's discoveries of the mental apparatus, and one would imagine that nowhere would this be more so than in issues of sexual dysfunction. The life drive, Eros, underpins all evolutionary drive in all living matter. The biochemical *push* starts from the ground up, electron gradients exhibiting a forward thrust that corroborates the forward thrust of development and time. The sexual drive is a potent force in human life, pressing forward in a constant and unwavering fashion, waning only temporarily before recharging itself and breaking the peace in its ongoing and intractable character. The libidinal drive not only presses somatic feelings of arousal that require discharge but also mental ones. In fact, human sexuality appears to be contained largely in the mental realm, filled with associative links, fantasy, and the cathexes of old imagos from early attachments. The infantile imagos wend their way inescapably through the streams of sensual currents, influencing their form and character and the future direction they will take as puberty and (ultimately) the efflorescence of adult sexuality erupts into life in the second phase of psychosexual development.

The positive association of early psychosexual development driven by the intense longings and loves of early attachments, drive the powerful imprinting that the libidinal pressures exert. In other words, libidinal pressures are not unclothed, so to speak, formless and without content. Rather, libidinal pressures become clothed in the form of early attachments and the subjective associations of how those imagos were navigated. All subsequent erotic attachments must be influenced by these early longings and cathexes. In other species, it appears the sexual instinct is unformed and unbridled, and will find a mate based on more primitive and instinctual promptings. But humans are never free in this fashion, never expressing their sexuality in an unbridled fashion, nor free of the early imprints that accompany such promptings. Nor are humans ever free of the taboos which accompany early psychosexual development. Freud wrote about these elements:

DOI: 10.4324/9781003628972-8

These affectionate fixations of the child persist throughout childhood, and continually carry along with them erotism, which is consequently diverted from its sexual aims. Then at the age of puberty they are joined by the powerful 'sensual' current which no longer mistakes its aims. It never fails, apparently, to follow the earlier paths and to cathect the objects of the primary infantile choice with quotas of libido that are now far stronger.

But, this developmental step in humans is not without complication. Freud adds that it runs up against the obstacles that have been erected in the meantime by the barrier against incest and so must make an effort to pass on from these objects, which are unsuitable in reality, and contend with finding other, extraneous objects with which a real sexual life may be carried on. "These new objects will still be chosen on the model (imago) of the infantile ones, but in the course of time they will attract to themselves the affection that was tied to the earlier ones. A man shall leave his father and his mother—according to the biblical command—and shall cleave unto his wife; affection and sensuality are then united. The greatest intensity of sensual passion will bring with it the highest psychical valuation of the object—this being the normal overvaluation of the sexual object on the part of a man".[1]

The transition from familiar to unfamiliar objects in post-pubescent and adult sexuality is essential if the barrier against incest is to be navigated. At least, this is true at a conscious level. Conscious acknowledgment that a sexual partner in any way represents the parental object must present as anathema to internal acceptability, since the power of the incest taboo is sufficient to make such association repugnant to consciousness. And yet, psychoanalytic investigation makes clear that old parental imagos remain powerfully imbedded in memory, together with its patterning and emotional cathexes. Early psychosexual development does not get left behind in the advent of object sexuality of later attachments. This might be regarded as both a blessing and a curse in that the familiarity of old object-attachments informs later ones, but this presents also a significant challenge in that they must also be simultaneously repressed from conscious awareness. Early familial attachments, as we know, become subject to various taboos and prohibitions, which, if able to 'leak' into later attachments, will invariably violate incest prohibitions and generate complicated feelings. Nature in her wisdom has anticipated this problem of early love-objects, including those tinged with sensual and somatic associations and phantasies, complicating later post-pubescent efflorescence.

Taboos and their Defences

If old (unconscious) imagos[2] and associations to parental objects leak into sensual life, it would set about a major and inextinguishable conflict which would risk the obstruction of sensual currents and inhibit erotic life to the point of risking effective reproduction, and leading, I should add without sounding too much like a writer of fiction, to the possibility of human extinction. Some couples in the modern era reproduce through medically-assisted reproduction for this reason, even when no medical grounds indicate fertility issues.

It is no wonder that, we could perhaps melodramatically suggest, the prohibition and psychological barrier against incest[3] remain stronger than the murder of one's parents. And yet, feelings of longings, love, and phantasies abound in these child-to-parent relationships. The mental apparatus requires mechanisms to both enable the blossoming of childhood love and fantasy in both the interests of bonding, attachment, and the benefits of nourishment, safety, and belonging that accrue, but simultaneously also requires a mechanism to disable these same longings later in life once the innocence of childhood is past and adult objects are required for bonding and reproduction. Whereas in the prepubescent stage of life the sensual and affectional currents[4] tend to mix and mingle through the innocence of childhood phantasy and love to parental objects, in the post-pubescent stage these currents must now separate from these same parental objects.

This defusing of these currents at home must fuse again outside of family ties, consciously freed of earlier associations, finding their denouement in an object upon whom both love and lust can again merge, fulfilling Nature's procreative requirement in the interests of the collective. Civilisation, we could suggest, offers a method to inhibit those childhood impulses that would compromise this sexual and reproductive imperative, by psychic and genetic separation that incest would violate and over time, reducing the viability of the human gene. As the biologist Lane suggests, that without generating chromosomes with different combinations – enabling adaptation to changing environments and conditions, human adaptation through evolutionary variation becomes limited. Sex allows selection to act on all genes individually, says Lane, and hence selection, "like God, can now see all our vices and virtues, gene by gene. That's the great advantage of sex".[5] Lane explains that "Sex is needed, to maintain the function of individual genes in large genomes, whereas two sexes help maintain the quality of mitochondria",[6] mitochondria being the energetic source that powers biological cells and life itself. Junk genes also get sidelined over time, an imperative that would be interfered with through incestuous violations and enactments. Incestuous phantasies can only prosper in the early stage of pre-pubescent sexuality when the mental and physical do not coincide in sensual life.

Like in other areas and processes of the psyche, its ability to navigate compromise-formations is highly developed, even where some economic costs are incurred or symptoms might manifest. Freud's great insight into the pathway of sexual development through the oedipal stage, enables a sensual current to emerge at around age three years. This stage facilitates the child mentally taking the opposite sex parent as an object, albeit in phantasy, and supplementing the earlier affective currents of childhood, the purer emotional loves (and hates) that are essential to sustaining the identity and cohesion of the child and family system. Pure love, in these affectional currents, are supplemented developmentally by sensual currents in this new phase, which retain the innocence of childhood and are largely relegated to the sphere of phantasy (unconscious) and fantasy (more conscious) through imagination and play. Children imagine themselves being able to marry their opposite sex parent, have them to themselves, and compete against the same sex parent for pride of place in the opposite parent's heart. The doctor-doctor games of this period and natural curiosity of childhood become apparent in these enactments of sensual awareness and the role of difference in provoking feelings of curiosity, envy, and the urge to enact through play. Accompanying this mental development are also the urethral sensations that prompt children in this stage to touch and fiddle with their genitals as sensations of urinary-like urges make their presence felt and disrupt the (genital) quiet of the pre-oedipal period.

The necessity for time to separate parental longings and imagos from the advent of adult object eroticism relies on the ability of the psyche to separate these two psychical stages. Notwithstanding some gender differences in development, to which I will return later, Freud noted that the oedipal stage "is literally smashed to pieces by the shock of threatened castration. Its libidinal cathexes are abandoned, desexualised and in part sublimated...".[7] It is as if the sexualised association to parental objects ceases to be and consciously appears as if it has never been. Freud adds, "In normal, or, it is better to say, in ideal cases, the Oedipus complex exists no longer, even in the unconscious; the super-ego has become its heir".[8]

However, oedipal associations and longings are never actually entirely lost to the mind, for how can memory ablate itself without deleterious effects? Since, encoded as it is through early development, its function remains essential to healthy navigation of life. Memory does not erase itself selectively, and yet we also know that specific memories can disappear from conscious awareness *as if* they never existed. Included in this paradoxical state of affairs is not only early memory from infancy that cannot be cognitively 'declared', since it is in a state that neuroscience refers to as non-declarative and imprinted pre-cognition, and yet exerts an emotional influence on the mental apparatus throughout time. It includes currents that are both in-mind and out-of-mind simultaneously, a paradox achieved through the mechanism of repression, that encodes association in memory but keeps such memory out of conscious awareness.

The notion of a mind split between 'topographical' layers of consciousness was one of Freud's great discoveries, and one that we can all resonate with – knowing and not knowing our internal worlds simultaneously. This capacity of the human psyche to repress much of its contents in the interests of internal psychic conflict resolution, remains an essential component of navigating a psychological world, in which competing needs and demands and the complications of ambivalence abound. The tremendous challenge of both loving and hating the same object, since it is only through investment in the object in the interests of mental and physical survival that frustrations and hurts also abound, means that the psyche is wracked with internal conflicts from the outset of life. It is not only the sensual currents that bump into the challenges of the reality-principle, requiring them to remain contained in the unconscious despite retaining the capacity to exert influence over consciousness and conscious object choice. To the complexity of the affectional current, I wish to now turn.

Ambivalence

The longing for primary attachments through both affectional and sensual phases of development invariably puts the human mind into conflict with itself. Only with affectional *investment* can loss be incurred, whether of a symbolic or material kind. Overvaluation of the love-object must build itself into the annals of attachment, as we shall discuss, but so too the potentiality for loss when emotional (over)investment is made. As an example of this, I noted earlier that, as Freud suggests, in marriage, and according to the biblical command to leave parental objects in favour of non-familial ones – in this way affection and sensuality are then united. "The greatest intensity of sensual passion will bring with it the highest psychical valuation of the object—this being the normal overvaluation of the sexual object on the part of a man".[9]

But long before this, sensual current emerges during the oedipal stage, in which powerful longings to possess the love-object and pair with them occurs (so common in childhood phantasies of marrying their parent, often openly expressed). However, life yields obstacles to the mental development, and so too introduces the reality principle that, according to Freud, "proved to be a momentous step",[10] leaves frustration and loss in its wake because of the tension between phantasy and reality, the wish and its impossibilities in the real world. Indeed, "an organisation which was a slave to the pleasure principle and neglected the reality of the external world could not maintain itself alive for the shortest time, so that it could not have come into existence at all".[11]

Where love and longing go, so follows invariably experiences of loss, frustration and hurt, the obstacles and taboos of the real world, generating the curse of the human condition of ambivalence, something as best we can tell does not plague other creatures. Longings, or the life drive which *pushes* feelings and fantasies of attachment, and which have so much more contact with our internal perception, are themselves disruptors, emerging as "breakers of the peace", as Freud put it.[12] This suggests that longing and loss are intertwined, since more often than not the longings of childhood meet with the reality of their frustration, both as a product of external competition of the other parent, but also because, in time, the emergence of the taboo against incest must smash these wishes and neutralise them as a threat. Of course, through adulthood love and longing is also met with the reality of disillusionments, losses, and heart-break.

We know from psychoanalytic work, and indeed from common everyday experience, that frustrations of wishes, fantasies, longings are invariably met with an ego-deflation, hurt, and heartache, engendering a rupture of psychic homeostasis. In turn, any rupture of homeostasis must be accompanied by an activating of the mechanism of the mental apparatus whose job it is to restore homeostasis, namely the conservative or aggressive drive, whose path once activated will be determined by individual circumstance and developmental history. But in general, we can safely assert that love and hate are bedfellows of the human psyche, tensioning against each other constantly. Ambivalence is the unavoidable curse of the human experience. As the oedipal stage comes to an end, repression exerts its stuff and unyielding power, in normal circumstances, to force a radical separation of early childhood longings and oedipal fantasies and feelings from post-pubescent erotic objects. This 'airtight' mechanism must allow old associations and imagos to parental objects to flourish and revive themselves in adult love attachments, but at the same time remain stripped of any vestiges of the sensual element. When this barrier against incest fails, so too does sexual capacity and performance.

When Repression Fails

This paradoxical demand of the human mind, that requires parental associations to influence future outcomes in memory's *feedforward* process, whilst at the same time stripping it of the memory of sensual currents, relies to some extent on different mechanisms for boys' and girls' developmental pathways. In boys, the threat of the rivalry with the father for the mother's affections must invite retaliatory phantasies and the fear that this rival may inflict genital harm, leasing to a gradual relinquishing of the sensual attachment to the mother, since "the complex is not simply repressed, it is literally smashed to pieces by the shock of threatened castration. Its libidinal cathexes are abandoned, desexualised and in part sublimated".[13] It is *as if* the oedipal longings and fantasies are no more, and yet memory must retain them in the unconscious, especially since the earlier rivalry must induce a threat to homeostasis. For girls, the threat of castration has already had its effect, in fact triggering oedipal longings, and hence "it may be slowly abandoned or dealt with by repression, or its effects may persist far into women's normal mental life".[14] In other words, for girls' oedipal memories retain a more benign character and do not require the same level of psychic abandonment. For boys, despite the evidence of his previous 'love affair' with his mother at the time of its oedipal ascendance, in its place is generally an 'obliteration' of this memory. Few men will acknowledge any feelings or memories of their love affairs with their mothers during this early phase of development and yet at the time its presence was usually easily noticeable and obvious to both the boy and those around him. The necessity for this layer of repression is that it both enables the development of the sensual attachment to adult women later in life but simultaneously strips it of any associative violations of the incest taboo.

These developmental trends are suggestive of how most pathways are navigated, but this speaks little to the complex nuance and individual subjectivity that pertains in each case of development. For example, some boys find their mothers intrusive, forceful, or enmeshed psychologically; this physical or emotional over-exposure lending itself to conditions where the borders between enactment-reality and taboo can become too thinly spread and compromise the repression layer that should put the child's love affair with his mother to rest at the end of the oedipal period.[15] Later sensual adult attachments triggering these associative memories of the maternal object, cannot easily dispense with the violation of the earlier taboos that embed as a signal of psychical danger and risk for the boy. The strength of the sensual currents often presses forward to overcome initial barriers against incest, since the erotic object may benefit in the early flushes of attraction and romance from a separation from any maternal association. But with time, for example, in some cases, what Freud referred to as psychical impotence occurs, in which it "manifests itself in a refusal by the executive organs of sexuality to carry out the sexual act, although before and after they may show themselves to be intact and capable of performing the act, and although a strong psychical inclination to carry it out is present".[16] The failure of repression of the oedipal association leads to a psychical leakage, so to speak, of an "incestuous fixation on mother or sister, which has never been surmounted, plays a prominent part in this pathogenic material and is its most universal content".[17]

The power of the erotic drive relies, in other words, on a separation of the two fundamental elements of love – namely, the affectional current so prevalent in early infancy and childhood for those who preserve and promote the child's well-being and life, and the sensual currents that make their presence felt in later development. Initial erotic ascendance relies on a separation of these currents, later a fusion of them, as a more mature love draws the familiarity of attachment together with the unfamiliarity of *otherness*.[18] In some cases, where psychical impotence or sexual dysfunction inhibits full satisfaction of the erotic instinct, often for both partners, this often represents a leakage of early parental attachment and its issues. It fosters an apparent violation of the incest taboo by forming mental associations of the current adult attachment to the early parental one, posing for the psyche an impossible dilemma. As Freud suggested that psychoanalysis has shown us that when the original object of a wishful impulse has been lost as a result of repression, "it is frequently represented by an endless series of substitutive objects none of which, however, brings full satisfaction. This may explain the inconstancy in object-choice, the 'craving for stimulation' which is so often a feature of the love of adults".[19]

Two sets of processes may emerge to complicate this matter. The leakage across the repression barrier, described above, is itself a disruptor to the psyche and hence triggers the aggressive drive in its attempts to manage this violation of homeostasis. But also, very often, we see in a deeper analysis that men with psychical impotence retain anger to their mothers from early age complications, which render the sexual organ in a state in which it may be said that it is not a case of cannot perform but that it 'refuses' to perform for the perceived demands[20] of the partner. In other words, says Freud: "Firstly, as a result of the diphasic onset of object-choice, and the interposition of the barrier against incest, the final object of the sexual instinct is never any longer the original object but only a surrogate for it".[21] More often than not, however, masturbation to phantasy or pornography demonstrates that the organ works perfectly well from a medical point of view. Its refusal to perform often represents a (passive) aggressive response, and may be regarded as a psychical protest, a silent resistance to maternal associations, and a refusal to succumb to the threat of engulfment, control, humiliation, or even castration. Further, completion of the sexual act for some men leads to the condition of *la petite mort*, a post-orgasm sensation likened to a 'little death', or what can also be referred to as *post-coital tristesse*, in which the experience of evacuation is akin to evisceration, a brief weakening of consciousness, the hollowing out of libidinal energy and psychical potency, as the male organ becomes flaccid and unable to function, at least temporarily. This experience is for some men depressing, leading to a literal diagnosis of post-coital dysphoria (PCD)[22], and sometimes leading to sex being avoided in an anticipatory manner. It is often accompanied by feelings of loss, sadness, anxiety, agitation, aggression or feelings of deep depression, which remits spontaneously over a period of hours to a few days. Distilled, loss accompanies the association and the completion of the sexual act, rather than the satiation and gain of libidinal engagement.

Incest and the Aggressive Drive

It might be said then, that various associative elements can break through the repression layer to impair sexual function in men. I do not include in this mix ejaculatory issues, such as the experience of a relatively 'premature' fulfilment of the sexual drive in men, since the universal nature of this problem, particularly in young men, suggests that the evolutionary pressure to copulate may carry through in development to pester men in their difficulty delaying the orgasm response in themselves in order to satisfy their partner.

Less frequently, some men struggle with delayed or even impossible climax for reasons that are more obscure than the more often reported clinical problem of sexual dysfunction, and the frustration that failure of the executive organ to perform causes in both men and women. Psychogenic dysfunction suggests a *refusal* of the organ to function, sometimes from the outset of foreplay but for some men erection is fine until the requirement for penetration, when the organ loses its power and resolve. Unconscious perceptions of being devoured may be associated with the archetype of the '*vagina dentata*',[23] a reference to the notion that the vagina has 'teeth' which can lead to being castrated and effeminised. The loss of the organ through a feminine control and imagined aggression is not the same as the threat of castration from the father, a fate from which oedipal desires and fantasies manifest. Rather, in men for which this unconscious phantasy springs, the capacity to be lost to maternal/ feminine controls renders the act of penetration one perceived of as absorption, mastication, or castration, not necessarily by the father competitor in the classical oedipal drama, but by the feminine object herself. The 'devouring' feminine replaces the male drive to 'possess' the sexual object, to penetrate the object in the service of both sexual gratification and reproduction.

Such associations are not manifest but reside in the recesses of the unconscious through history. This memory holds an association of the threats associated with (early) desire for the maternal object, and hence a loss of both agency and dominance. Stripped of ideology, the male psyche strives for an element of possession of the object and the desire to dominate in the service of this end. Disruption to the fulfilment of this quest meets with the threats to the phantasy which can become embedded in memory and 'leak' into adult sexuality, creating a conflict between two parts of the psyche: the one responding to instinctual promptings hardwired-in, as it were, to consummate the sexual act in the service of libidinal desire, universal, powerful and essentially irresistible, but the other turning against it, pushing back through associative memories that are deeply personal and attempting to neutralise the threats that this drive can mobilise. Principally, the incest taboo confronts this libidinal 'breaker of the peace', and tries to render it harmless and ineffectual, employing the mental mechanism designed for this purpose. The aggressive drive becomes mobilised not only against the object of desire now associated with prohibition, but also against the drive itself. Two parts of the psyche now come into conflict with each other, with one pushing for desire and the other pulling back in its attempt to neutralise such desire. For some, this conflict cannot be resolved, since the power of the drive against its opposition remains too threatening psychically. The somatic compromise-formation, strictly speaking not somatic at all, but a product of the psychical conflict, leads to the organ itself saying "no", it cannot both perform and honour the taboos that performance represents. Erectile refusal, an aggressive compromise, becomes to that psyche an 'obvious' solution –

mobilising the mechanisms required to restore homeostasis within an impossible bind of mental disruption.

La Petite Mort

A further word is in order on a dysfunction that follows, rather than precedes intercourse, and the consummation of the sexual act. As mentioned earlier, *la petite mort* is an expression that means "the brief loss or weakening of consciousness" and in modern usage refers specifically to "the sensation of post orgasm as likened to death". The first attested use of the expression in English was in 1572 with the meaning of "fainting fit".[24] The phenomenon of the 'little death' is reflected in the dysthymic consequence for some men following orgastic release. Many men, not just those suffering with a clinical consequence, report the experience of loss following release, feeling evacuated and depleted and in a sense rendered impotent by the experience. Albeit temporary, the loss of potency for some men evokes a need to separate and disengage in order to restore and replenish energetically the lost potency. Some men experience severe symptoms in this regard, to the point that a diagnosis is depression is warranted, except that after a few hours or a few days the depression spontaneously remits, case dependent, but is invariably triggered by the experience of orgasm and ejaculation.

The distinguishing characteristics of POIS are: the rapid onset of symptoms after ejaculation; the presence of an overwhelming systemic reaction. POIS symptoms, which are called a "POIS attack", can include various symptoms but in essence, as an online anonymous self-report study found, that 80% of respondents always experienced the symptom cluster involving fatigue, insomnia, irritation, and concentration difficulties. The symptoms usually begin within 30 minutes of ejaculation, and can last for several days, sometimes up to a week. In some cases, symptoms may be delayed by two to three days or may last up to two weeks. The feature we can observe in this syndrome is the profound sense of loss that accompanies orgastic release, rather than the gain we often associate culturally with sexual possession of the object and subsequent release. But as we hopefully know by now, loss triggers a state of disequilibrium, which must trigger the aggressive drive in the service of restoration, and since the aggression is not turned *out* against the object, the sense of loss is introjected and leads to the 'impoverishment of the ego', in which all libidinal energy is lost and the aggressive drive is activated. Unmetabolised, depression follows.

So, we observe two essential elements in the mobilisation of the aggressive drive in the genesis of sexual dysfunction in men: a 'no' to the risk of devourment and loss through the sexual act and a violation of the incest taboo which sets disruption to psychic equilibrium at risk; and secondly, a response to orgasm which triggers the loss-disruption-restoration cascade.

Whether a trigger for, or a response to, the aggressive drive is activated to return the disrupted homeostasis to homeostasis.

But what about women? Is the mechanism the same?

Women and Sexual Dysfunction

Like with men, women can suffer with related conditions in the sexual response: disorders of arousal, desire, orgasm, and of vaginal acceptance of penetration. Most often, these maladies are psychically driven and whilst the arousal response may diminish in time for women in regular relationships, it may not fully reflect the inner desire that she has for sexual play and coitus. A deeper analysis of the lack of the arousal response in women does not appear to benefit from a linear comparison to the arousal response of men, namely erectile refusal is not invariably comparable to a poor lubrication or engorgement response in women, since the complexity of the female hormone system as well as the sensitivity to emotional context may complicate direct parallels.

However, the malady of vaginismus (a barrier against penetration), or for some women dyspareunia (penetration is possible but with pain) may be compared more to the erectile refusal of men and the usually psychogenic contribution deeper mental attitudes might play in its cause. Erotic life in women is more contextually determined than for men, influenced by the feelings, atmosphere, and quality of attachment that evolves beyond the initial flushes of attraction. When the libidinal drivers have particular valence, as they do in the initial stages of attraction, the contextual elements may recede and pave the way for sexual experiences in which no obstacles to sexual function present themselves, even in cases where they may be more generally present. Libidinal ascendance, it seems, has the ability to override inhibitions and temporarily enable obstacles to be overcome psychically. But with time, inhibitions associated with erotic life have a way of returning, serving two masters at the same time: firstly, being *pushed* into life from the age-old libidinal/ life drive and being infused with tremendous energy and power but simultaneously having to submit to the drive to restore homeostasis from this disruptor. This dialectical tension between activation and restoration, the breaking of the peace and the restoration of the peace, plays itself out in both acute short-term ways but also over time as the initial ascendance of the libidinal drive gives way to a return to balance in which all manner of old unconscious associations return. As it does, so, in couples, conflict creeps in where only joy and positive projection held sway. Old oedipal associations, long since 'forgotten' to consciousness, trend upwards back into a sphere of psychical influence. Accordingly, incest taboos may act to inhibit libidinal desires, leading also to organ refusal, and a muscular tightening reflecting a 'no' assertion against penetration.

Whilst this 'return of the repressed' remains an inevitable element of intimacy, I mentioned above that female sexuality tends also to be more context-bound and effected by both emotional currency and life challenges. Pregnancy and birth, for example, invite a host of reality-based and intra-psychic associations. Freud made mention of the antecedents that trigger maternal cravings, in particular the internalising of the phallus-baby, which leads to her primary preoccupation becoming directed at the baby, rather than her partner to whom great attachment may have been present in the making of the baby. In girls, the losses associated with envy issues and the rupture of the oedipal phantasy suggests it too must activate a restorative response to these homeostatic disruptions. Writes Freud:

> She slips - along the line of a symbolic equation, one might say—from the penis to a baby. Her Oedipus complex culminates in a desire, which is long retained, to receive a baby from her father as a gift—to bear him a child. One has an impression that the Oedipus complex is then gradually given up because this wish is never fulfilled. The two wishes—to possess a penis and a child—remain strongly cathected in the unconscious and help to prepare the female creature for her later sexual role.[25]

Once achieved, and the phallus is acquired, so to speak, in the form of a baby in adulthood, the desire for her partner may drastically fall away. In addition, the now symbolically de-phallused partner may lose his attractiveness, no longer holding the power of seduction and reproduction and hence finding himself treated with elements of derision and contempt.

The Phallic Container[26]

Early motherhood is also a period in which the mental merger of one mind occurs with another for the betterment of the infant, but which represents a unique process through the lifespan in which two minds merge without a mental skin or barrier between them (except in psychotic states where mental boundaries become diffuse). For the baby this is a perfect and necessary condition. But not so for the mother in whom the disequilibrium induced by this merger is constant, a state of disequilibrium from the endless stream of projections from the infant, driven by the need for the mind of the mother to offer a metabolic function to make meaning out of the infant's state of *meaninglessness*, or in Bion's terminology, to turn beta elements into alpha elements.[27] This leads to the activation of the aggressive drive in the mother (albeit at times in a covert and unconscious form) in an attempt to reregulate and restore homeostasis in her own mind, in response to the endless stream of projective disruptions, as disruptive as projections must be, and as powerful as the baby's inducements will be to coerce a response in the mother to respond to its needs. Since the baby has free access to the mother's mind in the early post-partum months, states of disequilibrium abound for the mother, and homeostatic mechanisms must activate in response.

However, such a psychical immune response cannot be enacted against the infant since Nature protects it in the interests of the evolutionary imperative, that favours the infant surviving both physically and mentally. This triaging of need places infant, mother, other children, and then the father of the child or the couple relationship in an order of psychical priority, often at the cost of the marital or couple relationship. Defensively, introjection is one common strategy of protecting the infant from maternal aggression but this too has limitations in impairing maternal function through depression. Some of this aggressive affect must find a way out and invariably the husband/father becomes the container for these affective imbalances, or what I refer to as the phallic container, since the father represents several layers of psychic association. These include, the penis-baby acquisition, rendering him 'de-phallused' in her mind once the baby itself is acquired. Denigration of the symbolically *de-phallused* husband fuelled by the diversion of maternal hate from her infant, creates later problems for the couple, including sexual ones on both sides.

This diversion has adaptive value in protecting the baby from maternal enactments but the cost to the marital dyad of such aggressive displacement can be high indeed. Nature triages the infant's interests ahead of that of the couple initially, but, in its wake, intimacy and sexual interest can wane. The vaginal-resistance to the phallic-other intruding back into this mental space can lead to its refusal to function, paradoxically, even when she might desire it consciously. The displacement of hostilities from the mother-infant dyad into the couple space is bound to contaminate sexual desire, and when surmounted through conscious will, can run into the resistance the body musters in compliance with the unconscious directive, as it were, to manifest the aggressive feelings in the service of restoring some form of homeostasis.

Hostility displaced into the object renders the required elevation moot, for without some idealisation and objectification of the erotic-object, heightened arousal suffers. Libidinal energy has the strange capacity of promoting idealisation of the object but in the post-partum period the lion's share of the libidinal drive is directed at the infant and away from the father of the infant, and additionally, the lion's share of the hostility is directed away from the infant and into the husband. In men, this process of 'double emasculation' succumbs erotic life to inhibition, and both arousal and entry resistances and refusal often emerge. For women, vaginal tightness or spasm, loss of lubrication, and pain become expressions of this underlying aggressive mobilisation. Vaginal refusal may emanate from unconscious sources, and in a sense by-pass conscious feelings and evaluation, but the body registers the internal conflict of old oedipal associations, displaced aggression in the service of homeostatic demands to protect the infant, or real resentments at the husband's poor responsiveness, and keeps score, as it were, to reflect the unresolved discontents.

What emerges into clarity is that sexual problems across the spectrum often have psychogenic contributions, underneath which lie the activation of the aggressive drive in the service of restoration, and it is this element that contributes most to sexual dysfunction. Common contributions of anxiety or other feelings apply partially since these can never exist *sans* the activation of the drive whose aim is restoration, namely aggression. Where this is not processed, the body reflects it, through both arousal and refusal responses for both men and women. As I mentioned, Freud noted the centrality of the sexual in psychopathology, and the contribution of noxae of sexual life "as the most important causes of the neurotic disorders that are so common".[28] But Freud could also be forgiven for not yet recognising the second component to this point which emerged later in this 1920 theory of the dual-drive nature of the psyche, is that sexual noxae, invariably subjective, individually perceived, and psychically constructed, only represent a problem in that noxae create states of disequilibrium, which must trigger a restorative response and bind escalating free energy, even when this increasing arousal is from an unconscious source. The aggressive drive tasked with this job embroils itself in the unresolved leftovers from earlier childhood failures of resolution, and it is this response that plays such a central role in the genesis of sexual problems in adult life.

Notes

1 Freud, S. (1912) On the Universal Tendency to Debasement in the Sphere of Love (Contributions to the Psychology of Love II). *The Standard Edition of the Complete Psychological Works of Sigmund Freud* 11:170–190, p.181.

2 See for example: Freud, S. (1933) New Introductory Lectures On Psycho-Analysis. *The Standard Edition of the Complete Psychological Works of Sigmund Freud* 22:1–182, p.64; see also Freud, S. (1924) The Economic Problem of Masochism. *The Standard Edition of the Complete Psychological Works of Sigmund Freud* 19:155–170, p.168.

3 Freud, S. (1912) On the Universal Tendency to Debasement in the Sphere of Love (Contributions to the Psychology of Love II). *The Standard Edition of the Complete Psychological Works of Sigmund Freud* 11: 170–190, p.184.

4 Freud, S. (1912) On the Universal Tendency to Debasement in the Sphere of Love (Contributions to the Psychology of Love II). *The Standard Edition of the Complete Psychological Works of Sigmund Freud* 11: 170–190, p.183.

5 Lane, N. (2016) *The Vital Question: Why is Life the Way it Is?* London: Profile Books, p. 214.

6 Lane, N. (2016) *The Vital Question: Why is Life the Way it Is?* London: Profile Books, p. 241.

7 Freud, S. (1925) Some Psychical Consequences of the Anatomical Distinction between the Sexes. *The Standard Edition of the Complete Psychological Works of Sigmund Freud* 19:241–258, p.257.

8 Freud, S. (1925) Some Psychical Consequences of the Anatomical Distinction between the Sexes. *The Standard Edition of the Complete Psychological Works of Sigmund Freud* 19:241–258, p.257.

9 Freud, S. (1912) On the Universal Tendency to Debasement in the Sphere of Love (Contributions to the Psychology of Love II). *The Standard Edition of the Complete Psychological Works of Sigmund Freud* 11:177–190, p.181.

10 Freud, S. (1911) Formulations on the Two Principles of Mental Functioning. *The Standard Edition of the Complete Psychological Works of Sigmund Freud* 12:213–226, p.219.

11 Freud, S. (1911) Formulations on the Two Principles of Mental Functioning. *The Standard Edition of the Complete Psychological Works of Sigmund Freud* 12:213–226, p.219.

12 Freud, S. (2015) Beyond the Pleasure Principle. *Psychoanalysis and History* 17:151–204, p.203.

13 Freud, S. (1925) Some Psychical Consequences of the Anatomical Distinction between the Sexes. *The Standard Edition of the Complete Psychological Works of Sigmund Freud* 19:241–258, p.257.

14 Freud, S. (1925) Some Psychical Consequences of the Anatomical Distinction between the Sexes. *The Standard Edition of the Complete Psychological Works of Sigmund Freud* 19:241–258, p.257.

15 See for example, Richard Wood's fascinating chapter on his own experience of maternal enactments in his book on malignant narcissism. Wood, R. (2024) *A Study of Malignant Narcissism: Personal and Professional Insights.* Routledge: London/ New York.

16 Freud, S. (1912) On the Universal Tendency to Debasement in the Sphere of Love (Contributions to the Psychology of Love II). *The Standard Edition of the Complete Psychological Works of Sigmund Freud* 11:177–190, p.179.

17 Freud, S. (1912) On the Universal Tendency to Debasement in the Sphere of Love (Contributions to the Psychology of Love II). *The Standard Edition of the Complete Psychological Works of Sigmund Freud* 11:177–190, p.180.

18 It is common sense that novelty in erotic life promotes it – and since men have an extraordinary strong 'scopophilic instinct' and are visually driven, erotically activated by visual cues, women tend to reinvent themselves through creating difference in their dress, enhancements, hair styles, etc.

19 Freud, S. (1912) On the Universal Tendency to Debasement in the Sphere of Love (Contributions to the Psychology of Love II). *The Standard Edition of the Complete Psychological Works of Sigmund Freud* 11:177–190, p.189.

20 For some men, the sexual act is less about *penetration* and more about an experience of *engulfment*, representing loss of the sexual organ and hence a form of psychical castration.

21 Freud, S. (1912) On the Universal Tendency to Debasement in the Sphere of Love (Contributions to the Psychology of Love II). *The Standard Edition of the Complete Psychological Works of Sigmund Freud* 11:177–190, p.189.

22 Also known as Postorgasmic illness syndrome (POIS) is a syndrome in which human males have chronic physical and cognitive symptoms following ejaculation. The symptoms usually onset within seconds, minutes, or hours, and last for up to a week.

23 *Vagina dentata* (Latin for *toothed vagina*) is a folk tale tradition in which a woman's vagina is said to contain teeth, with the associated implication that sexual intercourse might result in injury, emasculation, or castration for the man involved. See also, https://en.wikipedia.org/wiki/Vagina_dentata

24 https://en.wikipedia.org/wiki/La_petite_mort

25 Freud, S. (1924) The Dissolution of the Oedipus Complex. *The Standard Edition of the Complete Psychological Works of Sigmund Freud* 19:171–180, pp.178–179.

26 See my paper for a deeper exploration of this phenomenon, in which maternal aggression from infant disruption gets diverted into the father as a mechanism to protect the

infant: Perkel, A. (2006) The Phallic Container in the Couple: Splitting and Diversion of Maternal Hate as Protection of the Infant. *Psycho-analytic Psychotherapy in South Africa* 12(2), pp.13–38.

27 See for example, Bion, W.R. (1959) Attacks on Linking. *International Journal of Psychoanalysis* 40, pp.308–315.

28 Freud, S. (1907) The Sexual Enlightenment of Children (An Open Letter to Dr. M. Fürst). *The Standard Edition of the Complete Psychological Works of Sigmund Freud* 9:129–140, p.131.

Chapter 8

Addiction

The Helplessness Model

Addiction, it might be said, is characterised by replacement of need-fulfilment in the real word by an internal artificial version of it. One could suggest that the pleasure principle replaces the reality principle, but not as in psychotic states of a denial of reality but in the ability to control and regulate reality *at will*. Addicts do not appear to split the internal from the external to the extent of psychotic denial of reality, but do control internal reality through denial of the helplessness that underpins it. I will return to this distinction shortly, but for the moment note the difference between psychotic denial of reality and denial of the helplessness underlying a belief in control. An old therapist joke, albeit not the best joke in the world, goes something like this: the patient resists the therapist's interpretation that the patient is addicted to smoking, an addictive pattern over which the patient exerts no control. The indignant patient says, "Addicted? I am *not* addicted. Giving up smoking is the easiest thing in the world! I've done it a hundred times!" Addiction replaces real-world work requirements to fulfil needs with a form of omnipotent control. As Solms et al., make the point:

> Substance abuse appears to employ brain mechanisms that were evolutionarily designed to reward biologically useful activities (like copulation, as opposed to masturbation). This is what pleasurable affects are *for*, evolutionarily speaking; they reward biologically useful actions, and thus motivate animals to perform the work that is necessary to achieve them. The word 'abuse' in 'substance abuse' refers to the fact that the pleasure is attained without the natural effort and persistence it was designed to reward.[1]

It is an oft-touted notion in treatment circles that addiction is linked to helplessness. In a study in 2011, for example, it was concluded that "... addicts had higher levels of learned helplessness. A direct relationship was found between learned helplessness and frequency of addiction treatments".[2] In this vein, the articles abound in the addiction literature, mostly suggesting that individuals who feel powerless in their life may turn to substance abuse

DOI: 10.4324/9781003628972-9

as a means to escape this discomfort. In the beginning, they may feel that alcohol and drugs help, "but in reality, their problems are only starting. Others developed learned helplessness as a result of their addiction. This occurs because of failed attempts to quit or control their substance abuse".[3]

This narrative of helplessness pervades the lay literature and most of the professional addiction treatment models we see today, and as authors such as Khantzian state, addicts "self-medicate states of subjective distress and suffering".[4]

Deeper analyses of the psychical thrust to addiction links helplessness to different elements, such as Jones, who writes that, "It is my belief that for many the use of substances reflects a powerful life and death struggle to hold on to one's vital and authentic sense of self",[5] perhaps which can be viewed as a tussle between helplessness and omnipotence. Dodes writes, for example, that "In many cases addictive behaviour serves to ward off a sense of help-lessness or powerlessness via controlling and regulating one's affective state. Addicts have a vulnerability to feelings of powerlessness, which reflects a specific narcissistic impairment. The drive in addiction to re-establish a sense of power is, correspondingly, impelled by narcissistic rage".[6] In other words, even deeper thought into the addiction theories suggest that powerlessness and helplessness represent both a driver for the addiction and a consequent 'side-effect' of it too. The idea of these attributes being central to addiction persists. In other studies, it is argued that results reveal that male drug abu-sers, for example, demonstrated dysfunctional attitudes and learned help-lessness in their study. In addition, dysfunctional attitudes and learned helplessness significantly predicted the coping styles of these male drug abusers. "However, although learned helplessness affected coping styles, it did not mediate the relationship between dysfunctional attitudes and coping styles".[7]

Typical cultural approaches to addiction also invariably link these mental states of helplessness (and powerlessness) and thereby also underpin treat-ment modalities across the spectrum of programmes, and including the tra-ditional "12-Step program" of Alcoholics Anonymous and related programmes, that encourage acquiescence and submission of the patient to the treatment paradigm, acknowledge their helplessness/powerlessness, and thereby submit to a 'prostrate' mental attitude. Submission is encouraged to the programme, a Higher Power, sponsors, and their own 'disease' fault lines – that is, pathological cracks in their psychic apparatus – for which no real remedy is possible except through this submission and the recognition of these fault lines. For other authors, substances provide an addict "with an 'ersatz self-object' experience... reflecting what they refer to as the 'mega-lomaniacal' self, through which the addict can wield magical control over his environment".[8] In other words, rather than helplessness being the pre-dominate state underlying the addiction drive, there is a defence against helpless – an omnipotence or 'megalomaniacal' thrust. I will return to this important distinction shortly.

The Sexual Model

It may raise some eyebrows, but a deeper analysis yields a more textured view of addiction, such as Freud's comments to Fleiss in a letter dated 1897:

> ...It has dawned on me that masturbation is the one major habit, the 'primal addiction' and that it is only as a substitute and replacement for it that the other addictions-for alcohol, morphine, tobacco, etc.—come into existence. The part played by this addiction in hysteria is quite enormous; and it is perhaps there that my great, still outstanding, obstacle is to be found, wholly or in part. And here, of course, the doubt arises of whether an addiction of this kind is curable...[9]

In a paper on the subject of masturbation, Freud noted, "To break the patient of the habit of masturbating is only one of the new therapeutic tasks which are imposed on the physician who takes the sexual aetiology of the neurosis into account; and it seems that precisely this task, like the cure of any other addiction, can only be carried out in an institution and under medical supervision".[10]

Freud takes this further on noting that, the same thing applies to all treatments for breaking an addiction. Their success will only be an apparent one, he argues, so long as the physician contents himself with withdrawing the narcotic substance from his patients, without troubling about the source from which their imperative need for it springs. 'Habit', he suggests, is a mere form of words, without any explanatory value. "Not everyone who has occasion to take morphia, cocaine, chloral-hydrate, and so on, for a period, acquires in this way an 'addiction' to them. Closer enquiry usually shows that these narcotics are meant to serve—directly or indirectly—as a substitute for a lack of sexual satisfaction; and whenever normal sexual life can no longer be re-established, we can count with certainty on the patient's relapse".[11]

In comments about the symbolic ideas in Dostoevsky, Freud notes that, "The 'vice' of masturbation is replaced by the addiction to gambling; and the emphasis laid upon the passionate activity of the hands betrays this derivation".[12] He goes on to suggest that, "If the addiction to gambling, with the unsuccessful struggles to break the habit and the opportunities it affords for self-punishment, is a repetition of the compulsion to masturbate, we shall not be surprised to find that it occupied such a large space in Dostoevsky's life. After all, we find no cases of severe neurosis in which the auto-erotic satisfaction of early childhood and of puberty has not played a part; and the relation between efforts to suppress it and fear of the father are too well known to need more than a mention".[13]

As I mentioned earlier, these comments may raise an eyebrow in the reader, for what on earth does addiction, masturbation, and ancient psychical history have in common, least of all in informing why some people succumb to it? Freud himself was cognisant of the risks we carry in reading the data backwards, suggesting we become aware of a state of things which also confronts us in many other instances in which light has been thrown by psycho-analysis on a mental process. "So long as we trace the development from its final outcome backwards, the chain of events appears continuous, and insight which is completely satisfactory or even exhaustive", he writes. "But if we proceed the reverse way, if we start from the premises inferred from the analysis and try to follow these up to the final result, then we no longer get the impression of an inevitable sequence of events which could not have been otherwise determined. We notice at once that there might have been another result, and that we might have been just as well able to understand and explain the latter. The synthesis is thus not so satisfactory as the analysis; in other words, from a knowledge of the premises we could not have foretold the nature of the result".[14]

Deconstructing the reasons and links addiction occurs in later life to its roots in early infancy is possible, and yet taking the elements of early history and trying to determine future outcomes is impossible. The variables remain too great. And yet, we notice certain drivers, or better those drives that underpin the tendency to addiction in the last analysis. In later psycho-analytical practice, authors such as Khantzian have argued that, "In the author's experience, this perspective has evolved through four stages: viewing addiction as (1) a special adaptation, (2) an attempt to self-medicate and/or change unbearable or confusing affect states, (3) evolving into an understanding of addictions as self-regulation disorder, and (4) an exploration of the nature of the 'disordered person(ality)' that predisposes individuals to become, remain, and relapse to addictive behaviours".[15] Whilst earlier models in psychoanalysis stressed the pleasurable/ libidinal aspects, he argues that "Any theory or explanation of addiction that does not address what it is in the workings of the mind (i.e., the inner psychological terrain) and a person to predispose and cause them to repeatedly relapse to addictive drugs is incomplete."[16] And indeed, this point is valid and essential but to which many theorists only pay half attention – that being, the first half of the driver for addiction. Libidinal, pleasure-seeking substitutes for real-world SEEK-ING[17] to achieve homeostatic 'celebration' and avoid unpleasure. But homeostatic parameters are invariably meted by the tensions that both drives invite – and omnipotent controls, that is that mechanism designed to respond to deviations from homeostasis, are part of this. Khantzian makes the point that, "In the author's experience, substances of abuse are and become compelling because in susceptible individuals they help to cope with unbearable painful feelings and/or to adapt to external realities that are otherwise unmanageable".[18]

Unbearable feelings are simply deviations from homeostasis that defy remedy. For the infant, over-flowing frustrations that the mother cannot or does not remediate generates increasing arousal, heightened free energy, and hence a mobilisation of the defences of the aggressive drive emerging in the service of restoration and conservation, and this increasingly helpless rage, proving ineffective in prising a remedy out of the mother, becomes central in the genesis of addiction. It is not always misattunement by the mother – think of a baby left to cry in the neonatal ICU because medical intervention takes precedent over the 'softer' needs of the infant.

Addiction and Free Energy

We do have to maintain caution in the causal chain linking early history to addiction, since Freud's caution is noteworthy, that:

> Even supposing that we have a complete knowledge of the etiological factors that decide a given result, nevertheless what we know about them is only their quality, and their relative strength. Some of them are suppressed by others because they are too weak, and they therefore do not affect the final result. But we never know beforehand which of the determining factors will prove the weaker or the stronger. We only say at the end that those which succeeded must have been the stronger. Hence the chain of causation can always be recognised with certainty if we follow the line of analysis, whereas to predict it along the line of synthesis is impossible.[19]

Authors such as Brickman have lamented in their writings the 'folly' of psychoanalytic speculation that appears to drive the narrative backwards and hence becomes ineffective for real-world interventions.[20] It can appear absurd *from an outsider perspective* to follow interpretations made upon the individual patient. Even when the law of subjectivity dictates that individual dynamics require a retrospective analysis that can never be predicted forward, despite the role of memory in doing precisely that, the publication of case studies can to an outsider seem far-fetched and more suited to the projections of the clinician than the feedforward mechanisms of the patient. As an example, Brickman criticises Garma for his finding that one of his patient's peptic ulcerations was caused by "a fantasy of an internalised oral/ aggressive biting maternal imago",[21] and cynically suggests this sort of interpretations can run riot in violations of sound clinical evidence. On the other hand, the mind-body cross over is consistent with current neuroscience and the link between drives, affects, feeling states, and these subjective experiential phenomena as playing a critical role in the functioning of neurological and somatic processes. This 'dual-aspect monism', as Solms would describe his theoretical neuroscientific orientation,[22] makes brain-mind-soma indisputably connected, not as dual mechanisms running in parallel but as different mechanisms making up the whole of the machine. Solms adds that, from a neuroscientific point of view, and in his view, the free-energy principle is a unifying principle of both brain and mind functioning; "it provides a monistic explanation of both physiological and psychological phenomena".[23] Internalised oral aggression, from *this* perspective, can certainly bring somatic zones into service of the unmetabolised or ineffective mental processes. Excessive affects that cannot be processed at the mental level are inclined to find a pathway through the somatic to 'bind' the excess neuronal energy from which affects and mental experience emerge, in the service of homeostatic restoration and maintenance. Solms notes that, "Variational free energy is a function of information exchange (not thermodynamic exchange) between a system and its environment".[24] Feeding the notion of helplessness, he argues that, "Certainly, to my way of thinking, the distinction between stereotyped (both innate and over-learned) and voluntary action is the essence of the difference between Freud's primary and secondary processes".[25]

An infant struggling with interoceptive or exteroceptive impingements and states of disequilibrium will protest through *inductive-crying* to force responsiveness from the maternal environment. When this fails, beyond a threshold, *helplessness* can prevail, exceeding the mental capacity to minimise free energy at the age and stage of the infant. If homeostatic balancing cannot be achieved through using conscious error predictions and 'reconsolidating' of memory, as an adult might be able to do, to remedy past frustrations, the infant remains stuck in a helpless state. If emotional binding or cathexis of excessive feelings remain inadequate, then free-energy will trend to increase, making the system of the mental apparatus less stable and threatening some form of mental decompensation – but from the subjectivity of the infant-without-worldy-perspective, this experience would represent a trend to entropy – the infant may feel themselves to be heading to destruct and die. In psychoanalytic terms, if the mind cannot bind the excess emotional energy of the system coming from early non-declarative memory systems, when cognitive facility is yet undeveloped, that being, for example, in the early oral stage of psychosexual development of the first year, then it must find a way to bind this energy and to balance the books of free-energy, minimising it to restore some semblance of homeostasis. From this perspective, then, such interpretations as Garma's mentioned above are not inherently quite so far-fetched.

If non-declarative memory traces represent automatised versions of old experience, in the after-glow of the primitive psyche's development, experiences of helplessness to influence outcomes (such as an infant in an incubator) can become imprinted, encoded into memory, even when not consciously or cognitively recalled. These may become automatised, nondeclarative circuits in memory which can be seen to ally with compulsions, or compulsive repetitive cycles from which conscious relief proves both resistant and often-time nigh impossible. Addictions seem to have this characteristic – automatised compulsions that remain extremely resistant to change, even in the face of their obvious destructive consequences and effects. Solms regards addictive repetitions as achieving immediate gratification without doing the necessary mental work, since, in my view, the mental work required exceeds the infantile part of the addict's capacity to remedy. Or, as Kinet points out, according to Bion, the patient "avoids *suffering the process of thinking*".[26] This is well-put, but might be thought of as missing two fundamental points, further consolidated in his statement (referencing Solms work) that although this is harmful and destructive, it "is not a result of a supposed death drive but a failing defence mechanism on the part of the Ego".[27] Let me address the implications of this point.

Omnipotence and Cardboard Bridges

If addiction is rooted in the very earliest stages of development where dys-regulation was prevalent and re-regulation to a homeostatic affective state was not achieved by the maternal mind-as-container, the helplessness and increasing mobilisation of frustration, and hence also of the aggressive drive being unleashed by the infant must eventually meet with an ignominious end at some point – even an infant can eventually realise its attempts to mobilise a remedy through screaming is proving ineffective. The infant must at some point give up, go quiet, dissociate, shut down its affect-protest, leading to a 'narcissistic' retreat from object-dependency to an internal but primitive self-soothing. This renders investment in the omnipotence of the care-giver to remedy needs subject to withdrawal, de-cathexis in the interest of finding the next best option to nudge towards homeostatic balance. This psychic man-oeuvre, coming at a time in early development when memory imprints to form the register of severe states of such disequilibrium, must then form part of the non-declarative and more fixed-patterning, that we note so character-istically in substance addiction. It is invariably rooted in early oral stages of primary narcissism so characteristic of the addict, a form of pre-genital 'masturbation' that Freud alludes to in his work.[28] The nett result of early injury and dysregulation means that addicts "are either flooded with unbearable painful affects (emotions), or they are devoid of or cut off from their feelings", says Khantzian.[29] A deeper probe into these extremes would suggest that the infantile part of the addict, to which they regress in the ser-vice of the addiction, had been stressed beyond their capacity to re-regulate and beyond their capacity to *induce* re-regulation from the caregiver through crying. As noted elsewhere, I have made the point that crying in infancy is driven by the aggressive drive as a mechanism to induce response from the auxiliary ego of the maternal object, to mobilise her to assist in restoring the infant to homeostasis, which it cannot do for itself in its early stages of helplessness and dependency.

Here, it may seem as if I part ways with authors such as Khantzian, Kinet, and Solms in suggesting that the regulating-preservative mechanism being evoked in early dysregulation is rendered ineffectual in prolonged dysregulation, but that it is precisely this death drive function, or this aggressive drive function, that is being required to do its work, but without recourse to object-inducement or other mental means in this early non-cognitive phase of development. Khantzian does acknowledge that in one part of the addictive process lies "the operative motive is to *control* feelings",[30] but this notion of control is not fully weighted for significance. Control suggests an omnipotence defence over the helplessness of the infantile part of the addict's experience, encoded in the memory of severe dysregulation. Turned inwards through primitive phantasy, this aggression can become omnipotent as a defence against the helplessness, and in later life turns to the ability to *omnipotently* control mental states without having to do the work necessary in the real world of frustrating objects. As Solms et al. note, "The motivation to perform the effortful work to achieve biologically useful goals in an indifferent and even hostile world is substituted by mere self-administration of pleasure-producing (or unpleasure-reducing) substances".[31] Normal satisfaction of needs requires mental work, since needs can never be fully met in isolation from the real world *out-there*. To paraphrase Solms' point that we feel like this *"about that"*,[32] means that internal needs require an engagement with objects in the real world to complete their satisfaction. Not so with addiction – whereby the outer world is effectively dispensed with to perform the work required, and in exchange a pill, prick, pinch, or clip can do the same thing sans such mental work. Feeling states too can, henceforth, disregard objects in the real world and substitute them internally. Solms et al., add that, "Part of the affective prize is thus attained without actually taking part in the social pursuit and competition for gratification. The biological purpose of reward is cheated. A cheap form of affect has been traded for reproductive fitness".[33]

Having one's fingers on the levers of (mental state's) control reflects an omnipotent-aggressive mechanism to create mental order and stasis out of the chaos and frustrations of the real world, without having to do the work required in this real world for it. Kinet cites the Dutch poet Sjoerd Kuyper's lines that I think captures this well: "If everything went well", he writes, "We started in such a cradle. Objectively: we were crippled by impotence. Subjectively: we were filled with omnipotence; or with reflections in a Golden I".[34]

The lessons of the addict's history speak to the pointlessness of so doing, replacing the real world with the omnipotent control of mental states though addictive replacement. Its rooting in pre-cognitive stages of development, that is, non-declarative automatised memory systems, gives addiction its hallmark resistance to change, insight, and efficacy. Insight tends to be of a pseudo-sort in addiction, often to manage others in their lives and sometimes to satisfy the internal, unconscious primitive manoeuvres that reality can be replaced by the use of the aggressive drive through phantasy and control, through pestering the arousal of helpless rage into the satisfaction of (a 'delusional' independent) omnipotence over helplessness. It is not the help-lessness of the addict that is central, so much touted by addiction theories and models, but the omnipotent aggression encoded in non-declarative, compulsive, and repetitive automatised predictions.

As we have suggested, one of the key hallmarks of addiction is replace-ment of the work required to meet needs in the real world with omnipotent control over the levers of mental and neurological systems. For Freud, authors such as Fonagy and Target note, "psychic reality poses a danger when there is imperfect discrimination ('reality testing') between stimuli from the outer world and those that arise as products of unconscious processes".[35] They add that, "Thus, there is normally a powerful developmental push towards integrating the modes of experiencing inner and outer reality, which allows the child to distinguish much more confidently between his internal and external experience".[36]

It could be said that the pleasure principle replaces the reality principle rather than supplementing it. Control driven by primitive oral aggression enables the compulsive nature of these repetitive patterns to embed when emotional work in later life makes itself felt, often in adolescence or early adulthood. Since life-drive emergent feelings require work in the real world to maintain homeostatic parameters, as do the needs these generate, and since helplessness may have dominated in the real world of early develop-ment, internal automatised mechanisms come to dominate the mental land-scape of the addict. Real-world work is no longer required – a pill, drink, or lever can move the needle up or down, left or right, and emulate real-world effects and need-satisfaction without the hopeless necessary requirement for work in a world encoded in memory as frustrating and 'murderous'. This is like buying a university degree rather than studying for it. The illusion of skill might prevail but not the reality that a false certificate represents. Kinet's point that pleasure is associated with consumption of an "object that satisfies a need", because the thing is "attractive and delicious" and pleasure results from "tension reduction and restoration of homeostasis"[37] is valid for the addict – but of course, the solutions to life-drive needs employing artifi-cial omnipotence get us so far, and no further, for, to paraphrase Freud, "... we might build bridges just as well out of cardboard as out of stone...and might use tear-gas as a narcotic instead of ether".[38]

The Intolerability of the Liminal Space

If, as Freud suggested, a drive appears as a concept on the frontier between the mental and the somatic, "as the psychical representative of the stimuli originating from within the organism and reaching the mind, as a measure of the demand made upon the mind for work in consequence of its connection with the body",[39] we notice that this liminal space between the body and emergent mind in addiction remains blurred.[40] To borrow Fonagy's concept, when overwhelmed by affects originating from somatic sources (in infancy) the ability for the infant to 'mentalise' these affects becomes impaired without adequate inputs from the maternal other. Target and Fonagy note that, current psychological theories stress mainly cognitive precursors of theory of mind in which the child is seen as an isolated processor of information, "engaged in the construction of a theory of mind from first principles, accumulating representations of the world through observation". From a psychoanalytic viewpoint, they argue, this is a barren picture that ignores the central role of the child's emotional relationship with the parents or other caregivers "in fostering the capacity to understand interactions in terms of mental states".[41]

They further argue that in the space between caregiver and infant, a host of mental processes occur. Citing seminal authors such as Bion and Rosenfeld, they argue that, at the heart of the child's relationship to the object lies the object's capacity to create a world for the child in which he may experience himself as a feeling, wanting, thinking being. They suggest that,

> Psychoanalysts take it for granted that the child's emotional experiences are not built in, but can only be properly developed in relationships which sustain those experiences, through what Kleinian analysts term 'healthy projective identification'. Unconsciously and pervasively, the caregiver ascribes a mental state to the child with her behaviour, this is gradually internalised by the child, and lays the foundations of a core sense of mental selfhood.[42]

When the quality of mental translation and reverie is sub-optimal, the infant may be forced to resort to its own primitive versions of mentalising, or making meaning out of *meaninglessness* [43] for its own account. Thus, say the authors, "We believe that moving away from the separation of pretend and psychic equivalent modes of experiencing psychic reality requires the prior development of a healthy core self, as described above. It is the child's capacity to depict mental states symbolically that enables him to construct the world of subjectivity, in which feelings and thoughts can be real at the same time as not corresponding exactly to external reality, or to other people's versions of it".[44]

Whilst these authors grapple with development over time and the later stages of infancy, their concepts can be seen to apply from the outset. Psychical reality can replace external reality when the burden of sensory and affective accretions become excessive and free energy remains unbound or uncathected. Freud was fully aware of how the internal intra-psychic can either replace or command a virtual replacement of external frustration that exceed, what Fonagy thinks about as, a capacity for, albeit primitive, 'mentalising'. In Bion's terms, the beta function remains transcendent – not psychotic but impaired in the liminal space towards alpha-function – so that internal resources dominate over external ones with the magical powers such a *phantastical* solution bestows. As Solms et al., put it, referencing Freud's link of a narcissistic tendency that replaces the need to do mental work: "Substance abuse, like masturbation, represents a failure to negotiate the transition from infantile self-soothing to mastery of the real external world – the arena of all the competitions that we simply have to enter in order to survive and reproduce".[45]

Infants in this early oral phase overwhelmed by the impingements of their own situation and body may be forced to find a route through the intolerability of somatic demands; attempting to induce a return to homeostasis versus the inability to so achieve, given the immaturity of the mental apparatus in the early months. Making meaning out of the *meaningless* state is a most important developmental task to avoid the pull of psychosis in which, to use Bion's notion, beta elements prevail and a form of mental primordial soup remains the dominant experience. Retreat into internal omnipotent control enables a binding of free energy, a reduction of arousal, but with it a phenomenon is which form of autistic shell is revisited, which Freud describes as, "A neat example of a psychical system shut off from the stimuli of the external world, and able to satisfy even its nutritional requirements autistically (to use Bleuler's term [1912], is afforded by a bird's egg with its food supply enclosed in its shell; for it, the care provided by its mother is limited to the provision of warmth",[46] that is to the *idea* of the maternal provision rather than her mental embodiment.

Without the benefit of the 'mentalising' function of the (m)other, affective overload, the precursor to consciousness and cognition, embeds itself in a two-poled mental development: namely, an initial state of helplessness to remedy the *experience* of disequilibrium through crying, as an aggressive inducement from the object-environment, followed by a turning inwards and cathecting this aggressive energy at imaginary omnipotent objects. This latter manoeuvre appears frequently in the psychic make-up of addiction – an element of early helpless aggression over the failure of supply, to an omnipotent defence through which affective supply is easily and readily controlled – at the 'push of a button', so to speak. This is like having the ability to dial-a-fix and push affect needs up, down, or sideways without the usual necessity for mental work, and, as mentioned, appears to underpin the phenomenon. Important to note is that the prevailing concept of addiction-helpless may be true as the underlying trigger for a more significant 'solution' but ends up being no solution at all. There simply is no artificial substitute for the work required to reregulate needs and feelings since these can invariably only be met in the outer world or real objects, real attachments, real sex, real food, real highs and lows, and so on. In other words, real embodiment is required to satisfy needs rather than the artificial or virtual embodiment that can come through chemical or electronic substitutes.

The infant that has struggled in the liminal space, intolerable as it can become when prolonged, where there is enough development and mentalising to progress beyond the psychosis of denial of reality and substituting it for an internal reality addiction, can take root. It is to a stage and state in which it substitutes the frustration of the ineffectualness of the aggressive drive mobilising, for the phantasy of omnipotent control over the source of supply and the fulfilment of needs. In babies left to cry, for example, for medical reasons or poor maternal attunement, the infant may hover in this liminal space and fixate there, encoding into memory the need for omnipotent control for future feedforward use. Omnipotent control that bypasses the real work required to fulfil needs and satisfy feelings can become embedded as a psychical 'solution' in the mental realm in infancy and later returned to when life presents its challenges and frustrations.

Beyond Liminality

It can be seen, as most theorists would happily agree, that whatever we call it, the mentalising function of the maternal object plays a critical role in assisting the infant to convert beta into alpha elements, to make meaning out of experience, and to find emotional containment. It enables the transcending of the somatic *into* the emergent mental through the 'doorway' of the liminal space – that transitional, in-between, emergent space so common in nature. Such is the function of the maternal mind that without this attunement being proper, amplified, effective, and reasonably accurate, the liminal space between internal affects and their signals of regulation-dysregulation, pleasure-unpleasure, become blurry – rather than crisp – in the mentalising function of the infant. Transitional spaces abound in nature and life, from the inanimate to the animate, the objective to the subjective, and the raw undigested to the 'mental solids' that Solms argues is achieved through the cortical function in higher order humans.[47] This is significant, because Solms offers us a neuroscientific rendering of the mental functions of turning the beta into alpha in Bion's model, or primary process into secondary process in a Freudian sense, in which raw affects are stabilised and cathected in order to bind the free energy and minimise it in the interests of stability, given mental representation and meaning through ideation, and the throttling of the entropic tendency of too much free energy that comes from excessive emotional arousal.

To reiterate, the Free Energy Principle suggests that nature must bind free energy to minimise it in the interests of economic functioning, achieving much by expending little, since the 'predictive brain' is revealed neuroscientifically to be 'lazy', at least over the long term, "vigilant for every opportunity to achieve more by doing less", as Solms points out.[48] When affect dysregulation in the early infant exceeds its capacity to 'bind' or 'cathect' this energy, added psychical manoeuvres will be required to prevent the slip into total fragmentation or psychosis, and with addiction we notice that replacing the need to seek satisfaction in the real world (too frustrating) with the internal (but as yet undeveloped) world leads to omnipotent phantasies and compromise remedies. These enable the infant in later post-pubescent or adult life to control and regulate internal states without the need for the mental work required in the real world.

It appears from clinical observation that many addicts suffer from a blunting of inner affects in the normal course, and as Solms et al. point out from a neuroscientific point of view, "that individuals with blunted SEEKING capacities come to learn (especially if not otherwise helped by parents, educators and the like) that substances which produce massive surges of D2-mediated activity enable them to *gain access to pleasurable experiences and objects in the outside world* that would otherwise be relatively inaccessible to them".[49] Put in psychological terms, the over-arousal of unpleasure affects that suffered poor remediation from the (m)other in early oral development, means that the infant's feelings were pushing for life-drive needs to be met in the interests of homeostatic settling. However, when homeostatic (life) drive needs are failing to be met, and extorting a real satisfaction of the libido is failing, frustration increases, mobilising the aggressive (death) drive to bind the excess free energy, and which seems, eventually, to lead to a shutting down of the aggressive protest as its effectiveness at remedy proves increasingly ineffectual, and in some senses counter-helpful as it increases rather than decreases frustration and the pain of a poor remedy. Of course, this is not always a result of an inattentive mother but sometimes circumstance, such as the infant's own medical or somatic challenges, which create the experience of over-arousal and for which no soothing is possible. As I mentioned, think of an infant left to cry out in an incubator due to illness or vulnerability in the post-partum period. No fault if the Neo Natal ICU is required to maintain biological survival. Whilst not an automatic predisposing factor, such helpless rage from circumstances such as these, seem to be a characteristic of many addicts.

Such are these characteristics we observe in the various forms of addiction, that I regard disruption in the liminal space to be central to its dynamic. Excess affects (and rising free energy) become omnipotently controlled (bound), and through (primitive) phantasy and defence reduced to a more manageable level. Of course, this mechanism serves a conservative function, restoring to homeostasis a dysregulated mind whose function is to enable conservation of the self-organising system, of which the mind plays its role in a liminal space between the internal and external worlds. This liminal space applies at two levels: between the infant and the external world is the maternal bridge, the mind of the mother interpreting, regulating, mediating between the infant and its experience of reality; but also, there lies between the unconscious primitive brain sensations and experiences and the emergent psychic apparatus being formed, a liminal layer wherein the unconscious meets consciousness-forming. In these two spaces in addiction, it appears that disruption plays a part and the layer remains poorly formed. The subjective experience of this is that affects, needs, and feelings, responding to the stresses of life and living, do not metabolise well, and the aggressive drive initially mobilised remains ineffective, leading to mental defences having to play their part and fixating there.

Much addiction research focuses on the pleasure-seeking aspects of addiction, including some neuroscience, noting as Solms et al. do, that "it appears that the main focus of the addiction process must still fall back, to a substantial degree, on the pleasurable aspects of rewards. This, and not just the primary SEEKING instinct or the drugs that stimulate it (or the paraphernalia associated with those drugs), seems to remain the ultimate psychological object of addiction, at least at the higher levels of the mental apparatus".[50] But omnipotent control over pleasure is a potent defence against the helplessness of increasing unpleasure pushing the infant (and the infant within the adult addict) outside their viable homeostatic bounds.

Hence, addicts feel the need to unwind, down or up regulate through artificial means. And the immediate sensation is, of course, pleasurable. But pleasure is also the tempering of unpleasure, finding synthetic (that is omnipotent) means to reregulate. Since regulating back to homeostasis, when life-drive measures do not succeed, falls into the domain of the aggressive drive, we can argue that the pleasure-seeking elements of addiction represents only part of the story. Effectively, an omnipotent response driven by the conservative drive – namely, the aggressive (death) drive – takes over from the work of the mind in the real world and replaces it with the capacity and yen to simply switch on and off at will what needs are required, and which feelings drive the chase for regulation and re-regulation, that is, to also down-regulate emotional pain often linked to perception of loss and longing.

Interestingly, neuroscientists link the brain circuits for opioid addiction with attachment and separation, seeing attachment as a primary form of addiction. "Anyone who has fallen in love knows the truth of this statement. Being in love with someone is almost indistinguishable from being addicted to them. This, surely then, is the major biological endophenotype that is hijacked by substance abuse".[51] If the implication of this is that,"(a)ddiction, like masturbation, is a substitute and replacement not only for general mastery of the object world, but specifically for the attainment of a secure love object",[52] we can note that the 'substitution and replacement' ("to actually replace the object"[53]) by the addiction for the real world is a process of aggrandisement, omnipotence, control over not only the external world, but the addict's own brain pathways. This magical power to achieve homeostatic settling points without the need for mental work is in itself driven by the substitution for the failure of protest in the real world (of the infant) to induce homeostasis through protest, crying, and so on, with an internal resort of the death drive through retreat into omnipotent phantasy, binding arousal through its primitive mental representations. This locates the death drive centrally on the genesis of addiction rather than the helplessness model which represents only the first part of the causal chain. Khantzian makes the point poetically that, "The 'marginal person' in each of us can consider the potentials and limitations in one another's perspectives and then we must wait on the rare 'Renaissance person' who can ultimately bridge the different domains and explain how they all come together. This is how we advance our sciences and our civilisation, and it is how we address what ails us as individuals and as a society".[54] Indeed, as different theorists notice the different sides of the same complex phenomenon, each represents a partial truth of the whole. What remains is to put the theoretical pieces together.

The integration of modern neuroscience and psychoanalysis brings to the fore that the two primary drives that occupy every organic entity, the libidinal drive to evolutionary variation and the conservative one maintaining the Markov blanket of an organic self-organising entity, underly the addictive process too. However, the form this takes is in the foregrounding of the conservative-aggressive response to excessive helpless rage, often manifest through early crying and other homeostatic regulatory mechanisms being exceeded, leading to omnipotent phantasy and mental defences mobilising as a binding mechanism of homeostatic re-regulation. The regression to this part of the psyche relies on the reactivation of the aggressive drive in the form of omnipotent control over states of dysregulation and in this world of phantasy, the addict no longer has to lean into or rely on external objects and external reality for remedy. The substance, over which full control is apparently present, does the job better – were it not, of course, for the caveat that dependency on substances rather than objects solves one set of problems for the infant-in-the-addict, but generates much bigger ones over time, since needs can only be fulfilled in the real world of objects and supplies.

Notes

1 Solms, M., Pantelis, E. and Panksepp, J. (2015) Neuropsychoanalytic notes on addiction, p.176. In Solms, et al., *The Feeling Brain*. Routledge: London/ New York, p. 175.
2 https://www.ncbi.nlm.nih.gov/pmc/articles/PMC3905522/
3 https://www.12keysrehab.com/addiction-and-learned-helplessness/
4 Khantzian, E. J. (2003) Understanding Addictive Vulnerability: An Evolving Psychodynamic Perspective. *Neuropsychoanalysis* 5:5–21, p.11.
5 Jones, D. B. (2009) Addiction and Pathological Accommodation: An Intersubjective Look at Impediments to the Utilisation of Alcoholics Anonymous. *International Journal of Psychoanalytic Self Psychology* 4:212–234, p.216.
6 Dodes, L. (2017) Addiction, Helplessness, and Narcissistic Rage. *Psychoanalytic Quarterly*, LIX, 1990; published online (2017): https://doi.org/10.1080/21674086. 1990.11927278
7 Wang, C., Zhang, K., and Zhang, M. (2017) Social Behaviour and Personality. *An International Journal* 45(2), pp. 269–280(12).

8 Jones, D. B. (2009) Addiction and Pathological Accommodation: An Inter-subjective Look at Impediments to the Utilisation of Alcoholics Anonymous. *International Journal of Psychoanalytic Self Psychology* 4:212–234, p.215.

9 Freud, S. (1897) Letter 79 Extracts From The Fliess Papers. *The Standard Edition of the Complete Psychological Works of Sigmund Freud* 1:272–273, p.272.

10 Freud, S. (1898) Sexuality in the Aetiology of the Neuroses. *The Standard Edition of the Complete Psychological Works of Sigmund Freud* 3:259–285, p.275.

11 Freud, S. (1898) Sexuality in the Aetiology of the Neuroses. *The Standard Edition of the Complete Psychological Works of Sigmund Freud* 3:259–285, p.276.

12 Freud, S. (1928) Dostoevsky and Parricide. *The Standard Edition of the Complete Psychological Works of Sigmund Freud* 21:173–194, p.193.

13 Freud, S. (1928) Dostoevsky and Parricide. *The Standard Edition of the Complete Psychological Works of Sigmund Freud* 21:173–194, p.194.

14 Freud, S. (1920) The psychogenesis of a case of homosexuality in a woman. The Standard Edition of the Complete Psychological Works of Sigmund Freud 18, p.167.

15 Khantzian, E. J. (2003) Understanding Addictive Vulnerability: An Evolving Psychodynamic Perspective. *Neuropsychoanalysis* 5:5–21, p.6.

16 Khantzian, E. J. (2003) Understanding Addictive Vulnerability: An Evolving Psychodynamic Perspective. *Neuropsychoanalysis* 5:5–21, p.8.

17 To use Panksepp's neurobiological nomenclature for the libidinal drive that seeks pleasure to avoid unpleasure and return an organism to homeostasis. See Panksepp, J. & Biven, L. (2012) *The Archaeology of Mind: Neuroevolutionary Origins of Human Emotions.* New York: Norton.

18 Khantzian, E. J. (2003) Understanding Addictive Vulnerability: An Evolving Psychodynamic Perspective. *Neuropsychoanalysis* 5:5–21, p.8.

19 Freud, S. (1920) The psychogenesis of a case of homosexuality in a woman. The Standard Edition of the Complete Psychological Works of Sigmund Freud 18, 1955, p. 167.

20 Brickman, B. (1988) Psychoanalysis and Substance Abuse: Toward a More Effective Approach. *Journal of the American Academy of Psychoanalysis* 16:359–379, p.366.

21 Garma, A. (1958) Peptic Ulcer in Psychoanalysis, Williams and Wilkins, Baltimore, cited in B. Brickman, (1988) Psychoanalysis and Substance Abuse: Toward a More Effective Approach. *Journal of the American Academy of Psychoanalysis* 16:359–379, p.366.

22 Solms, M. (2020) Response to the commentaries on the "New Project". *Neuropsychoanalysis* 22:97–107, p.99.

23 Solms, M. (2020) Response to the commentaries on the "New Project". *Neuropsychoanalysis* 22:97–107, p.99.

24 Solms, M. (2020) Response to the commentaries on the "New Project". *Neuropsychoanalysis* 22:97–107, p.99.

25 Solms, M. (2020) Response to the commentaries on the "New Project". *Neuropsychoanalysis* 22:97–107, p.101.

26 Kinet, M. (2024) *The Spirit of the Drive in Neuropsychoanalysis.* Routledge: London/ New York, p.96.

27 Kinet, M. (2024) *The Spirit of the Drive in Neuropsychoanalysis.* Routledge: London/ New York, p.96.

28 See Freud, S. (1928) Dostoevsky and Parricide. *The Standard Edition of the Complete Psychological Works of Sigmund Freud* 21:173–194, p.193.

29 Khantzian, E. J. (2003) Understanding Addictive Vulnerability: An Evolving Psychodynamic Perspective. *Neuropsychoanalysis* 5:5–21, p.14.

30 Khantzian, E. J. (2003) Understanding Addictive Vulnerability: An Evolving Psychodynamic Perspective. *Neuropsychoanalysis* 5:5–21, p.15 (italics mine).

31 Mark Solms, Eleni Pantelis, Jaak Panksepp (2015) Neuropsychoanalytic notes on addiction. *The Feeling Brain*. London/ New York: Routledge, p.176.

32 Solms, M., (2022) The Hidden Spring: A Journey to the Source of Consciousness.

33 Solms, M., Pantelis, E., and Panksepp, J. (2015) Neuropsychoanalytic notes on addiction. *The Feeling Brain*. London/ New York: Routledge, p.176.

34 Kinet, M. (2024) *The Spirit of the Drive in Neuropsychoanalysis*. London/ New York: Routledge, p.101.

35 Fonagy, P. & Target, M. (1996) Playing With Reality: I. Theory Of Mind And The Normal Development Of Psychic Reality. *International Journal of Psychoanalysis* 77:217–233, p.218.

36 Fonagy, P. & Target, M. (1996) Playing With Reality: I. Theory Of Mind And The Normal Development Of Psychic Reality. *International Journal of Psychoanalysis* 77:217–233, p.219.

37 Kinet, M. (2024) *The Spirit of the Drive in Neuropsychoanalysis*. Routledge: London/ New York, p.121.

38 Freud, S. (1933) New Introductory Lectures On Psycho-Analysis. *The Standard Edition of the Complete Psychological Works of Sigmund Freud* 22:1–182, p.176.

39 Freud, S. (1915) Instincts and their Vicissitudes. *The Standard Edition of the Complete Psychological Works of Sigmund Freud* 14:109–140, p.121–122.

40 Liminality is a term used to describe the psychological process of transitioning across boundaries and borders. The term "limen" comes from the Latin for threshold; it is literally the threshold separating one space from another. It is the place in the wall where people move from one room to another. Often a door is placed across the threshold to close up and restrict access between rooms. The concept was first applied to psychology as the technical name for the perceptual threshold, the degree of stimulus intensity that would just be noticed as audible or visible or detectable in any sensory mode. But its contemporary usage comes from the anthropologist Arnold van Gennep (1873–1957). In his study of religion as a cultural artefact, he saw that many, if not all, of the rituals across cultures have the function of moving a person from one status or social circumstance to another. In https://link.springer.com/referenceworkentry/10.1007/978-1-4614-6086-2_387#:~: text=Liminality is a term used, from one room to another.

41 Target, M. & Fonagy, P. (1996) Playing With Reality: II. The Development Of Psychic Reality From A Theoretical Perspective. *International Journal of Psychoanalysis* 77:459–479, p.461.

42 Target, M. & Fonagy, P. (1996) Playing With Reality: II. The Development Of Psychic Reality From A Theoretical Perspective. *International Journal of Psychoanalysis* 77:459–479, p.461.

43 See my concept on this in Perkel, A. (2023). *Unlocking the Nature of Human Aggression: A Psychoanalytic and Neuroscientific Approach*. London/ New York: Routledge.

44 Target, M. & Fonagy, P. (1996) Playing With Reality: II. The Development Of Psychic Reality From A Theoretical Perspective. *International Journal of Psychoanalysis* 77:459–479, p.462.

45 Solms, M., Pantelis, E., and Panksepp, J. (2015) Neuropsychoanalytic notes on addiction. *The Feeling Brain*. London/ New York: Routledge, p.176.

46 Freud, S. (1911) Formulations on the Two Principles of Mental Functioning. *The Standard Edition of the Complete Psychological Works of Sigmund Freud* 12:213–226, p.219.

47 "The answer to our question, 'What does cortex contribute to consciousness?', then, is this: it contributes representational memory space. This enables cortex to

stabilise the objects of perception, which in turn creates potential for detailed and synchronised processing of perceptual images. This contribution derives from the unrivalled capacity of cortex for *representational* forms of memory (in all of its varieties, both short and long-term). Based on this capacity, cortex transforms the fleeting, wavelike states of brainstem activation into 'mental solids.' It generates *objects.* Freud called them "object-presentations" (which, ironically, predominate in what he called the 'system unconscious')." Solms, M. (2013) The Conscious Id, *Neuropsychoanalysis*, 2013, 15(1), p.12.

48 Solms, M. (2021) *The Hidden Spring: A Journey to the Source of Consciousness.* London: Profile Books, p. 176.

49 Solms, M., Pantelis, E., and Panksepp, J. (2015) Neuropsychoanalytic notes on addiction. *The Feeling Brain.* London/ New York: Routledge, p.179.

50 Solms, M., Pantelis, E., and Panksepp, J. (2015) Neuropsychoanalytic notes on addiction. *The Feeling Brain.* London/ New York: Routledge, p.179.

51 Solms, M., Pantelis, E., and Panksepp, J. (2015) Neuropsychoanalytic notes on addiction. *The Feeling Brain.* London/ New York: Routledge, p.180.

52 Solms, M., Pantelis, E., and Panksepp, J. (2015) Neuropsychoanalytic notes on addiction. *The Feeling Brain.* London/ New York: Routledge, p.181.

53 Solms, M., Pantelis, E., and Panksepp, J. (2015) Neuropsychoanalytic notes on addiction. *The Feeling Brain.* London/ New York: Routledge, p.181.

54 Khantzian, E. J. (2003) Understanding Addictive Vulnerability: An Evolving Psychodynamic Perspective. *Neuropsychoanalysis* 5:5–21, p.18.

Chapter 9

Eating Disorders
The Breast

Let us begin this chapter with a reminder. The maternal breast remains one of the most powerful and enduring of *leitmotifs* in the human psyche. This soft but prominent part of a woman's body captivates both grownups and infants alike, loaded with powerful symbolism of both erotic and maternal associations. As an archetype of the human psyche, it occupies an extraordinary place of symbol and power, compelling and evocative, as Freud notes, the "...child's first and most vital activity, his sucking at his mother's breast, or at substitutes for it, that must have familiarised him with this pleasure".[1] Yet, strangely, this human feature can straddle competing worlds, some may say opposing ones, of two incompatible and yet conflated emblems, namely, the purely erotic with all its sexual (profane) effects and the purely maternal, with all its pure and entirely desexualised and apparently innocent and pure elements. There is probably no other symbol in the human condition capable of mustering this much power, this much evocative association, and this much ambiguity, as Freud suggests: "There are thus good reasons why a child sucking at his mother's breast has become the prototype of every relation of love. The finding of an object is in fact a refinding of it",[2] and yet simultaneously this symbol occupies two incompatible and contradictory mental spaces.

The breast is in many psychical respects, an emblem that is all powerful and consuming, dominating the earliest of object relations, introducing to the infant its own ego development from raw id drives and reflexes (such as the sucking and rooting reflex), turning raw primary process into what Solms calls "mental solids" over time. Melanie Klein describes it thus:

"The way in which this is achieved is through its earliest object relations. The breast, on which the life and death instincts are projected, is the first object which by introjection is internalised. In this way both instincts find an object to which they attach themselves and thereby by projection and re-introjection the ego is enriched as well as strengthened".[3]

For both infant and grown-up, the breast occupies a unique place in fostering both the physical nourishment required to sustain life, but also to provide the conduit for the flow of mental projections between mother and

DOI: 10.4324/9781003628972-10

infant in the early stages of life. The breast also represents an invitation, a mechanism to captivate scopophilically the visual lens of men along a pathway of arousal whose evolutionary aim is copulation and the fertilisation of new life. This ambiguity of place, between the profane and the pure, the erotic and the maternal, is a fascinating example of how nature straddles two faces in many of its functions, but which demands navigation in the many conflicts this ambiguity can engender. Our focus in this chapter is less about its erotic power, as significant as this is, but more on the maternal function the breast plays, not only as an obvious source of nourishment physiologically, but for the exceedingly powerful psychical role this organ plays in the mental development of the infant, becoming, as Freud noted, "the prototype of every relation of love".[4] For Klein, this function is even more considered and significant, writing:

> I have often expressed my view that object relations exist from the beginning of life, the first object being the mother's breast which is split into a good (gratifying) and bad (frustrating) breast; this splitting results in a division between love and hate. I have further suggested that the relation to the first object implies its introjection and projection, and thus from the beginning object relations are moulded by an interaction between introjection and projection, between internal and external objects and situations.[5]

It may appear obvious that for the infant the breast is associated with all that is good, sustaining, comforting and soothing, that Klein suggests "springs from the power of the instinctual desires which aim at unlimited gratification and therefore create the picture of an inexhaustible and always bountiful breast—an ideal breast".[6] The infant seeks the breast, what Klein refers to as "taken in under the dominance of the sucking libido",[7] and draws both mental and physical nourishment from it, owing its survival and development to the libidinal drive (what neuroscientists think of as the SEEKING system[8] interfacing with a maternal CARE system) that pushes it to bond with the mother and her representative in the form of the breast. The breast represents many layers of the human psyche, from the outset of life, serving as the main conduit through which re-regulation is achieved for a new-born infant. We could suggest that the breast is the chief mechanism through which both somatic and psychic regulation is achieved and for which there is no *ideal* substitute. For most theorists of infant development in psychoanalysis, the breast plays an outsized role in its extension of the maternal psyche and in many respects the access point of the infant to the maternal mind, especially in the early stages of the symbiotic orbit and its autistic stage,[9] as Mahler puts it, and as Klein suggests, "From the beginning of life the two instincts attach themselves to objects, first of all the mother's breast".[10]

Of course, the breast does not metabolise anything and has no mind as such, yet carries extraordinary weight in its role in human development and mental processing. It represents to the infant just such a thing – a mechanism and conduit capable of providing, absorbing, *metabolising*, and responding – initially only as a 'part-object' rather than the extension of the whole object, which emerges psychically only with time and development. The extension of the breast into the maternal object as a *whole* person owning the breast emerges over time. In the early phases of development, the good and bad experiences at the breast become also good and bad experiences *of* the breast, and link to two primary fundamental drives present from the outset, namely, the tension between the good and bad, pleasure and unpleasure, the seeking-libidinal to meet needs when homeostasis is deviant, and the conservative-aggressive, which is aroused to bind excess arousal when needs are being frustrated.

These drives have a relationship not only to the infant but to each other, working in tandem to limit surprisal and combat the risks associated with free energy rising. Freud noted that the drives have a relationship to each other, albeit an incomplete model, regarding the fusing and defusing of the drives, "'This hypothesis opens up a line of investigation which may someday be of great importance for our understanding of pathological processes.' For fusions may be undone, and such defusions of instincts may be expected to bring about the most serious consequences to adequate functioning".[11] Klein argues that the two primary drives play a pivotal role both in and at the breast, agreeing with Freud but embellishing on the relationship between the drives, that the development of the ego in connection with the functioning of the two instincts occurs by the introjection of the mother's feeding breast, which lays the foundation for all internalisation processes. "According to whether destructive impulses or feelings of love predominate, the breast (for which the bottle can symbolically come to stand) is felt at times to be good, at times to be bad." She explains that the libidinal cathexis of the breast, together with gratifying experiences that go with this experience, "builds up in the infant's mind the primal good object, the projection on the breast of destructive impulses the primal bad object". Since both these aspects are introjected, the life and death instincts, which had been projected, "again operate within the ego". This leads to the need to master persecutory anxiety and, as she describes, "gives impetus to splitting the breast and mother, externally and internally, into a helpful and loved and, on the other hand, a frightening and hated object. These are the prototypes of all subsequent internalised objects".[12]

Projection and Splitting

It thus may be viewed that from the infant's perspective and subjectivity, the breast can be *associated* with all things good, the rudimentary mind of the infant experiencing and over time *interpreting* this part-object as a psychical representative of the whole maternal object. She can have an (uncanny) ability to respond to states of dysregulation originating in the somatic realm, and restore homeostasis to the infant's body as if by magical means of attunement. This allows for the re-regulation of the infant's emotional states and particularly when they threaten with an experience of entropy, or annihilatory anxieties when frustration is too abundant. Since as we know from Solms,[13] for example, when crying signals disruptions and deviation from perfect homeostasis, even the primitive feelings of infancy begin to provide the *qualia* from which objective somatic states can be experienced (leading to, and in the subjective realm), and require a response in its aim to restore homeostasis when it is disrupted. So, the emerging *mind* of the infant develops the capacity to be a representative of its own somatic states of stasis or dysregulation, that being the movement away from or towards states of comfort, or what Freud would refer to as pleasure versus unpleasure in his earlier work on the pleasure-principle. It forms from a formless state and associates (that is projects) its internal mental states onto and *into* the breast, which is also the locus and source of its ability to regulate and reregulate.

But the breast is not always so perfectly responsive, attuned, or alive to the immediate needs of the infant. In this stage of development, which Freud identified as dominated by oral reflexes and needs, oral frustrations are also inevitable. Whilst the positive libidinal drive dominates the yearning and *push* to attach to the breast, frustration must activate the drive designed for restoration and conservation, namely, the aggressive drive, which activates infantile crying aimed at inducing a response from the environment. It may be successful or partially so, or sometimes not at all, and the infant must either give up or find alternative mechanisms to manage the prolonged states of frustration, discomfort, or homeostatic disruption. Put differently, the breast can become associated with bad feelings. Klein understood this splitting of good and bad in these primitive mental days in development, noting, and as regards splitting of the object, we have to remember, she says, that in states of gratification love feelings turn towards the gratifying breast, while in states of frustration hatred and persecutory anxiety attach themselves to the frustrating breast. "This twofold relation, implying a division between love and hatred in relation to the object, can only be maintained by splitting the breast into its good and bad aspects".[14]

If we remember Klein's implied point that primitive and developing minds rely on primitive mechanisms that are *emergent* and *in process*, then feel-good and feel-bad become reference points for emergent consciousness. Neuroscientifically, Solms makes a similar point that,

"The internal aspect of consciousness 'feels like' something. Above all, the phenomenal states of the body-as-subject are experienced *affectively*. Affects do not emanate from the external sense modalities. They are states *of the subject*. These states are thought to represent the biological value of changing internal conditions (e.g., hunger, sexual arousal). When internal conditions favour survival and reproductive success, they feel 'good'; when not, they feel 'bad.' This is evidently what conscious states are *for*. Conscious feelings tell the subject how well it is doing. At this level of the brain, therefore, consciousness is closely tied to homeostasis".[15]

Now, of course, this is not suggesting that an infant has the sentient, reflexive consciousness of an older child or adult – clearly this is acquired over decades in humans – but that when states of disequilibrium predominate, they tip the valenced perception of the infant into a state of 'feel bad', which must evoke a mechanism to pull the infant back towards homeostasis or it risks perishing. The infant cannot unilaterally achieve any physical or psychical remedy in its fused merger with the maternal object – it is obviously helpless and further, trapped in a *meaningless* psychical state initially – for which the mind of the mother must be recruited to both read and respond to the baby's signals of breaches to homeostasis. The breast serves such a function for both physical and psychical restoration, providing all the goodness but also when failing, must be perceived to be the source of frustration and badness. Feel-bad sources are by their nature, or by *its* nature in the breast – persecutory, and must induce an aggressive response from the infant, fussing, niggling, or crying to *induce* a response from the environment to being about quiescence. This induction is a forceful process – it *induces* – and this induction can be understood to originate from the restorative drive, that is, the death drive. Hate, as Klein identifies it, is embedded in these processes since it captures the internal state of the infant in a feel-bad state, it enables a crude rudimentary feeling experience to signal unpleasure. As she says, "This struggle has the effect that in so far as the infant wants to preserve the loved aspects of the good mother, internal and external, he must continue to split love from hate and thus to maintain the division of the mother into a good one and a bad one".[16] Another way of putting this, is that in this early stage where mentation is yet undeveloped, states are either good or bad, and rather undifferentiated in this regard – hence the polarity of good *or* bad, rather than good *and* bad, a character also, for example, of later borderline states, to which such personalities regress.

Hate and Its Objects

The projection that Klein identifies onto, and in her preference *into* the maternal breast when states of disequilibrium create ruptures to homeostasis, become associated with the 'badness' of the breast. Or, more simply, the breast itself *becomes* bad through projection of the aggressive response evoked by its perceived frustration or failure. Anna Freud, addressing slighter later development, nonetheless captures the inner tensions of the infant and their navigating a 'solution' to the inevitable challenges of life, notes that,

Simultaneously the ego begins to correlate conflicting emotions and tendencies instead of giving alternate expression to them. This means suppressing one or the other side of them (love or hate, active or passive desires, etc.), and creates new conflicts between ego and id. But although all these efforts are made by the ego to assert itself against the instincts, no real ego superiority is established in the first period of childhood.[17]

The conflict between ego and id is rudimentary and primitive, the primitive ego representing a gradual emergence of a layer of psychic skin, or as Bion refers to the process of turning beta into alpha elements, in which "beta-elements are stored but differ from alpha-elements in that they are not so much memories as undigested facts, whereas the alpha-elements have been digested by alpha-function and thus made available for thought. It is important to distinguish between memories and undigested facts—beta-elements".[18] This process is never purely reality-driven without deep associative elements influencing perception. The infant does not conclude the breast/ world is bad by reading a newspaper; it concludes this according to the trend that it *feels* in its feel-good or feel-bad dichotomy. When it is feel-bad, the aggressive mechanism (of psychical immunity) activates feelings that trigger representations for which 'conscious' associations are created.

This primitive 'thinking' is a form of making meaning out of the (primordial) *meaningless* state, but as we can note, driven by *affects* that imbue the breast with associations of badness. Frustration activates feelings in the infant that are at once both aggressive and persecutory – the aggression is within but also without, creating paranoid ideation for which the infant has little remedy but to try preserve the good breast by separating out the bad one and projecting it into the external world. "However, even at this early stage, and even under very favourable conditions, the conflict between love and hate (or, to put it in Freud's terms, between libidinal and destructive impulses) plays an important rôle in this relation. Frustrations, which to some extents are unavoidable, strengthen hate and aggressiveness",[19] notes Klein, because in neuroscientific terms, it is this drive that must activate to bind excess arousal when needs are not being adequately or quickly enough addressed.

This projection as a psychic mechanism has survival value and enables the psyche to preserve itself, by separating sources of pleasure from those of pain, the latter, which it seeks to externalise. Freud made the point that in the process of projecting inner conflicts outwards, the psyche "has separated off parts of its own self, which it projects into the external world and feels as hostile. After this new arrangement, the two polarities coincide once more; the ego-subject coincides with pleasure, and the external world with unpleasure…".[20]

In relation to the breast, the infant comes to, as Freud put it, feel the 'repulsion' of the object, and hate it, suggesting that this hate can be intensified to the point of an aggressive inclination against the object – an intention to destroy it... "Indeed", he asserts, "it may be asserted that the true prototypes of the relation of hate are derived not from sexual life, but from the ego's struggle to preserve and maintain itself".[21] 'Maintain itself' reflects the need in early life to channel the bad affects (frustration and hatred) into more harmless objects via phantasy. Such phantasy is not the sort like an adult daydream – these primitive ideational representations are deeply and powerfully affect-driven, since, in early life, affects and feel-good or feel-bad deviations from homeostasis predominate. Add to this that the differentiation between internal and external reality is still diffuse, and the boundary between the mother's and the infant's minds are indistinguishable, from the infant's point of view at least, which renders the breast (and mother) both a loved and hated object. Without adequate resolution through maternal metabolising, or for prolonged discomforts due to other biological or medical factors in either mother or infant, this can lead to a fixation of these affects projected into the breast, and stick there intrapsychically as an association to the mother and what her breast represents. More precisely, primitive defensive manoeuvres of splitting, projection, and introjection become fixated in some infants, and the excessive rising free energy of arousal bound, automatised in implicit memory through these defences, and stored for later 'efficient' navigation of life's frustrations when triggers present.

Di-phasic Return of the Repressed

Such unconscious fixations, described above, are well known in psychoanalytic work and theory, and it is a short step to recognising that when the breast remains hated, and there is a persecutory connection the bad breast may have for the infant, one of the unfortunate manifestations may be its association also to food, feeding, and nourishment. In other words, in the persecutory milieu of the frustrated infant, the milk of the breast may be experienced as sour, poison in fact, that is best kept out for survival. In time, these associations recede from conscious awareness, in that no obvious recollection of issues at the breast appear to remain from this non-declarative form of early memory. The maternal object may be beloved and valued, and the old rages and persecutory anxieties disappear. That is, until the second wave of psychosexual development takes hold as puberty ascends and the return of many earlier pre-latency memories becomes re-referenced. In terms of the neuroscience of memory, the implicit nature of early infantile experience makes it also 'non-declarative', as mentioned before – these encoded experiences cannot be consciously declared except through the *emotional* life it brings to triggers and their associations.

But the influence of these early memories is nonetheless great – in fact greatest – since the earliest imprints and memories carry enormous emotional valence given that the experience for the infant is total rather than partial, as occurs with older children and adults. Kinet elaborates on this point, arguing that as early as the end of pregnancy, relational and affective patterns are recorded in implicit memory. "The earliest experiences stored there for a structural part of this unconscious and assert their influence on adult life. In this way, they permanently influence later relationships' depth and emotional colour".[22] These imprints play a pivotal and outsized role in later personality and object-attachment since their valence is intense and subjectively encoded. Notes Kinet, "The 'natural' ways a person is present in the world and interacts with others belongs to the domain of implicit memory... So, this implicit knowledge is not remembered but enacted or acted out".[23] In other words, initially intangible emotional states can become deeply concretised and acted out in concrete fashions, rather than mentalised and metabolised in later life. The infant's early hatred of the breast that persecutes it through frustrations and disruptions may often then wend its way into later post-pubescent mental life, associating not with the breast per se, but with other sources of nourishment, sustenance, soothing, and of course, food in its most concrete form.

Anna Freud wrote that when the second wave of psychosexual development emerges at puberty, old pre-latency organisations and affects return, overthrowing ego superiority, because "of the biological increase in pregenital tendencies during pre-puberty, and genital tendencies during puberty, the libidinal forces rise in strength. Throughout adolescence ego forces and id forces struggle with each other for the upper hand, a combat that is responsible for many of the conflicting and abnormal manifestations of that period".[24]

Whilst Anna Freud's focus, alongside her father, was in observing the diphasic nature of libidinal ascendance in puberty with all its associated disruptions, she too missed one of the implications of this period – which is also the return of the repressed aggressive attacks of infancy: namely, the hate, frustrations, reservoir of implicit memory also re-engages to create manifestations for some adolescents that the breast and all it represents is best *pushed* away. Food, the breast's representative and substitute, may take on the mantle of the hated, persecutory, poisonous. Denial to the self of food entrenches itself in the anorexic psyche, since introjection of the hated may be too threatening and its expulsion (projection, that is), and denial, all defences of the early oral period, hold sway. Food must be put into the outside world but not ingested (introjected) because it will destroy the self. Anorexics may protect the mother in the outer conscious world through a great interest in food and its preparation for others but refuse its ingestion, at an unconscious level as an expression of hating the mother breast – that is, an aggressive derivative. Anorexia appears to be about control at the level of the superficial conscious – but the implicit component is the derivative of the aggressive drive in the form of the hate of the bad breast, a drive that carries over from the earliest oral period.

Ingestion is countered through ejection, or a concrete form of denial in which the closing of the mouth shuts the external world out from the internal one – in its most primitive forms taking on the character of psychotic states but in its lesser form, that is developmentally a little later, a denial of the external in its more concrete forms. The bad breast is denied access to the inner world and the splitting of the good and bad enables the hatred of the bad breast to concretise in the form of food without directly attacking or destroying, in phantasy, the maternal object. On this point, Anna Freud added, how the concretisation of earlier defences can then manifest:

> The sorting and interpretation of stimuli as they arrive leads to a sharp distinction between the child's own self and the objects outside; before this faculty is developed, the infant has been able to feel himself at one with the world around, to ascribe anything pleasurable to himself, and anything disturbing as 'outside'. The development of the function of memory is equally disturbing, since it aims at retaining memory traces irrespective of their quality; the infant gives preference to pleasant memories and rejects painful ones.[25]

The Hidden Monstrous

Anna Freud elaborates on some of these mechanisms,[26] without over-stating the developmental timeline from which development allows these mechanisms to emerge, but nonetheless captures the way the infant's mind has to do work to keep its own psychical integrity from rupturing through excessive deviations from homeostatic settling points. The earliest of excessive disruption to homeostasis for the infant becomes encoded in implicit memory, particularly when connected to oral needs and the emergent emotional representations of these needs. The obvious connection of breast-mother to oral frustrations and oral gratifications, risks return in the second wave of psychosexual development at the onset of puberty. Eating issues and associations of food with bad-object representations appears often in the psychic lives of adolescents struggling with disorders and disruptions to food and its symbolic representation. The surfacing of aggressive dynamics can be enormous and powerful and yet invisibly expressed through control, and as Sue Austin in her work with anorexic patients has noted, "Anyone who has worked with people who have anorexia knows that these aggressive, rejecting, refusing dynamics can be extraordinarily powerful...".[27] In fact, she uses the word "monstrous"[28] to capture the hidden aggressive dynamics that underlie the eating disordered. The inner monster reflects the disruption to stasis from the earliest oral experiences, associating the breast with bad, the source of dysregulation rather than its remedy for it – or, perhaps more accurately – the infant develops the capacity to split the good from the bad breast, as Klein suggests, and put into the outer world the source of the bad and preserve for the inner the good.

Such projection forms an integral part of these processes, aimed at preservation of the dependency; that is, the infant cannot destroy its sources of nourishment even when these sources are associated with frustration. Preservation of the object-breast is preservation of the infant-self, the maternal object being in the early stages indistinguishable, merged, and of one mind.

The essence of oral dysregulation is the evocation of an aggressive drive aimed at preservation from the bad feelings of dysregulation, blurring the distinction between the inner and outer worlds. Persecution from the breast or from internal impingements, such as gastric disturbance, can become associated, informing the infant that feel-bad has replaced homeostasis and the predicted remedies back to it has been exceeded. The aggressive drive in its primitive form is associated with feelings of a primitive form – undifferentiated and intense – feel-bad being all-bad – hate and the monster, hate *of* the monster, hate *being* the monster. This wrestling with the inner demon of hate for the ingestion of food is often coupled with a great love and obsession with food for the outer world, often exhibiting "a need to feed everyone else in an excessive way", as Sandler and Freud put it.[29]

Anna Freud addresses this issue in a discussion on the topic, noting, "If you can't get what you want yourself and enjoy it yourself because it's prohibited by internal conflict, well at least somebody else can get it, and you can enjoy it there through what you call vicarious enjoyment-which is certainly worthwhile. But that isn't all. At the same time the process liberates, or creates an outlet for the aggression. What I meant was that originally the individual wants to pursue his or her instinctual aims aggressively".[30]

In other words, what Anna Freud is observing is the underlying aggressive driver for both the denial of food to the self, given its associations to the hated maternal breast and rejection/ control over it, but also the added element of food being 'induced' into the environment, posited there in a manner of control and vengeance against the projected persecutor in the outer world. This paradoxical element of the eating disordered, also reminds us that the aggressive drive and subjective feelings of hate remains a key element in the disorder. The reported symptoms of low self-esteem about body, and even body dysmorphia, are secondary to the fixation of the hate and its merciless hold in the unconscious that prohibits and prevents resolution, since this drive must act to preserve the inner infant from the prospect of annihilation through the ingestion of the 'poison' of the bad-object.

Early survival depends on, says Klein, the splitting of the good and bad since this enables the infant "to derive a certain amount of security from his relation to the loved mother and therefore to develop his capacity for love". In the normal course, there is sufficient integration and metabolising for this to remain unhindered and not become fixated or encoded into implicit memory – says Klein, "If splitting is not too deep, and integration and synthesis at a later stage are not impeded, this is a precondition for a good relation to the mother and for normal development."[31] But when this splitting is terribly deep and the cleavage persistent under the pressures of excessive distress, frustration, and a poor metabolic or mentalising function, the cleavage may persist in a fixated form in implicit memory, for which access is difficult and working-through complicated, except through the concrete enactment of the infant in its later second-phase of psychosexual development.

However, integration evokes pain of loss and Klein makes her point that "The need for integration, moreover, derives from the unconscious knowledge that hate can only be mitigated by love; and if the two are kept apart, this mitigation cannot succeed. In spite of this urge, integration always implies pain, because the split-off hate and its consequences are extremely painful to face; the incapacity to bear this pain re-awakens a tendency to split off the threatening and disturbing parts of impulses."[32] In the eating disordered, the split must remain in place to avoid the threat of disintegration under the merciless pressures of persecutory frustrations, albeit unconscious.

Eating disorders are not only about disordered eating but about the inner conflicts that rage against the breast and the hate that accompanies the early imprints of manifest aggressive responses to deviations from homeostatic settling points that have exceeded the mental threshold, given the infant's young age, to restore equilibrium through protest, crying, and other expressions of the aggressive drive. Anorexia is, therefore, a disorder of hate (a death drive derivative) – and where the poor self-esteem and dysmorphia appear to rage, it is apparent that poor self-esteem is also about attacks against the self, and they are in part intra-punitive. The centrality of the aggressive drive is unavoidable and the intra-punitive is a branch of the death drive that could not manifest and instead expresses itself in this indirect form.

Notes

1 Freud, S. (1905) Three Essays on the Theory of Sexuality (1905). *The Standard Edition of the Complete Psychological Works of Sigmund Freud* 7:123–246, p.181.
2 Freud, S. (1905) Three Essays on the Theory of Sexuality (1905). *The Standard Edition of the Complete Psychological Works of Sigmund Freud* 7:123–246, p.222.
3 Klein, M. (1958) On the Development of Mental Functioning. *International Journal of Psychoanalysis* 39:84–90, p.89.
4 Freud, S. (1905) Three Essays on the Theory of Sexuality (1905). *The Standard Edition of the Complete Psychological Works of Sigmund Freud* 7:123–246, p.222.
5 Klein, M. (1946) Notes on Some Schizoid Mechanisms. *International Journal of Psychoanalysis* 27:99–110, p.99.
6 Klein, M. (1946) Notes on Some Schizoid Mechanisms. *International Journal of Psychoanalysis* 27:99–110, pp.101–102.

7   Klein, M. (1946) Notes on Some Schizoid Mechanisms. *International Journal of Psychoanalysis* 27:99–110, p.101.

8   See Panksepp, J. & Biven, L. (2012) *The Archaeology of Mind: Neuroevolutionary Origins of Human Emotions*. New York: Norton.

9   See Margaret Mahler's view, who notes: "The infant seems to be in a state of primitive hallucinatory disorientation, in which need satisfaction belongs to his own omnipotent, *autistic* orbit". The newborn's waking life centres around his continuous attempts to achieve homeostasis. The baby cries and the mother hopefully tries to soothe it. Mahler observes that: "Beyond a certain, but not yet defined degree, the immature organism cannot achieve homeostasis on its own. Whenever during the autistic or symbiotic phase there occurs 'organismic distress'—that forerunner of anxiety proper—the mothering partner is called upon, to contribute a particularly large portion of symbiotic help toward the maintenance of the infant's homeostasis. Otherwise, the neurobiological patterning processes are thrown out of kilter. Somatic memory traces are set at this time, which amalgamate with later experiences and may thereby increase later psychological pressures". Margaret Mahler (1967) On Human Symbiosis and the Vicissitudes of Individuation. Journal of the American Psychoanalytic Association, 15, 740–763, p. 745.

10 Klein, M. (1958) On the Development of Mental Functioning. *International Journal of Psychoanalysis* 39:84–90, p.85.

11 Freud, S. (1924). The Economic Problem of Masochism. The Standard Edition of the Complete Psychological Works of Sigmund Freud 19:155–170, p.414. Freud, S. (1933) New Introductory Lectures On Psycho-Analysis. *The Standard Edition of the Complete Psychological Works of Sigmund Freud* 22:1–182, p.105.

12 Klein, M. (1958) On the Development of Mental Functioning. *International Journal of Psychoanalysis* 39:84–90, p.85.

13 Solms, M. (2013) The conscious Id. *Neuropsychoanalysis*, 15, 5–19.

14 Klein, M. (1946) Notes on Some Schizoid Mechanisms. *International Journal of Psychoanalysis* 27:99–110, p.101.

15 Solms, M. (2013) The conscious Id. *Neuropsychoanalysis*, 15, 5–19.

16 Klein, M. (1975) 14. On Mental Health (1960). *Envy and Gratitude and Other Works 1946–1963* 104:268–274, p.271.

17 Freud, A. (1945) Indications for Child Analysis. *Psychoanalytic Study of the Child* 1:127–149, p.142.

18 Bion (1962) *Learning from Experience*. London: Jason Aronson, p.9.

19 Klein, M. (1975) 14. On Mental Health (1960). *Envy and Gratitude and Other Works 1946–1963* 104:268–274, p.271.

20 Freud, S. (1915) Instincts and Their Vicissitudes. The Standard Edition of the Complete Psychological Works of Sigmund Freud 14,109–140, p. 134.

21 Freud, S. (1915) Instincts and Their Vicissitudes. The Standard Edition of the Complete Psychological Works of Sigmund Freud 14,109–140, p. 134.

22 Kinet, M. (2024) *The Spirit of the Drive in Neuropsychoanalysis*. Routledge: London/ New York, p.32.

23 Kinet, M. (2024) *The Spirit of the Drive in Neuropsychoanalysis*. Routledge: London/ New York, p.33.

24 Freud, A. (1945) Indications for Child Analysis. *Psychoanalytic Study of the Child* 1:127–149, p.142.

25 Freud, A. (1945) Indications for Child Analysis. *Psychoanalytic Study of the Child* 1:127–149, p.144.

26 Anna Freud elaborates: "The weak and immature ego of the child fails to stand up to the impact of these dangers. It consequently attempts to undo its own

achievements as fast as they are made. It tries not to see outside reality as it is (Denial); not to record and make conscious the representatives of the inner urges as they are sent up from the id (Repression); it overlays unwelcome urges with their opposites (Reaction-Formation); it substitutes for painful facts pleasurable fantasies (escape into Fantasy-life); it attributes to others the qualities it does not like to see in itself (Projection); and it appropriates from others what seems welcome (Introjection); etc". Freud, A. (1945) Indications for Child Analysis. *Psychoanalytic Study of the Child* 1:127–149, p.145.

27 See the diary entry of a patient Austin cites as an example of this point: "All that is left is the will, clenched iron-fisted will. Radar on hyper-alert. Siege. Minefields. There is no hope other than defiance. The last soldier on the battlefield. Anything other than fighting feels like giving up and burrowing into rotting, dead corpses, and I cannot be grateful for that. Food is sickening, full of worms. So is my body. It's all poisoned. Keep your maggoty, therapeutic intimacy. I WON'T be grateful. I HATE anyone who TRIES TO GIVE ME THINGS AND MAKE ME/IT BETTER. Let me go. Your hope is my betrayal and my humiliation". Austin, S. (2009) A Perspective on the Patterns of Loss, Lack, Disappointment and Shame Encountered in the Treatment of Six Women with Severe and Chronic Anorexia Nervosa. *Journal of Analytical Psychology* 54:61–80, p.63.

28 Austin, S. (2009) A Perspective on the Patterns of Loss, Lack, Disappointment and Shame Encountered in the Treatment of Six Women with Severe and Chronic Anorexia Nervosa. *Journal of Analytical Psychology* 54:61–80, p.63.

29 Sandler, J. & Freud, A. (1983) Discussions in the Hampstead Index on 'The Ego and the Mechanisms of Defence': XI. A Form of Altruism. *Bulletin of the Anna Freud Centre* 6:329–349, p.343.

30 Sandler, J. & Freud, A. (1983) Discussions in the Hampstead Index on 'The Ego and the Mechanisms of Defence': XI. A Form of Altruism. *Bulletin of the Anna Freud Centre* 6:329–349, p.343, p.344.

31 Klein, M. (1975) 14. On Mental Health (1960). *Envy and Gratitude and Other Works 1946–1963* 104:268–274, pp.271–272.

32 Klein, M. (1975) 14. On Mental Health (1960). *Envy and Gratitude and Other Works 1946–1963* 104:268–274, p.274.

Chapter 10

Personality and Its Disorders: Derivations and Deviations

The Ghost in the Room

It is probably fair to suggest that the term 'personality' represents one of the most significant, and yet at the same time, broadest, and most vague of concepts in social and scientific discourse. It may only be a slight exaggeration to say that not a soul on earth has not and does not refer to personality and its types as both adjectives and nouns in cultural, social, and romantic discourse. In psychology, psychiatry, and other professional and scientific spaces the term also merits enormous passion, interest, and presence. Everybody understands what is meant by the term 'personality' – and so too its deviations – types, traits, and disorders are commonly used to understand others and in the clinical context most professionals will resort to various descriptors to understand the nature of any particular patient and, by implication, how their interior worlds interface with their environments and attachments. Freud considered the concept in writing about Leonardo da Vinci, that "...the behaviour of a personality in the course of his life is explained in terms of the combined operation of constitution and fate, of internal forces and external powers".[1]

This depiction seems scarcely adequate to capture the complexity of what constitutes difference in people, despite Freud obviously comprehending this complexity. He notes, for example, as mentioned in previous chapters, that agencies of the mind come into contest, "If these strivings, which are incompatible with the subject's present-day individuality, acquire enough intensity, a conflict must result between them and the other portion of his personality, which has maintained its relation to reality". He adds that symptoms emerge, as we hopefully know by now, due to conflicts within the personality and the drives: "This conflict is resolved by the formation of symptoms, and is followed by the onset of manifest illness. The fact that the whole process originated from frustration in the real world is reflected in the resulting event that the symptoms, in which the ground of reality is reached once more, represent substitutive satisfactions".[2] I want to emphasise here the mention of frustration, which although we have addressed this in previous chapters, will be visited again in this one, as a key bridge between the drives, along with other concepts, to remind the reader of the factors that

DOI: 10.4324/9781003628972-11

create this complex 'entity' know as personality. For those familiar with the material my apologies for repetitions, as with throughout the text, but for those not, I hope this will facilitate an ease of discussion.

However, as profound and groundbreaking as Freud's insights were, there is scarcely an adequate description of what constitutes this entity we glibly and universally refer to as 'personality'. One description relates, "Personality is the way of thinking, feeling and behaving that makes a person different from other people. An individual's personality is influenced by experiences, environment (surroundings, life situations) and inherited characteristics. A person's personality typically stays the same over time".[3] This might be regarded as a credible description of personality, coming from the American Psychiatric Association (APA), one of the most renowned of mental health organisations. And yet, if one stops to think about it, this description offers little by way of explanatory power, despite tapping into complex issues related to subjectivity, perceptions, personal history, and the old apparent dichotomous nature-nurture debate, as if body and mind are immutable. How can it be suggested that personality stays the same over time? Nowhere in the developmental trajectory can this be said to be true, even without psychotherapy or treatment. People evolve developmentally throughout the lifespan. Some residues of history remain encoded in memory and are returned to repeatedly as we know, through the repetition compulsion, that Freud so brilliantly identified, and which neuroscience would agree performs the function of being a mechanism to automatise predictions through efficient use of memory in the unconscious, and which also acts as a registrar of states of disequilibrium. In this sense, core personality may appear to remain stuck without treatment and yet these regressive repetitions of patterns of behaviour do not account for the whole of the person.

On the other side of an apparent dichotomy, from the normal we have the 'abnormal', the pathological, the disordered personality. To be regarded as personality-pathological, the APA suggests that:

> To be classified as a personality disorder, one's way of thinking, feeling and behaving deviates from the expectations of the culture, causes distress or problems functioning, and lasts over time. The pattern of experience and behaviour usually begins by late adolescence or early adulthood and causes distress or problems in functioning. Without treatment, personality disorders can be long-lasting.[4]

This, too, is all true from decades of clinical theory, research, and evidence. But it also presents challenges in its adequacy and explanatory power. Describing clusters of traits that characterise personality types is enormously helpful in clinical practice, since it enables better descriptors and methods for communicating in the real world of clinical work, which makes diagnosis of disordered personality useful and appropriate. The APA describes personality disorders as "long-term patterns of behaviour and inner experiences that differ significantly from what is expected",[5] particularly in the areas, as they put it, of thinking about oneself and others, of responding emotionally, of relating to other people, and of controlling one's behaviour. Further, by clustering these descriptors into discernible patterns that characterise various personality types, we do find useful nomenclature for describing, diagnosing, and treating these patterns, though often with poor outcomes and results that might be better described as a snail trans-navigating large swathes of territory rather than an eagle in thermal flight. It begs the question: what drives these deviations from normative?

According to the National Library of Medicine, "The precise aetiology of personality disorders continues to elude scientists, giving rise to wide-ranging hypotheses. Psychoanalysts suggest that these disturbances result from a failure to progress through proper psychosexual development. For example, classic Freudian drive theory postulates fixation at different stages manifests as separate disorders; dependent, obsessive-compulsive, and histrionic personality disorders are consequences of fixation at oral, anal, and phallic stages, respectively".[6] In short, these disorders are viewed, to distil it simply, as driven by libidinal elements that suffer some form of internal conflict and hence deviation-through-fixation. Anna Freud reflected that, "Analytic psychology, on the other hand, ascribes to the innate instincts the main role in shaping the personality. It is the claim of the instinctive urges on the mind which results in the development of new functions, the so-called ego functions".[7] She adds, "This never-ending series of inner conflicts serves as a constant stimulus towards higher development of mental functioning and finally determines the shape of the child's personality."[8] Additionally, she notes, that, "What we call character formation is, roughly speaking, the whole set of attitudes habitually adopted by an individual ego for the solution of these conflicts: the choice of which instinctive urges to help towards satisfaction, which to oppose, and what methods to adopt in its defence against the threats represented by a powerful outer world as well as a powerful inner world".[9] Rooted in the two primary drives of sexuality and aggression, Anna Freud does add texture to her analysis by suggesting that a quantitative factor can be factored in to account for differences in individual personality, noting, "This fusion of sexual and aggressive urges is normal and typical. Variation in the quantities of energy contributed from the two groups of instinctive tendencies account for a wide range of individual differences".[10]

The Quantitative Factor

There is not much to disagree with in these descriptions of personality. But they do not do enough to assist in understanding why and how these perturbations of personality emerge. Are there reducible mechanisms within the mental apparatus that might assist in making better sense of these deviations, from what I suggest is more *normative* rather than a normal-abnormal dichotomy? Whilst Anna Freud does note that this 'quantitative factor', as she calls it, allows for a less dichotomous distinction between normal and abnormal personality, she suggests that, "So far as the upbringing of children is concerned, these quantitative fluctuations account for the difference between manageable and unmanageable, 'good' and 'bad' children",[11] which assists with the idea that personality *variation* is built in from the ground up, and that the *quantity* of instinctual energy that becomes bound up, inhibited, or defended against in the course of development will be a key element in deviations from normative, since, as she adds, "Most of these variations are within the range of normality".[12]

Deconstructing this 'quantitative' factor points us in the direction of an important consideration: how mental energy gets discharged or bound-up through mental process from the outset of life. Libidinal energy prompts development in a forward direction and drives human needs that respond to states of disequilibrium. If needs are met easily, homeostatic parameters are reset, at both biological and psychological levels, even if, ultimately, psychological parameters emerge in evolution in the service of neurobiological ones, since as Solms puts it, "Conscious *feelings* tell the subject how well it is doing. At this level of the brain, therefore, consciousness is closely tied to homeostasis".[13] But if needs are frustrated and the buildup of energy in the direction of discharge is thwarted, this represents a threat to biological or psychological homeostasis and will activate the mental immune response, namely the aggressive drive, in the service of remedy, in the service, that is, of binding excess free energy.

Anna Freud, in making sense of personality formation as a "never-ending series of inner conflicts" which has a key role that "finally determines the shape of the child's personality",[14] is noting that there is no escaping the tensions of the two primary drives from the outset in the formation of personality. This is so, since all organic life is premised on the tension between the ability to grow, adapt, procreate and alter genetically in response to impingements that unsettle homeostasis on the one hand, and preservation and conservation of biopsychosocial identity on the other. As mentioned earlier, this tension which Freud so brilliantly identified in this later work,[15] suggests that unbound energy threatens disruption and entropy if left unchecked, and that according to Friston's Free Energy Principle, the mental apparatus must strive to bind excess energy and reduce excitations to as low as possible to maintain homeostatic parameters of the individual identity. Solms adds to this neuroscientific point, that "the fundamental driving force behind the volitional behaviour of all life forms is that they are obliged to minimise their own free energy. This principle governs everything they do".[16] Put differently, the drives that underpin the mental apparatus in humans, sources itself from a much wider evolutionary imperative. Anna Freud put it like this: "We may say equally, with regard to 'aim', that clinically speaking, i.e. on earth, both libido and aggression pursue their own limited and mundane aims while serving at the same time the vaster biological purposes of life and death".[17]

As mentioned previously, the science of economics also suggests that any biological system must do what it can to minimise free energy, and expend only what it must to maintain homeostatic parameters. Wasteful expenditure of resources will over time handicap the evolutionary advantage required to keep persisting. Accordingly, Solms makes the case that minimising free energy becomes the task of all homeostatic systems, and that according to Friston's Law, systems will minimise expenditure of energy, the work required to maintain homeostasis, or what we might refer to as a preservatory function. The tension between stasis and adaptation, embedded in all living matter from the outset, governed by the free energy principle and the requirement to minimise the expenditure of free energy, can become exceeded in the mental sphere, and when it does, we can note that Anna Freud's quantitative factor begins to apply. It makes sense that excess mental energy will require a response – distress exceeding the parameters of the individual (especially in infancy) to manage disequilibrium will require that this excess energy gets 'bound', or to use Freud's term, cathected, to minimise it. In this regard, we can think of perturbations of excess *quantitates* of mental energy as leading to deviations from normative parameters in mental development in infancy. Freud noted that the task of the mental apparatus is to find mechanisms to bind excess energy emanating from outside or inside the individual:

> A failure to effect this binding would provoke a disturbance analogous to a traumatic neurosis; and only after the binding has been accomplished would it be possible for the dominance of the pleasure principle (and of its modification, the reality principle) to proceed unhindered. Till then the other task of the mental apparatus, the task of mastering or binding excitations, would have precedence—not, indeed, in opposition to the pleasure principle, but independently of it and to some extent in disregard of it.[18]

At a broad level, this quantitative factor must gear itself according to the biological parameters of any species, but for the human mental apparatus excess dysregulation suggests also an elevated level of mental energy that requires cathecting – and given the limitations of the infant at various developmental stages – such excess energy nudges the infant in the direction of existential, that is, entropic failure. It must, therefore, find a mechanism to bind it or mental fragmentation can result. This quantitative factor is a crucial concept underlying deviation from normal parameters in and of the mental apparatus.

The Qualitative Factor

Both Freud's and Anna Freud's observations that excess mental energy requires binding (that is, it must be 'cathected'), to promote homeostasis and hence survival, must apply, however, in two ways: firstly, according to the available means present for the infant at their age and stage developmentally; secondly, according to how the subject *perceives* their experience, based on their temperament, history, biology, and so on, that is, their unique subjectivity. The available means for a three-hour old baby differs from that of a three-day old or three-month old or three-year old baby. Freud himself had suggested a caution: there is a need by the mental apparatus which endeavours to keep the quantity of excitation present in it as low as possible or at least to keep it constant[19] should not be seen in a purely *quantitative* sense. "It appears", he suggested, "that they depend, not on this quantitative factor, but on some characteristic of it which we can only describe as a qualitative one".[20] This *qualitative* element implies that from the perspective of the organism, an *interpretation* gets made about a stimulus or impingement that requires some form of evaluation in order to determine a course of 'action' or 'work' to meet a need (even if this course of action is fussing, niggling, crying or screaming for an infant) – but this can only apply from the subjectivity of the infant and its available means. This subjectivity permeates all living organisms in simpler or more complex ways, suggesting that once the quantum leap is made from the inanimate to the animate, an element of subjectivity *must* emerge, from which a system, in becoming biologically self-organising (as a living entity), must have a view point of its relation to and in the world, *viewed through the lens of its available means*. It must strive to ward off any possible ways of returning to inorganic existence other than those that are immanent in the organism itself,[21] as Freud put it, and find ways to persist, as it were, as a living entity.

It appears to me that the embedded contention between Anna Freud and her father is how subjectivity and interpretation of dysregulation emerges in the individual. Like her father she noted that there was aggression in the mix of early infantile libidinal urges or pushes from the beginning of life, which was, she notes, "at first attributed to the crude nature of infantile sexuality itself, later on recognised as the expression of the second group of instincts— the destructive urges". She emphasises from this that: "Aggression, destruction, their expressions and their development are as much in the centre of interest for dynamic psychology now as the development of the sexual function was at the beginning of the century".[22]

But unlike her father, it is not clear that Anna Freud fully engaged with the *qualitative* factor. If we can now accept that the aggressive drive serves a crucial and parallel role to the libidinal one in development, as Anna does suggest – its function being a conservative one, that is, a mechanism of preservation which job it is to activate a mental immune response when needs are unable to fulfil their homeostatic function and equilibrium is threatened – then the qualitative factor must play a role *from the outset of experience*. As soon as homeostasis is ruptured through the process of being born into the real world, *experience* is being activated and made manifest. Subjectivity is born in tandem with the body.

In neuroscientific terms, when free energy is increasing because the normal parameters for maintaining homeostasis are being exceeded *for the age and stage of the infant-child*, then the conservative drive must activate along some pathway to fulfil its function. 'Age and stage' are a broad description for infants in general and the mechanisms and means they have at their disposal at any given time – a three-month-old infant cannot control its bowels yet but it can control its mouth. This too is interpreted and used according to their subjectivity – a subject has to be registering their own internal state *in relation to* the external environment. Both these contexts, we might say, are crucial since neither can operate sans the other and neither can be construed as purely objective.

Both the inner and outer worlds of the individual are subject to experience and interpretation from the outset of its life. To use a simple example, a thinner infant or one more sensitive temperamentally may experience the same apparent room temperature differently – one *feeling* cold, another *feeling* hot depending on a host of factors, the one eliciting a niggling-crying response and the other not. Of course, such simple examples never apply alone in the myriad complexity of human experience – but I make the point simply that in principle there is a *measure of relativity* always in process from the outset of life.

Relativity is a concept that lends an important dimension to the struggles of living organisms to persist, and especially in the multi-dimensional world of the human mind-body system. A *subject* must be registering the internal state of their own biological systems, since as modern neuroscience suggests, the subjective experience of feelings registering the internal state of the body, in its relation to the external world, provides the most efficient economically effective method for the complex individual to avoid entropic pressures, and as Nick Lane puts it biologically, to fulfil "an imperative to persist, to stay alive and to reproduce, come what may".[23] The subject must register the state of its own internal object world, in its relationship to the external environment, in order to activate both conscious and unconscious feelings to both register these states and activate an appropriate response to restore homeostasis. Feelings *must be felt* and hence consciousness of the subject must play a pivotal role in its function of serving homeostatic requirements and avoiding entropic pressures. Consciousness of what is felt becomes essential. As Solms argues neuroscientifically, that, consciousness registers the state of the *subject*, not of the object world. "The sentient subject is first and foremost an affective subject", he says, which only then can *experience* perceptual and cognitive representations. "That is why—to state the obvious—there can be no objects of consciousness without a subject of consciousness to experience them. The subject of consciousness is primary. The secondary (perceptual and cognitive) form of consciousness is achieved only when the subject of consciousness *feels* its way into its perceptions and cognitions, which are unconscious in themselves. The pseudopodia of an amoeba, palpating the world, come to mind".[24]

So, we might agree, then, that you and I might experience everything, including apparently objective stimuli such as temperature in slightly different (but psychologically significant) ways, and 'palpate' the world through different subjectivity and experience, from the outset. The earlier in life, the more so this applies. We might also agree that putting on a jersey when cold will not remedy states of thirst. These needs must be biologically and consciously registered and differentiated at a conscious and subjective level to be appropriately interpreted. Only in this way can consciousness of feelings instigate effective and appropriate action for remedy, even when such action for an infant involves crying and through this mechanism *inducing* a remedy through its objects in the real world. It is worth being reminded that both internal and external worlds are kinetic, fluid, and effected by an extraordinary complex set of variables – and these variables make up a unique set of characteristics for the individual *subject*, through which all variables will be experienced and interpreted. This subjectivity will apply itself in both the internal psychobiological environment and the external world of attachments, objects. At no time does the infant/ individual escape this relationship inter-play – even though its ego is still "weak and undeveloped", as Kinet puts it, and "simply tries to 'make the best' of a difficult job".[25]

We might, therefore, also suggest that the qualitative factor over-rides any purely quantitative factors in humans, since when a quantum of energy is disrupting stasis and the psyche cannot immediately bind it to restore equilibrium, then defensive manoeuvres will begin to exert their role as the guardians of stasis. Since, as dealt with more extensively in my previous book,[26] the guardian of stasis ultimately rests on the conservative-aggressive drive, it must find a pathway that is available developmentally to fulfil this function. From here we begin to note the emergence of defensive mechanisms, according to the means available for the infant to bind excess energy. Projection, introjection, denial, for example, and later, reaction-formations, isolation, retentions and expulsions, and sublimations serve this purpose, depending on the age of the infant when these bindings of excess energy will be required, as "the organs for discharge are increasingly geared to the qualitative transformation and quantitative mitigation of the drive, i.e. to the defence against it".[27] But, as Anna Freud also more poetically put it, "We call a 'good lover' one who is faithful to his objects, i.e. constant in cathecting them. In contrast, the 'good hater' is promiscuous, i.e. he has free aggression at his disposal and is ready to cathect with it on a non-permanent basis any object who, either by his actions or his characteristics, offers adequate provocation".[28]

This broadening of the aggressive response is based on injury being encoded in memory to which the individual returns repeatedly in navigating life. Noteworthy, of course, is that any objective measure for 'provocation' is subsumed by perception, driven by experience, the foundation of subjectivity. This shifts us from a purely quantitative model of aggression striving to reduce tensions of unpleasure, to one in which the qualitative factor, that is its subjectivity, interprets experience and acts through projection when such experience is encoded for future reference. The quantitative factor no doubt precedes the qualitative one, since such encoding depends on unpleasure exceeding a threshold that threateningly breaches homeostasis; but we can also see that as development unfolds, the infant applies old filters to what is experienced as excessive, and hence the qualitative factors might also be shown to precede the quantitative one. What one infant finds acceptable, another might experience as highly dysregulating.

What is, therefore, *perceived* as disrupting stasis and trending towards a maximising of free energy, will elicit a restorative response in the service of restoration and preservation. Eissler had described an "initial stage of 'self-preservation intensely cathected with aggressive energy' and later stages of 'narcissism and ambivalence serving as the steering-wheels for aggression', 'narcissism … taking hold of aggression and using it for its own purposes'",[29] this linking aggression with preservation of the self and narcissistic injury. Eissler further notes in his writing, that biologically, the aggression is linked to the suggestion that "the death drive reaches its goal through the conversion of free energy into bound energy",[30] a prescient comment predating Friston's concept that free-energy requires binding as a counterpoint to entropic pressures, a concept which, as mentioned earlier, Solms more recently leans on in understanding the neuroscience of consciousness.[31]

When injury *by association* is re-triggered, the aggressive response finds itself activated, for which a target must be found. Whereas libidinal energy tends to cathect in specific and individual ways, one loves most *specifically* rather than generally, aggression and hate can free-float once activated, and search for objects against which it can rail. Dysregulation that leads to unpleasure, activates and mobilises the aggressive drive, and whilst, as Anna Freud suggests, "studies confirm the assumption that the infant's experiences of pleasure promote libidinal growth while the massive experience of unpleasure promotes aggression",[32] the function of 'unpleasure' or injury promoting aggression is because this drive is tasked with the role of conservation, preserving the infant through reducing or binding excess mental energy, which unchecked threatens entropic failure as free-energy is maximised rather than minimised, the latter being a requirement for maintaining homeostasis and the organism's identity.

Relativity, Subjectivity, and Preservation

We can see that subjective difference, or subjectivity, is here operating at two levels: firstly, that what is regarded as a disruptor (to stasis) is itself subjective and interpreted through individual history (as it is encoded in memory) and experience (as it gets encoded into memory); secondly, how the infant/ individual responds 'defensively' to remedy such excess is also subjective – not only as a by-product of age-and-stage mechanisms but also becomes each and every subject will experience their lives in different ways, from the very outset of life as it exits the womb. That is, as Anna Freud mentioned, "identity also with regard to the compromises which are formed between the drives and the defending forces, i.e. the neurotic symptom formation which results".[33]

Every human being has a face, which we can depict in broad terms but to be meaningful, we must concede that each and every face is infinitely variable and every one different from another. Mentally, the potential number of brain states is virtually infinite, and in converting meaning (that is, ideas or cognitions/ ideation about what internal states represent), prompts the mental apparatus to move from an undifferentiated state to a highly differentiated one, what Eissler describes as such, that, we observe clinically that it is the libidinal inflow from external sources that initiates and maintains "structuralisation of the psychic apparatus...". According to this view, he adds, "the 'silent work' of the death drive would therefore show two aspects: one within the body, the other within the psychic self. Both aspects would be characterised by an accumulation of irreversible structure formation".[34]

This links also to preservation through identity, since the "smooth functioning of the organism depends on its cohesiveness",[35] which relates to directing the mental apparatus towards self-interest, or essential and necessary narcissism, the investment in one's own body and system, first and foremost. Deviations from optimal can occur, however. Eissler notes that, "In a harmonious personality, the narcissistic cathexis is distributed in such a way as to guarantee optimal functioning. But narcissistic cathexis may also be unevenly distributed",[36] leading to the advent of, what we might describe as, exaggerated defence mechanisms, which become overly fixated, and to which the individual returns repeatedly through regression. Defence mechanisms, to remind the reader, are intertwined with the aggressive drive, whose function is to assist the infant to bind excess mental energy, minimise free energy, and strive for restoration, *given its age-related available means*. But narcissism also serves a less tangible purpose, elegantly put by Eissler, in writing about its function of protecting us: "Aside from the importance of narcissism for psychobiological reasons, it must be considered that it is the indispensable counterpoise to man's frightening irrelevance in the cosmos. Vis-à-vis the vastness of the globe which he inhabits, and the still greater vastness of the firmament to which he raises his gaze, without a healthy narcissism he would be crushed by the infinities that surround him".[37] Narcissism is thus also a defence against the experience of deep insignificance, itself a threat to sense of self, albeit of a more universal existential nature.

What Eissler is also describing, and which is corroborated well by modern neuroscience, is that the mental apparatus serves the maintenance of the biological entity by making meaning out of states of *meaninglessness*, and forming the 'mental solids', as Solms puts it, to represent internal states efficiently and effectively. The higher-level brain structures of the cortex enable humans to *represent* feelings, and 'stabilise' the objects of perception. This allows emotional experience of unpleasure to be encoded into memory, and *represented* in the form of ideas or mental solids and which Freud referred to as object-presentations.[38] In this way, experience at a *feeling* level can be formed into ideas that represent emotional experience and hence create more efficient ways to bind free energy, or cathect it, in the service of conservation. But the mental apparatus forms a life-of-its-own quality too, in which psychological needs in and of themselves are formed into structures, in which emotional needs diverge into a vast array of qualitative elements, fulfilling functions that are not purely related to biological homeostasis, despite originating from, and for this purpose. Psychical homeostasis too, in which the 'promiscuous good hater' and the 'faithful good lover' vie for their respective dominance in the *mental* balance of the individual, can be observed to have its own emergent life, divorcing its function of pure biological representation.

We must, first and foremost, persist in life. Writes Eissler, "Narcissism, by its enforcement of self-centredness, is the first prerequisite of survival; it provides man with a firm platform from which he can venture forth into the adventure of living, without running the risk of squandering his valuable heritage".[39] The essence of human aggression, compared to other species, is that human aggression, through being aided by cognitive representations and the encoding of (injurious) experience in memory, to which the organism returns repeatedly under the pressure of the repetition compulsion, becomes perverse. It can separate from its original purpose of conservation and preservation and develop a life-of-its-own duality. Remember also the point I made in Chapter 1 about human aggression's capacity for becoming perverse because it is directed by narcissism and ambivalence, and hence constitutes a supreme danger to man and culture - it can be scaled through intellect beyond its immediate preservatory function. The lion and its potential prey are able to mingle peacefully together so long as the lion is satiated, but with the first signs of the lion's eros-driven need for food in the service of homeostasis, however, its prospective victims disperse in a hurry, preserving their eros-driven need to avoid premature entropy. "Here we observe aggression wisely distributed, limited to the area where it belongs—namely, self-preservation",[40] Eissler noted, without the perverse elements we see in humans, and without, I might add, anything personal in the mix. It could be anyone in the herd for lunch, not anyone in particular.

In humans, the complexity of the mental apparatus frees the species from the constraints of 'tooth and claw', but simultaneously creates the conditions for anomalous self-destructiveness to self and conflicts with others, the tendency to exact specicidal enactments which, on the face of it, make little evolutionary sense. Which brings us back to the function of the aggressive drive in the formation of personality, how both quantitative and qualitative elements fuse in its formation. It also adds weight to my central thesis that there is no dispensing of the death drive and its function of conservation/ preservation, and as mentioned in Chapter 2, puts me in a little contention with Solms' conclusion that since all feelings, which represent life-drive pressures are in themselves homeostatic, there is no need for a separate death drive concept. But I also remind the reader of my earlier question: when needs are being frustrated, what then? What binds the rising free energy in the direction of entropy? Life-drive promptings through consciousness cannot always fulfil their homeostatic function – additional mechanisms must evolve, we should assume, since here we still are on this planet.

Memory that Cannot be Remembered

I have suggested that both quantitative and qualitative aspects of development and its challenges play their roles in the genesis of personality, and the deviations that apply to the pathologies that 'hijack' its pathways. As we know, Freud had suggested that the sexual instincts, "to which the theory of the neuroses gives a quite special place…",[41] remained indispensable to his model of mind and its deviations and symptoms. But if this is true, that the sexual instincts play the central role in psychopathology and the advent of deviations and distortions in personality, then how do we explain the malignant aspects of personality that emerge? The libidinal drive, or more broadly Eros, prompts the development of the individual organism but by coalescing into greater unities, guarantees the survival and prolongation of the individual and its species. The collective, in general, prompts an organism into a better state of sustainability – and as Freud points out, when germ cells combine, they increase this likelihood, since the essence of the processes to which sexual life is directed is the coalesce of two cell-bodies. "That alone is what guarantees the immortality of the living substance in the higher organisms".[42] And yet, most significant is the fact that this function of the germ-cell is reinforced, or only made possible, "if it coalesces with another cell similar to itself *and yet differing from it*".[43]

This notion of 'differing' is as significant as the organic requirement to join with others who share a species-specific genetic identity. Defining self-identity at all levels must exert itself vigorously both before and after joining with another, in terms of modern neuroscience which suggests that any organism must form a self-organising system that retains cohesion in the face of entropic threats, whether emanating from within and from without the organism. This Markov blanket enables Self to differentiate from Other – and so is born the dramatic paradox in human attachments that the intense and insatiable desire to bond libidinally with an Other, also becomes infused with its opposite tension to assert separateness and individuality. Couples universally get into conflict once the intense flushes of romance wane and the balancing act between attraction and unity battling it out against separateness and self-identity makes its presence felt.

In this regard, Freud deeply recognised the link between the biological evolutionary underpinning and the emergence of psychical tensions in more complex organisms, suggesting, if I may repeat, that accordingly, we might attempt to apply the libido theory which has been arrived at in psycho-analysis to the mutual relationship of cells, supposing that the life or sexual drive which is active in each cell takes the other cells as their object, and in so doing they "partly neutralise the death instincts ... in those cells and thus preserve their life; while the other cells do the same for them, and still others sacrifice themselves in the performance of this libidinal function".[44]

As mentioned, the system seeking to fly the flag for *preservation* of self-identity in humans falls, ultimately, to the death drive, whose function is less about promoting death as it is about preserving homeostasis, to assist that an organism follows its natural path through its phylogenetically typical life cycle. In broad terms, this aggressive drive functions in every human when under psychic threat of any sort – and is central in the development of deviations in personality. In some personalities, the *perception* of injury and threat becomes so extreme and entrenched that these defences, or this psychical immune system, takes on wildly deviant proportions in response to perceptions of injury, and becoming entrenched by what we can term psychical malignancy. The presentation of this malignant personality is what, in modern terms, we refer to as the narcissistic personality, which may present in either benign or malignant forms – but the 'malignant' variant helps to illustrate how personality disorders are formed out of deviations in the aggressive drive, rather than the libidinal one that Freud emphasised, since it is only in the overvaluation of the love object through libidinal investment that such injury in the face of frustration or disappointment becomes possible.

The question of *proportionality* also becomes central. As argued above, a certain amount of narcissistic investment, that is, libidinal energy, must also be directed at the self and self-needs, since without this seeking to fulfil self-needs, entropic pressures must increase. The younger the infant, the greater the intensity of its as-yet-undifferentiated experience, prompting an extortionate amount of libidinal demand and bonding with the maternal love object, and simultaneously, as Melanie Klein argues, an equal amount of hate and frustration when this investment is somehow failed in its perceived reciprocity. The perfect mother that can deliver perfectly is met, alas, with the imperfect mother who frustrates the infant from time to time.

These inevitable maternal failures, at least from the infant's point of view, may rouse affects that exceed the infant's capacity to metabolise them, from time to time – that is, to bind or cathect the excess mental energy as demanded by the need for a biological system to minimise free energy. Often, it is not the mother but the infant's own body that creates psychic ruptures but the infant expects the mother to remedy these states of disequilibrium and when she cannot, will not, or does not, amounts to the same experience – excess mental energy that cannot be bound or cathected. In such cases, these dramatic experiences find themselves encoded into (implicit) memory, to which that individual will return repeatedly under the pressures of regression. Since the aggressive drive aims to cathect excess mental energy and strives to minimise it in the service of homeostasis, it is this reactive mechanism that will be revived and activated when frustration or injury is perceived and *felt* later in life too.

Adult narcissistic personalities return repeatedly to these early experiences of injury, activating *affective* arousal that, whilst often appearing quite disproportionate to the perceived provocation, is proportionate to the original and early insults and breaches of their mental skin. It is *as-if* the infant within the adult is roused from its latent slumber in the unconscious and earlier injury and its responses are made manifest. This element of 'malignancy' is not simply a binary of those who are 'diseased' and those who are not – but a question of degree. The quantitative factor suggests that earlier experiences exceeded the capacity of an infant to bind the excess mental energy when needs are not met and a resort occurs to what available defences were in play at the time. The qualitative factor is that not all infants are of the same sensitivity, and amongst the myriads of variables that make up unique psychobiological experience, subjective interpretation of said experience adds a unique valence to each case. From their own perspective, they are the victim of excess distress, catalysing a rage response to restore homeostasis and bind the excess mental energy that has been unleashed.

We might suggest that the notion of malignancy in personality refers to a response that is generally regarded as disproportionate to the outsider but feels proportionate to the person themselves. Their emotional response becomes 'automatised', in neuroscientific terms, and as Solms argues it, "All nonfalsified predictions are repeated (are stored in the corticothalamic 'preconscious' and automatically executed), unless and until a prediction error arises."[45] A prediction error is simply a way of saying that action plans become automatised for efficient navigation of needs but sometimes these fail and, when subject to errors, require updating.[46]

During early development, memories of emotional distress and trauma become encoded for future use, in which, as Solms explains it, the consolidation of such deeply automatised predictions involves transferring them from cortical to *subcortical* memory systems, of which the best-known subcortical memory systems are the "emotional" and "procedural" systems.

"The crucial thing to note about these systems is that they are non-representational, *nonthinkable* associations; they are 'nondeclarative.' This means they are *not subject to updating in working memory*".[47]

Memory can thus be seen to serve two requirements: it must encode the drive experiences that promote needs through feelings that approach homeostatic settling points for the individual (pleasure); but it *must* even more efficiently encode memory that moves the individual away from homeostatic settling points (unpleasure). The greater the valence of unpleasure, the greater the threat of entropy through excess free energy that requires binding and hence the greater the requirement to encode such experience into memory. Memory can thus be seen to serve two masters: the life drive and its libidinal pressures to efficiently fulfil needs in the service of homeostasis – and secondly, to fulfil the requirements of the conservative drive to encode threats to homeostasis when free energy is increasing, either through aversive threats (such as those which violate the needs for safety, for example) or through the obstruction of need-fulfilment. Memory encodes the trends to pleasure or unpleasure, life drive and death drive requirements.

The significance of this point is crucial to understanding why narcissistic (and borderline) personalities (Cluster B personality types, using psychiatric nomenclature), and especially malignant variations thereof, repeatedly and seemingly in irrational ways react to the world as if it were attacking them, their defenses serving the function, as Richard Woods eloquently describes it, "of protecting this emaciated core".[48] Wood's point is that malignant narcissistic personalities struggle with love and he ponders whether the core function of their narcissism was to protect them against love – "as if love were an unbearable threat".[49] Wood's point makes sense in the context of early experience in which libidinal drives, the SEEKING[50] of need-fulfilment through attachment and oral satisfaction, are infinitely intense and infinitely dependent on the maternal object. When needs are failed, we might rather say that homeostatic requirements are failed, and libidinal pressures to attach and bond are disrupted, then states of disequilibrium become prolonged, exceeding the infant's capacity to bind this negative arousal and their states of unpleasure. Annihilatory threats prompting violent rage (think an inconsolable screaming infant) will attempt to induce a restorative response from the environment – but in infancy it can only be done through crying, screaming, fussing, niggling, and so on, aimed at inducing a response from the mother to fulfil the functions the infant cannot unilaterally.

But let's face it, if an infant is struggling with unbearable impingements from its own body, reflux, colic, other medical abnormalities that require invasive interventions, even the best mothering and what Winnicott might call 'good-enough' maternal attunement,[51] will fail to regulate the baby. From the infant's perspective, this can quickly become associated with maternal failure, prompting memory formations encoding the oscillations between love and hate, or attachment needs and retraction from the persecutory mother. This may lead to what Woods eloquently describes as follows: "By implication, such a personality has faced so much repeated, intolerable violation and threat that it must insulate itself against its own humanity, ensuring it remains untouched by interactions that require vulnerability and openness to others".[52]

Put differently, these early injuries may or may not be a result of maternal failures, but the core personality will have been injured by states of arousal exceeding their capacity and hence fixating in early forms of memory, to which a return will be inevitable, even when such memory is implicit and not available for conscious and cognitive recollection. From the infant's perspective, their own subjectivity, their rage is proportionate to the experience of a helpless annihilatory threat. To love, even in infancy, is to be humbled. "The effect of dependence upon the loved object is to lower that feeling: a person in love is humble. A person who loves has, so to speak, forfeited a part of his narcissism, and it can only be replaced by his being loved. In all these respects self-regard seems to remain related to the narcissistic element in love",[53] wrote Freud, since an investment of great intensity that unrequited, or perceived as such when the infant experiences failures to re-regulation, must activate states of disequilibrium and loss – and I should add, hence, a restorative-aggressive response. This applies in infancy as it does in adulthood, albeit the intensity may vary, depending on how regressed the victim is when their heart is hurt.

However, the destructive patterns we see in Cluster B personality types manifest their repeating cycles without insight or even regret, since, access to these memories is not possible. They are contained implicitly, and yet still maintain the role of registering states of noxious stimuli and trying to combat them through re-regulation. Solms addresses the point of inaccessible yet powerfully protective-destructive (depending from which vantage point you are placed vis-a-vis the narcissist), declaring that what these two non-declarative memory systems have in common is that they *by-pass thinking*, which happens a lot in earliest childhood while the cortical memory systems are still maturing. But this does not mean that they by-pass *affective* consciousness. "Just because we cannot 'declare' our automatised predictions does not mean we cannot *feel* their causes and consequences".[54]

Early aversive experience that exceeds the capacity to bind the energy being unleashed, hence threatening entropy in free energy terms, tends to become encoded in early non-declarative memory, constantly being enacted but impossible to recall directly in cognitive or verbal terms. These automatised *emotional* reactions take on their own life in response to associations that trigger these responses. As mentioned above, Solms explains the paradox of memory that cannot be remembered, in that non-declarative memory systems have in common the by-passing of thinking, but this does not mean that they by-pass *affective* consciousness. Although we cannot directly "declare" our early memories does not mean we cannot *feel* their causes and consequences.[55] In personality disorders, these early insults to psychic integrity – experience of negative arousal exceeding manageable levels – becomes encoded in these 'mindless repetitions'. Solms adds that, "Nondeclarative memories are purely associative (and permanently unconscious) action tendencies of the kind described above: X simply triggers Y, with nothing in between, as with Pavlov's dogs. No thinking occurs, not even implicitly. This leads to endless, mindless *repetition*, which is why 'transference' is so important in psychoanalytic treatment".[56]

What Solms is describing is how early insults to psychical integrity *from any source* will become encoded, even if the infant will interpret these injuries as related to maternal failure, since the separation barrier between the minds of mother and infant are porous in the early months and functions (almost) as a singular integrated unit, as Winnicott reminds us, at least from the perspective of the infant. These memories cannot be remembered cognitively or consciously, since they predate ideational-cognitive development, but they are 'remembered', encoded for future reference, and ignited into the present when perceived emotional injuries occur. Kinet, describing this process, suggests that the ways of being in the world can be understood as memories, but memories that are 'expressed' in how a person is and behaves. "So, this implicit knowledge is not remembered but enacted or acted out. It is unconscious knowledge, not dynamically unconscious through repression, but not conscious, i.e. flowing 'naturally' beyond consciousness".[57]

These 'memories-that-cannot-be-remembered' nonetheless play a crucial role in influencing development and the life of later attachments, and begin at the beginning. As mentioned in the introduction, but worth repeating in this context, Kinet adds to our point, that as early as the end of pregnancy, relational and affective patterns are recorded in implicit memory. The domain of implicit memory is unconscious, not repressed and not recallable through words. These earliest experiences are stored and form a structural part of the unconscious, asserting their influence on adult life, and in this way, "they permanently influence later relationships' depth and emotional colour".[58]

Woods, in describing his own personal experience of such a process in relation to his own malignantly narcissistic father, notes, with the great depth of insight coming from being a psychologist having experienced these dynamics first-hand, how, "The quality of personal righteousness that attended his rage flooded me, *obscuring any capacity for perception or for thought*".[59] Of course, Woods is not only describing his own experience of early automatised emotional reactions in childhood, but also the projected experience of his father's mind in regressive free-fall, back to a place that Woods observed over and over in childhood, how "any perceived or actual slight could produce - did produce - storms of retribution he seems unable to contain. Once the ugliness of a counterattack began, he was caught in its grip".[60]

This depiction is helpful in getting the feel of the regressive, automatised dynamic that 'afflicts' this type of personality. Injury triggers regression to early states of automatised emotional reactivity, that almost unstoppable, must play itself out like a tornado burning off its energy, and so, from its own perspective, it *must*.

Proportionality and the Binding of Free Energy

I will focus not on every personality disorder, since the tedium of so doing might alienate even the most interested reader. I intend to use the narcissistic personality, and in particular, the malignant variant thereof, to illustrate that the libidinal emphasis accounts for only half its aetiology. This is true of all personality types, that in their variability become extreme and fixated. It is a type in which, as Woods puts it, "His internal world increasingly consolidates his perception of the external world as being characterised by malicious intent. In this fashion, he comes to live in a projected world, one defined by his expectation that others can be expected to be as rapacious as he is".[61] We can note the various concepts we have been discussing: subjectivity, memory, fixation, regression, free energy and its binding, and so on.

From our discussion above, it can be seen that the origin of this malignant tendency places the adult narcissistic personality in the place of the perpetual and eternal 'victim'. The carnage they might create from an outside perspective may be entirely at odds with their own perception of injury and threat, including, perhaps especially, from those closest to them. Perhaps, as Wood suggested above, one of the core functions of the narcissistic defence is to protect the narcissist against the *unbearable threat of* love (these being life drive needs for attachment), and he notes that over and over he observes in his clinical work with these personalities, that when the narcissist's self is threatened in some important manner, their need for psychological safety inevitably trumps empathy – "it was all about protecting the self", he observed.[62]

But if this be true, how would the greatest malignancy of character be borne of love in attachment when this is precisely what he destroys over and over in his later adult life? Over time, we observe that this excessive use of primitive defences, rooted in the good-bad split, leads to a terrible cycle of impoverishment of the self, demanding greater use of the defensive system, leading to what Klein describes as, "the weakening and impoverishment of the ego resulting from excessive splitting and projective identification". She adds that, "This weakened ego, however, becomes also incapable of assimilating its internal objects, and this leads to the feeling that it is ruled by them. Again, such a weakened ego feels incapable of taking back into itself the parts which it projected into the external world".[63]

Regression to such early pre-cognitive states of *affect* in infancy, to a time in which the primacy of dependency and attachment to the maternal object holds virtually all libidinal energy, takes us back to the first months of life and especially the first four months of life, before the depressive position begins its ascendance, noted Klein, "in about the second quarter of the first year" when "marked steps in integration are made".[64] Klein adds that, "The very experience of depressive feelings in turn has the effect of further integrating the ego, because it makes for an increased understanding of psychic reality and better perception of the external world, as well as for a greater synthesis between inner and external situations".[65] The depressive position, as Klein terms it, is actually a developmental achievement!

This time-frame is based upon two developmental elements: firstly, a state of normal primary narcissism in which "His Majesty the Baby"[66] takes a grand and central place in all the universe; and secondly, Klein's observations of what she termed the "paranoid-schizoid" phase in which the good or bad, love or hate are split into separate mental spaces (in order to preserve the good from the bad). The bad-hate is nothing more than the activation of the aggressive drive trying to reregulate. Adult regression to this phase evokes implicit memory systems that have encoded experiences of injury and excessive dysregulation but which cannot be recalled cognitively or in words, but as mentioned, only enacted repeatedly. Also, as we noted above, the neuroscience enables us to understand how this 'automatised' *affective* reactivity can return in such compelling ways when perceptions of injury present to the adult narcissist. But it does not explain the disproportionate intensity of "being caught in its grip", as Woods describes it, from which the emotional tornado can be unleashed from what may appear to be even trivial and benign triggers, "like a dangerous moment, one in which one misstep could cause real jeopardy".[67]

Klein helps to make sense of this in describing the origins of this tendency by suggesting that certain paradoxical elements are in play. If aggressive elements in relation to an object are predominant and strongly stirred by the frustration of parting, the individual feels that the split-off components of his self, projected into the object, control this object in an aggressive and destructive way. She notes that at the same time the internal object is felt to be in the same danger of destruction as the external object in whom one part of the self is felt to be left. "The result is an excessive weakening of the ego, a feeling that there is nothing to sustain it, and a corresponding dependence on people".[68] In other words, defences against the failures of attachment can also predispose to excessive loneliness and anxious dependency.

Regression to early stages of development, and we might say, the earlier the greater this is true, invokes affective valence and intensity that is inversely proportional to age. The younger the infant, the more it lives in a world of undifferentiated pleasure-unpleasure and of "undigested facts",[69] to use Bion's term. Hence, too, their emotional experiences are greater in intensity and scope. Experience at very young age is global and all-encompassing, *meaningless* and without specificity and location. Making meaning out of this state requires the forward libidinal pressure, time, and the maternal mind's engagement to mediate between the internal and the external environment where needs *must* be met. Forming cognitive representations and thinking requires, to use Bion's concept, maternal "linking",[70] enabling the infant to form mental differentiation, meaning, and location somatically, out of states of unpleasure (that is, disruption and threats to biological, somatic, and emotional homeostasis). It can be said that as experience becomes differentiated, the infant can mentally process states of unpleasure as coming from a source that is not representative of all sources. Partial experience of unpleasure represents to the infant a lesser threat, a lesser mental pressure signalling entropy. Binding, or cathecting partial states of negative arousal requires less mental energy for the infant than trying to bind global and excessive quanta of mental energy. With age, as the weeks and months pass, the infant can differentiate one source from another, *hence minimising free energy through less mental effort*, unless excessive or prolonged trauma recurs which breaches this emergent differentiation. However, if in later life massive trauma assaults the otherwise manageable levels of daily challenges, and which breaches the mental capacity to reregulate and bind the excess free energy, then post-traumatic reactions may emerge with which we are familiar.

As we have discussed previously, the task of the mental apparatus is to both drive need-fulfilment (libidinal drive) but also to bind excess mental energy, striving to minimise free energy to manageable levels of stasis (aggressive drive). As we know, one of the earliest and most important functions of the mental apparatus is to bind the instinctual impulses that impinge on it, and to replace the primary process prevailing in them by the secondary process "and convert their freely mobile cathectic energy into a mainly quiescent (tonic) cathexis".[71]

The implication of these psychic requirements, is that the younger the infant, the less the differentiation of experience, the greater the affective intensity of such experience, the more polarised and undifferentiated it is – in Melanie Klein's formulation, being *split* into a binary of pleasure-unpleasure, or good-bad poles – as she writes, that "object relations exist from the beginning of life, the first object being the mother's breast which is split into a good (gratifying) and bad (frustrating) breast; this splitting results in a division between love and hate".[72] Klein was prescient, I believe, in noticing that the earlier the dysregulation, the greater the intensity of a tendency to split into binaries, to master undifferentiated negative stimuli, from whatever source, and to mobilise its only available but primitive defences, to reduce entropic pressures by reducing free energy through a separation of sorts between the pleasure and unpleasure divide.

As the infant evolves, at around four months of age, Klein observes, this requirement for primitive splitting is supplemented by a greater capacity to integrate the good and the bad into one, driven, I believe, by the emergent capacity to differentiate *meaningless* states of unpleasure into more meaningful and *manageable* sources of unpleasure. This advent coincides with the improving mental capacity to differentiate, to form the 'mental solids' that enable ideational representation to form, for embryonic, albeit primitive, *thinking* to begin crystallising, and for higher cortical functions to evolve which can, like the ego, mediate between the internal and external worlds. Emotional splits, infused with some ideational representation to differentiate affective experience, also then enables a greater diffusion of mental energy, a more differentiated binding of somatic and psychical disruption into smaller and smaller chunks of dysregulation. These smaller chunks of affective unpleasure, enabled by mental differentiation, require, then, also less mental energy to cathect or bind them, to reduce free energy, and to promote psychic integrity.

The Psychical Immune Response

Narcissistic personalities have invariably suffered injury, by life's sins of omission or commission, including impingements from within their own bodies that exceed the threshold capacity for the infant to reregulate on its own, or through the auxiliary mental and physical efforts of the mother. Remember Wood's description, that the internal world increasingly consolidates the "perception of the external world as being characterised by malicious intent" – since sources of bad-unpleasure tend to be projected outwardly to preserve the inner world. Klein was, I believe correct, in naming this mechanism's part of the paranoid response, in that the inner/bad is encapsulated and expelled through projection into the outer world, which in turn becomes 'bad', and a source of 'persecution', whether intended or not, but management of external bad is easier than internal bad, from which escape is impossible. To remind ourselves of how Freud had explained this phenomenon, that firstly, feelings of pleasure and unpleasure are like an index of what is happening in the interior of the mental apparatus – think of my concept on an internal 'barometric sensor' to register, measure, and signal a widening of the gap between the internal 'atmosphere' of eros-driven homeostatic needs and their increasing frustration. This predominates over all external stimuli, and has a particular way of dealing with any internal excitations which produce too great an increase of unpleasure – that is deviates from homeostatic settling points. There is, writes Freud, a tendency to treat them as though they were acting, not from the inside, but from the outside, so that it may be possible to bring the shield against stimuli into operation as a means of defence against them. "This is the origin of projection, which is destined to play such a large part in the causation of pathological processes".[73]

This is a crucial and general point: in the helpless dependency of infancy, when 'bad' feelings of unpleasure are registered, whether from an internal source, or because needs are not being fulfilled in the external world where needs *must* be met, the resulting state of frustration and dysregulation can be projected into the external world and its objects, from whence these feelings then seem to emanate. From thereon, the source of unpleasure is in the external world and from thence is impinging upon the mind-body of the infant, threatening it in the direction of entropy. Such a 'pathogenic attack' in the mental realm must mobilise an immune response to this threat, in much the same way the body's immune system is mobilised in response to biological pathogens. Both immune responses are aggressive in nature, emotionally and biologically violent, in fact, but whose aims are entirely benign and striving merely for the restoration of homeostatic parameters. Should the pathogenic attacks be neutralised, the aggressive immune response should dissipate back to a latent state.

Sometimes, it is simply incidental that the greatest mental damage to a narcissistic personality (and others) derives from such early insults to psychic integrity. For example, a hungry infant trying to suckle to satiate its internal need, one leading to a state of disequilibrium, whose maternal breast is unable to create sufficient supply, will likely prompt arousal states of unpleasure that is no-one's fault and yet can breach its mental capacity to bind the rising excess mental energy. The same can occur with internal states that disrupt, such as colic, reflux, or other gastric disorders. Paradoxically, the more the well-intentioned mother is trying to sooth her baby's discomfort through offering the breast, the more the infant is starving, feeling unsettled, prompting the aggressive drive to do what it must to bind this excess. Of course, other times, maternal neglect, depression, simple mis-attunement, or leaving the baby to cry, can have this effect too, driving the infant to states of apoplexy and affective frenzy and trauma, to which the adult narcissistic returns repeatedly under the pressure of these sorts of (now automatised) emotional triggers.

The mental immune response, that being the mobilisation of the conservative-aggressive drive, develops a *proportionality* that correlates inversely with developmental age. The earlier injuries become encoded in memory as fixations, and hence appear disproportionate to the adult triggers, but entirely proportionate from the perspective of the infantile stage within. This developmental floor that is being *affectively* revisited – is a descent into the depths of implicit memory that cannot be accessed through cognition, words, or ideation, since these are yet undeveloped, but nonetheless exert a powerful emotional influence. The current emotional excess makes sense from the developmental vantage of the infant prone to undifferentiated pre-cognition experience, in which splitting into binary mental states is prominent. It derives, as mentioned, from what Klein described in the splitting process, the polarities of good-bad derived from undifferentiated pleasure-unpleasure in the earliest phases of life. Wood described this process as allowing the individual to "break the world up into binary schemas that permit one to apply gross, sweeping generalisations to others that render them inordinately good or inordinately bad".[74] It is a mechanism borne of the undifferentiated experience of pleasure-unpleasure in which the unpleasure polarity cannot effectively bind excessive dysregulation. A baby in distress left to cry, for example, may itself induce this experience for the infant – crying being an expression of the aggressive-restorative drive aiming to induce a response in care-givers to restore homeostasis. If this is ineffective, despite the infant's escalation of this drive, then biding excess negative arousal may trend to become traumatic for the infant – trauma being, as we discussed in the Chapter 5 on anxiety, excess mobilisation of an aggressive drive that remains frozen or ineffective.

But the remedy the infant applies, given its available means of defence for binding of excess arousals, also has a cost and psychical consequences in the economics of the mind, as Klein wrote that, "So far as the ego is concerned, excessive splitting off of parts of itself and expelling these into the outer world considerably weaken it. For the aggressive component of feelings and of the personality is intimately bound up in the mind with power, potency, strength, knowledge and many other desired qualities".[75] These are the underpinnings we see in the narcissistic personality.

The Malignant Factor

The question of *malignancy* now bears exploring. Why is it that the narcissistic personality, as with other personality disorders, produce malignant effects on their attachments, and their own internal worlds, when their primitive injuries are triggered? It seems counter-intuitive to their resolute striving for remedy of their perceived injuries that they should create in their attachments just the opposite. We could suggest, that narcissistic personalities return to a non-declarative period of primitive development under trigger-pressure, in which pre-cognitive affect is awoken, by association, to create a cascade of processes in which unbound mental free energy threatens subjective entropy. This must catalyse the conservative drive, phylogenetically inbuilt, to do its work of cathecting or binding this excess, undifferentiated arousal, and returning the infant to a semblance of mental (and somatic) homeostasis. This drive, although designed to maintain homeostasis and is 'peace-loving' in this regard, preferring its latent state rather than a manifest one, once activated turns to aggressive manoeuvres to do its job of returning the infant (or the infant within the adult) to an expectation of perceived stasis.

However, as we know, it can only resort to those manoeuvres which are at its disposal at any particular stage of development, and so regression to early memory-encoded reactivity will vary not in a binary sense of normal or abnormal, but along a continuum of earliest to later age-wise, in developmental terms. The earlier a personality regresses, the greater the intensity of the aggressive response even to apparently benign triggers, give the early limitations of available means. Malignancy, this suggests, is not a matter of a distinct category, but rather an intensity of aggression that becomes disproportionate to the trigger, but only from the subjective perspective of an outsider. Each disorder finds its 'floor' to which regression settles, early fixations that allow for different defensive manoeuvres, and hence flavour, as it were, the nature of the pathology that manifests later. The malignant aspect is a matter of the intensity of affect being stirred from primitive sources, in which all the machinations of mind, that Klein well-described, take hold, and in the earliest months tend to be more binary.

So, we are suggesting that the malignant elements of narcissism are in part a matter of *proportionality*, in which the global nature of early experience is revisited rather than the partial nature of experience in later development. This touches the quantitative aspect of personality, in which breaches to the threshold of the infant to reregulate is exceeded, accordingly becomes encoded as memory, and revisited under the pressures of the repetition compulsion. This activates its functional role in the psyche's *feedforward* process, attempting to make predictable the links between internal and previously learned expectations and current external stimuli and events; it is aimed at generating an expected context for the selected associative sequence. *This is the product of all our learning.* In other words, says Solms, when a need (of either drive) propels us into the world, "*we do not discover the world afresh with each new cycle.* It activates a set of predictions about the likely sensory consequences of our actions, based upon past experience of how to meet the selected need in the prevailing circumstances".[76] In other words, both drives tend to become automatised in the interests of the mental economy and efficiency in the world.

But we can also quickly notice that not all infants suffer in the same way to states of disequilibrium or to the same stimuli, encoding their affective learning at different levels. Some seem temperamentally more sensitive, and more prone to bring their subjective lens to bear in ways that *amplify* experience of frustration, pain, or dysregulation. It would make sense that subjectivity adds its lens to all experience *from the outset of life* and that even in early infancy, interpretation of experience, albeit of a primitive kind, prevails. This includes, of course, its relationship with the maternal container and her capacity to attune and mediate between the internal and external. This emotional mediation will influence outcomes and whether the emotional threshold is breached and the aggressive drive mobilised and demobilised as homeostasis is restored, or becomes encoded in memory, because the threshold is breached and extreme mobilisation of the aggressive drive is required through its available means at the time.

We must concede, therefore, that in real life, both quantitative and qualitative factors are in play in the development of personality. Or, perhaps more accurately, that the qualitative factor mediates the quantitative one, determining the extent to which the aggressive drive is activated and stored for future revisitation (regression). The revisitation to encoded memory of this sort of high valence and intensity forms the basis of what we call malignancy in the narcissistic personality, a quality that seems to metastasise into their attachments and leave the personality denuded and enfeebled over time, a precarious adjustment that is, ultimately, flawed and "destined to end itself in personal disintegration"[77] but driven by what Shaw argues is "the gravity and the extent of developmental trauma they have suffered".[78] The term 'trauma' may be misleading, in being suggestive of experiences out of the ordinary – but it should be remembered that the qualitative factor may lead one infant to experience their dysregulation as traumatic and unbearable, which for another may be tolerable and better metabolised. To this extent, the experience of trauma is also partly subjectively mediated, and may prevail, as Mika suggests, "even when there is no evidence of overt abuse and/or neglect in his biographical data".[79]

Wood, in his compelling work on the malignant variant of the narcissistic personality, and his narrative of his own personal experience of having a father in this category, relayed this element of subjectivity well, in relating how any misstep with his father could cause "real jeopardy" – an extension of his father's "real core, an irreparably injured child seeking solace for damage that no one could fix. The exaggerated, dramatic, and even absurd presentation of this pain belied its immensity".[80] This captures these elements discussed above – how subjectively driven perception of early trauma, in which dysregulation thresholds are breached, leads to an exaggeration in the aggressive drive's attempts to mobilise and reregulate. This can become fixated and hence returned to repeatedly, with the aggressive drive developing the character of *perversion*, separated in a conscious sense from its original triggers and activated in the presence of any associative ones in later life. This malignant aspect captures the disproportionate quality, in which the personality experiences even benign triggers as existentially threatening, and warranting of a highly mobilised aggression response, which effects are devastating on others and further enfeebles the person themselves, but which aim is noble – primitive attempts to protect the self from the experience of irreparable, annihilatory harm. Relating his father's reactivity, Wood notes how: "He did sound like a small and defenceless child in great pain, a child who expected, no demanded that others heed his cry",[81] despite the immense damage this father caused in his life to others and especially to his only child, the writer.

What, then, is the malignant factor? It is, in short, the return to a restorative-aggressive response upon which the personality comes to rest as their foundation of implicit memory, the internal guardian becoming perverted as a result of excessive early mobilisation of the conservative-aggressive drive. Its aims are benign (to the self) – restoration of perceived injury and threat (and rising free energy in the wrong direction to homeostasis) – its effects invariably malignant (to others), manifesting in aggressive modes of operating in a world perceived as dangerous, injurious, humiliating, and hence game for (defensive) attack. Wood puts it well when he writes: "The greater people's fear of their inner world, the more likely they seem to be to build rigid, inflexible structures, including unyielding moral schemas meant to protect them, to define what they can and can't feel, to limit and constrain their thought, and to deny the presence of impulses deemed to be unacceptable",[82] excessively weakening the ego as Klein would describe it. But beneath the malignant psychic exoskeleton usually lies the agonising knowledge of a feeble and helpless self, one invariably tortured and tormented by feelings of pending annihilation if constant vigilance and fight is not in an ongoing state of alert and mobilisation.

Malignancy and Counter-Attack

We can easily notice in clinical work and in life that narcissistic personalities are caught in a perpetual state of expectation of attack or actual attack – sensitive to feelings diminished or injured – and using counter-attack to the slightest provocation they might experience "because it creates safety" to perceptions of non-recollectable early trauma, and in the process, says Wood, "insulating itself against its own humanity",[83] ensuring it remains untouched by the requirements for vulnerability. Strength, to the narcissistic-leaning personality, means shutting others down and any real or perceived attack upon the self produces reflexive and ruthless counter-attack meant to devastate the other. I think Wood's descriptions are rich and compelling, describing how such behaviour can and often does emerge in response to seemingly small sleights, objectively out of all proportion to the injury being sustained. He describes how the malignant narcissist "is therefore living in a solipsistic world, one defined by their own voice, their own emotional vicissitudes, their own needs, and their own prerogatives of action. It is a profoundly lonely, isolating place, but one that offers insulation against a world the malignant narcissist has learned - through unendurably painful experience - is malevolent".[84]

It is a world driven by early splitting mechanisms, in which the bad experience is projected outwardly to protect the enfeebled self from annihilation but which then places the malignant, bad parts of experience in the outer world, protecting the inner core from fragmentation and disintegration – that is, a primitive manoeuvre against entropy. We could suggest that counter-attack to any perceived slight that diminishes the person emotionally, is borne of the necessity to protect the self against the subjective pressures of entropy. An infant struggling to feed at a breast that unbeknownst to the mother is not producing milk, may, for example, create somatic dysregulation, and no amount of crying to induce a response to restore a state of pleasure would remedy this problem, at least not immediately. A few weeks of struggle in the earliest stages of life would imprint excessive threat in the memory of the infant, one in which free energy appears 'unbindable'. To an infant, this deficiency in capacity to cathect excess mental energy represents an existential threat that requires the mobilisation of all available defensive manoeuvres to strive for psychic protection and integrity, triaging needs so that immediate psychic integrity is sustained, even if at the cost of the capacity to properly love, trust, or attach in the vulnerability that dependency requires of us.

Counter-attack, a key hallmark of the narcissistically leaning personality, is, from their perspective, a mechanism to simply protect the self from psychic annihilation. Of course, this threat is disproportional because it stems from early, primitive injury but as human memory must encode states of extreme dysregulation to 'future-proof' the organism efficiently, so too this mechanism becomes embedded in future attachments, reminding the adult of early insults to psychic integrity, but from the band of memory that existed prior to the development of cognition, ideational representation of experience, and intellect – that is, as we discussed before, implicit memory which cannot be consciously declared but which nonetheless must be enacted, an implicit knowledge not remembered but enacted or acted out. "It is unconscious knowledge", as mentioned before, how Kinet describes it,[85] and can have deleterious effects for everyone, those around the narcissist, who gives up on the unbearable pain of love, bandages their wounds with heavy weapons of attack and guardedness, anticipating and pre-empting every conceivable slight and injury before it can penetrate into their increasingly emaciated and enfeebled core.

I have focused on the Cluster B personality disorder of narcissism, not because it is unique amongst the personalities, but because it lends itself to an insight into how the aggressive drive takes centre stage in its aetiology and development. We can never properly understand this configuration without understanding the centrality of the aggressive drive in its role as guardian of homeostasis, whose job is tasked with minimising free energy, cathecting and binding it in its attempts to restore some semblance of homeostasis. Its *aims* are benign, even when its *effects* are malignant. Other personality disorders present with some differences, depending on the configuration of the individual's history, familial dynamic, and of course, at what developmental stage in infancy and early childhood the fixations embed.

But invariably, we find, both theoretically and clinically, the developmental fixations that lead to extreme perturbations in some personalities, significant fixations along particular pathways, depend on mapping the pathway of the aggressive drive in that person and the available defensive manoeuvres for their age and stage. For, the libidinal drive may underpin psychopathology to the extent that yearning for love, attachment, security, having needs met in the external world where needs must be met, break the peace and stir dysregulation when such libidinally driven needs are extensively frustrated, but it also catalyses a cascading aggressive response attempting to bind the excess free energy and induce a remedy from the environment, and where these manoeuvres are effective, no fixation need arise.

As Freud had suggested that our mental apparatus as being first and foremost a device designed for mastering excitations, which would otherwise be felt as distressing or would have pathogenic effects. Working them over in the mind helps remarkably "towards an internal draining away of excitations which are incapable of direct discharge outwards, or for which such a discharge is for the moment undesirable".[86] But when remedy is undesirable or not available, and when the mental apparatus cannot perform the work required to achieve restoration, then the infant must find auxiliary mechanisms to achieve homeostasis through mobilising the aggressive drive along available pathways, from where their encoding in implicit memory is revisited, revived, and relived when later triggers present themselves. This is also the origin of feelings of hate, anger, rage, and the niggling, fussing, crying, screaming that infants commonly use to induce an environmental response, and particularly from its most devoted love-object.

Concluding Comments

It must be remembered that Freud had centralised libidinal pressures in the formation of the narcissistic character, suggesting that narcissism has the significance of a perversion that has absorbed the whole of the subject's sexual life, "and it will consequently exhibit the characteristics which we expect to meet with in the study of all perversions".[87] Freud did acknowledge the complexity of narcissism in writing that the disturbances to which a child's original narcissism is exposed, the *reactions* with which he seeks to protect himself from them and the paths into which he is forced in doing so – "these are themes which I propose to leave on one side, as an important field of work which still awaits exploration".[88]

It is my view, that as with his insights into the death-drive, Freud was both 100% right and 50% half-right. Libidinal pressures must keep needs alive in the interests of the individual, and must be directed at both objects (who fulfil needs in the real world – 'object-libido') and the infant's own ego ('ego-libido'),[89] for some investment in the self is a prerequisite for psychic and somatic survival. When libido is withdrawn from the self, as in depression, psychic impoverishment results. However, this is only part of the story: for where the libidinal drive and its needs are frustrated in the real world, whether for psychical or somatic supplies, the minimising of free energy and a return to homeostasis is delayed, prolonged, or endlessly frustrated *from the point of view of the infant/individual,* excessive states of dysregulation result – triggering the drive normally latent in its character to mobilise in the service of restoration and conservation. Its aim is to return the infant to homeostatic parameters but its effects now excessively mobilised, and at times encoded into memory for future reference and use, create a fixation, that when returned to under the pressure of later associative triggers, will activate the aggressive response beyond the proportionality prevailing in the current later situation. The malignant effects of personality disorders rest, therefore, not only on the libidinal promptings but in their excessive frustration and subsequent aggressive response.

The remaining question might be what form this aggressive response takes, depending on the infant and their circumstances: rage/hot or hate/cold and which defensive manoeuvres are available. These two forms are flagged in neuroscientific work suggesting that the aggressive response can take on various forms, or a combination of them.[90]

Whilst needs aim to meet homeostatic demands they are also disruptors. The question of diagnosis, formulation, and intervention depends on mapping the pathways that the conservative-aggressive drive takes in response. It is tempting to remain faithful to Freud's earlier formulations, as he tended to do paradigmatically, despite his brilliant breakthrough in formulating his dual-drive theory, which links human psychic development to the evolutionary imperative in life itself. But perhaps if we remain so faithful to our theoretical love-objects, then we too fall foul of being only 50% complete, and foul too of the question, as the Fool asks in Shakespeare's King Lear: "May not an ass know when the cart draws the horse?"[91]

Notes

1 Freud, S. (1910) Leonardo Da Vinci and a Memory of his Childhood. *The Standard Edition of the Complete Psychological Works of Sigmund Freud* 11:57–138, p.135.
2 Freud, S. (1912) Types of Onset of Neurosis. *The Standard Edition of the Complete Psychological Works of Sigmund Freud* 12:227–238, pp.232–233.
3 https://www.psychiatry.org/patients-families/personality-disorders/what-are-personality-disorders
4 https://www.psychiatry.org/patients-families/personality-disorders/what-are-personality-disorders
5 https://www.psychiatry.org/patients-families/personality-disorders/what-are-personality-disorders
6 https://www.ncbi.nlm.nih.gov/books/NBK556058/
7 Freud, A. (1949) Aggression in Relation to Emotional Development; Normal and Pathological. *Psychoanalytic Study of the Child* 3:37–42, p.37.
8 Freud, A. (1949) Aggression in Relation to Emotional Development; Normal and Pathological. *Psychoanalytic Study of the Child* 3:37–42, p.38.
9 Freud, A. (1949) Aggression in Relation to Emotional Development; Normal and Pathological. *Psychoanalytic Study of the Child* 3:37–42, p.38.
10 Freud, A. (1949) Aggression in Relation to Emotional Development; Normal and Pathological. *Psychoanalytic Study of the Child* 3:37–42, p.41.
11 Freud, A. (1949) Aggression in Relation to Emotional Development; Normal and Pathological. *Psychoanalytic Study of the Child* 3:37–42, p.41.
12 Freud, A. (1949) Aggression in Relation to Emotional Development; Normal and Pathological. *Psychoanalytic Study of the Child* 3:37–42, p.41.
13 Says Solms, M. "The internal aspect of consciousness 'feels like' something. Above all, the phenomenal states of the body-as-subject are experienced

affectively. Affects do not emanate from the external sense modalities. They are states *of the subject.* These states are thought to represent the biological value of changing internal conditions (e.g., hunger, sexual arousal). When internal conditions favour survival and reproductive success, they feel 'good'; when not, they feel 'bad.' This is evidently what conscious states are *for.* Conscious feelings tell the subject how well it is doing. At this level of the brain, therefore, consciousness is closely tied to homeostasis." Italics mine on the word 'feelings'. Solms, M. (2013) The Conscious Id. *Neuropsychoanalysis* 15(1), p.7.

14 Freud, A. (1949) Aggression in Relation to Emotional Development; Normal and Pathological. *Psychoanalytic Study of the Child* 3:37–42, p.38.

15 Freud, S. (2015) Beyond the Pleasure Principle. *Psychoanalysis and History* 17:151–204.

16 Solms, M. (2021) *The Hidden Spring: A Journey to the Source of Consciousness.* London: Profile Books, p.177.

17 Freud, A. (1972) Comments on Aggression. *International Journal of Psychoanalysis* 53:163–171, p.171.

18 Freud, S. (1920) Beyond the Pleasure Principle. *The Standard Edition of the Complete Psychological Works of Sigmund Freud* 18:1–64, p.35.

19 Freud, S. (1920) Beyond the Pleasure Principle. *The Standard Edition of the Complete Psychological Works of Sigmund Freud* 18:1–64, p.9.

20 Freud, S. (1924) The Economic Problem of Masochism. The Standard Edition of the Complete Psychological Works of Sigmund Freud 19:155–170, p. 414.

21 Freud, S. (1920) Beyond the Pleasure Principle. *The Standard Edition of the Complete Psychological Works of Sigmund Freud* 18:1–64, p.39.

22 Freud, A. (1949) Aggression in Relation to Emotional Development; Normal and Pathological. *Psychoanalytic Study of the Child* 3:37–42, p.39.

23 Nurse, P. (2020) *What is Life?* Oxford: David Fickling Books, p. 20.

24 Solms, M. (2017) What is "the Unconscious", and Where is it Located in the Brain? A Neuropsychoanalytic Perspective. *Annals of the New York Academy of Sciences,* 1406 (2017) 90–97. New York Academy of Sciences, p.92.

25 Kinet, M. (2024) *The Spirit of the Drive in Psychoanalysis.* London/ New York: Routledge, p.89.

26 Perkel, A. (2023) *Unlocking the Nature of Human Aggression: A Psychoanalytic and Neuroscientific Approach.* New York/ London: Routledge.

27 Freud, A. (1972) Comments on Aggression. *International Journal of Psychoanalysis* 53:163–171, p.167.

28 Freud, A. (1972) Comments on Aggression. *International Journal of Psychoanalysis* 53:163–171, p.166.

29 Eissler cited in Freud, A. (1972) Comments on Aggression. *International Journal of Psychoanalysis* 53:163–171, p.165.

30 Eissler, K. R. (1971) Death Drive, Ambivalence, and Narcissism. *Psychoanalytic Study of the Child* 26:25–78, p.33.

31 Solms, M. (2021) *The Hidden Spring. A Journey to the Source of Consciousness.* London: Profile Books.

32 Freud, A. (1972) Comments on Aggression. *International Journal of Psychoanalysis* 53:163–171, p.169.

33 Freud, A. (1972) Comments on Aggression. *International Journal of Psychoanalysis* 53:163–171, p.166.

34 Eissler, K. R. (1971) Death Drive, Ambivalence, and Narcissism. *Psychoanalytic Study of the Child* 26:25–78, p.37.

35 Eissler, K. R. (1971) Death Drive, Ambivalence, and Narcissism. *Psychoanalytic Study of the Child* 26:25–78, p.51.

36   Eissler, K. R. (1971) Death Drive, Ambivalence, and Narcissism. *Psychoanalytic Study of the Child* 26:25–78, p.52.
37   Eissler, K. R. (1971) Death Drive, Ambivalence, and Narcissism. *Psychoanalytic Study of the Child* 26:25–78, p.52.
38   "The answer to our question, 'What does cortex contribute to consciousness?', then, is this: it contributes representational memory space. This enables cortex to *stabilise* the objects of perception, which in turn creates potential for detailed and synchronised processing of perceptual images. This contribution derives from the unrivalled capacity of cortex for *representational* forms of memory (in all of its varieties, both short and long-term). Based on this capacity, cortex transforms the fleeting, wavelike states of brainstem activation into 'mental solids.' It generates *objects*. Freud called them 'object-presentations' (which, ironically, predominate in what he called the 'system unconscious')". Solms, M. (2013) The Conscious Id, *Neuropsychoanalysis*, 15(1), p.12.
39   Eissler, K. R. (1971) Death Drive, Ambivalence, and Narcissism. *Psychoanalytic Study of the Child* 26:25–78, p.54.
40   Eissler, K. R. (1971) Death Drive, Ambivalence, and Narcissism. *Psychoanalytic Study of the Child* 26:25–78, p.55.
41   Freud, S. (1920) Beyond the Pleasure Principle. *The Standard Edition of the Complete Psychological Works of Sigmund Freud* 18:1–64, p.39.
42   Freud, S. (1920) Beyond the Pleasure Principle. *The Standard Edition of the Complete Psychological Works of Sigmund Freud* 18:1–64, p.56.
43   Freud, S. (1920) Beyond the Pleasure Principle. *The Standard Edition of the Complete Psychological Works of Sigmund Freud* 18:1–64, p.40 (italics mine).
44   Freud, S. (1920) Beyond the Pleasure Principle. *The Standard Edition of the Complete Psychological Works of Sigmund Freud* 18:1–64, p.50.
45   Solms, M. (2017) What is "the Unconscious," and Where is it Located in the Brain? A Neuropsychoanalytic Perspective. *Annals of the New York Academy of Sciences*, 1406 (2017) 90–97. New York Academy of Sciences, p.93.
46   Solms notes: "This (prediction error) releases what Friston[24] calls 'free energy'—that is, increased *entropy*. In terms of information theory, increased entropy implies increased *uncertainty*; and in arousal terms, uncertainty implies *salience* (see Pfaff[31]). *Prediction error therefore renders preconscious predictions salient again.* Salience is signaled by arousal. An unmet need is what activates ('hypercathects,' as Freud put it) the memory traces that were meant to satisfy it. Only ERTAS arousal can produce the level of activation that is necessary for reconsolidation to occur. In this way, prior predictions (what Freud called 'wishes') are subjected—reluctantly—to the reality principle, and they are updated." In Solms, M. (2017). What is "the Unconscious," and Where is it Located in the Brain? A Neuropsychoanalytic Perspective. *Annals of the New York Academy of Sciences*, 1406 (2017) 90–97. New York Academy of Sciences. p.93.
47   Solms, M. (2017) What is "the Unconscious," and Where is it Located in the Brain? A Neuropsychoanalytic Perspective. *Annals of the New York Academy of Sciences*, 1406 (2017) 90–97. New York Academy of Sciences. p.94.
48   Wood, R. (2024) *A Study of Malignant Narcissism: Personal and Professional Insights.* New York/ London: Routledge, p.17.
49   Wood, R. (2024) *A Study of Malignant Narcissism: Personal and Professional Insights.* New York/ London: Routledge, p.66.
50   The SEEKING system is part of the forward neurological drive in humans. See Panksepp, J. & Biven, L. (2012) *The Archaeology of Mind: Neuroevolutionary Origins of Human Emotions.* New York: Norton.

51 Winnicott, D. W. (1975) *Through Paediatrics to Psychoanalysis, Collected Papers.* London: Hogarth Press.

52 Wood, R. (2024) *Psychoanalytic Reflections on Vladimir Putin: The Cost of Malignant Leadership.* London/ New York: Routledge, p.6.

53 Freud, S. (1914) On Narcissism: An Introduction. *The Standard Edition of the Complete Psychological Works of Sigmund Freud* 14:67–102, p.98.

54 Solms, M. (2017) What is "the Unconscious," and Where is it Located in the Brain? A neuropsychoanalytic perspective. *Annals of the New York Academy of Sciences*, 1406 (2017) 90–97. New York Academy of Sciences, p.94.

55 Solms, M. (2017) What is "the Unconscious," and Where is it Located in the Brain? A Neuropsychoanalytic Perspective. *Annals of the New York Academy of Sciences*, 1406 (2017) 90–97. New York Academy of Sciences, p.94.

56 Solms, M. (2017) What is "the Unconscious," and Where is it Located in the Brain? A Neuropsychoanalytic Perspective. *Annals of the New York Academy of Sciences*, 1406 (2017) 90–97. New York Academy of Sciences. p.95.

57 Kinet, M. (2024) *The Spirit of the Drive in Psychoanalysis.* Routledge: London/ New York, p.33.

58 Kinet, M. (2024) *The Spirit of the Drive in Psychoanalysis.* Routledge: London/ New York, p.32.

59 Wood, R. (2024) *A Study of Malignant Narcissism: Personal and Professional Insights.* New York/ London: Routledge, p.63 (italics mine).

60 Wood, R. (2024) *A Study of Malignant Narcissism: Personal and Professional Insights.* New York/ London: Routledge, p.63.

61 Wood, R. (2024) *Psychoanalytic Reflections on Vladimir Putin: The Cost of Malignant Leadership.* London/ New York: Routledge, p.9.

62 Wood, R. (2024) *A Study of Malignant Narcissism: Personal and Professional Insights.* New York/ London: Routledge, p.66.

63 Klein, M. (1946) Notes on Some Schizoid Mechanisms. *International Journal of Psychoanalysis* 27:99–110, p.104.

64 Klein, M. (1946) Notes on Some Schizoid Mechanisms. *International Journal of Psychoanalysis* 27:99–110, 105.

65 Klein, M. (1946) Notes on Some Schizoid Mechanisms. *International Journal of Psychoanalysis* 27:99–110, 105.

66 Freud, S. (1914) On Narcissism: An Introduction. *The Standard Edition of the Complete Psychological Works of Sigmund Freud* 14:67–102, p.91.

67 Wood, R. (2024) *A Study of Malignant Narcissism: Personal and Professional Insights.* New York/ London: Routledge, p.79.

68 Klein, M. (1946) Notes on Some Schizoid Mechanisms. *International Journal of Psychoanalysis* 27:99–110, p.99, p.104.

69 "Beta-elements are stored but differ from alpha-elements in that they are not so much memories as undigested facts, whereas the alpha-elements have been digested by alpha-function and thus made available for thought. It is important to distinguish between memories and undigested facts—beta-elements". Bion, W. (1962) *Learning from Experience.* London: Jason Aronson, p.9.

70 'Linking' is a technical term that Wilfred Bion used to refer to the child and the maternal enabling of the child's mind to make links between emotional experience, events that impinge, and how this interface are mentally processed. This is not automatic but requires the maternal mind to facilitate this developmental process.

71 Freud wrote: "Our views have from the very first been *dualistic*, and to-day they are even more definitely dualistic than before— now that we describe the opposition as being, not between ego instincts and sexual instincts but between life

instincts and death instincts". He follows: "We have found that one of the earliest and most important functions of the mental apparatus is to bind the instinctual impulses which impinge on it, to replace the primary process prevailing in them by the secondary process and convert their freely mobile cathectic energy into a mainly quiescent (tonic) cathexis. While this transformation is taking place no attention can be paid to the development of unpleasure; but this does not imply the suspension of the pleasure principle. On the contrary, the transformation occurs on *behalf* of the pleasure principle; the binding is a preparatory act which introduces and assures the dominance of the pleasure principle". In Freud, S. (1920) Beyond the Pleasure Principle. *The Standard Edition of the Complete Psychological Works of Sigmund Freud* 18:1–64, p.62.

72 Klein, M. (1946) Notes on Some Schizoid Mechanisms. *International Journal of Psychoanalysis* 27:99–110, p.99.

73 Freud, S. (1920) Beyond the Pleasure Principle. *The Standard Edition of the Complete Psychological Works of Sigmund Freud* 18:1–64, p.29.

74 Wood, R. (2024) *Psychoanalytic Reflections on Vladimir Putin: The Cost of Malignant Leadership*. London/ New York: Routledge, p.10.

75 Klein, M. (1946) Notes on Some Schizoid Mechanisms. *International Journal of Psychoanalysis* 27:99–110, p.102.

76 Solms, M. (2021) *The Hidden Spring: A Journey to the Source of Consciousness*. London: Profile Books, p. 141.

77 Wood, R. (2024) *A Study of Malignant Narcissism: Personal and Professional Insights*. New York/ London: Routledge, p.11.

78 Shaw (2014) cited in Wood, R. (2024) *A Study of Malignant Narcissism: Personal and Professional Insights*. New York/ London: Routledge, p.25.

79 Mika (2017) cited in Wood, R. (2024) *A Study of Malignant Narcissism: Personal and Professional Insights*. New York/ London: Routledge, p.34.

80 Wood, R. (2024) *A Study of Malignant Narcissism: Personal and Professional Insights*. New York/ London: Routledge, p.79.

81 Wood, R. (2024) *A Study of Malignant Narcissism: Personal and Professional Insights*. New York/ London: Routledge, p.79.

82 Wood, R. (2024) *A Study of Malignant Narcissism: Personal and Professional Insights*. New York/ London: Routledge, p.97.

83 Wood, R. (2024) *Psychoanalytic Reflections on Vladimir Putin: The Cost of Malignant Leadership*. London/ New York: Routledge, p.6.

84 Wood, R. (2024) *Psychoanalytic Reflections on Vladimir Putin: The Cost of Malignant Leadership*. London/ New York: Routledge, p.6.

85 Kinet, M. (2024) *The Spirit of the Drive in Psychoanalysis*. Routledge: London/ New York, p.33.

86 Freud, S. (1914) On Narcissism: An Introduction. *The Standard Edition of the Complete Psychological Works of Sigmund Freud* 14:67–102, pp.85–86.

87 Freud, S. (1914) On Narcissism: An Introduction. *The Standard Edition of the Complete Psychological Works of Sigmund Freud* 14:67–102, p.73.

88 Freud, S. (1914) On Narcissism: An Introduction. *The Standard Edition of the Complete Psychological Works of Sigmund Freud* 14:67–102, p.92 (italics mine).

89 Freud, S. (1914) On Narcissism: An Introduction. *The Standard Edition of the Complete Psychological Works of Sigmund Freud* 14:67–102, p.70.

90 Panksepp, J. & Biven L. (2012). *The Archaeology of Mind: Neuroevolutionary Origins of Human Emotions*. New York: Norton. p.165.

91 https://en.wikipedia.org/wiki/Cart_before_the_horse

Chapter 11

On Treatment Implications
A Game Fought out by Masters

Freud drew the analogy in his openings remarks of his paper on beginning the treatment, that anyone trying to learn the game of chess through books will soon discover that the complexity of real-life engagement belies what any text can capture. He declared, that "This gap in instruction can only be filled by a diligent study of games fought out by masters."[1] This caution is well-made, for the complexity of treatment process can never be taught through text, nor is there any point at which the skill is fully learned.

Psychological treatment is a complex and intricate process, ill-suited to neat algorithms and recipes, reliant on both technical and interpersonal skill, in which the cut-and-thrust of transference and counter-transference can work its efficacy. But treatment is guided by common paradigmatic themes, two of which stand out as universally common – namely, empathy with the suffering and hurt of the 'victim' within the patient and secondly, particularly for those psychodynamically inclined who work in deeper ways, an emphasis on the libidinal drive and its frustrations in the aetiology and causation of psychopathologies and the genesis of symptoms. Freud made the point that, "The first of these two alternatives can be carried out in two ways: in reality, or in the transference—in either case by exposing the patient to a certain amount of real suffering through frustration and the damming up of libido."[2] Even in normal development, Freud emphasised that "the transformation is never complete and residues of earlier libidinal fixations may still be retained in the final configuration",[3] and added that "If this is the correct answer to our question, we may say that analysis, in claiming to cure neuroses by ensuring control over instinct, is always right in theory but not always right in practice."[4]

Of course, Freud was never suggesting that libidinal pressures are the sole cause of symptoms but that "instinctual conflicts"[5] form this foundation. In contention, was what the form of these conflicts take – between ego and id, ego and superego, reality and wish? All of these are significant in the formation of symptoms, but all also suggest that libidinal pressures meet a counter-cathexis in the form of back-pressures that seek to neutralise these, or at least render them constrained in the real world of psychical risks,

DOI: 10.4324/9781003628972-12

threats, ambivalences, and the frustrations of reality. Psychical conflicts form the basis of neurotic symptoms, between drives and between agencies of mind, and the task of treatment is to assist in their resolution. Few clinicians of any persuasion would disagree with this concept, the thrust to healing being engineered by resolution of conflicts, injuries, cracks in the psychic foundation.

However, a deconstruction of these seemingly obvious aims runs into difficulties. We know that the ego makes use of various procedures for fulfilling its task, "which, to put it in general terms, is to avoid danger, anxiety and unpleasure. We call these procedures 'mechanisms of defence'",[6] writes Freud, but centralises what is being defended against is from, or in, the libidinal realm – sexual promptings create affects, violate taboos, prompt desires and yearnings for which there is, for children especially, no solution possible. The psychical manoeuvres required to maintain homeostatic parameters becomes 'expensive', "The dynamic expenditure necessary for maintaining them, and the restrictions of the ego which they almost invariably entail, prove a heavy burden on the psychical economy",[7] but whose aim is to "serve the purpose of keeping off dangers",[8] such dangers being predominantly interpreted from within the psychic apparatus and the navigation of competing needs and wishes which must be fulfilled in the real world.

At the same time, Freud astutely points out that therapeutic change uncovers not only defences against internal impulses and wishes in the patient, but also resistances to change. In the work itself, the progress of treatment inevitably becomes corrupted by a countervailing drag, and that we see that there is a resistance against the uncovering of resistances, and the defensive mechanisms are resistances not only to the making conscious of contents of the id, "but also to the analysis as a whole, and thus to recovery".[9]

In other words, Freud's bitter experience uncovered also a further truth about treatment resolving symptoms through the making conscious of unconscious conflicts within the psyche and freeing the ego from these constraints and conflicts. Cure, or a closer approximation to it, seems to meet an unfortunate fate in the hands of a 'resistance to uncovering resistances', impasses in treatment that signal repetition and a faithfulness to familiar patterns, even when they are unhelpful or destructive to the patient. The apparent contradiction lies buried deep in the nature of life and the mental apparatus as a whole, because as Valdrè notes, "we know how to recognise external aggression, but what is difficult is the recognition of *internal* aggression, and even more so if this procures paradoxical enjoyment".[10]

The Grand Conflict

As previously discussed in this book, two great forces work their way through the annals of evolutionary history, reaching its pinnacle in the human mind. But no matter how high the grand thrust of evolution drives development, there is also a grand drive that must preserve the biological identity of every organism, according to their phylogenetic memory encoded genetically. Evolution through variation and adaptation to change and challenge is met with the need to preserve identity and the homeostatic parameters *that are familiar*. This grand balancing act between evolutionary variation and conservation of what is familiar, finds its way into treatment as well, where psychotherapeutic intervention's *raison d'être* driving change from old patterns that have created symptoms, meets with resistances that push back to old familiarities, however maladaptive they may have become. The greatest impediment to resolution and growth therefore seems to emanate from within the patient themselves, and their resolve to preserve the familiar, if at all possible, even if at the cost of change and progress, which initially, at any rate, seems to come at a large mental cost. The mental work required for growth can at times seem so much greater to the patient than does staying in the realm of the familiar, those automatised defences doing their job, at least once their symptoms creating discomfort have receded and are causing less trouble to daily functioning.

Treatment takes its toll, therefore, on the side of change versus conservation in the patient but also in the clinician for whom the frustrations of resistances defy any common sense and oftentimes seems to undo all the progress of the hours. Just as the patient feels better, so their resistances appear full-frontal, and strive to represent the conservative self, balancing the grand force that suggests too much variation leads to loss of identity and hence a form of psychical entropy, versus the drive to maintain what is, so long as the symptoms emerging from inner conflicts are not so great that they too threaten entropy and psychic disintegration. Freud noted that, "we are reminded that analysis can only draw upon definite and limited amounts of energy which have to be measured against the hostile forces. And it seems as if victory is in fact as a rule on the side of the big battalions".[11]

But now we must deconstruct what these terms 'resistances' and 'defences' mean – for the suggestion above is that it seems to strive for conservation of the self-identity of the individual, their personal Markov blanket, which defines its Self and all that makes up this character. Freud astutely pointed out that these phenomena are unmistakable indications of the presence of a power in mental life, which we call the instinct of aggression or of destruction according to its aims, and which we trace back to the original death instinct of living matter. "It is not a question of an antithesis between an optimistic and a pessimistic theory of life. Only by the concurrent or mutually opposing action of the two primal instincts—Eros and the death-instinct—never by one or the other alone, can we explain the rich multiplicity of the phenomena of life."[12]

The two grand forces of evolution and nature never relinquish their grip on the mental apparatus, forcing the conclusion that the tendency to a conflict is something special, something that is newly added to the situation, irrespective of the quantity of libido. Freud remonstrates that "An independently-emerging tendency to conflict of this sort can scarcely be attributed to anything but the intervention of an element of free aggressiveness"[13] – for which Freud notes that, "our two primal instincts, Eros and destructiveness, the first of which endeavours to combine what exists into ever greater unities, while the second endeavours to dissolve those combinations and to destroy the structures to which they have given rise".[14]

Prescient in his later thinking, Freud seemed to move away from a purely libidinal model of treatment and its resistances, into the link to the conservative drive and its representative of aggression. He also seemed to recognise, at least conceptually, that defences serve the purpose of binding excess mental energy in the service of restoration (toward homeostatic parameters – away from unpleasure) so that conservation of the individual can prevail against the pressures of variation and change, particularly when eros-driven needs are meeting with a 'brick wall'. In other words, if we remind ourselves what defences are for? In essence, defences serve the purpose of binding increasing free energy in the service of restoring the mental state to a quiescent one when libidinally driven needs are not met timeously to restore homeostasis, but this can only be achieved through developmentally available means at the infant's disposal. This is the origin of symptoms too, as we have discussed, that the experience of deviations from homeostatic settling points elevate arousal of unpleasure in infancy, which carries a disproportionate intensity of affects that require binding.

But so too, in the treatment process we encounter resistances to change – not to the alleviation of symptoms and suffering per se, but to change that is fundamental and enduring. It is as if in the treatment process too, as in life, one psychic drive pushes the patient to change and variation in their personal circumstances when there are challenges, as if their instincts 'rush forward', whilst others 'jerk back' – an oscillating rhythm that makes treatment so challenging for the clinician. As mentioned, wrote Freud of these drives in tension with each other *from the outset of life*, the organism itself moving with a "vacillating rhythm", with one group 'rushing forward' so as to reach the final aim of life as swiftly as possible but the other group 'jerking back' to a certain point to make a fresh start and so prolong the journey of life.[15]

This concept is helpful, in that in the treatment process the strange and often-frustrating paradox of the patient communicating both the desire for change and the desire to leave change aside, can render the clinician frustrated and helpless. The request is to remove the discomfort of symptoms so that previous homeostatic parameters can be restored, but once this aim is achieved, the patient manifests resistances, often presented in the form of pragmatic concerns, such as sudden financial considerations becoming foregrounded, and the treatment becoming unaffordable. The timing of such 'practical' concerns invariably have significance. Underlying these resistances one can often note the emergence of the previously latent conservative drive 'jerking back' to some familiar place, in which older mental configurations can be left intact that in the absence of symptoms remains unconsciously preferable. No matter that the older configurations, that being the defensive systems remaining intact to remediate old and unresolved injuries, once symptoms resolve and the patient feels better, so resistances have a way of presenting themselves, serving a grander underlying master of the conservative drive's role in restoring the familiarity of homeostasis.

Treatment itself suffers this grand fate. Freud expressed it that the repression of the unconscious instincts and of their productions, which has meanwhile been set up in the *subject*, must be removed. "This is responsible for by far the largest part of the resistance, which so often causes the illness to persist even after the turning away from reality has lost its temporary justification". The analysis has to struggle against the resistances from both these sources, which accompany the treatment step by step. Freud adds to this point, that, "Every single association, every act of the person under treatment must reckon with the resistance and represents a compromise between the forces that are striving towards recovery and the opposing ones which I have described."[16]

This tussle between Eros and the conservative drive manifests in treatment through this endemic resistance. But Freud also places the reason for the resistance at the door of libidinal pressures, and the vicissitudes of the sexual paths attempting to find a route to fulfilment and consciousness against the restrictions, taboos, and frustrations of the real world. Put differently, the resistances are not about sexuality, or at least, these breakers of the peace that drive needs, making their presence felt through manifest feelings, are only half the equation. Inevitably, as discussed, so is mobilised the aggressive response in the service of restoration of stasis and the requirement to bind excess free energy when unpleasure is exceeding pleasure, feel-bad is dominating over feel-good.

Latent Versus Manifest Interpretation

It is a general tendency in psychotherapeutic work to allow the patient's associations and unconscious material to find its own way to the surface. More specifically, interpretation does not lead the patient – rather, the patient's associations lead the interpretation, and when preconscious and nearing the surface of consciousness is made manifest by the clinician through putting into words what is being presented and reflecting these back to the patient in a form that links unconscious to conscious processes, turning meaningless, affective states into ones that can be mentalised. In this unfolding, and the links that are made, so too the abreactive process of re-triggering and releasing old affects can take place, and in this fashion facilitate the forward thrust of libidinal growth. Alongside Freud's cautions mentioned above, Barratt argues too that, "Indeed, it must be emphasised that psychoanalysis cannot be practiced formulaically".[17] Nonetheless, he also goes on to argue that "The psychoanalyst's intent is to facilitate the patient's readiness to let go the obstructions to free-associative discourse; that is, to facilitate his or her potential for release from repetition-compulsivity",[18] that is, automatised defences, and I might add, their resistances. Barratt adds that through a more passive, receptive, egalitarian, quiet, and contemplative posture, traditional analysis, and other psychotherapeutic treatment modalities, adopt a meditative posture of equanimity in which a passive receptacle, a receiver of the pressing upwards of unconscious material, is encouraged.[19] When unconscious material 'ripens' for interpretation, this critical timing is triggered for the therapists reflective or interpretative inputs.

This approach makes sense when dealing with the libidinal drive that SEEKS,[20] creating a forward thrust to life and its attachments, presenting in the transference relationship old patterns, imagos, and projections that require remedy to free the patient from their old habitual defences that create symptoms over time. It is a reactive form of interpretation, but it makes sense since the forward thrust of life drive elements will press forward to make their presence known, playing itself out in 'felt' and often direct ways when associations in life and the transference relationship are manifest and present. This is because the nature of Eros is to make its presence felt in the form of needs and feelings, to have a connection to our inner perceptions, a psychobiological drive that pushes and prompts, emerging, as Freud noted, to remind ourselves, as breakers of peace and constantly producing tensions whose release is felt as pleasure.[21]

The conservative-aggressive death drive is different to the libidinal-Eros drive. It presents in a latent state, unobtrusively, like the immune system of the body that does not seek to make its presence felt, unless striving to restore homeostasis when it is disrupted, because needs are frustrated. The libidinal promptings stir needs into consciousness through feelings, in order to meet the needs of homeostasis – but when these strivings are perceived of as unreciprocated, obstructed, frustrated, or prolonged, especially in infancy, then the aggressive drive must do its work to manage the excess arousal and free energy, finding ways to 'bind' it or risk entropy. This is where the death drive does its work, binding mental energy to reduce arousal and restore the perception of homeostatic parameters, even when the needs remain unfulfilled. If, for example, prolonged crying by an infant does not have the desired effect of returning the primary caregiver to it, it must relinquish this desire which is pressing the infant beyond manageable levels of dysregulation – and so it might shut down emotionally, retract its 'feelers' from the external environment, and make a 'decision' to not depend on anyone. Such detachment from attachment-needs can embed as a defensive response to any attachments later in life, where internal stasis is preferred to the excess arousal from investment in the outer world. The binding of excess free energy, through defensive means available to the infant-child at the time when they require activation, can then leave the defensive manoeuvres back to a state of perceived stasis, and hence also draw the death drive back into its latent state.

This latent state does not always *present* in therapy, though will invariably be present and influencing both therapeutic outcomes and the origins of the pathologies presenting for treatment. The various manifestations of this drive, hot, cold, or competitive aggression, will play an outsized, albeit often invisible-to-the-naked-eye role, so to speak. This is the nub of the issue and its significance. Let us revisit Freud's point regarding treatment that the portion of libido that is capable of becoming conscious and is directed towards reality is diminished, and the portion that is directed away from reality and is unconscious, and which, though it may still feed the subject's phantasies, nevertheless belongs to the unconscious, is proportionately increased. "The libido (whether wholly or in part) has entered on a regressive course and has revived the subject's infantile imagos. The analytic treatment now proceeds to follow it; it seeks to track down the libido, to make it accessible to consciousness and, in the end, serviceable for reality." Where the investigations of analysis come upon the libido "withdrawn into its hiding-place", a struggle is bound to break out in which all the forces that have caused the libido to regress "will rise up as 'resistances' against the work of analysis, in order to conserve the new state of things". He adds that "if the libido's introversion or regression had not been justified by a parti-cular relation between the subject and the external world—stated in the most general terms, by the frustration of satisfaction —and if it had not for the moment even become expedient, it could never have taken place at all".[22]

Freud's points capture several important issues: his emphasis on the sexual drive in the aetiology of psychopathology and also therefore of its centrality in treatment; but also, his recognition, perhaps without emphasis, that the resistances are tied up with the need to 'conserve' – the universal tension between variation and conservation that haunts all living substances, an oscillating dance of nature, that inhabits the transference dynamic of all treatment. But the dance of libido with conservation, variation with self-identity, coalescing through evolution with the Markov blanket is a dance in which it takes One-to-Tango, at least on the manifest face of it. The unob-trusive nature of the psychical death drive makes it more difficult to *feel* internally and in the therapeutic relationship. Note also, the element of *frus-tration* we discussed in Chapter 2, as manifesting in the therapeutic setting also, and hence triggering resistances that require surmounting.

Memory, and its tendency to automatise programmes for efficient naviga-tion of life, is central to all psychotherapies, since in memory is 'bound' both the traumas of history and the repetitive solutions the patient has found to manage them. This important point can be distilled: *memory can be seen to encode two things: a drive that promotes towards homeostatic settling and a drive that retards (binds) towards homeostatic settling.* The psyche must remember efficiently how to navigate the environment towards the fulfilment of needs, but it must also rapidly encode into memory experiences that threaten entropy, obstruct homeostatic settling, and are therefore aversive. Memory serves the requirements of the pleasure-unpleasure principle by encoding efficient navigation towards or away from that which moves the individual towards or away from homeostatic parameters – feel-good or feel-bad. Life-drive pressures to meet needs that are registered consciously as feelings, aim to promote pleasure and the approach to homeostatic settling points which are subjectively experienced as good; but also, memory must encode aversive or frustrating experiences that move the individual away from homeostasis and towards unpleasure, which, as mentioned, increases free energy and threatens entropy, and when this occurs, defences must be brought to bear to do their job of binding it and reducing arousal back to the experience of a quiescent state, even when to some extent an illusory one.

The aggressive drive is activated in response to this second problem in which the needle is being pressed towards unpleasure and away from homeostasis – and the greater the threat and aversion, the greater this memory must encode it and employ its weapons of defence. Remembering to take the sunblock is useful but remembering to not put your fingers on a hot stove is essential. In short, memory serves both masters of the life and death drives simultaneously, but it is the death drive pathways aimed at binding excess, that promotes defensive pathways that fixate and are returned to repeatedly – this latter being causal in the genesis of symptoms and psychopathology but also the resistances in treatment.

Memory encodes to promote a drive that promotes homeostatic settling and a drive that retards homeostatic settling; the former drives homeostatic settling through efficient feed-forward implicit knowledge that certain feelings with certain valence prompts certain action in the real world to fulfil whatever needs are prompting, in their specificity – so that the remedy for air hunger is different to the remedy for food hunger – both register feelings of unpleasure, but in different ways that require different remedies; the second function of memory is to record threats to meeting needs through any excessive deviation from need-fulfilment – whether over or under-indulged – and is hence secondarily mobilised against entropic pressures and in the interests of homeostatic parameters. This is the function of the aggressive drive – to lay in stealth awaiting mobilisation in the face of entropic pressures brought about by the failure of the libidinal drive to meet required needs to stay alive and trending in the direction of pleasure, rather than unpleasure.

The defensive requirements to bind this excess energy, when free energy increases and threatens (subjective) entropy, falls to the defensive systems available to the individual at their levels of mental development, but given the latent nature of the conservative drive, being background in the absence of unpleasure, makes its presence in the treatment process usually more difficult, since, as Freud noted, this drive seems to do its work "unobtrusively".[23] This character requires treatment to take two competing stances in managing the dance and tensions of the two primary drives: regarding life-drive pressures, it requires a receptacle to absorb and contain needs, feelings, and transference requirements in a more passive style, one in which the blank but empathic screen can enable a neutral space for unconscious material to find its way to the surface; but it also requires attention to the character of the core conservative death drive that does not seek to make its presence felt and remains often unfelt in doing its work for the mental apparatus, leaving the aggressive pathways of hot, cold, introjected, projected, inverted, and so on, not being manifest unless the clinician actively identifies, names, and surfaces these elements, whether or not they are brought to the surface by the patient. As an example, a depressed patient, and especially one suffering from post-partum depression, may *never* name their rage (at their infant) or even be aware of it without this being 'outed' through clinician linking. A mother struggling with post-partum depression will unlikely recognise her feelings of violence being introjected in the face of unboundaried infantile demands and attacks which, by definition, unsettle her homeostatic parameters and evokes a counter-aggressive mobilisation – but which cannot be expressed at her baby and turns in against her own ego. So difficult are these *feelings* of hate or violence, that they find no conscious place at all in her mind, and yet once named by the clinician, will invariably *be there* and then emerge into the foreground of conscious thought.

This example is a single one, but applies to treatment in general – that the making manifest of the aggressive elements, so central in the genesis of psychopathology and symptoms, requires active interpretation rather than passive receptivity, no matter how psychoanalytical the style of the clinician. Our treatment task remains, as Freud noted, and we all would likely agree: "In consequence of the special character of our discoveries, our scientific work in psychology will consist in translating unconscious processes into conscious ones, and thus filling in the gaps in conscious perception...."[24] – but what can be added to this general comment is that whilst any depth-oriented clinician would agree that the bringing into consciousness is a key task of treatment to alleviate symptoms and bring about fundamental change to prevent their recurrence, not everyone would agree that for the process to be effective and efficient, two forms of approach are simultaneously required. One of these engages the life-drive demands that tend to make themselves manifest because they are the psychical representative of the stimuli originating from within the organism and reaching the mind, as a measure of the demand made upon the mind for work in consequence of its connection with the body[25] in a more *passive* manner, since these feelings will emerge according to their own volition, but also with the death drive defences and their effects, which will not become manifest without judicious but *active* ferreting, formulation, and interpretation.

Kohut, the famous self-psychologist, I think captured this tension in technique rather well – writing about empathy and the abuse of the concept in treatment approaches, when he wrote,

> That I have a sense of responsibility about the abuse of this concept. The fact again that people have acted as if I were abusing it makes me go up on a high horse, and say, 'These idiots, they don't read what I write!' ... They will claim that empathy cures. They will claim that one has to be just 'empathic' with one's patients and they'll be doing fine. I don't believe that at all! What do I believe? Before I go into the more exact practical statements aimed to contribute a little bit of antidote to the sentimentalising perversions in psychotherapy about curing through love, through empathy, through kindness, through compassion, to just being there and being nice and 'Yes, I understand you'; before I go into that, I think what I need to do, if I take you seriously, and I think I should, is to define empathy on the various levels on which this concept can be used.[26]

Kohut grapples with the concept of empathy because, I suspect, he recognised the strange duality it demands in attuning to both drives of the mental apparatus, commenting, "Empathy serves also, and this is now the most difficult part—namely, that despite all that I have said, empathy, per se, is a therapeutic action in the broadest sense, a beneficial action in the broadest sense of the word... Namely, that the presence of empathy in the surrounding milieu, whether used for compassionate, well-intentioned therapeutic, and now listen, even for utterly destructive purposes, is still an admixture of something positive."[27] Kohut is bringing to the fore, perhaps for different reasons, the latent nature of the aggressive components, commenting how early dysregulation creates a mobilisation of a response that is not always manifest, lost in the milieu, as he puts it, and hence non-declarative, at least not without an *active* interpretation from the clinician. Referring to early experience, he writes that the loss of an empathic and understanding milieu, the loss of understanding in childhood, can become internalised like a fish in water does not always recognize its medium. He wrote:

> There are children with horrible mothers and fathers, misunderstanding their kids, reacting to them in horrible ways (oh, of course, they show the scars when they grow up); but the worst suffering I've seen in adult patients is in those very subtle, and difficult to uncover, absences of the mother—because her personality is absent. *Nothing will be told about it, because the patient assumes this is the milieu in which people grew up.*[28]

Of course, an absent mother must evoke dreadful feelings of abandonment and unsafety in an infant, threatening homeostasis, frustrating need-fulfilment, and hence mobilising some form of the death drive response. However, because this represents the internal milieu of the patient, their underlying aggression may seem quite latent, as if simply a normal part of their interiority. I quote Kohut, a little generously I concede, because I think intuitively he is recognising the strange duality required in psychotherapeutic intervention, and that empathic attunement (to libidinal pressures and their frustrations) reflects only half the intervention required, and which constitutes a partial error in many treatment approaches within the psychodynamic tradition, not as a measure of quantity (of sessions per week or month) but as a measure of the requirement to attune to both drives, which manifest in two different directions, and although Kohut does not make this link, he does seem to grapple with this duality. He submits that the most important point about the analytic cure carries qualities beyond interventions on the level of interpretation, "understanding", repeating and confirming what the patient feels and says, which he regards as only the first step; interpretation involves moving from confirming that the analyst knows what the patient feels and thinks and imagines (that he's in tune with his inner life), to the next step of giving of interpretations which represents a move from a lower form of empathy to what he calls a higher form of empathy. Kohut suggests that treatment requires a "fine understanding of the various secondary conflicts that intervene as far as the expression of these [childhood wishes and needs] are concerned. The paradigm, or should I rather say (because that's now a loaded word too, for some crazy reason), the prototype, the prototype of this shift—this two-step moves from understanding to explaining—is, in childhood, a particular situation that I described, hopefully with feeling, in my new work...".[29] Interpretation and empathy must involve, I suggest, those manifest and latent elements of both drives, rather than only those that are manifest.

Freud had counselled that therapeutic technique involves something "very simple", as he put it, which "rejects the use of any special expedient (even that of taking notes). It consists simply in not directing one's notice to anything in particular and in maintaining the same 'evenly-suspended attention' (as I have called it) in the face of all that one hears".[30] Thus, the clinician should "'simply listen, and not bother about whether he is keeping anything in mind.'"[31] I believe such a quality requires attention to both drives – which require different approaches – about which I shall have more to say in a bit. Nonetheless, in contrast to this conventional and more familiar approach, what I think Kohut is noting at this 11th hour of his life, his last public address before he died just a few days later, was linking traditional, more passive approaches of empathic attunement to life-drive processes, feelings, dreams, phantasies, needs, frustrations – but highlighting, in his own way, that whereas traditional technique might stop at this level of empathy, it misses the other half of the treatment requirements. What he calls "inter-pretation" is not only in the traditional sense of making links to unconscious elements, but also to move from the passive to active method by fore-grounding the pathways the aggressive drive might take in its defensive con-stellations in response to these life drive injuries, and the failure of need-fulfilment in early life that prompts the infant towards meeting homeostatic maintenance and limiting or minimising entropic pressures through binding, or at least minimising free energy.

Duality in Drive – Duality in Technique

Freud had suggested that the clinical attitude requires a form of neutrality, not only empathy, in which, to put it in a formula: "he must turn his own unconscious like a receptive organ towards the transmitting unconscious of the patient...",[32] and like a telephone receiver intercepting and interpreting impulses into something meaningful, suggested the need to make interpreta-tion "from the derivatives of the unconscious which are communicated to him, to reconstruct that unconscious, which has determined the patient's free associations".[33] Free association in Freud's paradigm generally involved the unlocking of repressions that have steered sexual elements into various defensive constellations, or put neuroscientifically, that steer feeling-driven needs into memory constellations that have found *imperfect but automatised solutions to insoluble problems* of infancy and childhood. Because such imperfect solutions are encoded in memory, they are revisited repeatedly, as is required to navigate life efficiently (we cannot invent anew a solution for old problems every time we encounter them – for the economics of life would prohibit this as a good method for surviving over time). This tendency to revisit, the repetition compulsion, makes sense from the vantage point of the fixation in the child, who has found a mental solution, however imperfect that solution may be. But in treatment we have to tackle these repetitions, freeing the psyche "from the stasis constituted by the repetitive configurations, permutations, and transformation of representationality",[34] as Barratt puts it. Barratt adds, eloquently suggesting that, "Free-associa-tive discourse is inherently healing in that it mobilises the subject's libi-dinality or life's energies in a way that appreciated the holistic connectivity of the human bodymind with the expressiveness of free-associative discourse."[35]

However, Barratt's point about "stasis", mentioned above, is also sugges-tive of an element often unspoken in treatment, since stasis is also repre-sented by the aggressive-conservative death-drive. Barratt's point focuses the treatment on the "libidinality" and "free energies" of the patient as a pro-moter of healing, as was Freud's focus on the libidinal elements, whilst of course deeply insightful and appropriate, tends to leave aside the activation of the aggressive drive, which Freud identified and Barratt recognises, and this dual drive element gives rise to the requirement, in my view, of a dual approach to interpretation.

The one requirement is not new to any practicing psychotherapist, the empathic attunement to the libidinal conflicts stirred by needs and losses, unrequited longings and hurts, narcissistic injuries and so forth, which emerge as feelings, needs, which *make their presence felt* through their contact with internal perception, and hence to which the more passive, reflective, and time-biding approach to associations is effective. The same cannot be said of this effective approach to the aggressive drive's role – since its latent, stealth-like nature often does not, and will not always make itself felt, even after years of treatment. It has to be *actively* named, noted, mentioned as an antidote to its latent unobtrusive tendencies, mapped through early development and personality, and brought into the open *for* the patient to recognise its place in their psychic makeup. Since the aggressive drive has a role as an inner guardian, empathy to this function means recognising its reactivity to old insoluble problems in which excess arousal in response to needs that were not met (timeously), must be bound to reverse entropic trends, or at least the subjective experience of same. To an adult, a crying baby is not at risk for entropy – but for the crying baby, without means or meaning, the intensity of such experience can certainly *feel* like it threatens fragmentation/ annihilation/ entropy.

Therapeutic intervention requires, in my view, two components: the one we are all familiar with, empathy to injury and distress, loss and longing and a passive receptivity to what the patient brings from their conscious and unconscious experience and their feelings about their lives; but also, it requires attention in an active manner to the more stealth-like activations of the aggressive drive in response to these failures of libidinal pressures to find their adequate fulfilment. Only in this dual fashion, it seems to me, can treatment efficacy be fully realised, improving outcomes for symptoms but also in a time-frame that is prudent. Attending to only half the technique, may prolong both treatment and its efficacy. The essential debate of many treatment approaches, including classic psychoanalysis, rests on the active versus passive approaches to intervention. Based on the theoretical positions argued above, and premised on modern neuroscientific views, is that this split is a synthetic one; both passive (to active libidinal associations) and active (to passive death drive manifestations) interventions and interpretations are required for a full and effective treatment of symptoms, psychopathology, and personality.

As Freud said, treatment is like a game fought out by masters, but not only in a theoretical sense of modelling from the greats, or even from supervisors with experience, but by paying attention to the two grand masters of the drive – both life and death drive pathways in psychogenesis, and their dual roles in the genesis of symptoms and psychopathology, and evenly attending in both passive *and* active ways to the dual manifestations they bring to bear in human psychology. It should be remembered that whereas eros/ the libidinal drive promotes the requirement to meet needs and is thus also a disruptor, by increasing excitations until needs are met, when they are not, the death drive aims to retard free energy, to bind it, to reduce excitations to as low a level as it can, or even to a quiescent state. This is the nature of defences, that aim to bind this excess arousal through available means, developmentally.

Like Waiting for Godot

It is, therefore, also this duality that requires a dual-nature intervention, a two-pronged approach to how psychic material, conscious and unconscious, and its associations and enactments, are handled. This is true whether the unconscious memory that is being sought and elicited through associations are born of declarative or non-declarative systems, implicit or not to the patient's cognitive conscious. For when a patient "simply tries to 'make the best' of a difficult job",[36] as Kinet puts it, they lean deeply into their familiar and historically predictive methods for binding excess mental energy, this mental task is essentially mobilising the death drive though its defensive mechanisms and pathways to complete the job of restoring what becomes consciously experienced as homeostatic – even when such familiar ground underpins damaging patterns and repetitions that promote symptoms.

Reworking old memory systems and their prediction errors,[37] particularly early ones that are non-declarative (and hence powerfully etched onto the psychic landscape), rely on their working through via repetition in treatment (in the transference) since these patterns cannot be cognitively retrieved but only enacted in the treatment and in life. But, since the conservative drive may not always present *itself* through such a therapeutic endeavour, given the latent nature of this drive, and despite everyone's best intentions, suggests that active extraction becomes essential for therapeutic efficacy *in a reasonable time*, rather than a proverbial passive approach of waiting for the Godot,[38] a situation that strives, according to the Irish critic Mercier, to achieve a theoretical impossibility – "a play in which nothing happens, that yet keeps audiences glued to their seats".[39] And then, to make matters worse, of what Barratt likes to call the "workplaying alliance"[40] of psychotherapy, writes Mercier, "What's more, since the second act is a subtly different reprise of the first, he has written a play in which nothing happens, twice."[41] Barratt reminds us that free-associative discourse is inherently healing in that it "mobilises the subjects libidinality or life energies" – and adds that the "pluritemporality of embodied experience is only repressively disclosed to self-consciousness by way of its disguised expression *in the streaming of thoughts and feelings*"[42] but one from which one can "never be fully free".[43]

A full intervention in treatment requires duality, a two-tiered system technically, to meet the dual nature of the psychical system itself. As discussed, the expression of thoughts and feelings and these derivatives of the libidinal drive, make their presence felt through internal perception, whereas the conservative drive does its work unobtrusively. This tension and drive-difference leaks into the therapeutic endeavour, the life drive making more contact with our internal perception and manifest, while the death drive does its work unobtrusively and tends to remain more latent.[44]

Accordingly, the 'streaming of thoughts and feelings' tends to reflect the libidinal elements which make their presence felt because of the inbuilt phylogenetic and broad organic *push* that this drive musters in the interests of meeting needs and adapting to challenges through evolutionary variation. I also want to remind the reader in this context of treatment, how the evolutionary biologist Nick Lane's points out that as he reflects on his depiction of the origins of life finds himself also using the term *drive*, as in life drive, since he says, "there isn't a better word" to capture the idea that it is not passive chemistry "but it is *forced*, pushed, driven by the continuous flux of carbon, energy, protons. These reactions *need* to happen...".[45] Libido in humans is not a passive energy – it *pushes* for expression, for the drive to procreate in the service is not only self-survival but that of the species. This is where Barratt's point retains muster – and most therapeutic engagements rely on this drive for the work of psychotherapy to be done. But half the psyche remains, thereby, unrepresented, or at best, under-represented. The death drive seeks to remain background, unobtrusive, as Freud describes it, and hence does not inevitably press forward into proprioceptive consciousness. The conservative drive requires an invitation to attend awareness, to be brought forward into consciousness, and to contradict its nature of preferring the latent state to the manifest one. This more active approach may well horrify clinicians trained in the traditional models of psychoanalysis, and to which most modern therapeutic approaches owe their basic technique, and yet this dual-aspect component to treatment across the symptoms and syndromes we encounter, would, in my experience, benefit significantly from both an efficacy and an economics of time point of view.

But in addition, prioritising the life drive push-elements creates a contradiction: it neglects the essential theoretical discovery Freud made that libidinal drives create feelings and affects which in turn disrupt homeostasis in the interests of serving homeostasis, that the pleasure principle seems actually to serve the death instincts. As Freud noted, "It is true that it keeps watch upon stimuli from without, which are regarded as dangers by both kinds of instincts; but it is more especially on guard against increases of stimulation from within, which would make the task of living more difficult."[46] Hence, whenever feelings pursue needs in the external world to reduce excitations exceed their capacity to achieve their goals, especially in infancy and childhood when needs in conflict sometimes cannot be met or resolved, then the increase in free energy will demand the activation of the death drive, in the interests and service of restoration and conservation, and sometimes, this will be in the resistances of treatment itself. Leaving this unaddressed in treatment is like waiting for nothing to happen whilst glued to our seats, and like Beckett's Godot, doing that twice, and for a small fee.

Notes

1 Freud, S. (1913) On Beginning the Treatment (Further Recommendations on the Technique of Psycho-Analysis I). *The Standard Edition of the Complete Psychological Works of Sigmund Freud* 12:121–144, p.123.
2 Freud, S. (1937) Analysis Terminable and Interminable. *The Standard Edition of the Complete Psychological Works of Sigmund Freud* 23:209–254, p.231.
3 Freud, S. (1937) Analysis Terminable and Interminable. *The Standard Edition of the Complete Psychological Works of Sigmund Freud* 23:209–254, p.229.
4 Freud, S. (1937) Analysis Terminable and Interminable. *The Standard Edition of the Complete Psychological Works of Sigmund Freud* 23:209–254, p.229.
5 Freud, S. (1937) Analysis Terminable and Interminable. *The Standard Edition of the Complete Psychological Works of Sigmund Freud* 23:209–254, p.231.
6 Freud, S. (1937) Analysis Terminable and Interminable. *The Standard Edition of the Complete Psychological Works of Sigmund Freud* 23:209–254, p.235.
7 Freud, S. (1937) Analysis Terminable and Interminable. *The Standard Edition of the Complete Psychological Works of Sigmund Freud* 23:209–254, p.237.
8 Freud, S. (1937) Analysis Terminable and Interminable. *The Standard Edition of the Complete Psychological Works of Sigmund Freud* 23:209–254, p.237.
9 Freud, S. (1937) Analysis Terminable and Interminable. *The Standard Edition of the Complete Psychological Works of Sigmund Freud* 23:209–254, p.239.
10 Valdrè, R. (2025). *The Death Drive: A Contemporary Introduction.* New York/London: Routledge, p.89.
11 Freud, S. (1937) Analysis Terminable and Interminable. *The Standard Edition of the Complete Psychological Works of Sigmund Freud* 23:209–254, p.240.
12 Freud, S. (1937) Analysis Terminable and Interminable. *The Standard Edition of the Complete Psychological Works of Sigmund Freud* 23:209–254, p.243.
13 Freud, S. (1937) Analysis Terminable and Interminable. *The Standard Edition of the Complete Psychological Works of Sigmund Freud* 23:209–254, p.244.
14 Freud, S. (1937) Analysis Terminable and Interminable. *The Standard Edition of the Complete Psychological Works of Sigmund Freud* 23:209–254, p.246.
15 Freud, S. (1920) Beyond the Pleasure Principle. *The Standard Edition of the Complete Psychological Works of Sigmund Freud* 18:1–64, pp.40–41.
16 Freud, S. (1912) The Dynamics of Transference. *The Standard Edition of the Complete Psychological Works of Sigmund Freud* 12:97–108, p.103.
17 Barratt, B. (2013) *What is Psychoanalysis: 100 Years after Freud's 'Secret Committee'.* London: Routledge, p.131.
18 Barratt, B. (2013) *What is Psychoanalysis: 100 Years after Freud's 'Secret Committee'.* London: Routledge, p.138.
19 Barratt, B. (2013) *What is Psychoanalysis: 100 Years after Freud's 'Secret Committee'.* London: Routledge, p.138.
20 This capitalised notation refers to Panksepp's neurobiological identification of a system that describes the forward thrust of an organism. See Panksepp, J. & Biven, L. (2012) *The Archaeology of Mind: Neuroevolutionary Origins of Human Emotions.* New York: Norton.
21 Freud, S. (1920) Beyond the Pleasure Principle. *The Standard Edition of the Complete Psychological Works of Sigmund Freud* 18:1–64, p.63.

22 Freud, S. (1912) The Dynamics of Transference. *The Standard Edition of the Complete Psychological Works of Sigmund Freud* 12:97–108, p.103.
23 Freud, S. (1920) Beyond the Pleasure Principle. *The Standard Edition of the Complete Psychological Works of Sigmund Freud* 18:1–64, p.63.
24 Freud, S. (1938) Some Elementary Lessons in Psycho-Analysis. *The Standard Edition of the Complete Psychological Works of Sigmund Freud* 23:279–286, p.286.
25 Freud, S. (1915) Instincts & Their Vicissitudes. *The Standard Edition of the Complete Psychological Works of Sigmund Freud*, 14:109–140, p.122.
26 Kohut, H. (2010) On Empathy: Heinz Kohut (1981)2. *International Journal of Psychoanalytic Self Psychology* 5:122–131, p.124.
27 Kohut, H. (2010) On Empathy: Heinz Kohut (1981)2. *International Journal of Psychoanalytic Self Psychology* 5:122–131, p.126.
28 Kohut, H. (2010) On Empathy: Heinz Kohut (1981)2. *International Journal of Psychoanalytic Self Psychology* 5:122–131, p.127 (italics mine).
29 Kohut, H. (2010) On Empathy: Heinz Kohut (1981)2. *International Journal of Psychoanalytic Self Psychology* 5:122–131, p.128.
30 Freud, S. (1912) Recommendations to Physicians Practising Psycho-Analysis. *The Standard Edition of the Complete Psychological Works of Sigmund Freud* 12:109–120, pp.111–112.
31 Freud, S. (1912) Recommendations to Physicians Practising Psycho-Analysis. *The Standard Edition of the Complete Psychological Works of Sigmund Freud* 12:109–120, p.112.
32 Freud, S. (1912) Recommendations to Physicians Practising Psycho-Analysis. *The Standard Edition of the Complete Psychological Works of Sigmund Freud* 12:109–120, pp.115.
33 Freud, S. (1912) Recommendations to Physicians Practising Psycho-Analysis. *The Standard Edition of the Complete Psychological Works of Sigmund Freud* 12:109–120, pp.115–116.
34 Barratt, B. (2013) *What is Psychoanalysis: 100 Years after Freud's 'Secret Committee'*. London: Routledge, p.127.
35 Barratt, B. (2013) *What is Psychoanalysis: 100 Years after Freud's 'Secret Committee'*. London: Routledge, p.127.
36 Kinet, M. (2024) *The Spirit of the Drive in Psychoanalysis*. Routledge: London/New York, p.89.
37 Solms deals with this central concept of memory as it relates to prediction and prediction errors. Solms, M. (2021) *The Hidden Spring: A Journey to the Source of Consciousness*. London: Profile Books, pp. 184–185.
38 *Waiting for Godot* is a play by Irish playwright Samuel Beckett in which two characters, Vladimir (Didi) and Estragon (Gogo), engage in a variety of discussions and encounters while awaiting the titular Godot, who never arrives. *Waiting for Godot* is Beckett's reworking of his own original French-language play, *En attendant Godot*, and is subtitled (in English only) "a tragicomedy in two acts". In a poll conducted by the British Royal National Theatre in 1998/99, it was voted the "most significant English-language play of the 20th century". https://en.wikipedia.org/wiki/Waiting_for_Godot
39 Vivien Mercier is an Irish Literary Critic – cited in https://en.wikipedia.org/wiki/Waiting_for_Godot
40 To borrow playfully Barratt's use of the term that analysis is a therapy-play space. p.149.
41 Vivien Mercier, Irish Literary Critic – cited in https://en.wikipedia.org/wiki/Waiting_for_Godot
42 Barratt, B. (2013) *What is Psychoanalysis: 100 Years after Freud's 'Secret Committee'*. London: Routledge, p.128 (italics mine).

43 Barratt, B. (2013) *What is Psychoanalysis: 100 Years after Freud's 'Secret Committee'*. London: Routledge, pp.127–128.
44 Freud, S. (1920) Beyond the Pleasure Principle. *The Standard Edition of the Complete Psychological Works of Sigmund Freud* 18:1–64, p.63.
45 Lane, N. (2016) *The Vital Question: Why is Life the Way it Is?* London: Profile Books, p.135.
46 Freud, S. (1920) Beyond the Pleasure Principle. *The Standard Edition of the Complete Psychological Works of Sigmund Freud* 18:1–64, p.63.

Conclusion

The nature of the death drive, and its various aggressive derivatives, is paradoxical and elusive, and yet plays a central role in psychogenesis, and perhaps *the* central role in the genesis of symptoms and psychopathology, and the formation of personality. It is also such an unpalatable dimension of human existence, especially given its potential for its scalability into destructiveness, and its capacity for perversion in humans. It is also a truth we have to dissect, face square-on, understand fully. As I mentioned in the preface, when Bob Dylan wrote that Oedipus went looking for the truth and when he found it, it ruined him, prompting him to turn his back on the truth, he was reflecting how so often in life, the truth brings its own sets of pain and challenge, and which we turn our noses from that which is malodorous. Some things are, perhaps, better left unseen and unsaid. This is not only a bitter-sweet *philosophical* reflection – science, too, is never free from emotional drivers – if the science of subjectivity and consciousness is to be believed. We try our best to mitigate subjectivity by good methods of research but in the end, what we feel drives so much of what we think, not the other way round. And this is the great breakthrough of neuroscientists such as Damasio, Panksepp, and Solms,[1] who note that affects and feelings drive consciousness, and the mental representations these form to 'ideate' them for future reference and meaning. *This* feeling means *that*. Air hunger feels different from food hunger. It's the best way, perhaps the only way, to survive and fulfil the ultimate dictate of evolution: which is to persist. Life is good, death is bad. Thinking, and our ways of thinking about things in the world, emerge from this reality.

Maybe, as Dylan wrote, the truth *can* be a "cruel horror of a joke", but if we in our studies of the mind do go sniffing, foraging, do SEEK, and do stumble on the truth, it might be prudent to not "sit on it and keep it down". This is the great legacy of the greats – they notice simple things and turn toward them with curiosity – and in particular Freud's bold and courageous discoveries that, especially in his day, were not easily received. But Freud was also the first to recognise his own limitations and those of his time, and credit future science and biology with its discoveries-to-come, as he wrote,

DOI: 10.4324/9781003628972-13

"we may expect it to give us the most surprising information and we cannot guess which answers it will return in a few dozen years to the questions we have put to it",[2] which might alter the way we think about his work and the mind.

And as neuroscience has evolved, this is precisely what has occurred, through bold initiatives by contemporary thinkers, some of whom we have leant on in this book, such as Solms, Friston, Kandel, and Panksepp, and which both verify, and in places refute, some of Freud's key assumptions. The death drive, and its place in the mind, is one very contentious construct of Freud, and some contemporary scientists and thinkers make the claim that there is no need for the concept. This book makes the opposite claim – that the death drive not only exists, not only that it has a relationship to the life drive and is directly bridged to it, but also, that this is the most critical and principal agent in the genesis of symptoms and psychopathology. Whilst Freud was bold yet humble, I should add that the thinkers in this book who challenge some of Freud's assumptions, like many great conquistadors of knowledge, bring their own brand of humility, being open to debate, refutation, rethinking. Whilst paradigms can be sticky masters exhibiting a Velcro effect, the greats invariably open themselves to challenge, and this book hopefully celebrates that notion.

Gloomily, albeit poetically, Dylan captures a universal problem of paradigms – and the succumbing to the dictates of the pleasure principle we all can suffer from, the intrinsic desire to move away from those things we find less palatable to those we find more so, even theoretically. No-one worth their scientific salt does so out of intellectual dishonesty or lack of courage – the greatest and boldest of thinkers have fallen foul of this problem, as mentioned earlier.

In my previous book, I attempted to take the reader on an exploratory journey that brought into focus the strange paradoxes of human aggression and its role through the lenses of biology, psychology, psychoanalysis, and the current neurosciences. Using various examples of the destructive effects of human aggression, I sought to demonstrate the distinction between its benign aims and its malignant effects, in its role as guardian of psychic homeostasis, and the conservation of subjectivity. I also touched upon the implications of this analysis in the genesis of symptoms – but which required a significant fuller treatment. In this book, I have attempted to elaborate on this undertaking, centralising the function of the death drive and its aggressive derivatives in the formation of symptoms and hence also of its role in treatment, suggesting from the evidence that a dual-drive model of mind requires a dual-approach intervention strategy in treatment. The traditional passive approaches are lengthy and costly, and in some respects also violate the model of mind that modern neuroscience would suggest validates Freud's dual-drive model of mind, locating it in the evolutionary context, and the underlying biological underpinnings from which human aggression springs.

This role of the death drive, that Freud so cleverly and deftly formulated, has remained, however, on the margins of mainstream psychoanalysis and psychological thinking, sometimes regarded as an unsavory concept reflecting an aspect of human function best disposed of and constrained, an imperative of which we are reminded daily of the atrocities we see in the media. The awful effects of aggression in both domestic and geo-political spaces give pause for thought, and most would wish it gone from the human condition. But doing so, would leave the human psyche unbound, unguarded, without a mechanism to conserve it when free energy is pushing the organism towards entropy, without a form of psychical immunity. Psychical aggression, like the immune system of the body, is tasked with the requirement to maintain and conserve its charge, but from the vantage of a pathogen disrupting the homeostasis of the organism, woe betide its own destiny, whose fate will be one of short shrift.

In this technical sense, that Freud termed the death drive, and from which aggression emerges in the service of conservation and binding excess free energy that threatens the subject, this mechanism is essential, and as I hope to have shown with the few examples of psychopathology I covered, *the* central driver of problems and maladies of the mind. Remaining with Freud's own paradigmatic bias, centralising the libidinal in the genesis of symptoms, is an example of the sticky Velcro nature of paradigms, from which gravitational pull even the great master himself did not fully escape. Although he wrote, that our views have "from the very first been *dualistic*, and to-day they are even more definitely dualistic than before..."[3], in the end, he remained largely wedded to the profound but earlier formulations of his scientific career. But to be fair, as mentioned, Freud actively conceded that only time and the development of biology and neuroscience would deliver to us the answers required to possibly shift the paradigmatic emphasis from the libidinal to the aggressive, from life drive to death drive, in the genesis of psychopathology and symptoms.

With the advent of affective neuroscience, the neuroscience of consciousness, and the righting of the model of mind from whence consciousness arises, we also encounter in scientific thought the role of free energy, the Markov blanket, and the tension between subjectivity and identity versus the threats of diffusion and entropy. Life's continuance, at both personal and species levels, requires these drives to find balance. When they do not, when problems cannot be solved in early development, the psyche must use whatever available means it has to reduce excitations through meeting needs, and when needs are not met and free energy increases, defences must activate to bind this excess, and manage energetic constancy for the mind. These defences, with which we are so familiar in psychoanalysis, are driven by the death drive, psychical immunity aiming to reduce pathognomonic effects, but when fixated at these points in development, are returned to repeatedly under the pressures of the repetition compulsion, built upon the mind's bedrock of memory as a mechanism to automatise effective management of complexity, and its feedforward process to help efficient and optimal circumnavigation of life. But as always, the costs can be in the form of symptoms, the drag of increased thrust, the balancing of the energetic requirement of life in general. It is also the blessing and the curse of the mind's capacity for automatising, the good and the bad, for better and for worse.

All organic activity must navigate such balances between the tensions and challenges of living, moving forward through creative adaptation or variation, and maintaining selfhood and identity. If only, we can at least dream, common sense would enable humans to find the balance without recourse to manifest expressions of aggression and violence against others, or the compromise-formations that lead to symptoms and psychopathology. But as Anna Freud remarked to an analyst she was supervising: "The trouble with common sense is that it is so uncommon".[4] The complexity of the human mind keeps us perpetually guessing, navigating the oscillations around the mean, finding homeostasis for only brief moments until something internal or external disrupts it, pushes us to *do* something, to action a need, to wriggle and move, to express, abreact, and seek. Simultaneously, we jerk back, find it all too much, require a recalibration that allows us to exhale, breath more gently, forget for a bit that our heart beats, despite the fact that it simply does, outside our notice, until a disruptor prevails again, and our hearts break, and it makes the soma knock on the door of the psyche, or the psyche on the door of the soma. It's an integrated and dialectical marvel.

The trouble, also, is that not only are human needs met in the real world, but in the real world of objects and attachments, who, unfortunately, have minds of their own, and react and respond according to their own internal histories and makeups, adding layers of complexity to how needs get met, especially complex ones like sex, love, and dependency. Such complexity relies on complex mechanisms of both brain and mind. There's simply no escaping it, since the greatest imperative of life is to persist, to stay alive, and maintain our viable parameters to do so. The life-drive prompts needs, which prompt feelings, to register which needs must be met, and when they are not, and free energy increases, when our core comes under the perception of threat from internal or external sources, and arousal is heightening, frustration is triggered and then the death drive mobilises, often with some form of aggressive manifestation to bind this excess, and help return to the perception of homeostasis. It starts with the first cry of the human infant. How strange that the first act of any human life is driven by the death drive!

Alas, it is often the *perception* of stasis that prevails – especially in infancy and childhood when options for remedy remain so curtailed and limited. The infant can only use those defensive manoeuvres that are available to it at the time – but it is also these effective mechanisms that become fixated, engraved into memory to which, under the pressures of the repetition compulsion and its automatised 'algorithms', the adult returns over and over, using old methods to try solve new problems in life. It is here that things become unglued, maladaptive, unhelpful – the advantage of the feedforward of efficient automatised memory systems that make the best of a bad lot, continue to ply their wares in the post-childhood new worlds that require updated methods to operate. Yet, this 'updating', when old methods no longer work, invariably succumb to these old methods encoded in memory, a memory that has no reference to time, in an unconscious system that cannot always be thought about in thoughts, or spoken about in words, yet creates experience that feels as real as the day is long, and finds itself enacted in patterns that are bad for us, despite ourselves and our best intentions, and so in its wake brings those maladies of mind that plague us all, at least, from time to time.

This is also the requirement for treatment, analysis, psychotherapy, to address old automatised repertoires and methods that no longer serve the present efficiently enough and update them. Bringing repetitious automatons out of the unconscious shadows and into conscious awareness enables a working-through, a making of a different use of the two drives to maintain health – less rigid, less automatised, better balanced. Essential to this process is the role not only of the libidinal drive in its forward push to bring needs into conscious awareness so they can be acted upon and met, but also the death drive whose function, like the immune system of the body, brings its benign aims to the mix, doing what it can to conserve, preserve, and return to a quiescent state, our mind-body system. As mentioned throughout this book, it does so by attempting to bind free energy, and respond to it as if neutralising a pathogenic disruption.

Valdrè wrote in her conclusion to her book on the death drive, "If we tune into these counterintuitive, profound and paradoxical aspects of human nature, aware that we also have them in ourselves, then analytic work, so complex and almost impossible, becomes like art, among the most authentic of human experiences".[5] Of course, this is in many respects so true – and yet, I can't help thinking about Anna Freud's comment about the promiscuity of hate, and how unresolved resentments and anger do their work relentlessly, trying to undo the tensions, bind excess emotional and mental energies, return the mental apparatus to a quiescent state in the interests of continuing to get through another minute, another day, another year. The ugly side of human aggression has a rosy side too – to represent subjectivity on the stage of the real world, doing what it can to 'work things through', to find a different solution to old-world problems, despite the maddening pull of the repetition compulsion that does not judge the desirable or undesirable in a person's defences – but simply represents them based on encoded automatisms that do their work economically, albeit sometimes painfully, which is what the 'consciousness' of psychotherapeutic treatments are for. That is, to make different meaning out of what was, to unravel the timelessness of the unconscious, and to bring into alignment the patient's current subjectivity with their current real-world environment; to align their infantile selves with their adult selves, to dance the dance of integration of past and present, of the two drives.

So, that when treatment works, taking into account the primacy of the aggressive drive in the genesis of symptoms and psychopathology, so too, to parody Dylan, can Oedipus uncover the truth and not be ruined by it, but enhanced by the unsavoury knowledge that within the victim within, lies a perpetrator within, a 'promiscuous' one, whose noble intent must be embraced as the best of life's challenging lot.

Afterall, mostly, it's in the phantasy that the mischief lies.

Notes

1 Solms, M. (2017) What is "the Unconscious," and Where is it Located in the Brain? A Neuropsychoanalytic Perspective. *Annals of the New York Academy of Sciences* 1406, 90–97.
2 Freud, S. (1920) Beyond the Pleasure. On Metapsychology: The Theory of Psychoanalysis. London: Penguin, p. 334.
3 In Freud, S. (1920) Beyond the Pleasure Principle. *The Standard Edition of the Complete Psychological Works of Sigmund Freud* 18:1–64, p.62.
4 Schwartz, C. The Freuds. In A. Blauner, Ed. (2024). *On the Couch: Writers Analyse Sigmund Freud*. Princeton University Press: Oxford, p.117.
5 Valdrè, R. (2025) *The Death Drive: A Contemporary Introduction*. New York/London: Routledge, p.90.

Acknowledgements

True pioneers of knowledge seem often to carry a magical mix of high passion, determination, persistence, and a taste for drama. Yet the higher they climb the academic and scientific ladder, the greater seems to grow their humility and openness to the evidence and alternative scientific views, even when these refute or challenge their own work. In this category, I must credit Prof. Mark Solms in three respects: firstly, his observations and theories have led to a thousand pennies dropping in my mind, linking biology and neuroscience to psychoanalysis and the functioning of the brain-mind-body system; secondly, where I diverge from his interpretations of some of the data, he has remained magnanimous and entirely comfortable to consider an alternative voice and to be complimentary of a manuscript whose *raison d'etre* directly challenges one or two of his own conclusions; thirdly, his unwavering generosity of spirit. To Mark Solms, a true scientist and a mensch, once again, a great debt of gratitude.

For her wonderful warmth and ongoing support for my works, my Editor Zoë Meyer of Routledge, my deep thanks! I also thank the reviewers whose comments on an earlier draft of this manuscript helped sharpen my pencil. Also, for comments on earlier drafts of this manuscript, my deep gratitude to the two other pioneers in their own rights, Jenny and Michaela.

I have been blessed to be in a professional community whose vitality and vibrance has never waned, and for their wonderful support and spiritedness I owe an ongoing and unrepayable debt, a professional family without whom all this work would seem pointless. I remain particularly indebted to my many colleagues from the various professional groups I have worked with, including the Association of Couple Psychoanalytic Psychotherapists (ACPP), the South African Psychoanalytic Confederation (SAPC), the South African Psychoanalytic Initiative (SAPI) and in particular the SAPI Instinct Group (a wonderful incubator of ideas), the South African Psychoanalytic (SAPI) College, the Cape Town Society for Psychoanalytic Psychotherapy (CTSPP), the Mind-body Behavioural Medicine Group, the International Journal Couple and Family Psychoanalysis, and my colleagues on the editorial boards of the *Psychoanalytic Psychotherapy in South Africa* journal, and the journal *Couple and Family Psychoanalysis*. For all the other colleagues over the years who have directly or indirectly added to my thinking, and there are many, my gratitude.

A book such as this has clinical implications and applications, and hopefully for the better in treating those who struggle with the maladies of the mind. My countless hours in the clinical saddle have taught me a great deal, for which textbooks and academic papers are little substitute, though so terribly important in learning a craft that is truly mastered in the hoary years when one's bottom is calloused from sitting but one's mind is yet sharp and elastic. Trying to learn to fly an aircraft through books or even simulators would be little comfort to any passengers on board, let alone the pilot, especially when turbulence hits or the unexpected intrudes into the routine. There is a saying in aviation: rather be on the ground wishing you were in the air than in the air wishing you were on the ground. Psychological treatment can be like that, and remaining plugged into professional community and its life is essential to the development of technique. Psychotherapies of all sorts require endless time in the saddle, countless hours of supervisions, reading, discussions, conferencing, and the like – but mostly, suffering the bruising encounters and resistances that rattle any clinical smugness that might creep in, reminding one that clinical work is challenging, the mind infinitely complex and unique, and the insights we garner evolve through many years of personal and communal reflection. In this regard, I must credit my patients for the many insights and learnings I have taken from the immense privilege of being granted access to working so deeply in the interior of people's minds and their lives, of going into psychical places not even they have ventured, grappling with the vexing paradoxes of knowing stuff about their inner worlds that even they may not yet know, and which no text could teach. I hope that this book will do credit to these theoretical and clinical complexities and perhaps even contribute to better methods of intervention to relieve suffering and the often-painful affliction that life is.

I should also recognise that one of the best ways to learn is to share ideas, and one of the more humbling and yet most powerful of experiences of professional learning is writing. I have learned a great deal in writing papers and books, despite nursing the not-so-occasional bruising from feedback which sharpens one's thinking. I hope the reader, both professional and non-professional alike, will reflect a little, too, from engaging with these ideas, and debate them. In 1875, whilst still young, Freud wrote in a letter to an Eduard Silberstein: "Never before have I enjoyed that pleasant sensation, which may be called academic happiness, and which mostly derives from the realisation that one is close to the source from which science springs at its purest and from which one will be taking a good long drink". I must therefore also acknowledge those readers who have engaged with these ideas here in the spirit of that good long drink. To life!

Bibliography

Abram, J. (2013). Response by Jan Abram. *International Journal of Psychoanalysis* 94, 121–124.

Austin, S. (2009). A Perspective on the Patterns of Loss, Lack, Disappointment and Shame Encountered in the Treatment of Six Women with Severe and Chronic Anorexia Nervosa. *Journal of Analytical Psychology*, 54, 61–80.

Barratt, B. (2013). *What is Psychoanalysis: 100 Years after Freud's 'Secret Committee'*. London: Routledge.

Beckett, S. (2011). *Waiting for Godot: A Tragicomedy in Two Acts*. New York: Grove Press.

Bion, W.R. (1959). Attacks on linking. *International Journal of Psychoanalysis*, 40, 308–315.

Bion, W. R. (1962). *Learning from Experience*. London: Jason Aronson.

Brian, D. (1996). *Einstein: A Life*. New York: John Wiley & Sons.

Brickman, B. (1988). Psychoanalysis and Substance Abuse: Toward a More Effective Approach. *Journal of the American Academy of Psychoanalysis* 16, 359–379.

Damasio, A. (2018). *The Strange Order of Things: Life, Feeling, and the Making of Cultures*. London: Penguin Random House.

Darwin, C. (2003). *The Origin of Species: By Means of Natural Selection of the Preservation of Favoured Races in the Struggle for Life*. New York: Signet Classic.

Dodes, L. (2017). Addiction, Helplessness, and Narcissistic Rage. *Psychoanalytic Quarterly, LIX*, 1990; published online (2017): https://doi.org/10.1080/21674086. 1990.11927278.

Dylan, B. (2005). *Chronicles. Volume One*. London: Pocket Books Simon & Schuster.

Eigen, M. (2012). On Winnicott's Clinical Innovations in the Analysis of Adults. *International Journal of Psychoanalysis*, 93, 1449–1459.

Einstein, A. (1995). *Relativity*. New York. Prometheus Books.

Eissler, K. R. (1971). Death Drive, Ambivalence, and Narcissism. *Psychoanalytic Study of the Child* 26, 25–78.

Fechner (1873). Einige Ideen zur Schöpfungs-und Entwick-lungsgeschichte der Organismen, 1873 (Part XI, Supplement, 94). Cited in Freud, S. (1920). Beyond the Pleasure Principle. *The Standard Edition of the Complete Psychological Works of Sigmund Freud*, 18, 1–64.

Fonagy, P. & Target, M. (1996). Playing With Reality: I. Theory of Mind and the Normal Development Of Psychic Reality. *International Journal of Psychoanalysis*, 77, 217–233.

Freud, S. (1897). Letter 79 Extracts from the Fliess Papers. In J. Strachey (Ed), *The Standard Edition of the Complete Psychological Works of Sigmund Freud*, 1, 272–273. London: Hogarth.

Freud, S. (1898). Sexuality in the Aetiology of the Neuroses. In J. Strachey (Ed), *The Standard Edition of the Complete Psychological Works of Sigmund Freud*, 3, 259–285. London: Hogarth.

Freud, S. (1901). The Psychopathology of Everyday Life: Forgetting, Slips of the Tongue, Bungled Actions, Superstitions and errors. In Strachey (Ed), *The Standard Edition of the Complete Psychological Works of Sigmund Freud*, 6, 7, 7–296. London: Hogarth.

Freud, S. (1901). On Dreams. In J. Strachey (Ed), *The Standard Edition of the Complete Psychological Works of Sigmund Freud*, 5, 629–686. London: Hogarth.

Freud, S. (1905). Three Essays on the Theory of Sexuality (1905). In J. Strachey (Ed), *The Standard Edition of the Complete Psychological Works of Sigmund Freud*, 7, 123–246. London: Hogarth.

Freud, S. (1905). On Psychotherapy (1905 [1904]). In J. Strachey (Ed), *The Standard Edition of the Complete Psychological Works of Sigmund Freud*, 7, 255–268. London: Hogarth.

Freud, S. (1906). My Views on the Part Played by Sexuality in the Aetiology of the Neuroses (1906 [1905]). In J. Strachey (Ed), *The Standard Edition of the Complete Psychological Works of Sigmund Freud*, 7, 269–279. London: Hogarth.

Freud, S. (1907). The Sexual Enlightenment of Children (An Open Letter to Dr. M. Fürst). In J. Strachey (Ed), *The Standard Edition of the Complete Psychological Works of Sigmund Freud*, 9, 129–140. London: Hogarth.

Freud, S. (1909). Family Romances. In J. Strachey (Ed), *The Standard Edition of the Complete Psychological Works of Sigmund Freud*, 9, 235–242. London: Hogarth.

Freud, S. (1910). Leonardo Da Vinci and a Memory of his Childhood. In J. Strachey (Ed), *The Standard Edition of the Complete Psychological Works of Sigmund Freud*, 11, 57–138. London: Hogarth.

Freud, S. (1911). Formulations on the Two Principles of Mental Functioning. In J. Strachey (Ed), *The Standard Edition of the Complete Psychological Works of Sigmund Freud*, 12, 213–226. London: Hogarth.

Freud, S. (1911). Psycho-Analytic Notes on an Autobiographical Account of a Case of Paranoia (Dementia Paranoides). In J. Strachey (Ed), *The Standard Edition of the Complete Psychological Works of Sigmund Freud*, 12, 1–82. London: Hogarth.

Freud, S. (1912). Recommendations to Physicians Practising Psycho-Analysis. In J. Strachey (Ed), *The Standard Edition of the Complete Psychological Works of Sigmund Freud*, 12, 109–120. London: Hogarth.

Freud, S. (1912). Types of Onset of Neurosis. In J. Strachey (Ed), *The Standard Edition of the Complete Psychological Works of Sigmund Freud*, 12, 227–238. London: Hogarth.

Freud, S. (1912). Contributions to a Discussion on Masturbation. In J. Strachey (Ed), *The Standard Edition of the Complete Psychological Works of Sigmund Freud*, 12, 239–254. London: Hogarth.

Freud, S. (1912). On the Universal Tendency to Debasement in the Sphere of Love (Contributions to the Psychology of Love II). In J. Strachey (Ed), *The Standard Edition of the Complete Psychological Works of Sigmund Freud*, 11, 177–190. London: Hogarth.

Freud, S. (1912). The Dynamics of Transference. In J. Strachey (Ed), *The Standard Edition of the Complete Psychological Works of Sigmund Freud*, 12, 97–108. London: Hogarth.

Freud, S. (1912). Types of Onset of Neurosis. *The Standard Edition of the Complete Psychological Works of Sigmund Freud*, 12, 227–238. London: Hogarth.

Freud, S. (1913). On Beginning the Treatment (Further Recommendations on the Technique of Psycho-Analysis I). In J. Strachey (Ed), *The Standard Edition of the Complete Psychological Works of Sigmund Freud*, 12, 121–144. London: Hogarth.

Freud, S. (1914). On the History of the Psycho-Analytic Movement. In J. Strachey (Ed), *The Standard Edition of the Complete Psychological Works of Sigmund Freud*, 14, 1–66. London: Hogarth.

Freud, S. (1914). On Narcissism: An Introduction. In J. Strachey (Ed), *The Standard Edition of the Complete Psychological Works of Sigmund Freud*, 14, 67–102. London: Hogarth.

Freud, S. (1915). Instincts and their Vicissitudes. In J. Strachey (Ed), *The Standard Edition of the Complete Psychological Works of Sigmund Freud*, 14, 109–140. London: Hogarth.

Freud, S. (1915). The Unconscious. In J. Strachey (Ed), *The Standard Edition of the Complete Psychological Works of Sigmund Freud*, 14, 159–215. London: Hogarth.

Freud, S. (1917). A Difficulty in the Path of Psycho-Analysis. In J. Strachey (Ed), *The Standard Edition of the Complete Psychological Works of Sigmund Freud*, 17, 135–144. London: Hogarth.

Freud, S. (1917). The Paths to the Formation of Symptoms. In Freud, S. (1917). Introductory Lectures on Psycho-Analysis. In J. Strachey (Ed), *The Standard Edition of the Complete Psychological Works of Sigmund Freud*, 16, 241–463. London: Hogarth.

Freud, S. (1917). Introductory Lectures on Psycho-Analysis. In J. Strachey (Ed), *The Standard Edition of the Complete Psychological Works of Sigmund Freud*, 16, 241–463. London: Hogarth.

Freud, S. (1917). Mourning and Melancholia. In J. Strachey (Ed), *The Standard Edition of the Complete Psychological Works of Sigmund Freud*, 14, 237–258. London: Hogarth.

Freud, S. (1918). The Taboo of Virginity (Contributions to the Psychology of Love III). In J. Strachey (Ed), *The Standard Edition of the Complete Psychological Works of Sigmund Freud*, 11, 191–208.

Freud, S. (1919). Letter from Sigmund Freud to Ernest Jones, February 18, 1919. In J. Strachey (Ed), *The Complete Correspondence of Sigmund Freud and Ernest Jones 1908–1939*, 28, 333–335. London: Hogarth.

Freud, S. (1919). Introduction to Psycho-Analysis and the War Neuroses. In J. Strachey (Ed), *The Standard Edition of the Complete Psychological Works of Sigmund Freud*, 17, 205–216. London: Hogarth.

Freud, S. (1920). Beyond the Pleasure Principle. In J. Strachey (Ed), *The Standard Edition of the Complete Psychological Works of Sigmund Freud*, 18, 1–64. London: Hogarth.

Freud, S. (1920). Beyond the Pleasure Principle. In J. Strachey & A. Richards (Eds), *On Metapsychology: The Theory of Psychoanalysis*. London: Penguin.

Freud, S. (1920). Letter from Sigmund Freud to Georg Groddeck, November 28, 1920. *The Meaning of Illness: Selected Psychoanalytic Writings Including his Correspondence with Sigmund Freud*, 105, 56. London: Hogarth.

Freud, S. (1920). The psychogenesis of a case of homosexuality in a woman, In J. Strachey (Ed), *The Standard Edition of the Complete Psychological Works of Sigmund Freud*, 167. London: Hogarth.

Freud, S. (1923). The Ego and the Id. In J. Strachey (Ed), *The Standard Edition of the Complete Psychological Works of Sigmund Freud*, 19, 1–66. London: Hogarth.

Freud, S. (1924). The Economic Problem of Masochism. In J. Strachey (Ed), *The Standard Edition of the Complete Psychological Works of Sigmund Freud*, 19, 155–170. London: Hogarth.

Freud, S. (1924). The Dissolution of the Oedipus Complex. In J. Strachey (Ed), *The Standard Edition of the Complete Psychological Works of Sigmund Freud*, 19, 171–180. London: Hogarth.

Freud, S. (1925). Some Psychical Consequences of the Anatomical Distinction between the Sexes. In J. Strachey (Ed), *The Standard Edition of the Complete Psychological Works of Sigmund Freud*, 19, 241–258. London: Hogarth.

Freud, S. (1925). An Autobiographical Study. In J. Strachey (Ed), *The Standard Edition of the Complete Psychological Works of Sigmund Freud*, 20, 1–74. London: Hogarth.

Freud, S. (1926). Inhibitions, Symptoms and Anxiety. In J. Strachey (Ed), *The Standard Edition of the Complete Psychological Works of Sigmund Freud*, 20, 75–176. London: Hogarth.

Freud, S. (1928). Dostoevsky and Parricide. In J. Strachey (Ed), *The Standard Edition of the Complete Psychological Works of Sigmund Freud*, 21, 173–194. London: Hogarth.

Freud, S. (1930). Civilisation and its Discontents. In J. Strachey (Ed), *The Standard Edition of the Complete Psychological Works of Sigmund Freud*, 21, 57–146. London: Hogarth.

Freud, S. (1933). New Introductory Lectures on Psycho-Analysis. In J. Strachey (Ed), *The Standard Edition of the Complete Psychological Works of Sigmund Freud*, 22, 1–182. London: Hogarth.

Freud, S. (1936). Inhibitions, Symptoms and Anxiety. *Psychoanalytic Quarterly*, 5, 415–443.

Freud, S. (1937). Analysis Terminable and Interminable. In J. Strachey (Ed), *The Standard Edition of the Complete Psychological Works of Sigmund Freud*, 23, 209–254. London: Hogarth.

Freud, S. (1938). Some Elementary Lessons in Psycho-Analysis. In J. Strachey (Ed), *The Standard Edition of the Complete Psychological Works of Sigmund Freud*, 23, 279–286. London: Hogarth.

Freud, S. (1940). An Outline of Psycho-Analysis. *International Journal of Psychoanalysis*, 21, 27–84.

Freud, A. (1945). Indications for Child Analysis. *Psychoanalytic Study of the Child* 1, 127–149.

Freud, A. (1949). Aggression in Relation to Emotional Development; Normal and Pathological. *Psychoanalytic Study of the Child* 3, 37–42.

Freud, S. (1956). Memorandum on the Electrical Treatment of War Neurotics (1920). *International Journal of Psychoanalysis*, 37, 16–18.

Freud, A. (1972). Comments on Aggression. *International Journal of Psychoanalysis*, 53, 163–171.

Freud, S. (2015). Beyond the Pleasure Principle. *Psychoanalysis and History*, 17, 151–204.

Garma, A. (1958), Peptic Ulcer in Psychoanalysis, Williams and Wilkins, Baltimore, cited in B. Brickman, (1988) Psychoanalysis and Substance Abuse: Toward a More Effective Approach. *Journal of the American Academy of Psychoanalysis*, 16, 359–379.

Goodwin, G.M. (2008). Major Depression is Sometimes Described as the Common Cold of Psychiatry. *Journal of Psychopharmacology*, 22(7 Suppl)3. doi:10.1177/0269881108094716.

Hawking, S.W. (1988). *A Brief History of Time: From the Big Bang to Black Holes*. London: Bantam Dell.

Hertog, T. (2023). *On the Origin of Time: Stephen Hawking's Final Theory*. London: Torva, Penguin.

Jones, D. B. (2009). Addiction and Pathological Accommodation: An Intersubjective Look at Impediments to the Utilisation of Alcoholics Anonymous. *International Journal of Psychoanalytic Self Psychology*, 4, 212–234.

Jones, E. (1963). *The Life and Work of Sigmund Freud*. New York: Anchor Books.

Kandel, E. (2006). *In Search of Memory: The Emergence of a New Science of Mind*. New York: WW Norton & Co.

Khantzian, E. J. (2003). Understanding Addictive Vulnerability: An Evolving Psychodynamic Perspective. *Neuropsychoanalysis*, 5, 5–21.

Kinet, M (2024). *The Spirit of the Drive in Psychoanalysis*. London/ New York: Routledge.

Klein, M. (1946). Notes on Some Schizoid Mechanisms. *International Journal of Psychoanalysis*, 27, 99–110.

Klein, M. (1958). On the Development of Mental Functioning. *International Journal of Psychoanalysis*, 39, 84–90.

Klein, M. (1975). On Mental Health (1960). *Envy and Gratitude and Other Works 1946–1963*, 104, 268–274.

Knafo, D. (2002). Revisiting Ernst Kris's Concept of Regression in the Service of the Ego in Art. *Psychoanalytic Psychology, Vol. 19 (1)*, 24–49.

Kohut, H. (2010). On Empathy: Heinz Kohut (1981)2. *International Journal of Psychoanalytic Self Psychology*, 5, 122–131.

Lane, N. (2016). *The Vital Question: Why is Life the Way it Is?* London: Profile Books.

Lemaître, G. In https://en.wikipedia.org/wiki/Georges_Lemaître.

Lubbe, T. (2011). *Object Relations in Depression. A Return to Theory*. London: Routledge.

Lyly, J. (1578). *Eupheus: The Anatomy of Wit*. London: Gabriel Cawood.

Mahler, M. S. (1967). On Human Symbiosis and the Vicissitudes of Individuation. *Journal of the American Psychoanalytic Association*, 15, 740–763.

Mahler, M.Pine, F. & Bergman, A. (1975). *The Psychological Birth of the Human Infant: Symbiosis and Individuation*. New York: Basic Books.

Mercier, V. Cited in https://en.wikipedia.org/wiki/Waiting_for_Godot.

Mika (2017). cited in Wood, R. (2024). *A Study of Malignant Narcissism: Personal and Professional Insights.* New York/ London: Routledge.

Mills, J. (2006). Reflections on the Death Drive. *Psychoanalytic Psychology,* 23(2), 373–382.

Nurse, P. (2020). *What is Life?*Oxford: David Fickling Books.

Panksepp, J. & Biven, L. (2012). *The Archaeology of Mind: Neuroevolutionary Origins of Human Emotions.* New York: Norton.

Perkel, A. (2006). The phallic container in the couple: Splitting and diversion of maternal hate as protection of the infant. *Psycho-analytic Psychotherapy in South Africa,* 12(2),13–38.

Perkel, A. (2023). *Unlocking the Nature of Human Aggression: A Psychoanalytic and Neuroscientific Approach.* London/ New York: Routledge.

Sacks, A. (2008). The Therapeutic Use of Pets in Private Practice. *British Journal of Psychotherapy,* 24, 501–521.

Sandler, J. & Freud, A. (1983). Discussions in the Hampstead Index on 'The Ego and the Mechanisms of Defence': XI. A Form of Altruism. *Bulletin of the Anna Freud Centre,* 6, 329–349.

Schroeder, G. (1997). *The Science of God: The Convergence of Scientific and Biblical Wisdom.* New York/ London: The Free Press.

Shaw, 2014, cited in Wood, R. (2024). *A Study of Malignant Narcissism: Personal and Professional Insights.* New York/ London: Routledge.

Solan, R. (1999). The Interaction between self and others: A Different perspective on narcissism. *Psychoanalytic Study of the Child,* 54, 193–215.

Solms, M. (2013). The Conscious Id, *Neuropsychoanalysis,* 15(1), 5–19.

Solms, M. (2015). Reconsolidation: Turning Memory into Consciousness. *Behavioural and Brain Sciences,* 38. e24. doi:10.1017/S0140525X14000296..

Solms, M., Pantelis, E., & Panksepp, J. (2015). Neuropsychoanalytic notes on addiction. In Solms, *et al.,* (2015). *The Feeling Brain.* London/ New York: Routledge.

Solms, M. (2017). What is "the Unconscious," and Where is it Located in the Brain? A Neuropsychoanalytic Perspective. *Annals of the New York Academy of Sciences,* 1406, 90–97, doi:10.1111/nyas.13437.

Solms, M. (2018). *The Feeling Brain. Selected Papers on Neuropsychoanalysis.* London/ New York: Routledge:.

Solms M.L. (2018). The Neurobiological Underpinnings of Psychoanalytic Theory and Therapy. *Frontiers in Behavioural Neuroscience,* 12, 294.

Solms, M. (2019). The Hard Problem of Consciousness and the Free Energy Principle. *Frontiers in Psychology,* 9, 2714. https://doi.org/10.3389/fpsyg.2018.02714.

Solms, M. (2020). Response to the commentaries on the "New Project". *Neuropsychoanalysis,* 22, 97–107.

Solms M. (2021). Revision of Drive Theory . *Journal of the American Psychoanalytic Association,* 69(6), 1033–1091. https://doi.org/10.1177/00030651211057041.

Solms, M. (2021). *The Hidden Spring: A Journey into the Source of Consciousness.* London: Profile Books.

Solms, M. (Ed), (2024). *The Revised Standard Edition of the Complete Psychological Works of Sigmund Freud.* New York: Rowan & Littlefield.

Target, M. & Fonagy, P. (1996). Playing With Reality: II. The Development of Psychic Reality From A Theoretical Perspective. *International Journal of Psychoanalysis,* 77, 459–479.

Valdrè, R. (2019). *Psychoanalytic Reflections on the Freudian Death Drive in Theory, the Clinic and Art*. New York/ London: Routledge.

Valdrè, R. (2025). *The Death Drive: A Contemporary Introduction*. New York/ London: Routledge.

van Gennep, A. (1873–1957). *Liminality*. In https://link.springer.com/refer enceworkentry/10.1007/978-1-4614-6086-2_387#:~:text=Liminality.

Wang, C., Zhang, K., & Zhang, M. (2017). Social Behaviour and Personality. *An International Journal*, 45(2), 269–280.

Winnicott, D.W. (1965). The Maturational Processes and the Facilitating Environment. *Studies in the Theory of Emotional Development*, 64, 1–11.

Winnicott, D.W. (1975). *Through Paediatrics to Psychoanalysis, Collected Papers*. London: Hogarth Press.

Winnicott, D. W. (1975). Chapter XVI. Aggression in Relation to Emotional Development [1950–5]. *Through Paediatrics to Psycho-Analysis* 100, 204–218.

Wood, R. (2024). *Psychoanalytic Reflections on Vladimir Putin: The Cost of Malignant Leadership*. London/ New York: Routledge.

Wood, R. (2024). *A Study of Malignant Narcissism: Personal and Professional Insights*. London/ New York: Routledge.

Index

For Product Safety Concerns and Information please contact our EU
representative GPSR@taylorandfrancis.com
Taylor & Francis Verlag GmbH, Kaufingerstraße 24, 80331 München, Germany

www.ingramcontent.com/pod-product-compliance
Lightning Source LLC
Chambersburg PA
CBHW050630280326
41932CB00015B/2595